Buddhist Philosophy

Losang Gönchok's Short Commentary to Jamyang Shayba's *Root Text on Tenets*

Buddhist Philosophy

Losang Gönchok's Short Commentary to Jamyang Shayba's *Root Text on Tenets*

by Daniel Cozort and Craig Preston

Snow Lion Publications
Ithaca, New York
Boulder, Colorado

Snow Lion Publications
P.O. 6483
Ithaca, New York 14851 USA
607-273-8519

www.snowlionpub.com

First Edition USA 2003

Printed in Canada on acid-free recycled paper

ISBN 1-55939-198-7

Library of Congress Cataloging-in-Publication Data

Blo-bzad-dkon-mchog.
[Grub mtha' rtsa ba'i tsig tik śel dkar me loṅ. English.]
Buddhist Philosophy : Losang Gönchok's short commentary to Jamyang Shayba's root text on tenets / by Daniel Cozort and Craig Preston.
p. cm.
ISBN 1-55939-198-7 (alk. paper)
1. 'Jam-dbyaṅs-bźad-pa Ṅag-dbaṅ-brton-'grus, 1648–1721. Grub mtha'i rnam par bźad pa 'khrul spoṅ gdoṅ lṅa'i sgra dbyaṅs kun mkhyen lam bzaṅ gsal ba'i rin chen sgron me źes bya ba bźugs so. 2. Buddhism—Doctrines—Early works to 1800. 3. Buddhist sects—Early works 10 1800. I Cozort, Daniel, 1953- . II Preston, Craig, (1950- . III. 'Jam-dbyaṅs-bźad-pa Ṅag-dbaṅ-brtson-'grus, 1648–1721. 'Jam-dbyaṅs-bźad-pa Ṅag-dbaṅ-brtson-'grus, 1648–1721. Grub mtha'i rnam par bźad pa 'khrul spoṅ gdoṅ lṅa'i sgra dbyaṅs kun mkhyen lam bzaṅ gsal ba'i rin chen sgron me źes bya ba bźugs so. IV. Title.
BQ4140.J363.B5713 2003
181'.043—dc22

2003014569

Contents

On Pronunciation

Since this is a book about Tibetan Buddhist philosophy, which is deeply connected to India, it contains many Tibetan and Sanskrit terms and names. For those without much background in these languages, they may be a stumbling block.

We have accordingly translated as many terms and titles as we can, supplying a glossary and bibliography for those who are interested in the originals. However, some Sanskrit terms have entered English dictionaries and, therefore, are neither translated nor italicized: Abhidharma, Arhat, Bodhisattva, Buddha, dharma, karma, nirvāṇa, samsāra, sūtra, tantra, vajra, yogi, Mahāyāna, Hīnayāna and Vajrayāna. A few Tibetan terms are also treated as English words: geshe, lama, and rinpoche.

Regarding personal names, we believe that it is important to render them in a reasonably pronounceable form, especially in the case of Tibetan, whose many silent letters lead to consonant-cluster nightmares like *'jams dbyangs bzhad pa* (Jamyang Shayba) or *blo bzang dkon mchog* (Losang Gönchok). It is much more difficult to remember what we cannot pronounce. What follows are some aids to pronunciation.

Pronouncing Tibetan

For easy pronunciation, we have used Jeffrey Hopkins' system of "essay phonetics,"which approximates Lhasa pronunciation.[1] The proper names of those who have established a form for their names in the West (and the name of Tibet's capital, Lhasa, which ought to be Hlasa) are the only exceptions. For instance, we use "Dzongkaba" to render *tsong kha pa,* although it is true enough that the forms "Tsongkhapa" and "Tsong-kha-pa" have more renown. (His is a rare name that can be pronounced more or less as it appears in transliterated form, and this has in some cases disguised the need for a pronunciation system.) Tibetan studies are still in a developing state and we feel that it is not yet too late for a different (and improved) convention to become accepted.

On page 291 there is a table that compares the pronunciation and transliteration system for each Tibetan consonant, and a list of all the Tibetan names used in the text in both "essay phonetics" and transliterated form.

---

[1]Hopkins, *Meditation,* 19–22.

Pronouncing Sanskrit

Sanskrit, fortunately, is generally pronounced as it looks. Unlike Tibetan, Sanskrit has no silent letters, and unlike English, it has few exceptional cases for pronunciation. However, it has *fifty* letters. In order to represent all fifty letters, some are represented by pairs of Roman letters and some have superscribed or subscribed diacritical marks.

We have decided to follow the standard transliteration scheme for Sanskrit because we feel that the reader can easily master the few cases that are more difficult, especially since some pronunciations are similar to those in European languages. Only a few Sanskrit letters represent sounds that English speakers do not usually, or ever, make. The following are the most problematic, with approximate pronunciation:

Letter	Description
kh, gh, jh, dh, bh, ph, th	aspirated (extra breath) version of k, g, j, d, b, p, and t. **Gh** and **ph** are troublesome because in English these combinations may both be pronounced "f"; likewise, **th** is usually the dipthong, as in "the." In Sanskrit they are just aspirated versions of g, p, and t. Example: Vaibhāṣika (a Buddhist school).
ḍ, ṭ, ṇ	retroflex version of the same letters without subdot. To pronounce a retroflex letter, touch the tip of your tongue to the roof of your mouth as you say it. Example: nirvāṇa.
jñ	"gya." Example: *jñāna* (wisdom).
ś and ṣ	"sh." Examples: *śunyatā* (emptiness), Vaibhāṣika.
c	"ch." Example: Candrakīrti (Mādhyamika philosopher).
a	as vowel sound in "sum." Example: *saṃsāra* (cyclic existence, i.e., the round of rebirth).
ā	as the a in "farther." Example: *saṃsāra.*
e	as vowel sound in "make." Example: *cetana* (intention).
ī	as vowel sound in "keen." Example: Candrakīrti.
ai	as vowel sound in "tribe." Example: Vaibhāṣika.
ṛ	"er" as in butter. E.g., ṛta is pronounced "erta." Example: *saṃvṛtisatya* (conventional truth).

Acknowledgments

We are deeply indebted to Jeffrey Hopkins, who has done more than anyone else to present Buddhism according to the Tibetan Gelukba tradition to a Western audience, both scholarly and general. He was our mentor for many years at the University of Virginia and has continued to encourage and help us ever since.

We first studied Losang Gönchok's text in a class with Professor Hopkins at Virginia that also included Jules Levinson, who made many contributions to the translation. At every meeting, we brought our attempts at translation to Professor Hopkins, who patiently corrected our mistakes and gave us a running commentary based on his own deep knowledge of Jamyang Shayba's *Great Exposition of Tenets* and the oral tradition he learned from Kensur Ngawang Lekden and many other eminent Tibetan scholars.[1] We have benefitted "initially" from working directly with him, in the "middle" from his many books that directly or indirectly concern tenets, and in the "end" from his generosity in sharing his work-in-progress on the *Great Exposition of Tenets* and Ngawang Belden's *Annotations.*

We were aware that Professor Hopkins' book about tenets, *Maps of the Profound,* would be published in the same year as this one. That motivated us to write ours as an introduction that might help others enter the more difficult terrain of his work. It also helped us to decide to adhere more closely (although not completely) to the translation equivalents he uses, so that it would not be unnecessarily difficult for the reader to go from one book to the other.

By the way, we did not finish the book in the aforementioned class. A year later, Daniel Cozort worked under Professor Hopkins' supervision to finish it as part of the research he undertook for his dissertation and he then had a series of classes over nearly a year with the late abbot of Loseling College of Drebung Monastic University, Kensur Yeshey Tupden, whose commentary illuminated many contentious issues. He later

[1]See Hopkins, *Meditation,* 12–17, for a complete explanation of his sources.

made revisions to the translation and added some notes but Craig Preston is largely responsible for bringing the translation into final form.

We are also indebted to our former fellow students and present colleagues who have worked on particular schools of tenets or on specific issues that concern several schools, among them: Elizabeth Napper, Anne Klein, Donald Lopez, Joe B. Wilson, Guy Newland, Georges Dreyfus, Jules Levinson, and John Beuscher. We have often referred to their books, articles, or manuscripts as we have attempted to condense and simplify the profound and difficult issues of Buddhist philosophy.

We are both grateful to our families and friends for their love and support.

Finally, we would like to thank our friends both within and outside of the academic community who read all or portions of the manuscript and helped it to take a shape that might speak better to its intended audience, those who are interested in the ideas of Buddhism but who have not studied the complex and sometimes difficult issues of philosophical tenets that are explicated here. In particular, Diana Cutler raised important qualms and made many editorial suggestions.

Preface

The text translated in this book is an explanation of Buddhist philosophy, with some attention paid also to non-Buddhist schools of thought, from the perspective of a particular but important corner of the world of Tibetan Buddhism. Although it is a relatively short work, it represents centuries of philosophical investigation and analysis.

Its form is that of a commentary on a "root text," Jamyang Shayba's *Roar of the Five-Faced [Lion]*. A root text is a poem meant to be memorized and to be supplemented by a written or oral commentary. Jamyang Shayba wrote his own commentary to *Roar* called the *Great Exposition of Tenets*, an enormous work that is the most exhaustive treatment of comparative philosophical tenets in the history of Buddhism.

The shorter commentary translated here, *The Clear Crystal Mirror*, was composed later by Losang Gönchok, who came from the monastery founded by Jamyang Shayba and probably grew up studying the latter's works carefully. It is a "word commentary," one that paraphrases and expands the root text, which because of its brevity can be rather like a telegram. It is much more accessible than the *Great Exposition of Tenets* but it preserves the breadth and profundity of Jamyang Shayba's thought and is informed by subsequent written and oral tradition.

Nevertheless, *The Clear Crystal Mirror* can be difficult, too. In the first place, Losang Gönchok presents philosophy by working school-by-school through the non-Buddhist and Buddhist systems of thought. He seldom makes explicit comparisons between the schools. Second, the issues with which he deals are in some cases extraordinarily complex, and even though he has attempted to simplify them, the text is sometimes too terse, sometimes too convoluted.

Accordingly, we have tried in our introduction (written by Daniel Cozort) to provide a simple and straightforward outline of the major points of comparison between the Buddhist schools. Then, in the translation section, we have supplied many explanatory notes for the text (written by both of us). We have tried to avoid burdening the reader with technical discussions and bibliographic notes. Our aim has been to introduce readers who have some background in Buddhism to the world of Buddhist philosophy, which, as our text reminds us, is not merely a world of intellectual games but a means to salvation.

The remainder of this preface explains the background of the text: its roots in the Tibetan Gelukba tradition; how Tibetan authors systematize the Indian tradition; the genre of tenets texts; the biographies of its authors; and the plan of the text. Readers who want to get right into the issues of Buddhist philosophy can skip ahead.

The Gelukba Tradition

This book is concerned with *Indian* Buddhist philosophy. Tibetan authors do not ever see themselves as innovators (although sometimes they are) but rather as interpreters—exegetes—of the glorious traditions that originate in Buddhism's birthplace.

However, *The Clear Crystal Mirror* represents a distinctly Tibetan approach and differs from what a non-Tibetan scholar might write about Indian Buddhism. It is also definitely a product of that particular Tibetan tradition called Gelukba, a monastic order to which both of our authors belonged. This is notable because the Gelukba tradition is more concerned than other Tibetan traditions with the sort of scholasticism represented here and because it has a unique way of presenting the subject of tenets.

The monastic order that came to be called Gelukba was established by the great scholar and reformer Dzongkaba Losang Drakpa (1357–1419). A child prodigy who studied with many great lamas around Tibet, especially with Rendawa of the Sagya order, he began to write philosophical treatises at the age of thirty-two. In his late thirties he had a vision of the Bodhisattva or Buddha personifying wisdom, Mañjuśrī, who is said to have taught him directly. Another important vision occurred during the composition of his greatest work, the *Great Treatise on the Stages of the Path.* This time, he is reputed to have learned directly from the spirit of the Indian paṇdit (scholar) Atīśa, who reinvigorated Tibetan Buddhism in the eleventh century and died in Tibet. Dzongkaba attracted many disciples with his brilliant synthesis of Indian philosophy and Tibetan commentary. In particular, his explanation of the Mādhyamika school, which Tibetans consider the highest of all, was ingenious, intricate, and persuasive.

Dzongkaba never announced the establishment of a new monastic order, but it began to form following on his founding of Ganden Monastery near Lhasa in 1410. Others started to call his followers "Gandenbas." It was not until later, when Dzongkaba's writings were criticized by writers of the Sagya order, that the Gandenbas distinguished themselves from Sagya by calling themselves, somewhat immodestly, Gelukbas ("virtuous ones"). They were also called the "New Gadamba," harking back to the Gadamba order established by Atīśa's disciple Dromdönba (1005–1064). Like Atīśa, Dromdönba, and especially the great scholar and translator Ngok Loden Sherab (1059–1109), Dzongkaba emphasized that monasticism should not be only about ritual but should involve the rigorous study of Buddhist philosophy.

Within the Gelukba order in Tibet, there were many great monasteries. The three close to Lhasa—Ganden, Drebung, and Sera, all established within a single decade by disciples of Dzongkaba—are special academic centers, granting the doctorate degree of geshe (*kalyanamitra*, "spiritual friend"). Students from as far away as Russia and Mongolia undertook long, difficult, sometimes dangerous journeys to reach Lhasa and suffered many privations once there in order to be worthy of this degree.

Each of the monasteries contained several nearly autonomous colleges. In these institutions there is a particular emphasis on the study of philosophy, and each of the colleges within the monasteries has a tradition, mostly oral, of points of difference with the other colleges. Jamyang Shayba and Losang Gönchok came from the philosophical tradition of the Gomang College of Drebung Monastery, although each spent most of his life far away from Lhasa in the Amdo region at Labrang Drashikyil Monastery, founded by Jamyang Shayba.

The Gelukba Approach to Tenets

How does our text differ in its approach from Western histories of philosophy? One major difference is that it scarcely discusses history. There are indications of the chronology of writers, to be sure, but we do not learn anything about the historical circumstances in which a school developed, where within India it was popular, how many people followed it, what kind of people they were, how long it lasted, or how it influenced other schools. Another difference is that it is not as complete as it might be. Some schools that no longer existed in northern India but were important (notably the Theravāda) are left out.

A more subtle difference is that these presentations of tenets are attempts to construct coherent, logically consistent, and complete systems of thought, even if the basis for doing so is a bit thin. The seminal Indian texts upon which the tenets of the various schools are based are often terse and sometimes cryptic. In an effort to clarify these texts, the Gelukbas sometimes resort to subtle qualifications that they interpolate into the explicit language of the original sources. They contend that they are merely drawing out the implications of a terse text, but others accuse them of doctoring the original.

To name a particularly important instance, the Gelukba tradition clarifies the difficult reasoning of Nāgārjuna, the founder of the Mādhyamika school, by modifying his main terms. Nāgārjuna is famous for the "tetralemma" that things are neither produced from themselves, from others, from both themselves and others, or neither from themselves nor others. That something is not produced from itself (as some non-Buddhist schools such as Sāṃkhya would contend) is not disputed; nor are the last two possibilities ever accepted. But since the world obviously says that things *are* produced by something other than themselves, the second term must be explained. Dzongkaba attempts to show that what Nāgārjuna meant was not that there is *no* production from other but that this production is not *inherently* other; it is only conventionally other. In the first two terms of the reasoning, then, Nāgārjuna rejects true or inherent existence (independent existence, or existence from a thing's own side) but upholds conventional existence (existence imputed in dependence on a thing's parts, etc.)

Dzongkaba was roundly criticized for this and other interpretations of Mādhyamika by the fifteenth-century Sagya scholar Daktsang Shayrap Rinchen (born 1405), known as Daktsang the Translator, and a good bit of our text is concerned with defending Dzongkaba (mainly by attacking Daktsang). We are not concerned here with whether Dzongkaba's additions are necessary to make sense of Nāgārjuna. The point is that what we read in the present work is really "Gelukba Mādhyamika" rather than Mādhyamika *per se*, if such a thing could be determined (and there is certainly no scholarly consensus on the meaning of Nāgārjuna, or for that matter, many of the other Indian Buddhist philosophers).

How much does it matter? In theory, little. The formulation of tenets is mainly a heuristic device. The purpose of tenets study, as we will discuss in the next chapter, is to use the temporary adoption of philosophical positions to work logically through many possibilities in order to arrive at an "established conclusion" (tenet) in which we feel confident. It is not supposed to be a matter of indoctrination in the "correct tenets" of Buddhism, even if it is true that in the end a particular school (the Prāsaṅgika) is labeled "correct" and that it is presumed that eventually we will reach the same conclusions as its proponents. Ideally, we are to study tenets so that our minds will be sharpened and our presuppositions exposed and scrutinized.

The Genre of Tenets Texts

Although the genre of tenets books reached its apogee with eighteenth-century Tibetan texts, perhaps with Jamyang Shayba's root text and its commentaries, it began in India.[1] The *Points of Controversy (Kathāvatthu)* records a third-century B.C.E.[2] debate between the Sthaviravāda and several other schools; while not a tenets book as such, it may be the first work to document tenets formation. Bhāvaviveka, retroactively considered to be the founder of the Svātantrika-Mādhyamika school, wrote the *Blaze of Reasoning* in the sixth century; Śāntarakṣita, the *Compendium of Principles* in the eighth century. Bhāvaviveka's text is used by Jamyang Shayba to sort out the Vaibhāṣika sub-schools. Jetāri, in his *Discrimination of the Sugata* in the tenth century, referred to the four schools.

In Tibet, two early books on tenets were Beltsek's *Explanation of the Stages of Views* and Yesheday's *Differences Between Views*, both from around 800. The great Nyingma scholar Longchen Rapjam wrote his *Treasury of Tenets, Illuminating the Meaning of All Vehicles* in the fourteenth century. In the fifteenth, the great Sagya scholar Daktsang wrote the *Ocean of Good Explanations, Explanation of "Freedom from Extremes Through Understanding All Tenets."* As we have mentioned, Jamyang Shayba wrote his great work on tenets at the end of the seventeenth century in no small part as a reply to Daktsang.

Jamyang Shayba's root text on tenets and his auto-commentary, published in 1689 and 1699 respectively, are the most comprehensive of the tenets texts.[3] They were followed about four decades later by the last of the large, comprehensive works on tenets, Janggya Rolbay Dorjay's *Clear Exposition of the Presentation of Tenets, Beautiful Ornament for the Meru of the Subduer's Teaching.* A smaller work that is even more comprehensive, treating the four orders of Tibetan Buddhism briefly, was subsequently written by his student, Losang Chögyi Nyima. There have been a number of smaller "primers" written after Jamyang Shayba. One, the *Presentation of Tenets, a Precious Garland* by Gönchok Jikmay Wangbo, the second Jamyang Shayba (i.e., his reincarnation), has been translated into English several times.

---

[1]See Hopkins, "The Tibetan Genre...," 172–3.

[2]C.E. (common era) is the era held in common with Christianity. C.E. and B.C.E. are neutral ways to designate the periods that are otherwise designated B.C. (before Christ) and A.D. (*anno domine*, year of our lord).

[3]Because the *Great Exposition* is itself sometimes obscure, an invaluable companion to it is Ngawang Belden's *Annotations*, which is even longer than the *Great Exposition.*

As may already be clear, the major figures of Gelukba tenets works form a close circle of reincarnate lamas (tulkus) with an "eastern" flavor. It is centered in Amdo, the eastern province of Jamyang Shayba's Labrang Drashikyil Monastery and Janggya's Gönlung Jambaling Monastery. In Jamyang Shayba's time, the area was controlled by Dzungar Mongolians. In fact, the Janggya lamas and Ngawang Belden, Jamyang Shayba's great annotator, were themselves Mongolians.

The first Janggya lama, Ngawang Chöden, tutored Jamyang Shayba in tantric studies. The second Janggya, Rolbay Dorjay (1717–1786), taught the second Jamyang Shayba lama, Gönchok Jikmay Wangbo (1728–91), and the third Tügen lama, Losang Chögyi Nyima (1737–1802).

Gönchok Jikmay Wangbo, in turn, taught Gungtang Denbay Drönmay, whose work clarifies a number of points involved in the Mādhyamika school critique of the philosophy of the Cittamātra school. Another of his students was probably Losang Gönchok, the author of our text.

The Root Text, Its Commentary, and Their Authors

Jamyang Shayba won his geshe degree at the Gomang College of Drebung Monastery, and thus his verses, and Losang Gönchok's commentary on them, surely reflect the traditions of oral debate at that college. Jamyang Shayba's own commentary is replete with hypothetical debates, some of which may have been drawn from real debates in the Gomang courtyard, where he served as abbot for seven years.

Jamyang Shayba's sixteen–folio[1] root text is entitled *Presentation of Tenets, Roar of the Five-Faced (Lion) Eradicating Error, Precious Lamp Illuminating the Genuine Path to Omniscience* and was written in verse in 1689. (We have decided, however, not to present it as poetry.) The verses have a strange relationship with the Dalai Lamas. According to Geshe Tupden Gyatso, a twentieth-century Gomang College scholar, they were written at the behest of Jamyang Shayba's student, Sanggyay Gyatso, while he was the regent of the great Fifth Dalai Lama. The request was made in the name of the Dalai Lama, who died in 1682 but whose death was concealed by Sanggyay Gyatso for fourteen years.

Jamyang Shayba's own enormous commentary on the verse treatise (530 folios in the Drashikyil edition, probably four times the length of *The Clear Crystal*

[1]A folio is a Tibetan book page, typically about four inches high but up to twenty-four inches long, printed on both sides, usually using woodblocks.

Mirror) was written ten years later. It is usually referred to as the *Great Exposition of Tenets* but its full title is the rather grand *Explanation of "Tenets," Sun of the Land of Samantabhadra Brilliantly Illuminating All of Our Own and Others' Tenets and the Meaning of the Profound, Ocean of Scripture and Reasoning Fulfilling All Hopes of All Beings*. It was published in 1699, the year before he became the abbot of Gomang.

Jamyang Shayba's full name is Jamyang Shayba Dorjay Ngawang Dzöndrü. He was born in 1648 in lower Amdo, the easternmost region of Tibet (now in Qinghai Province of the People's Republic of China), in the area of Ganggya Dingring.[1] A serious student, he became a novice monk in his teens, traveling to Lhasa at the age of twenty-one to enter the Gomang College of Drebung Monastery. At age twenty-seven he became a fully ordained monk, and at twenty-nine he entered the Tantric College of Lower Lhasa, Gyumay. Among his teachers were the great Fifth Dalai Lama, Losang Gyatso, whom he met when as a boy His Holiness stopped in Amdo on his way to China. Jamyang Shayba was also taught by the first of the line of reincarnating Janggya lamas, Ngawang Chöden.

At the age of thirty-three he entered a two-year meditation retreat in a cave near Drebung, thereby attaining yogic powers. He wrote prolifically for the rest of his life. Among the dozens of texts collected in the fifteen volumes of his "Collected Works" are his famous monastic textbooks on the five "root" topics: Valid Cognition; the Perfection of Wisdom; the philosophy of the Mādhyamika school; Abhidharma; and Monastic Discipline.

In 1709 Jamyang Shayba returned to Amdo at the invitation of the Dzungar Mongolians. In the following year he founded the Labrang Drashikyil Monastery (sometimes referred to as just Labrang), which grew into a major center of the Gelukba monastic order; a tantric college was also established there in 1717. Drashikyil's first abbot was Ngawang Drashi, who, using Jamyang Shayba's writings, authored the Collected Topics textbook still studied by those beginning the Gomang curriculum. Jamyang Shayba died at age seventy-three or -four in 1721 or 1722. His line has continued. The sixth Jamyang Shayba lama is currently building a new house at Labrang.[2]

About Losang Gönchok we know much less. If the author of our text is the Losang Gönchok who was a student of Gönchok Jikmay Wangpo, Jamyang

---

[1]The following account of Jamyang Shayba's life and literary activities has been gleaned from Lokesh Candra (45–9), who in turn relies on a sketch by a "Dr. Rinchen of Ulanbator." Some details have been added from Nietupski.

[2]Paul Nietupski, private communication.

Shayba's reincarnation, which seems likely, he was born in 1742 in Amdo and became a monk at a young age. He became a master of all texts, sūtra and tantra, and had many students at Labrang Drashikyil, his monastery. He died at the age of eighty, in 1822.[1]

The title of Losang Gönchok's commentary is *The Clear Crystal Mirror, A Word Commentary on Jamyang Shayba's Root Text on Tenets.* A word commentary is one that minimally paraphrases all of a root text so that its meaning can be understood. *The Clear Crystal Mirror* exceeds this requirement by explaining many issues at some length. It admirably compresses Jamyang Shayba's *Great Exposition of Tenets* without deleting important points. It avoids the copious citation of Indian sources and construction of hypothetical debates that swell Jamyang Shayba's own commentary, giving the student of Indian and Tibetan Buddhism an extensive but not unmanageable handbook of Buddhist philosophical discourse.

Jamyang Shayba's root text and Losang Gönchok's *The Clear Crystal Mirror* are clearly oriented toward demonstrating the superiority of the Prāsaṅgika-Mādhyamika school, which they, and all other Gelukbas, consider to be the greatest of the Indian schools and hence the one that actually reflects the thought of the Buddha. Nevertheless, there is great respect for the other schools of Buddhist tenets, since it is the presumption of the Prāsaṅgika school that the Buddha deliberately taught many kinds of doctrine in order to serve the needs of persons of different dispositions and capacities, and that understanding the views of the lower schools is the key to understanding the views of the higher schools.

Most of the text is devoted to Buddhist tenets, with only about forty pages given over to summaries of all of the major non-Buddhist tenet systems of India, provided principally, it seems, to demonstrate the uniqueness of Buddhist philosophy. Of the chapters on Buddhist tenets, much less space is given over to the lower schools than is given to the higher ones; in particular, the Prāsaṅgika school receives close attention. The order in which the schools are discussed reflects the Gelukba assessment of their respective proximity to the Buddha's own views; thus, we are led slowly through the nest of issues that constitute Buddhist philosophy until we reach the most subtle topics in the Prāsaṅgika inventory, the nature of Buddhahood and the practice of secret mantra, the swift method for attaining Buddhahood restricted to the most intelligent and compassionate of those with the Prāsaṅgika view.

---

[1]There are several persons with the name Losang Gönchok who lived around the same time and place. According to the database of the Tibetan Buddhist Research Center, the Losang Gönchok who lived from 1742–1822 was a student of Gönchok Jikmay Wangpo. Another Losang Gönchok, who was born in 1803, became the throne holder of Drashikyil.

Introduction to Tenets

"My doctrine has two modes,
Advice and tenets.
To children I speak advice
And to yogis, tenets."

—*Descent to Laṅkā Sūtra*

What Are Tenets?

In *The Clear Crystal Mirror*, Losang Gönchok summarizes the views, or "tenets," of some well-known Indian philosophical schools. He is mainly concerned with the Buddhist schools, of course, and within them is much more concerned with those that his tradition thinks represent the higher, most correct worldviews. In this introduction to his text, we would like to provide the reader with some perspectives on the nature of tenets and the principal issues about which the Buddhist schools disagree.

Tenets, Losang Gönchok tells us, are "established conclusions." That is, they are the end product of a process of reasoning that has considered various possibilities and has tentatively eliminated all but one. They are not mere beliefs; we cannot be real proponents of Buddhist tenets without having studied, debated, and struggled with the implications of our views.

This is important because, as we shall see, the real goal of tenets study for Gelukbas is that the student become a living, breathing Prāsaṅgika-Mādhyamika, a proponent of the greatest Buddhist school. To be a Prāsaṅgika is to be a master of the art of "flinging consequences *(prasaṅga)*"; it is to know how to take any statement and wring from it whatever might logically follow. Prāsaṅgikas are not supposed to preach doctrine at their opponents. They are to ask others for their opinions and pursue relentlessly all of their implications. This, it is thought, will enable those persons to see not only what is wrong with their views but to arrive at correct ways of thinking themselves. Those who are not Prāsaṅgikas have simply not thought deeply enough about the consequences of their own views.

But it is easy to see that there is a paradox in this, for if a tenet is a final conclusion, and the final conclusion of all reasoning is the Prāsaṅgika view, would it not follow that only Prāsaṅgikas have actual tenets? Only a Prāsaṅgika is someone who truly embodies the meaning of a tenet as a conclusion reached only upon eliminating *all* other possibilities.

So, we must say that while tenets are conclusions established by a process of reasoning, that process is not necessarily complete. A hypothetical Vaibhāṣika, for instance, may have no familiarity with the texts of the Mahāyāna Buddhist schools (Cittamātra and Mādhyamika), either by lack of exposure or because of regarding the latter as inauthentic, as not being true teachings of the Buddha. And even if we are aware of other positions and the reasoning that establishes them, we may not yet have properly understood them and are not in that sense "aware" of them. Thus, tenets are not necessarily final conclusions, even if they are "established."[1] Of course, is this not the nature of our knowledge in general? Our "facts" are merely empirical verities that can and often are altered or even discarded as our knowledge increases.

Did the Buddha Teach Philosophy?

Did the Buddha teach these systems of tenets? The answer to that question is both yes and no. First, we must remember that the Buddha taught a great deal. His teaching career of forty-five years resulted, long after his death, in enormous scriptural collections (canons) in the various countries to which Buddhism has spread. The Tibetan canon is the largest of all, with two divisions of 108 and 225 volumes. The Buddhist schools in general maintain that the Buddha was a master pedagogue who deliberately taught different points of view for the different kinds of persons who could benefit from them. It might even have been the case that different persons heard different teachings at the same time and place. According to the Mahāyāna schools, this was not merely a matter of differing styles or of emphasizing different aspects of the doctrine but sometimes involved views that are in direct contradiction.

For example, whereas in general the Buddha spoke of the things in the world as ordinary persons view them—as having an existence completely independent of the persons who apprehend them—in some teachings, such as the *Descent to Laṅkā Sūtra,* he said quite the opposite, that there is no world external to consciousness.[2]

---

[1]Some teachers go further and explain that to be a tenet-holder of a system, we must have realized the selflessness taught by that system (a topic we will discuss later). In that case, there would be very, very few tenet-holders.

[2]We are trying to give an example of teachings that contradict each other but as might be expected, this is controversial. So it must be borne in mind that since the Hīnayāna schools may not accept this sūtra as valid, it is not an example for them. Also, some Mahāyānists (Bhāvaviveka, the Svātantrika) felt that in this case, the Buddha's words had been misunderstood and he was not

(We will discuss this issue a little later.) For certain persons, this teaching is an appropriate "medicine" that helps them to overcome their attachments to material things. The "medicine" that will ultimately cure ignorance can be administered at a later time.

We will say more later about the number of schools and the problem of their identification. For now, we should just note that the higher schools in particular do not attempt to establish their superiority over the lower schools by claiming that the scriptures upon which others depend are inauthentic. They are perfectly willing to concede that all of the scriptures in the vast Tibetan canon are Buddha's but they insist that, of course, they cannot all represent the Buddha's own, true "final thought." Thus, one of the occupations of the higher tenet systems is hermeneutics, the science of interpreting literature.

Buddhist hermeneutics is a complex and interesting area of Buddhist philosophy that we will briefly examine later. It will suffice to say here that while the Buddha is the source of the various systems of tenets, Gelukbas consider that the scriptures relied upon by the systems lower than the highest, final system of Prāsaṅgika "require interpretation" in order to understand what the Buddha meant. They either are literally what he said (but do not represent his own final thought, which must be interpolated), or, although they *do* represent his own final thought, they need further clarification. To refer again to our example about the reality of the external world, Prāsaṅgikas claim that at certain times and places the Buddha deliberately taught that there are no external objects. This eventually resulted in the formation of the Cittamātra school. However, these statements require interpretation because they do not explicitly state the way phenomena actually exist (that they are "empty of inherent existence" or "not established by their own character").

Gelukbas make these judgments in a way that relates to what we have been saying about the nature of tenets. Scriptures are distinguished into definitive and non-definitive categories based upon what in them stands up to reasoning, for of course, the Buddha's own final thought must be logically impeccable. His own dictum, that his teaching ought to be analyzed the way a goldsmith tests a lump of ore, is used to separate the absolutely, literally reliable scripture from that which is only provisional. There are scriptures that are themselves about hermeneutics, showing how to distinguish the definitive and non-definitive. Cittamātrins use the *Sūtra Unraveling the Thought* and Mādhyamikas, the *Teaching of Akṣayamati Sūtra*. However, it is never enough to say that a position is correct simply because the Buddha said it was.

---

in fact contradicting any other teaching.

The Sources of Tenets

The Buddha's teaching as captured in his own discourses, the sūtras, is usually but not always clear and well-organized, and it is certainly not "systematic." He was not attempting to establish various philosophical schools but rather to meet the needs of his immediate listeners. Even if his teachings had been presented in that way, succeeding teachers in various historical and cultural circumstances would have to interpret them in order to bridge the gaps in understanding that naturally arise whenever the horizon of the text and the horizon of the reader are separated by history or culture. Exegesis, or scriptural interpretation, is inevitable, and it is from exegesis that Buddhist tenets are developed. This process began immediately after the Buddha's death.

The source of the tenets of the various schools are, then, not so much sūtras as exegetical works that developed a following for their particular views. They are relatively few in number:

- Vaibhāṣikas rely on the anonymous *Mahāvibhāṣā*.[1]
- Sautrāntikas rely on the works of Dignāga and Dharmakīrti, or Vasubandhu.
- Cittamātrins rely either on Dignāga and Dharmakīrti or on Asaṅga and Vasubandhu.
- Svātantrikas rely on Bhāvaviveka or Śāntarakṣita.
- Prāsaṅgikas rely upon Candrakīrti.

It is notable that most of these works were composed in the relatively brief period of the fourth to seventh centuries C.E.

To belong to a "school," therefore, really meant to have a kind of intellectual commitment. It is not like the kind of commitment that causes someone to be identified as a Shi'ite Muslim, a Protestant Christian, or a Shaivite Hindu, but is more like the kind of commitment that might cause someone to be identified as a political liberal, conservative, or moderate. It certainly did not lead to physical isolation and antagonism. The Chinese pilgrim Xuanzang visited India in the seventh century and found tenet-holders of all varieties living and studying together at Nālanda Monastery. It is hazardous and, we think, unhelpful to guess at the

---

[1]Because this text was not translated into Tibetan until the twentieth century, Tibetans actually understand the school from Vasubandhu's *Treasury of Abhidharma*.

affiliations any particular person had with a "school" unless they clearly identified it themselves. Then, as now, traditional Buddhist scholars have played roles in order to understand better the perspectives of their opponents. And of course, they have changed their minds as they have grown older.

So far we have established that the Buddha did not teach particular systems of tenets as such, although he taught about a great many subjects and, at least according to most Mahāyānists, articulated viewpoints that were apparently contradictory. The subsequent tradition organized and interpreted these teachings in various ways. Certain teachers developed followings. But are these "systems of tenets"? Not really, and that is where the genre of tenets texts comes in.

The seminal texts of Indian Buddhism are just a starting point for scholars like Jamyang Shayba or Losang Gönchok, who are system-builders. Just as the Sūtras are not systematic expositions of tenets, neither are the exegetical works that we have just identified. That they are analytical and have more the form of an argument does not mean that they are necessarily complete in themselves. For instance, Losang Gönchok explains at some length the "unique tenets" of the Prāsaṅgika school, which he traces back to Nāgārjuna. However, a close look reveals that Nāgārjuna himself made explicit assertions about only a few of the sixteen points presented by Jamyang Shayba; we arrive at the remainder by developing the implications of certain statements.

To give another example, as we shall see there are thought to be many different positions within the four schools and their sub-schools on what constitutes a "person," but few of these tenets are clearly stated in the texts. Gelukbas believe that only the Prāsaṅgika school correctly maintains that there is nothing within the mind-body continuum—the five aggregates—that *is* the "person"; rather, the person is something that is merely designated in dependence on mind and body. Everyone else gets it wrong, in one way or another. Some Cittamātrins, for instance, speak about a neutral, continuously operating consciousness that they call the mind-basis-of-all. Although no Cittamātrin ever baldly states that the mind-basis-of-all *is* the person, because of the way it is described and because it is said to travel from one lifetime to the next, we infer that this is their version of the person and ascribe it to them as one of their tenets.

What is the Value of Tenets Study?

Systematic philosophy is a Tibetan obsession, apparently building on late Indian Buddhism. East Asia went in quite a different direction, with schools based on particular sūtras that became virtual mono-texts for those who followed them. The

Tibetan tradition, by contrast, depends little upon sūtras themselves and heavily on the rich Indian commentarial literature, which lends itself more to system-building. Of course, that means that the Tibetan monk, compared to his Theravāda or East Asia counterparts, does much more reading.

Another tradition brought to Tibet from India is that of formal scholastic debating. Gelukbas are renowned for their belief in the value of study and debate, especially in comparison to some of the other orders of Tibetan Buddhism, which place more emphasis on the practice of meditation. It is not that they do not value meditation, at least in principle; but they see scholarship as an essential form of practice, too. As the contemporary Gelukba Geshe Jampa Gyatso, director of a teacher training program for Westerners (the Istituto Lama Tzong Khapa in Italy), says, "If one is ignorant, one cannot meditate. The Kadampa geshes have a saying that 'meditating without having listened to teachings is like someone without hands trying to climb a snow mountain.'"[1] Study and debate are supposed to remove misconceptions and sharpen the mind so that meditation can be more effective.[2]

This might be said to be a theme running throughout Tibetan Buddhism, inasmuch as all the orders, even those that do not emphasize study and debate, acknowledge the Great Debate in the late eighth century in which the Indian paṇḍit Kamalaśīla is reputed to have bested the Chinese meditation master named "Mahāyāna." That debate is said to have determined that Tibet would follow a "gradual" approach to enlightenment. There is still controversy over the site, date, and content of the debate, but it is true that the kind of philosophical study that emerged in Tibet is nourished by the idea that enlightenment is preceded by a lengthy, difficult process of perfection.

In the Gelukba monasteries, the positions of all schools are studied in order to fully understand the Buddhist context of the highest system, the Prāsaṅgika school.[3] Jamyang Shayba says in our text that "the views of the lower systems are a platform for [understanding] the views of the upper systems." We need a platform because it is too difficult and perhaps too dangerous to leap immediately to the study of

---

[1]Gyatso, "Climbing," 28.

[2]It should be noted that all of the time spent on debate comes at a price. Although Tibetan monks in general read more than other Buddhist monks, other orders may read more than Gelukbas. Dreyfus (*Sound*, 132) notes that Nyingma monks at the Namdroling Monastery just down the road from the Gelukba monastery of Sera in south India read and learn thirteen texts in half the time their Gelukba counterparts devote to five.

[3]The Gelukbas assert that all the major Tibetan sects are Prāsaṅgika, even if some of those sects do not explicitly identify themselves as such. For the Gelukba reasoning behind this assertion, see Hopkins, *Meditation*, 531–8—mostly a paraphrase of Janggya's *Presentation*, 291.9–9.8.

Prāsaṅgika (which would mean, basically, its explanation of emptiness). The twentieth-century Gelukba abbot, Kensur Yeshey Tupden, recommended that:[1]

> The student who has faith in emptiness but does not understand it begins by studying the Vaibhāṣika system, then Sautrāntika, Cittamātra, Svātantrika, and finally Prāsaṅgika. This method guards against undermining students' understanding of dependent arising, so that they will not [wrongly] conclude that validly established phenomena do not exist at all.

Kensur Rinpoche was concerned that a student, taught that nothing anywhere has any existence from its own side, but exists only as a nominal imputation (which is what "emptiness" means in the Prāsaṅgika system), might misunderstand what is meant and fall into some sort of nihilistic view. It is far better, it is thought, to begin with a strong affirmation of the world as it appears in all its variety and come to see what might be deficient in that view, than to begin with doubt and have to be convinced that the appearances of the world have value. (Of course, not everyone agrees. Bhāvaviveka, the founder of Svātantrika school, said that adopting the Cittamātra view and then using the Mādhyamika philosophy to reject the true existence of the mind is like wallowing in mud so that we can wash and get clean; it would be better not to get dirty in the first place.)

Beginning with the lower schools is also a "Prāsaṅgika" procedure, since Prāsaṅgikas work from the basis of other's views. We naturally are naive realists who believe in the true existence of whatever appears to our senses and doubt what does not. There is no harm, ultimately, in learning most of Buddhist thought from within that perspective, and there is the advantage that when the path of reasoning leads, as it inevitably will, to the established conclusions of the Prāsaṅgika, that the lessons learned will be all the more striking because of being hard-won.

Another way of putting this is that Gelukbas believe that the elimination of our ignorance depends upon accurately identifying, and then directly opposing through reasoning, the misconceptions we have about the reality of the self and the world. Dzongkaba says,

> One cannot see that there is no inherent existence without coming to disbelieve in the object of the conception of inherent establishment.[2]

---

[1]Klein, *Path*, 86.

[2]From Dzongkaba's *Middling Exposition of Special Insight*, unpublished translation by Hopkins, 26.

To "disbelieve" means to have believed and then to have abandoned one's belief. But how can this occur unless we have correctly ascertained our beliefs in the first place? One of the benefits of learning the tenets of the lower schools is that it may help us identify the beliefs that we may hold unconsciously, so that they can be subjected to analysis.

Still, it should not be thought that study and debate of tenets is itself liberating. Gelukbas emphasize that these are just steps upon the way. It is undoubtedly useful to eliminate the misconceptions that may match up with certain philosophical tenets but the final elimination of ignorance will depend upon identifying and rooting out a level of misconception that goes beyond any philosophical formulation. Erroneous tenets constitute mere "artificial" errors. Much more serious, and a universal problem rather than just a malady of philosophers, is the "innate" misconception of inherent existence that occurs simply through one's assent to the false manner in which ordinary things appear.

How Are Tenets Studied?[1]

The issues involved in books such as the present one are the very stuff of monastic education, permeating the curriculum. However, study of tenets books was not a formal part of the curriculum, except in a few places. One of them was Gomang College of Drebung Monastery, where monks normally memorized Jamyang Shayba's "root text" early in their studies, prior to the classes on the Perfection of Wisdom. They then had an outline of tenets to which they could make reference as they continued their studies, and which could be supplemented by commentaries, principally Jamyang Shayba's own *Great Exposition of Tenets.*

In the monastery, texts by renowned Indian scholars are formally the basis of study and students memorize those designated as "root" texts. Notably, sūtras (Buddha's discourses) are rarely studied. Even the Indian texts, translated from Sanskrit, are scarcely less difficult for young Tibetan monks than they are for us. Therefore, they rely upon Tibetan commentaries, such as those by Dzongkaba, and even more on special monastic debate manuals.[2] Each monastic college has its own. (Jamyang Shayba is the author of those used at Gomang College.) The debate

---

[1]Some of this section has been adapted from Cozort, "The Making..."

[2]However, Dreyfus notes (*Sound,* 116–7) that manuals are not used for the topics of monastic discipline and Abhidharma and that the commentaries the monks study are not exclusive to the Gelukba tradition.

manuals supply hypothetical debates, a systematic summary of "our own system," and responses to hypothetical objections.

Teachers teach the root texts and the debate manuals, following which students pair up to engage each other in long, formal sessions of dialectical debates on the material. The better students also read the Indian and Tibetan sources and the works of Gelukba founder Dzongkaba. (Some of the debate manuals are commentaries on Dzongkaba's Mādhyamika works, which are themselves commentaries on Indian texts.)

The Gelukba monasteries of Sera, Ganden, and Drebung awarded the geshe degree upon completion of a very ambitious curriculum and a final examination by debate.[1] Geshe Lhundup Sopa and Geshe Rabten completed the typical curriculum at Sera Monastery's Jay College, which they described in this way:[2]

- **Collected Topics on Valid Cognition.** The aspiring scholar, usually a young boy, is grounded in topics of logic, epistemology, and psychology for at least three years. He relies on his debate manual, the basis for which is the *Commentary on (Dignāga's) "Compendium on Valid Cognition"* by Dharmakīrti (seventh century). Much emphasis is placed on learning how to debate as the student considers topics such as sameness and difference, subjects and objects, karma, and parts and wholes. The topics of **Types of Mind** (literally, "awareness and knowledge," *blo rig*) and **Signs and Reasoning** are also studied at this time.
- **Perfection of Wisdom.** For five years, he studies seventy topics related to the spiritual path of Buddhist practitioners at all levels, based on Maitreya's (fourth century) *Ornament for Clear Realization*, various commentaries, and the Sera Jay debate manual.
- **Middle Way.** For four years, in two separate classes, he studies the Mādhyamika philosophy based on the debate manual, which is essentially a commentary on Dzongkaba's commentary on Candrakīrti's (seventh

---

[1]It should be noted that many monks, then and now, are not interested in or capable of advanced philosophical studies. However, it continues to be a very strong tradition, especially at the monastic universities that grant the geshe degree. It should also be noted that there are higher and lower types of the geshe degree and that examination by debate is not required for the lower type.

[2]Sopa, *Lectures*, 41–2. Time estimates are his but he notes that circumstances could easily extend the time required; brilliance and hard work could shorten it. Geshe Rabten (38) differs from this account only in noting that after the Abhidharma class there is a Karam (*bka' ram*) class that reviews discipline and Abhidharma in detail.

century) *Entrance to the Middle Way.* The ten Bodhisattva perfections and grounds are covered, although the main topic is emptiness.

- **Monastic discipline.** For four years, he studies Buddhist ethics as delineated in the rules of monastic life through the debate manual based on Guṅaprabha's (fourth century) *Sūtra on Discipline.*
- **Abhidharma.** For four years, he studies topics such as cosmology, meditative states, and psychology through commentaries on Vasubandhu's (fourth century) *Treasury of Abhidharma.*[1]

There were many small additions to this curriculum, such as the annual winter debating sessions on the Dharmakīrti's *Commentary on (Dignāga's) "Compendium on Valid Cognition"* and much time spent memorizing rituals and prayers. Students were organized into classes with teachers who met with them in the mornings and imparted a commentary on the text. Then, many hours were spent in memorization and debate. Monks were expected to learn by heart many texts, such as the Indian root texts for their classes, as well as the definitions, divisions, and illustrations of the debate manuals. They were not allowed to bring books to the debating courtyard but rather had to cite passages from memory. In Tibet, as many as eight hours per day were spent debating.[2] In India, Sera Jay's schedule includes two hours in the morning and two hours in the evening.

Viewed from the perspective of Western standards, it may seem that the education of a Sera monk is at once broad and narrow, deep and shallow. On the one hand, he learns only Buddhist philosophy. What he learns about Buddhist philosophy is also limited; there is nothing, for instance, from the East Asian or Theravāda traditions. He deals with only certain kinds of texts on a regular basis; he reads little of the Sūtra or even commentarial literature except what is filtered through the debate manuals. He reads a relatively small number of texts, considering how many years he is a student.

On the other hand, every student becomes an expert on every matter, great and small, that has occupied Buddhist philosophy. The debate manuals he uses, which

---

[1]The Abhidharma literature is comprised of analyses by Buddhist scholars of the material that is in the Buddha's discourses (sūtras). This process of analysis began very soon after the Buddha's death, and some Abhidharma-like material is even included in the sūtras themselves, which were not in final form for hundreds of years. But in the early Buddhist canon, the Abhidharma became a separate "basket" from the sūtras and the discipline texts (*vinaya*). Since the word Abhidharma can now be found in English dictionaries and since no translation of the term (such as "knowledge") is very meaningful, we have left it untranslated.

[2]Rabten, 50–1.

are anthologies of pertinent texts from across the Indian and Tibetan traditions, present him with multiple points of view, and he hears more from his teachers. Finally, he explores the topics in fine detail through testing them in the debating courtyard. For Gelukbas, it is much more important to memorize and debate than it is to read broadly.

When we studied tenets with lamas in India and America, our teachers subjected the texts to probing analysis and often tried to debate with us. Those from Drebung Monastery's Loseling College, which does not use Jamyang Shayba's texts, were particularly free with their criticisms of his assertions, although they sometimes agreed with him, even when it contradicted the explanations of their own debate manual author, Paṇchen Sönam Drakba (1478–1554).[1]

In terms of the content of the monastic curriculum, it is easy to see that monks are exposed to the different schools of tenets in stages. From the beginning, they learn logic, epistemology, and psychology in texts composed from the point of view of the lower schools. The Collected Topics book that is their starting point is a summation of some fundamental points from the same material, the writings of Dharmakīrti, that are the basis for the school of the Followers of Reasoning of the Sautrāntika and Cittamātra schools. They study Vasubandhu's *Treasury of Abhidharma* and his own separate explanation of it, respectively, the bases for the Vaibhāṣikas and for the Sautrāntikas Following Scripture. They study the main texts of the Mādhyamika school, which also serves as a study of the Cittamātra school inasmuch as those texts throughly explain and refute the school.

In the debating courtyard, therefore, everyone takes on the roles of proponents of the lower schools of tenets beginning with the Sautrāntika presentation. It is even the source of a Westerner's aphorism: "When you scratch a Gelukba geshe, there is a Sautrāntika underneath."

[1]However, on occasions of important public debate, such as those for the geshe degree, it is expected that a monk will uphold the manuals of his college. Also, the freedom of expression that characterizes the debating courtyard does not necessarily extend to publication, as Georges Dreyfus notes in his account of his own fifteen years as a monk *(Sound)*. In print, a monk is expected to hew to the positions established in his college.

What Are Buddhist Tenets?

We have now discussed how tenets have come about and how and why they should be an object of serious study. Before going on to some of the key issues that divide schools of Buddhist philosophy, we should briefly consider what unites them. One way to begin to explore that is to do what our text does and ask how Buddhism differs from the schools it rejects.

What Buddhists Have in Common With Other Indian Schools

The first part of Jamyang Shayba's root text concerns non-Buddhist Indian philosophies. It must be admitted that for the most part, he has misrepresented them, sometimes badly. However, there is value in these presentations, for they explain some of the concerns of Buddhist philosophy, both in the positive sense that Buddhists are in agreement with the general worldview of most of these schools and in the negative sense that some Buddhist tenets are rejections of their central assertions.

With a few exceptions, the Indian schools, Buddhism included, accepted the reality of rebirth and karma in a universe that is vast, perhaps infinite, and is populated by many types of beings who are experiencing different realities, mostly unaware of each other. Saṃsāra, the "wandering" of beings from one kind to another of these rebirths, life after life, is the basic problem. Although a small minority of living beings enjoy fabulous comforts and delights, most experience a great deal of suffering.

Although this may seem to be a pessimistic outlook on life, nearly all[1] of the Indian schools share a common hope of liberation (*mokṣa*) or passage beyond suffering (nirvāṇa). They agree that the cause of bondage is neither the machination of a malevolent spirit nor the misjudgment of a primordial ancestor, as we see so often in the world's religions. Rather, the cause of saṃsāra is our very own ignorance about our true nature, and therefore, we ourselves can do something about it. Thus, they also agree that personal experience leading to wisdom is the answer. Wisdom is supra-rational but reason is not rejected; it is the first step.

It is in their identification of ignorance that the schools vary considerably.

The **Sāṃkhya** school is the one on which our authors concentrate the most, perhaps because its description of self is the one with which Buddhism most clearly differs. The Sāṃkhyas are the principle "dualistic" school; they say that there are two eternal, uncaused principles, Nature (*prakṛti*, or *pradāna*) and Spirit *(puruṣa)*. Everything that exists, except Spirit, is included within Nature, even subtle states of consciousness that we might not expect to be lumped in with material constituents.

Our ignorance is that we mistakenly think that Nature itself or something within it is our true self. However, our true self is Spirit, that pure, indivisible, mere "witness" to events. The reason for this confusion is the very manifestation of Nature, which occurs through the interaction of the three "strands" of which it is composed. We can have direct experience only of that which has evolved from pure Nature. Spirit is experienced only indirectly, reflected to our ordinary mentality through the subtle level of consciousness called *buddhi*, the subconscious awareness. The most common error, therefore, is to mistake that subtle level of our own minds for the immutable and infinite Spirit.

The goal of spiritual discipline is to reverse the process of manifestation until even the subconscious awareness is withdrawn, at which point Spirit is isolated and ignorance is eliminated.

Advaita Vedānta is the principle "monistic" school, although it is treated very briefly here. Advaita Vedāntins say that our ignorance is to believe in our own reality, identifying "self" with our bodies and/or minds. However, only one ("mono") entity really exists; it is the Infinite, Brahman, which is permanent and indivisible. The spiritual path, primarily one of meditation, reveals the illusion in

[1]They are not mentioned specifically in our text but the Ajīvakas are one school that recognized the faults of saṃsāra without believing in an escape from it.

which we live and allows us to shed our birth identity and become, or merge with, the Infinite. (There are also dualistic Vedāntins, for whom our souls are not identical with the Infinite and who rely on a devotional relationship with God for liberation.)

Vaiśeṣikas and **Naiyāyikas** explain that the primary cause of fear, suffering, and death is ignorance in which the self is wrongly identified with the body. Self is an entity separate from the body and mind, and liberation comes from knowing this. (By the way, the Vaiśeṣikas are famous for their explanation of the composition of things by the aggregation of tiny particles, which has led some to conclude that there is a connection between this school and the Buddhist Vaibhāṣika school.)

Jainism (Nirgrantha) shares many views with Buddhism. Ignorance refers to our lack of understanding about the limits of our knowledge and the true cause-effect relationships in the world. We act with desire and hatred because of limited knowledge and the incorrect inferences that flow from it. Liberation from rebirth is not only a matter of knowledge, however, because karma, a material substance, encrusts the soul and can be removed only through asceticism. Knowledge prevents the further accumulation of karma. When liberation occurs, it is a state of bliss and omniscience, fused with the universe.

There are various theologies among the **Vaiṣṇavas** (those who worship Viṣṇu) and **Śaivas** (those who worship Śiva). Most of them are based on the philosophies of Sāṃkhya or Vedānta, with Viṣṇu or Śiva as the eternal principle with whom (or which) we seek union or who is reality itself.

In India there are always exceptions, and there was a school that rejected the prevailing viewpoint that we have been describing. The **Ayatas** differ from the preceding schools because they reject rebirth. Some of them also reject karma and the existence of beings other than those that appear on earth. Of all the schools discussed in our text, they are the only "proponents of annihilation" (that is, who say we are annihilated at death; we might call them "scientific materialists").

Some of the other schools are lukewarm in their concern with saṃsāra. **Mīmāṃsaka** developed as a response of Vedic priests to the criticisms of several schools, including Buddhism. It is mainly concerned with the interpretation of the wisdom texts, the Vedas, and how the performance of sacrifices can improve life now and prevent bad rebirth in the future. According to Losang Gönchok, it teaches that one type of rebirth, in the heaven of Brahmā, is permanent. However, liberation is just the dissolution of the mind and body at the time of death without subsequent rebirth. The schools identified as **Brāhmaṇa, Vaiyākarana**, and **Guhyaka** in our text are minor schools that are linked by similar concerns.

In summary, Buddhism shares the concerns of most of these schools: the problem of saṃsāra; its basis, delusion; its perpetuation, by karma; and the path of wisdom that leads away from it. In many ways, Buddhism stands in the middle of the views of these schools, since they include nihilists (who do not believe in future lives), eternalists (who believe in a permanent self, spirit or god), determinists (who think our lives are predetermined), and indeterminists (who think that events are random). It even forms a middle way not only between hedonists and ascetics (the middle way of behavior promulgated by the Buddha) but in style between the dry rationalists and the ecstatic devotionalists.

However, in one way Buddhism is quite distinct. It defines ignorance in a radically different way, one that is exactly the opposite of most of the non-Buddhist schools. In Buddhism, wisdom consists in understanding the *non*-existence of the self as it is defined in the non-Buddhist schools. Hence, the presentation of non-Buddhist tenets emphasizes the way in which the self is described, and, to a lesser extent, what is said about causality.

What Is a Buddhist?

Buddhism is not a "natural" religion, to use Joachim Wach's term, because we are not automatically Buddhists by birth (as we might be Hindus or Jews by birth, for instance, whether or not we ever become religiously observant). We have to *choose* to become Buddhists. And since it is a matter of choice, anyone can be a Buddhist; no one is excluded because they do not meet a standard of bloodline or ethnicity. That has helped to make Buddhism one of the few true "world" religions—religions that can easily cross cultural boundaries and become a global fellowship.

A Buddhist is simply a person who "goes for refuge" to the Three Jewels—the Buddha, his Teaching, and his Spiritual Community—which means that such a person considers them to be a haven from the terrors of saṃsāra. The *actual* refuge is the Teaching—in particular, true paths (the method) and true cessations (the elimination of the afflictive karma that causes rebirth). The Buddha is the teacher of the refuge, and the Spiritual Community is a congregation of helpmates and teachers. The Jewels act as helpers, not saviors; we must still make our own efforts.

Janggya says that going for refuge means: to know the qualities of the Three Jewels; to know the difference between them; to accept them; and not to go elsewhere for refuge.[1] He adds that it is not necessary to understand the Teaching fully in order to know its qualities and distinguish it from the other Jewels. We may go for refuge out of mere faith or out of a desire to avoid bad migrations.

Two particularly interesting points stem from this definition. First, it seems possible that we could *be* Buddhists without having formally identified ourselves in this manner. It is sufficient to meet the definition if we find ourselves fundamentally in agreement with the essential teachings of Buddhism and believe that it has salvific power, even if we do not practice it ourselves.

Second, it is clear that a Buddhist does not necessarily have a deep understanding of profound matters such as emptiness, as otherwise there would be few Buddhists! Nevertheless, being a Buddhist is not a matter of faith in the man, Buddha, or faith in claims that cannot be verified by reason; it is a matter of having concluded, insofar as we are able, that what the Buddha taught is correct.[2] In short, it is a matter of having "established conclusions," or tenets, that are Buddhist. (Then, depending on what they are, we may or may not be identifiable as belonging to a particular school of tenets.)

What is a Buddhist Tenet-Holder?

In the sense that anyone who takes refuge in the Teaching has arrived at certain conclusions that he or she feels are characteristically Buddhist, all Buddhists hold tenets. However, the tenets themselves might not be Buddhist, since they may not meet the standard of what are called "the four seals," described below. For instance, we might not understand properly the meaning of "selflessness," erroneously concluding that Buddhists reject any kind of self. In that case, although we might be Buddhists because of meeting the standard of taking refuge and might in a sense

---

[1] *Presentation*, 14.1.

[2] For *some* matters, Buddhists must take statements on faith. Although everything can be established by reasoning, sometimes this occurs only indirectly, as in the case of the subtle workings of karma. A "scriptural proof" is a statement such as, "Through giving, resources; from ethics, a good migration" (that is, if one performs acts of giving in this life, one will be born with good resources in a future life; if one practices good ethics, one will have a good rebirth). This is a "proof" only in the sense that once we have established by reasoning that the Buddha's teaching on the Four Noble Truths or emptiness is correct, we trust that his unverifiable statements are also correct.

even be holders of tenets because of having come to reasoned conclusions, we would not be holding a Buddhist tenet.

The "four seals" are tenets that are so called because they "stamp" a tenet as Buddhist. All Buddhist partisans, i.e., tenet-holders, propound the four seals, though they may disagree about certain aspects of them.

1 **All composed phenomena are impermanent**. This simply means that anything that has causes will change moment by moment, even if that change is imperceptible.[1]
2 **All contaminated things are miserable**. Everything in our experience is "contaminated" because it is ultimately the product of our ignorance. That is, intentional actions (karma) performed while misunderstanding the way things exist are the forces that cause our own births and the formation of the cosmos itself. All of these things are "miserable" in the sense that impermanence itself is a kind of suffering.
3 **All phenomena are selfless**. "Self" refers to what non-Buddhist schools describe as our true selves: a permanent (i.e., unchanging), unitary (i.e., indivisible), independent entity at the core of our being. No such "self" exists and there are no objects that are used by such a "self."
4 **Nirvāṇa is peace**. Nirvāṇa is not a place or a kind of consciousness but the absence of the afflictions of desire, hatred, and ignorance.

These characteristics are continuous with early Buddhism. The Buddha taught about the "three marks" of impermanence, selflessness, and suffering; the four seals are these three marks with the addition of the assurance of nirvāṇa. The four seals are also all implied in the teaching of the Four Noble Truths.

Alternately, the Buddhist view could be described as a middle way avoiding the two extremes of "permanence" or "nihilism." All of the non-Buddhist schools described in the first part of *The Clear Crystal Mirror* are guilty of one or the other. Let us discuss these a little further.

---

[1] "All composed phenomena" refers to things that have causes. Vaibhāṣikas deny the permanence of things merely on the grounds that they do not have continual existence but the other schools go further, understanding that things actually undergo change very rapidly at all times ("subtle" impermanence). The Vaibhāṣikas think that production, abiding, aging, and disintegration occur serially but the other schools say they occur simultaneously. That is, a thing lasts only for the moment of its production and must be reproduced in every succeeding moment until its final moment.

Proponents of Permanence are those who "deny too little." They say that something exists that in fact does not, such as a permanent self. It is the conception of a self found in the Hindu Upaniṣads: an individual soul (*ātman*) that is identical with Brahman—infinite being, consciousness, and bliss (*sat-cit-ananda*). Therefore, this soul/self is (1) permanent (in the sense of not changing moment to moment); (2) indivisible; and (3) independent (it is uncaused and does not produce an effect). Buddhists maintain that this is merely a *coarse*, or crude, false conception of a self. Therefore, its refutation would not be sufficient to win liberation from saṃsāra. We must overcome the most *subtle* false conception of a self. Also, this conception is merely *artificial*—one learned from parents or teachers—not one that we would naturally, innately hold.

Proponents of Annihilation are nihilists, those who "deny too much." They believe only what they see, hear, and so forth. In other words, they are skeptical materialists, and most secular Westerners would probably find much in common with them. They do not believe in karma or rebirth, for which Buddhists accuse them of lacking belief in inference itself. Specifically, they deny that persons can be designated in dependence on mind and body.

As we have seen, all non-Buddhist sects (except the Ayata, which is nihilistic) fall grossly to an extreme of permanence because of their assertion of a permanent, indivisible self. Each Buddhist school has its own interpretation of the "middle way" between the extremes of denying too much or too little, about which we will say more below. Of course, all views other than that of the Prāsaṅgika-Mādhyamikas fall to an extreme. The non-Prāsaṅgika Buddhist schools also fall to an extreme of permanence because they assert that phenomena truly exist. However, this error is considered to be less harmful than that of the non-Buddhists.

The views of the Buddhist schools are increasingly subtle as we consider in turn the Vaibhāṣika, Sautrāntika, Cittamātra, and Svātantrika-Mādhyamika schools. But because the views of the higher schools are quite subtle and require the refutation of grosser views, familiarizing ourselves with the views of a lower school can enable us to grasp the full meaning of the views of a higher one.

What Are the Buddhist Schools?

The idea of four schools of tenets was received from late Indian Buddhism. Within the four main schools, three are split into sub-schools and one sub-school is split into sub-sub-schools, for a total of eight schools (not counting the many sub-schools of Vaibhāṣika). In ascending order of proximity to the correct position of the highest school, the Prāsaṅgika school, they are as follows.

The Four Schools and Their Branches

- **Vaibhāṣika** (Great Exposition School)
- **Sautrāntika** (Sūtra School)
  - Sautrāntikas Following Reasoning
  - Sautrāntikas Following Scripture
- **Cittamātra** (Mind Only School)
  - Cittamātrins Following Reasoning
  - Cittamātrins Following Scripture
- **Mādhyamika** (Middle Way School)
  - Svātantrika (Autonomy School)
    - Yogācāra-Svātantrika (Autonomy Yogic Practice School)
    - Sautrāntika-Svātantrika (Autonomy Sūtra School)
  - Prāsaṅgika (Consequence School)

This hierarchy is highly disputable. For instance, there is little evidence of real Indian "schools" in the sense of lineages dedicated to a certain systematic view.

However, for Gelukbas this scheme represents the distillation of certain definite and strong currents in Indian thinking, based on the intellectual heritage translated from Sanskrit to Tibetan during the formative period of Tibetan Buddhism (sixth century C.E. onwards). What follows is a thumbnail sketch of each of them.

"**Vaibhāṣika**" is a cover term for many small sects that can be identified in early Buddhism. There are generally held to be eighteen sub-schools, although different ancient authors had different lists. Historically, the most important sub-school seems to have been the Sarvāstivāda. Their relationships are very complex, as our text indicates.

The term Vaibhāṣika means "follower of the *Mahāvibhāṣā*" (the *Great Exposition of Particulars*, an anonymous collection of teachings on the topics of the Abhidharma). However, not all of them follow that text, about which our authors knew little anyway because it had not been translated into Tibetan. Tibetan authors take Vasubandhu's fourth-century *Treasury of Abhidharma* as their main source for understanding Vaibhāṣika. Philosophically, Vaibhāṣikas are the most "realist" of the schools in the sense that they regard as truly real the tiny atoms out of which material things are made. Anything larger, constructed out of the aggregation of these atoms, is just "imputedly existent" and is "conventional" as opposed to "ultimate."

"**Sautrāntika**" just means "follower of Sūtra" (i.e., scripture), which in itself would seem to mean nothing because all Buddhist schools are followers of scripture. However, Sautrāntikas doubt that the Abhidharma literature or the Mahāyāna scriptures are the word of Buddha; therefore, they rely on their unique list of authentic scriptures. The Sautrāntikas probably began as dissenters from the Vaibhāṣikas, who rely on the Abhidharma to such a great extent.

Some are called Followers of Reasoning because they rely upon works by Dignāga and Dharmakīrti, who lived in the fifth and seventh centuries and are renowned for the development of logic and epistemology in response to Hindu schools. They differ from Vaibhāṣikas and the other Sautrāntikas in many small ways, such as the way in which they define ultimate and conventional truths. Others are called Followers of Scripture, which really means only that they are not the Followers of Reasoning. They rely on Vasubandhu's *Explanation of the "Treasury of Abhidharma,"* wherein he modifies some of the positions of his original Vaibhāṣika work. It is not clear that the Sautrāntikas existed very long, since the latter is their only unique text.

"**Cittamātra**" is a term applied to those who take literally the teaching in the *Saṃdhinirmocana Sūtra* and some other places that there is nothing external to consciousness, i.e., that the world is "mind only" (*citta-mātra*). Some are called Followers of Reasoning because, like their Sautrāntika counterparts, they rely upon the works of Dignāga and Dharmakīrti. The others are, of course, called Followers of Scripture. They follow the works of Asaṅga and Vasubandhu. (Asaṅga converted his half-brother, Vasubandhu, to the Mahāyāna; hence, Vasubandhu is an important source for three of the four main schools—Vaibhāṣika, Sautrāntika, and Cittamātra. Vasubandhu is even indirectly related to the Followers of Reasoning, both Sautrāntika and Cittamātrin, through his student Dignāga.)

The most significant of their differences from the Sautrāntikas is that they reject the existence of external objects. Also, the Followers of Reasoning argue that all persons eventually become Buddhas (a teaching known as "one final vehicle").

"**Mādhyamika**" just means "follower of the Middle Way," which is true of all Buddhist schools, but connects us to this school's foremost text, Nāgārjuna's *Mādhyamikakārikā* or "Treatise on the Middle Way." Nāgārjuna demonstrated that nothing truly or ultimately exists but that things do conventionally exist. That is, although things do not exist the way in which they appear, which is as if they had their own independent existence, they actually do exist.

Tibetan traditions consider the Mādhyamika school to have two branches, the split having taken place in the sixth century C.E. when Bhāvaviveka criticized Buddhapālita, who lived a century earlier, for his interpretation of the *Treatise on the Middle Way*. Candrakīrti (seventh century), in turn, defended Buddhapālita.[1] Bhāvaviveka's school is called Svātantrika ("Autonomy"), Candrakīrti's, Prāsaṅgika ("Consequence"). These names reflect two methods for helping others to realize emptiness, which in themselves are not very different. Bhāvaviveka would present the listener with a formal argument, a syllogism, whereas Buddhapālita and Candrakīrti would only present the consequences of an opponent's view.

However, Dzongkaba ascertained that there is a significant difference in view between the two because they have a different idea of "conventional truths," about which we will say more later. Svātantrikas include within existing phenomena (in the category of "conventional truths") some things that are unreal. These include

[1]This division was not recognized in India but was probably made in the late eleventh or early twelfth century after Candrakīrti's works were translated into Tibetan. The three texts in question are commentaries by Bhāvaviveka, Buddhapālita, and Candrakīrti on Nāgārjuna's *Treatise on the Middle Way*. For an extensive analysis of the Bhāvaviveka/Buddhapālita/Candrakīrti debate, see Hopkins, *Meditation*, 441–530 and the recent Dreyfus/McClintock volume.

optical illusions such as reflections or mirages, but more seriously, they also include truly existent things, things that seem as though they do not depend even on the awarenesses to which they appear. Although Svātantrikas themselves admit that nothing actually does exist this way, because they know that this is how things appear to ordinary people, they count such things as legitimately existent. Prāsaṅgikas also try to remain true to the conventions of the world, but they do not endorse truly existent things as conventional truths.[1]

Svātantrikas can themselves be divided into Yogācāra and Sautrāntika branches, the former relying on the views of the Indian abbot Śāntarakṣita, who was instrumental (along with Padmasambhāva) in establishing the first monastery in Tibet, Samye. The Yogācāra branch, like the Cittamātra school (Yogācāra, "practice of discipline," is an alternate name for Cittamātra), maintains that there are no external objects.

The Hierarchy of the Schools

The way in which these schools form a hierarchy is nothing that was self-evident in the Indian context. It has been constructed by Gelukbas who are looking at Indian Buddhist treatises through the lens of Dzongkaba's interpretation of Prāsaṅgika-Mādhyamika. It may not even be appropriate, for instance, to place the Sautrāntikas in the "Hīnayāna" camp; they may have been Mahāyānists who did not clearly identify themselves as such.

Nevertheless, it is fascinating to consider the criteria by which one school is "better" than another. They are not in order of founding, for instance, as we might expect. To be sure, the Vaibhāṣika school, the main type of which was the Sarvastivāda, does predate the arising of the Mahāyāna tradition and the founding of the Mādhyamika school, which can be roughly placed in the first century C.E. However, the Sautrāntikas and Cittamātrins rely upon works written in the fourth and seventh centuries C.E.

---

[1]Although it may not be obvious, there is a connection between the use of syllogisms as opposed to logical consequences and the way in which the Svātantrikas maintain that ruly existent things are conventional truths. Dzongkaba reasoned that if we rely on syllogisms, we must be assuming that there is an appearance common to both the stater and the hearer. Since at least one of the two persons, the one to whom the syllogism is directed, perceives truly existent objects, it must be the case that truly existent objects exist, at least on the level of conventional truths. If we rely on consequences, however, we are not stating any positive thesis but merely drawing attention to the deficiencies of the other person's view.

Rather, as indicated in the last chapter, the schools are arranged according to their approach to the "middle way" of denying the extremes of permanence and annihilation. Each succeeding school includes more in what it regards as "permanence" and less in what it regards as "annihilation."[1]

Roughly, we move gradually from radical "substantiality" to radical "insubstantiality" as we go from Vaibhāṣikas to Prāsaṅgikas. At the one end, Vaibhāṣikas call "ultimate truths" the substance particles out of which they say all things are built; they have substantial existence, by which they mean that they can be perceived without depending on anything else. At the other end, Prāsaṅgikas say that nothing substantially, truly, inherently, or ultimately exists (these terms all being equivalent); absolutely nothing has anything other than a mere nominal, imputed, interdependent existence, even the ultimate truth of all things, their emptiness of inherent existence.

Avoiding Permanence. We can see this movement as we consider how the schools claim to avoid the extreme of permanence. Each succeeding school enlarges the category of "permanence."

- Vaibhāṣikas think that it is sufficient to *deny the existence of a permanent, independent, singular self and to assert that anything that is caused, disintegrates.* (Some non-Buddhist schools, e.g., Sāṃkhya, claim that the cause continues to exist in the effect, since manifest existence is not new creation but an unfolding of what already exists in Nature, which contains all things.) However, they regard all things as substantially *established,* i.e., as having independent existence, and they regard irreducible particles as substantially *existent,* i.e., as being something we can recognize without depending on any other things.
- The Sautrāntikas Following Reason go further, maintaining that despite appearances, *things change rapidly, moment by moment* (a notion called "subtle impermanence"), and that *there are some things that exist not on their own but only by imputation,* such as space. However, they, like the Vaibhāṣikas, regard other things as having substantial existence.
- The Cittamātrins avoid the extreme of permanence by *denying that external objects truly exist* and by maintaining that *things are not by their own nature the basis of names* (i.e., that they do not have identity until we give it to them conceptually). They do not accept the existence of

[1]This way of putting it was suggested by Newland, *Appearance,* 59–60.

"indivisible particles," either. However, they do not apply the same criticism to the mind.[1]

- Mādhyamikas *deny that anything has true existence*, ultimately. However, the Prāsaṅgika branch goes further by denying that things have true existence in any way, even conventionally.[2]

Avoiding Annihilation. We can also see the movement from "more to less" when we consider how the schools avoid the extreme of annihilation. Each succeeding school accepts a greater level of non-existence.

- Vaibhāṣikas say that *all phenomena have substantial establishment.* They mean, basically, that all things exist independently of other things.[3]
- Sautrāntikas say that *things are established by their own character* as the bases of names and concepts and that the continuum of a product exists even after its destruction. (For instance, ashes exist after wood is burned.)
- Cittamātrins deny the existence of external objects but assert that those *non-external things are truly existent.*[4]
- Mādhyamikas deny the true existence of things, ultimately, and Prāsaṅgikas go further by denying the inherent existence of things in any sense, but they insist that *things do conventionally exist.*

---

[1]There is some controversy over whether Asaṅga asserts that the mind truly exists (see Nakamura, 279) but our texts do not reflect it.

[2]The twentieth-century Gelukba abbot Kensur Yeshey Tupden felt that the Cittamātrins come closer to the Prāsaṅgika view than do the other Mādhyamikas, the Svātantrikas, primarily because they give more primacy to the mind and less to the mind's object.

[3]In addition, those things that we can recognize even when they are physically broken or imaginatively separated (which, as we shall see, are what they regard as "ultimate truths") are also said to be *substantially* existent.

[4]Impermanent things *must* truly exist. There are *permanent* phenomena, too, and they are merely imputedly, not truly, existent. "Permanent" phenomena are so called because they have no causes but are just negations of some sort. For instance, space, the mere absence of obstructive contact; the mere absence of a marching band in my office; the mere absence of an inherently existent thing in my meditation (i.e., its emptiness)—all these are not caused and not changing moment to moment.

School	Avoids Permanence	Avoids Annihilation
Vaibhāṣikas	No permanent self; causes disintegrate	All things are substantially established
Sautrāntikas Following Reasoning	Subtle impermanence	Impermanent things are established by their own character
Cittamātrins	No external objects	Impermanent things truly exist
Svātantrika-Mādhyamikas	No true existence ultimately	True existence conventionally
Prāsaṅgika-Mādhyamika	No true existence even conventionally	Conventional existence

Hīnayāna vs. Mahāyāna

Buddhist schools are either Hīnayāna (Lesser Vehicle) or Mahāyāna (Great Vehicle).[1] There is no third "vehicle" to enlightenment, despite the fact that in contemporary Western literature the Vajrayāna (Diamond Vehicle), the tantric teachings, is sometimes called a third vehicle; it is simply tantric Mahāyāna. The Vaibhāṣika and Sautrāntika schools are considered to be Hīnayāna; the Cittamātra and Mādhyamika schools, Mahāyāna.

The grounds for distinguishing Hīnayāna and Mahāyāna are new ideas based on the Mahāyāna scriptures. What are these scriptures? We know that they were unknown to the world before about the first century. Jamyang Shayba explains that this is because after the Buddha taught them to appropriate audiences in his own time, they had to be hidden for four hundred years in the underwater world of the Nāgas so that they would not be misunderstood. They were recovered by the great

[1] Hīnayāna is an obviously pejorative term taken from the Mahāyāna sūtras. Some modern authors use "Theravāda" instead, reasoning that it is the sole modern heir of the Hīnayāna schools, but Theravāda historically was just one of many non-Mahāyāna schools. We use the term here mainly because it is the one employed by our authors. Roger Jackson has suggested that we think of "lesser" as meaning "fewer sūtras"!

Nāgārjuna, who was able to explain them properly, establishing the Mādhyamika school.

We might expect that the Hīnayāna would reject the authenticity of these newly discovered scriptures, and indeed they did. However, Jamyang Shayba, without explaining further, maintains that later Hīnayāna schools came to accept the authenticity of the Mahāyāna scriptures, although obviously they did not adopt new tenets.

Whatever is the actual case, it is clear that the Mahāyāna introduced new ideas that were not present in the scriptures followed by the Hīnayānists alone. Let us first look at three interrelated concepts: the *selflessness of phenomena*, the *obstructions to omniscience*, and the *Bodhisattva grounds*.

Selflessness of Phenomena. Both Mahāyāna schools (Cittamātra and Mādhyamika) maintain that we have misconceptions not only about the nature of the person, as "selflessness" implies, but about the nature of things in general. The same term, "self," is used to refer to a kind of misconception that actually has to do with things such as houses and cars. (Perhaps this is not so confusing, since sometimes we do talk about our possessions as though they were persons.) The Mahāyāna schools differ on their description of the selflessness of phenomena but we will explore that in another chapter.

Obstructions to Omniscience. The misconceptions about phenomena other than persons do not prevent one from becoming an Arhat, one who is liberated from saṃsāra. (Arhat was rendered in Tibetan as "Foe Destroyer," referring to the Arhat's destruction of the "foes" of the afflictions of ignorance, etc.) However, these misconceptions do obstruct omniscience, which is a very important quality of Buddhas. Since the aspiration of a Bodhisattva, the ideal person, is to become a Buddha, they must be eliminated.

The Hīnayāna schools do not speak of obstructions to omniscience as such. Vaibhāṣikas say that those rare persons who become Buddhas are able, by accumulating great merit, to remove "non-afflictive obstructions" that prevent ordinary persons from knowing the past or foretelling the future, from knowing what is happening in distant places, from knowing the specific karmic cause of events, and from knowing the special qualities of Buddhas. ("Non-afflicted" means "not connected with ignorance," which is why Hīnayāna and Mahāyāna are so different on this point.)[1] Buddhas are able to know anything to which they turn their attention (a more modest "all-knowingness" as opposed to the sense of omniscience in the Mahāyāna, which is that Buddhas know everything at every moment).

Bodhisattva Grounds. The scheme of Bodhisattva grounds is related to the ideas of the selflessness of phenomena and the obstructions to omniscience. These are ten gradations of the last major stage of the spiritual path leading to Buddhahood, the path of "meditation." They are set forth exactly as successive levels of the removal of the obstructions to omniscience, which in turn results from realizing the selflessness of phenomena. In other words, continued meditation gradually expands our abilities, our good qualities, and our scope of knowledge.

Bodhisattva Ideal. We have not mentioned the Bodhisattva ideal as a way to distinguish Hīnayāna and Mahāyāna. That is because our text makes clear that this would be incorrect. The Bodhisattva is distinguished by embodying *bodhicitta*—the selfless, altruistic great compassion that seeks Buddhahood in order to be maximally helpful to others. It is well known that the Mahāyāna tradition places great emphasis on the Bodhisattva ideal; most of its schools maintain that all persons eventually become Bodhisattvas themselves.

However, Jamyang Shayba considers this to be a distortion, since, although rare, there are Bodhisattvas within the Hīnayāna, too. To be a Bodhisattva is a matter of motivation, not philosophy, so it is conceivable that some persons would be Hīnayānists by tenet but Mahāyānists by path, and the reverse would be true as well. In fact, it is likely, since if it is so difficult to become a Bodhisattva, few holders of Mahāyāna tenets would be true Bodhisattvas.

Holding Tenets vs. Practicing the Path

One of the controversies in *The Clear Crystal Mirror* concerns attempts to correlate the three types of Buddhist practitioners (Hearers, Solitary Realizers, and Bodhisattvas) with particular schools. Jamyang Shayba says that such attempts are mistaken because all three types are found in each school.

---

[1]Guy Newland (*Appearance*, 23) makes the observation that since Vaibhāṣikas deny the ultimacy of most things, making it clear that they have only an imputed existence (one that requires dependence on other things), they also identify a sort of selflessness of phenomena.

A Hearer is one who hears doctrine, practices it, and proclaims it to others but who has not yet developed *bodhicitta* (altruistic compassion). Such a person may become liberated in a minimum of three lifetimes but will not become a Buddha until he or she switches to the Bodhisattva path.

Solitary Realizers are persons who have no teacher in their last lives; they also extend their practice for a hundred eons, which is why they get a similitude of a Buddha's body when they become enlightened. There are two types of Solitary Realizers: the *rhinoceros-like* who extend their practice because they believe they are to become Buddhas, and the *congregating*, who, because they had a teacher earlier in their last lives, are not so solitary.

Bodhisattvas have the extraordinary motivation to attain enlightenment for the sake of others. They also practice for an extraordinary length of time, up to three periods of "countless" great eons.

Any of these types can be found among any of the proponents of the tenet systems. For instance, a Hīnayānist *by tenet* can be a Bodhisattva *by motivation.* That is, there can be Hearers who, although they are Hīnayānists *by tenet* (i.e., are Sautrāntikas or Vaibhāṣikas), are Mahāyānists *by path* because of their altruistic motivation. Therefore, they respect Mahāyānists such as Nāgārjuna. The reverse is also certainly true. There are Mahāyānists by tenet who lack the Bodhisattva motivation and, therefore, are still Hīnayānists by path.

Summary

We have seen that the various schools of Buddhist tenets do not represent different types of practice or motivation. Their differences are philosophical.

The two Hīnayāna schools can be distinguished from the two Mahāyāna schools by their distinctive stances on the inter-related issues of the selflessness of persons, the obstructions to omniscience, and the Bodhisattva grounds. However, the principal means by which the schools are arranged in a hierarchy is through their take on the Buddha's middle way between the extremes of affirming or denying too much of how the world appears to us.

What Is Ignorance?

Why do we suffer and die? Buddhism answers: because we do not understand ourselves and our world. Suffering and death are not inevitable, as many religions teach; they are not our punishment for sin; they are not what a mythic ancestor chose for us. Rather, this regrettable condition is the result of a terrible misunderstanding.

It is important to keep in mind that the ignorance with which we are concerned is not a lack of knowledge, such as my ignorance of Swahili; it is bad knowledge, a *mis*-understanding, a *mis*-conception. To some degree, our ignorance is of our own making, since we may have been taught to believe in a false kind of existence. Buddhism indicts many of the non-Buddhist Indian schools, and by extension the world's largest religions, for teaching that there is a soul, or inner self, that is unchanging, independent of whatever is going on in our minds and bodies, and is singular. One of the four "seals" that mark a doctrine as Buddhist is the denial of precisely this sort of entity.

However, these sorts of ideas are "artificial"; they are constructions, ideas that must come to us from outside. Although they are very unhelpful, no Buddhist school regards them as being the real cause of our problem, which is a level of misconception that is somewhat more subtle and much more insidious, since it comes to us naturally—it is "innate." Ignorance is not, therefore, fundamentally a matter of taking the wrong stance, of having an incorrect philosophical position; it is a universal problem of the tutored and untutored alike.

We will look below at what the various schools identify as this innate ignorance but all of them involve the concept that with regard to a person or thing there is something that independently *is* that person or thing—the essence, or true reality of it—which then may be conceived in different relationships to the mind and body (in the case of the person) or to the parts of the thing. Put another way, they all involve something other than what wisdom understands, which is that nothing has that sort of independent existence.

To use a crude metaphor, ignorance is, in some way, to think of the self as our hard core, like the pit of a peach. Even after the flesh of the peach has dried up and blown away, the pit remains. All Buddhist schools reject the concepts of the non-Buddhist schools on the grounds that they see the self as a peach. However, most of the Buddhist schools also have a tendency towards "peachiness," one that is more subtle.

The Prāsaṅgika school says that the self is really an onion; if we peel away the layers (all the different aspects of mind and body), we find that the core is empty. What constitutes our aggregates of body and mind are our "layers." "Self" is just a convenient way to refer to the whole, but it is inevitably made into a peach pit rather than being recognized as the empty onion core it really is. There is no "essence" or intrinsic character to anything; our existence is relational and dependent. In the next chapter we will discuss the various choices Buddhist schools have made regarding the basis for designating a relational and dependent "self."

The following table shows the range of misconceptions and the harm that the various schools think they do.[1] It is arranged in terms of how these misconceptions prevent liberation from suffering or the liberation of the mind from its obstructions to omniscience. Only the elimination of those labeled "subtle" will change one's status but dealing with the "coarse" conceptions may be an important step towards that result.

The harmful misconceptions are listed in order of most coarse to most subtle from the point of view of the Prāsaṅgika school. Again, it is important to bear in mind that we are not discussing philosophical views but the sorts of innate misconceptions that ordinary people may have. Any given individual tends to one or another of them in ordinary situations. After the table we will sketch them individually.

[1]Adapted from Hopkins, *Meditation,* 300–1.

Conception	Obstructiveness	Schools
Permanent, single, independent person	Coarse obstruction to liberation	All schools (but Prāsaṅgika considers it an "artificial" conception)
Self-sufficient person	Coarse obstruction to liberation	Prāsaṅgika
Self-sufficient person	Subtle obstruction to liberation	All schools except Prāsaṅgika
Phenomena are naturally bases of names; subject and object are different entities	Subtle obstruction to omniscience	Cittamātra
Subject and object are different entities	Coarse obstruction to omniscience	Yogācāra-Svātantrika
True existence	Subtle obstruction to omniscience	Svātantrika
Inherent existence	Subtle obstruction to liberation	Prāsaṅgika
Appearance of inherent existence; *stains* of conceiving the two truths as different entities.	Subtle obstruction to omniscience	Prāsaṅgika

Permanent, Indivisible, Independent Person. This is the conception that there is a self that is uncaused and does not act as a cause, is without parts, and is independent of the mind and body. This is the classic formulation of the Indian Upaniṣads about the *ātman*, the individual soul that is in truth identical to the Infinite, the Brahman. It does not match exactly the concept of soul in any other religion, although in most religions there is at least one soul that survives death and, therefore, is independent of the mind and body in life.

Although all Buddhists reject this concept, even the Hīnayāna schools regard it as a "coarse" conception and think that there is a slightly more subtle level of ignorance. Therefore, overcoming this type of ignorance is not sufficient to win liberation. Prāsaṅgikas make the further qualification that this conception is not innate, or natural, but is the result of tutoring.

Self-Sufficient Person. This is the conception of a self that is not only permanent and unitary but is the "boss" of the mind and body. That the self is "self-sufficient" means that it can appear to the mind without depending on other objects, i.e., that it can appear to our minds without depending on the mind and body.

This conception prevails in our ordinary talk about the self. Do we not speak of "my body" or "my mind" as though the "I" is the owner or master of mind and body, which are like its possessions or subjects? When we reminisce, or plan for the future, do we not say "When *I* was five...," or "When *I* am sixty...," as though the "I" of the child, the adult, and the senior is exactly the same? In our hearts we feel that there is something irreducibly *me* here, which is special, unique, and unlike the mind and body, not changing all the time. Do we not describe a search for identity as "finding" ourselves, as though there was a "real" me underneath the flux of personality? Do we not believe that we have utter free will? In the West, at least, we believe in our individual integrity—that we can do without other people and just be ourselves (a richer, better version of what we are presently).

Most of the Buddhist schools consider this type of conception to be the crucial obstacle to liberation. The Prāsaṅgika school alone identifies a yet more subtle type of conception, the conception of inherent existence, which is described below.

Phenomena Are Naturally Bases of Names. When we see something familiar, it seems to be *naturally* the basis of the name we give it; that is, it does not appear to be something that *has to be named*. For instance, when we see a flat surface supported by legs, we immediately feel that it *is* a table, not merely that it is something to which we must attach the name "table." According to the Cittamātra school, the flat-surface-with-legs appears to our eye consciousness to be a table, and then we immediately conceive that this appearance is correct. (Prāsaṅgikas say that this is absurd, since if it were true, we would know flat-surface-with-legs as a table even if we had no concept of table or knew the name "table.")

Subject and Object Are Different Entities. This is the conception that our consciousnesses (eye, ear, nose, tongue, body, and mental) are independent of their objects, such that an object causes perception. For instance, we assume that first the sun rises, and then that the light entering our eyes leads to an awareness of the sun.

Cittamātrins (and Yogācāra-Svatantrikas) contend that there are no external objects; subject and object are caused simultaneously by a single karmic potency. Because they necessarily arise together, they are one entity, like flame and heat. This conception goes together with the previous one since it is precisely because we misconceive of things as naturally the basis of a name—again, as being something without having to be named—that we conceive of them as being different entities from consciousness.

True Existence. This is a conception that applies to all phenomena, not just persons. It is that any phenomenon has what we might call "pointable existence": that there is something—one of the aggregates or parts; their collection; or, something apart from them—that can be pointed to *as being* that phenomenon. For instance, it is said that when we refer to ourselves, we conceive of some aspect, such as the mind itself or the feelings, as *being* what we really are; when we point to a table, we feel that there is something that really *is* the table, such as its top or the mere collection of its parts. Somehow the table itself is *within* the parts of which it is made. This conception is subtler than the conception of a self-sufficient person because it usually does not involve conceiving that there is an entity apart from the mind and body that controls them.

Inherent Existence. This conception also applies to all phenomena. Like the conception of true existence, we conceive of something we can point to; however, we do not conceive of this as being anything from among the aggregates (or parts). Rather, the self or thing just seems to be indistinguishable from the aggregates or parts. The "I" or the "thingness" is somehow more important but not distinguishable from that to which it is intimately related. With another phenomenon, such as a table, the conception is that there is some "tableness" that pervades the table and is its real identity, without any conception that the table is some specific part, etc. Again, this conception is *innate*, not something learned.

***Appearance* of Inherent Existence.** As stated, this includes the "stains" of conceiving the two truths as different entities. Prāsaṅgikas do not differentiate between what we must understand to become liberated persons (Arhats) and what we must understand to become Buddhas. The conception of inherent existence is always the target. At one point along the path, our direct realization of the emptiness of inherent existence will eliminate all of the afflictions of ignorance, desire, and hatred that cause rebirth, and we will become Arhats.[1] We will never again conceive of things as inherently existing. However, because of our beginningless conditioning to this way of seeing things, they continue to *appear* to us in the usual, false way. There is no longer any danger that we might believe this appearance but nevertheless, it continues, only slowly giving way. Until it completely disappears, we cannot simultaneously know things and their emptinesses (which, as we will discuss later, are known as the "two truths"). Therefore, we are not omniscient.

In brief, all schools other than Prāsaṅgika are said to be "Proponents of True Existence" because they do not completely reject the idea that phenomena have some kind of "pointable" existence. Cittamātrins deny that *external objects* have true existence but they do not deny that *mere* objects or the *mind* does; Svātantrika-Mādhyamikas deny true existence *ultimately* but they say that *conventionally*, in the world, "truly existent" is the way things really exist. Only Prāsaṅgikas say that *even in the conventions of the world* nothing truly exists. That is, there is no valid cognition of any inherently existent object. Their rejection of it is total, so they are the sole "Proponents of Non-True Existence," or "Proponents of Only-Imputed Existence," since they say that things can only be said to exist as mere imputations or designations in dependence upon parts or thought.

If no other school recognizes the conception of inherent existence, does this mean that only Prāsaṅgikas can become liberated? Not exactly. The Prāsaṅgika school thinks that it is necessary to realize directly the absence of inherent existence in order to become liberated from saṃsāra. At the same time, they do not deny that non-Prāsaṅgikas can attain liberation. How can that be? We must recall that we are talking about innate conceptions that are identified and analyzed in meditation, not propositions that are argued in the debating courtyard. It is possible for anyone to realize something more subtle than what their own schools teach, if they are, in fact, even a proponent of tenets. That is, such people simply discover, in meditation, a deeper truth than they were seeking.

---

[1]The obstructions to liberation are eliminated at the seventh of the ten Bodhisattva grounds into which the fourth of the five paths is divided. The fifth path, the path of no more learning, is Buddhahood, when the obstructions to omniscience have been eliminated as well. To indicate how much more work must be done to eliminate the obstructions to omniscience (and how much greater are Buddhas than Arhats), it is said that this period is one of countless great eons.

Why Are We Ignorant?

Buddhists generally do not speculate about the causes of ignorance other than to say that it is as beginningless as the universe and perpetuates itself endlessly unless we are fortunate enough to encounter the Dharma and learn how to challenge it. It is felt to be enough to identify it as the problem and to find methods to overcome it. However, thinking that it might help our readers to understand how these conceptions might take form in themselves, what follows are some brief indications of how the operation of ordinary consciousness helps to create an illusory sense of self.

In the first place, consciousness (that is, mental consciousness, to use the Buddhist terminology) is primarily the ability to *imagine*. One of the ways we believe that we differ from the lower animals and from humans who lived more than a few millennia ago is our capacity to create mental analogues of ourselves and other things so that we might replay past events and plan for the future. To plan for the future implies goals and intentions, which are intimately bound up with our image of self. Indeed, the self might be described, as Csikszentmihalyi does, as the "dynamic mental representation we have of the entire system of our goals."[1] Our experience continually refers to this structure and brings to it a greater level of complexity. Perhaps ignorance about the self derives in no small part from this capacity to create an analogue of ourselves and imagine it interacting with other people and things.

Similarly, consciousness has a powerful capacity to create the illusion of a stable world around us. It is obvious that since we have at any given moment a limited scope of knowledge and do not have the ability to keep track of everything at once, consciousness must construct a picture of the world for us. It operates by what might be called "screening" and "story-making." First, it is necessary to screen out much of the sensory data available to us at any given moment, as we would otherwise be overwhelmed. We are able to do this with such success that sometimes, when we are very focused, we have virtually no awareness of anything except the task at hand.

Nevertheless, we have a remarkable sense of continuity, both of our own being and of our environments, due to the way that human consciousness fills in the gaps to make experience seem fluid, connected, and whole. It maintains the illusion that there is a continuous "me" keeping track of everything. Hour after hour, day after day, we maintain a description of ourselves and the world that is based upon only

---

[1] *Flow*, 35.

fragmentary information. Moreover, this is a highly conservative process, tending to resist strongly new information or perspectives that conflict with the storyline. We suggest that perhaps this powerful and extremely subtle feature of consciousness supports the illusion of a continuous, central self.

Another relevant aspect of consciousness is the way in which recognition occurs. The Buddhist epistemologists as represented by the Sautrāntika school give us the best discussion of perception, one accepted by the higher schools as well. How do we recognize things? The epistemologists answer that we all have a store of "generic images"—mental constructs of *types* of things. We have a construct for every phenomenon we are capable of recognizing. When we recognize something, we "match up" the external sense data with mental images of the *types* of things we are perceiving. To recognize a "tree," for instance, I make reference to my *idea* of "tree," which is not any specific, real tree but rather the amalgam of all trees I've ever experienced. My present perception then gets *mixed* with past experiences; it becomes impossible to experience anything nakedly, freshly. We suggest that perhaps the very existence of such generic, or *a priori*, images, makes us tend to *assume* "tree-ness" as something real, not merely a projection from our own side.

Finally, it seems obvious that we might indulge in the imagined self of ignorance in part because we are disturbed by aging, death, and the transience of the things of our experience. It is deeply unsettling to see everything in constant change. (Western existentialism focuses upon this experience of the mere "contingency" or non-necessity of everything.) It is comforting to assume that at the core, persons and other phenomena are stable.

Whatever might be the mechanisms by which we come to have an erroneous, overly solidified sense of self, it is clear that it is intimately connected with tendencies to be aggressive, acquisitive, intolerant, jealous, and miserly, to name but a few. Recalling Csikszentmihalyi's description of the self as a set of goals, we know that our primary goal is self-preservation and, beyond that, self-enhancement, as might occur through the extension of the self in representations such as material possessions, power over others, and identification with larger entities such as nations, political movements, religions, and so forth. Buddhism contends that to become aware of the construction of self and its ramifications is to become free of them. Perhaps this is what the Japanese Zen master Dogen meant when he said, "To study the self is to forget the self."

What Is a Person?

Buddhist philosophers use the word "person" more broadly than do most of us, since not only humans but also animals, hell beings, hungry ghosts, demi-gods, and gods are persons. But they also use the term in a special sense to designate that which is the most essential aspect of our individual beings. To put it another way, they ask, "What is it about me that constitutes my personhood? What is really *me*?"

One way to begin to answer this question is to make an inventory of the various aspects of living beings. We are all complex creatures, having a certain type of body and a mentality that can be distinguished into various kinds of consciousness, certain feelings, certain moods and motivations, and certain discriminations. The Buddha spoke often about the five "aggregates" of body and mind, categories into which he placed all of these elements.

But when we refer to the "person," or even "me," just what among these factors *is* it? Am I my body? My mind? Some combination of them? Problems immediately arise when we consider any of these possibilities, for both the body and mind change continuously, and some aspects of them may become absented. How can I identify "me" with my body if I lose my arms or legs in an accident, or if I receive mechanical or transplanted organs or joints? How can I identify "me" with my memories if amnesia or Alzheimer's might rob me of them? Am I whatever I am thinking, moment to moment? Do I cease to exist if I am not thinking, such as when I'm asleep or unconscious? Where is "me" if I'm in a coma?

As we have seen, one point that differentiates Buddhist schools from the non-Buddhists is that the latter tend to define a person as something that is the unchanging core of the body and mind but is different from either; it is emphatically *not* the body and *not* the mind. Religions that speak about the "soul" are generally referring to such an entity. For them, my soul is irreducibly *me*, from the moment of my conception to the moment of my death, and possibly also before and after the present life.

But Buddhists begin with the rejection of such entities, and, therefore, must answer the question, "What does 'person' refer to?" in some way that can rely upon the five aggregates of body and mind. It is not a question, as some have thought, of denying that the word "person" or "self" means anything at all. "Selflessness" has always meant the negation of some *concept about* the self rather than selfhood itself.[1] To deny selfhood would be to deny multiplicity and come to rest in a view, like the Indian Vedāntins, wherein the only real existence is that of God, or whatever term we might choose to use for the Infinite and All-Inclusive.

So, given the existence of five aggregates of mind and body, what should be regarded as the "person"? It is not a trivial question, since most of the Buddhist schools regard the person as that to which the seeds of intentional actions (karma) are infused or attached. Therefore, they sought to identify something that would be present continuously. (Which is not to say it would be unchanging; it only means that at all times there is something whose existence is not in doubt.)

Remembering, again, that the answers given by Jamyang Shayba for the various schools are sometimes based on inference rather than forthright assertions, let us survey the range of possibilities as he and Losang Gönchok explained them.

Mere Collection of the Aggregates. (Most Vaibhāṣikas) There are many kinds of Vaibhāṣikas, and this is one of the issues on which they disagree. However, most of them would say that the person is the "mere collection" of the five aggregates of body and mind, there being no "substantially existent" person. What they mean by "mere" is also what is meant by "not substantially existent": a person is something that comes to mind only in dependence on perceiving something else first. For instance, I cannot say that I have perceived a person until I have at least seen a body, heard a voice, or seen writing. The "person" is whatever is used within the five aggregates as a basis for recognizing someone as a person. It is not an independent category.

This understanding of "person" would seem to avoid the problems mentioned in relation to the non-Buddhist schools. It is not some sort of permanent, unchanging entity apart from mind and body; nor is it some aspect of the aggregates that would not be continuously able to provide a place to "point." But it is, to be sure, a slippery concept. It is supposedly not separate from the aggregates, yet it is not any of them itself.

---

[1]In general, there is no reason why "person" and "self" cannot be used interchangeably, once it is understood that when speaking of the selflessness of persons, "self" means a certain *kind* of self, not self in general. However, to avoid confusion we will use "person" in this section.

Inexpressible Reality. (Some Vaibhāṣikas—the Saṃmitīya schools) This is a very different sort of notion. The Saṃmitīyas say that the person is an entity that, although it definitely exists, cannot be ***said*** to be either the same as the five aggregates or different from them. It is "inexpressible." They reason that if it were identical to the five aggregates, it would cease at death; if it were not, it would be separate from them and, therefore, would be like the non-Buddhist *ātman*, which is eternal and beyond limits.[1]

This idea is in some ways close to that of the Prāsaṅgikas, for whom the person is also inexpressible in that way; but for Prāsaṅgikas, it is not a "substantial entity," one with its own independent existence. Nevertheless, the "inexpressible reality" is not a cogent assertion, since although it is supposed to be a substantial entity, it does not amount to anything to which we can point.

Continuum of the Aggregates. (Sautrāntikas Following Scripture, Kashmiri Vaibhāṣikas, and Sautrāntika-Svātantrika-Mādhyamikas) Perhaps these schools realized that there were significant problems with the possibility of "collection"; in any case, they identified as the person the continuum or stream—the mere successions of moments—of the mind and body. This, too, avoids the problems of identifying an entity that exists outside of the aggregates or cannot always be present. Change is always occurring in our bodies and minds, and quite possibly there are times when there is no particular functioning *consciousness*, but there is always *something* present such that we can say that a stream continues. During life there is always a body but even before and after life as well as during it there is a stream of moments of consciousness.

Mental Consciousness. (Sautrāntikas and Cittamātrins Following Reasoning) These followers of Dharmakīrti, who differ on other tenets, say that a subtle, neutral form of the mental consciousness is the person. In Dharmakīrti's system and

---

[1]This view, regarded by other Buddhist schools as heretical, was very popular. According to the seventh-century Chinese pilgrim Xuanzang, it was the view of 66,000 of 254,000 monks at that time. Considerable space is devoted in Losang Gönchok's commentary to defending the view that these schools *are* Buddhist. What he argues there is that just because they say that the person cannot be said to be *within* the five aggregates, they are not necessarily asserting its opposite, namely that the person exists *outside* the five aggregates. Only if they had, would they be outside the Buddhist view. However, Jamyang Shayba's own commentary in the *Great Exposition of Tenets* differs from Losang Gönchok's; he does not think that the Vatsiputriya sub-school's person is a substantial entity. Also, according to Gönchok Jikmay Wangbo, the Avantakas, one of the Saṃmitīya schools, maintain that the mind alone is the person.

in Buddhism generally, there are six types of consciousness. In addition to'the mental consciousness, which discriminates and cogitates, there are five consciousnesses associated with the senses.

This solution seems to suffer the objection that the mental consciousness does not operate continuously, at least at times of unconsciousness. Vasubandhu says in his *Thirty Stanzas* that there are five such states. Deep sleep (without dreams) and fainting are two that all of us experience (and along these lines there are several other types of unconsciousness that he might have included as well). Then there are two kinds of special meditative states, the absorptions of non-discrimination and cessation, which are devoid of feelings and discriminations. As a result of experiencing the absorption of non-discrimination, we might be born in a heaven (which in Buddhism is a temporary abode), specifically the Form Realm heaven called "Without Discrimination."

Subtle Neutral Mental Consciousness. (Svātantrikas) This is not the conceptual mind but a substratum without content. Some subtle form of the mental consciousness must always be present, it is thought, for consciousness does not arise by itself but is caused.[1] It cannot be caused by the body but must be caused by a previous moment of consciousness. Consciousness is a never ending stream. Hence, some kind of mental consciousness *must* be present, even when we are in a coma or in the circumstances named by Vasubandhu, which means that there is a subtle level of consciousness even if "coarse" feelings and discriminations are absent. This subtle consciousness cannot ordinarily be remembered, so the proof of its existence is merely that it is logically necessary.

Mind-Basis-of-All. (Cittamātrins Following Scripture and Yogācāra-Svātantrika-Mādhyamikas) These followers of Asaṅga introduce a new concept, that of the mind-basis-of-all, a neutral, continuously operating consciousness with no other function than to hold the seeds of actions. Indeed, the karmic latencies and the mind-basis-of-all are a single substantial entity; they are never found apart from one another and are different only conceptually.

Cittamātrins reject the other possibilities because they contend that all other consciousnesses are absent at some time or another. Sense consciousnesses do not operate continuously (and some cannot operate at all, if their physical basis is gone,

[1]There are three conditions for the production of a sense consciousness: an "empowering condition" such as an eye sense power, an "immediately preceding condition"such as a previous moment of consciousness, and an "observed object condition" such as an external object.

such as in the case of blindness). Even if that were not the case, they see a problem in designating the mental consciousness, even a subtle level of it, as the person because the mental consciousness can be virtuous or non-virtuous. They felt that whatever is the basis of seeds established by virtue or non-virtue should itself be neutral. Also, they asked,'if the seed-bearer were the mental consciousness, would not that mean that whenever we had a thought, there would be two simultaneous mental consciousnesses?

Mere I. (Prāsaṅgika) The Prāsaṅgika designation of the person aptly demonstrates why it might be best to approach Prāsaṅgika only after having considered the other schools, since it is a subtle view and one that follows upon the refutation of the others. Prāsaṅgikas consider all of the possibilities mentioned above to be indefensible, since they are all based upon the assumption of the "true existence" of the person that, when sought among the "bases of designation" such as the mind and body, can be found. Rather, Prāsaṅgikas say, an analytical search will not result in the finding of anything that exists independently. All things are "empty." Prāsaṅgikas also generally uphold the conventions of the world. Since the mind-basis-of-all is something unknown to ordinary persons, we should be skeptical of its existence.

The "mere I" is just that: the person is a name. It is a nominal designation made on the basis of the aggregates but it is not itself any of the aggregates. As we saw in the last chapter, the various possibilities outlined above assume substantial existence. That is precisely what is wrong with them.

Sometimes it is said that for Prāsaṅgikas, the subtle mental consciousness can also be designated as the person. The subtle mental consciousness certainly can give rise to the thought "I," and as long as it is understood that the "I" is merely designated *in dependence on* the mental consciousness rather than *being* the mental consciousness, there is no problem. The mind-basis-of-all and some other entities that will be discussed below, however, are unnecessary additions that go beyond worldly conventions.

The Transmission of Karma

The topic of the "person," as we said earlier, is linked to the topic of karma. The various possibilities mentioned here are ways to account for the transmission of karmic potentials from one life to the next. The problem faced by all Buddhist tenet systems, which share with most other Indian philosophical systems a cosmology based on the notions of karma and reincarnation, is that there must be a continual basis for such latencies; otherwise, actions and their effects would not necessarily be related.

We have already seen that most of the sub-schools comprising the Vaibhāṣika school (from what has been gathered from a close reading of Vasubandhu's *Treasury of Abhidharma*) identify the person as the mere collection of the aggregates. How do they explain how karmic latencies attach to this mere collection? The Vaibhāṣika schools introduce a factor called "acquisition," the function of which is to attach the latencies to the continuum of the sentient being who has acquired them.

Several other Vaibhāṣika sub-sects—the Sarvāstivāda, Vibhajyavāda, and Saṃmitīya—refer to a factor called "non-wastage" of actions, meaning that the potencies of karma persist until their fruition without being "wasted." In the case of other schools, no additional factors are mentioned: Kashmiri Vaibhāṣikas, Sautrāntikas, and the Sautrāntika-Svātantrika-Mādhyamika school consider the continuum of mind to be the basis of infusion, while Cittamātrins and the Yogācāra-Svātantrika-Mādhyamika school use the idea of a mind-basis-of-all.

Prāsaṅgikas criticize these "karmic seed-holders" because they are presented as substantially existent entities, as are the seeds themselves. They believe that it is not necessary to invent any of these possibilities. Rather, a fact about actions themselves, their "disintegratedness," which requires neither intervening causes nor making actions into permanent entities, is responsible for the production of effects. "Disintegratedness" is not a very elegant term but it refers to the state that exists once something has occurred and is now in the past. Jamyang Shayba explains at some length how this state can function to produce effects.

Here, the Prāsaṅgikas have changed the terminology of karmic cause and effect. It is no longer necessary to say that actions establish "seeds" for future effects or to say that they are held in a neutral medium until ripened by appropriate conditions into an individual fruition, for each virtuous or non-virtuous action has a later continuum—its continuum of disintegratedness—that serves to link the action and its effect. It might be said that for Prāsaṅgikas, the disintegratedness of actions simply performs the same functions that, in other explanations, are performed by a karmic seed.

Persons and Other Things

It is now obvious that it is quite difficult to identify a person, since unless we admit that nothing inherently *is* the person, that we only *designate* a person, we are misconceiving of it. But we should not think that the phenomenon of a person is any different than any other phenomenon.

For instance, what is a table? We might answer: it is a manufactured article on which objects can rest, consisting of a horizontal top and at least one leg that supports it. Has top and legs, acts as a platform. Right? But wait: can we point to something that *is* the table? It could not be the top alone, nor the leg or legs alone. If it is the *collection* of these parts, we have the difficulty not only of pointing to "collection," which is an abstract concept, but of explaining how there can still be a table if a part (say a brace or an ornamental foot) falls off, thereby changing the collection.

No, there is no table save the one that we designate upon perceiving the objects and relationships that meet our definition of table. And perhaps that is a good way to remember the meaning of "mere nominal designation": a table is something that fits the definition of table. By speaking of it in that way, we are reminded that the existence of things depends on *us.*

What Is the World?

Buddhist philosophers differ in their description of the world but all of them agree that it is impossible to speak of its existence without speaking of the mind.[1] What is the creator of the world? Not God but the mind. In the *Collection of Related Sayings*[2] the Buddha says:

> The world is led by mind and drawn along by mind. All phenomena are controlled by one phenomenon, mind.

Actions contaminated by ignorance give rise to the material worlds and bodies of all the different types of beings in saṃsāra. Actions are themselves primarily the mental factor of intention. In short, the worlds of rebirth and the bodies in which we live are products of our intentions.

Moreover, the very measure of existence is that something can be established by mind. In the monastic textbooks[3] used in Tibetan monasteries, "existent" and all of its synonyms emphasize this point. For example, here are some key terms and their definitions:

- existent: "that which is observed by valid cognition"
- established base: "established by valid cognition"
- object of comprehension: "an object of realization by valid cognition"

---

[1]This section is drawn largely from Cozort's *Unique Tenets.*

[2]Translation from Bodhi, 130.

[3]For example, the Collected Topics text entitled *Festival for the Wise* written by Jambel Trinlay is used by young students of Drebung Monastic University's Loseling College.

Also, all Buddhists accept that an external world is not absolutely necessary, since an entire realm of saṃsāra, the Formless, is populated by beings without bodies. Even in the other realms, it is possible to have vivid experiences without an external world through the medium of dreams, visions, or meditative states.

Given this emphasis on the primacy of mind, it should not be surprising that one of the major points of contention within Buddhist tenets is whether an external world exists at all. The Cittamātra school, as well as the Yogācāra branch of the Svātantrika-Mādhyamika school, relies on scriptures that seem to agree that there is no external world. The *Sūtra on the Ten Grounds* is the source of what is perhaps the most famous statement:

> [The Bodhisattva] thinks as follows, "What belongs to the triple world, that is (of) mere mind."[1]

The *Descent to Laṅkā Sūtra* says:

> [Objects] do not appear as external objects as perceived.
> The mind appears as various [objects].
> [Because the mind is generated] in the likeness of bodies [senses],
> enjoyments [objects of senses], and abodes [physical sense organs and environments],
> I have explained [that all phenomena are] mind only.[2]

In interpreting these passages, Gelukbas take "mind only" to mean that although minds and their objects, such as a visual consciousness and a visible object, seem to us to be unconnected entities, they are actually one inseparable entity. Minds and appearances arise simultaneously from a single cause, the ripening of a predisposition established by a previous action. Roughly speaking, the world is a film projected upon the screen of mind.

It would be easy to misunderstand this position. Cittamātrins are *not* denying the *existence* of the world. If the world is a like a film, something projected that appears to be something it is not, it is at least a documentary, not a cartoon. Something real is appearing to us, even if it does not exist in the way that it appears. It is not random or arbitrary. It appears to us in a particular way because of our individual karma.

---

[1]Translation from Honda, 189.

[2]This is translated by Hopkins, *Meditation,* 613.

When they say the world does not exist as something separable from mind, they are *not* saying that everything *is* mind. A table and the mind apprehending it are one entity with each other but they are not identical; neither *is* the other. Similarly, a table and the space it occupies are one entity but no one would claim that the space *is* the table or that the table *is* the space.

They especially are not saying that only *one* mind exists. There are as many minds as there are living beings, which is a vast, vast number.

But they *are* saying that the world does not exist as it appears, as something separate from our minds. According to our authors, they attempt to prove this remarkable position, so much at odds with common sense, with the following five arguments:[1]

1. No external objects appear to the wisdom consciousnesses of one absorbed in meditation on emptiness.
2. When different types of beings see fluid, they see different things in accordance with their own karma.
3. The same person seen simultaneously by enemies and friends can appear to be pleasant or unpleasant.
4. For yogis in meditation, earth can appear to be water.
5. Dreams and other experiences show that it is possible to have vivid experiences without real external objects.

These arguments can be resolved into three categories: (1) meditative experiences in which external objects are not found, either because there is simply an absence of any positive appearance or because an internal mental image has blocked out the appearance of external objects; (2) cases in which different types of individuals validly perceive different objects in the same place, which would seem to be impossible if external objects really existed; and (3) vivid experiences that occur in the absence of external objects. Let us explore these categories a little further.

---

[1]146.6 ff. There are other arguments not mentioned here. For instance, the Yogācāra-Svātantrikas ask: if a thing is supposed to depend upon being perceived by consciousness in order to establish its existence, how can it be said to exist before that? Yet the model of consciousness supposes that an object exists in the moment before it is perceived. Therefore, the model must be wrong; subjects and objects must arise together.

Meditative Experiences Devoid of External Objects

Asaṅga points out that no external objects appear to the mind at the time the mind is absorbed in meditative equipoise on emptiness. The Cittamātra school and the Mādhyamika school agree that at the time of direct realization of emptiness, when we are in meditative equipoise on emptiness, only emptiness itself appears to the mind. Asaṅga takes this as an indication that those objects do not exist.[1]

Prāsaṅgikas reply in two ways. First, it must be remembered that the mind that is absorbed in emptiness came about because it was involved in analyzing the way that objects appear to us naturally. Prāsaṅgikas would describe it as an examination of the existence of something inherently existent. When that something is not found, its lack of inherent existence—its emptiness—appears to the mind. Why *should* anything else appear?

The other Prāsaṅgika reply is that what establishes the existence—or non-existence—of anything is an ordinary valid awareness, that is, ordinary direct perception or inference that is not affected by causes of error. Since there is no such consciousness that certifies the absence of external objects, it cannot be said that they do not exist.

Different Valid Perceptions in the Same Place

The Mahāyāna schools also agree that there are cases in which different types of individuals validly perceive different objects in the same place. There were yogis who practiced a type of meditation in which, after much concentration on earth or water, they entered a trance in which all that appeared to their minds was water or earth, the water "totality" or earth "totality." This cognition is certainly considered valid.[2] Asaṅga raises the difficulty that if these appearances are valid and external to mind, would not the rest of us who cannot see the water or earth be wrong?

---

[1]Some Western scholars, such as Schmithausen (247), think that "mind only" means something else. It does *not* mean that no external objects exist but only that they cannot *appear* to the mind. He has suggested that the Cittamātra philosophy stems from the meditative experience of having the object itself disappear at the moment of realizing its emptiness.

[2]Jamyang Shayba (*Great Exposition of the Middle Way*, 638.7), considering a hypothetical debate about a yogi's cognition of the ground being covered with skeletons, denies that all such appearances are just imaginary form. To him it would absurdly entail that "the actual appearance of such emanated by the two [types of Hīnayāna] Arhats and Bodhisattva Superiors on the pure grounds is [an imaginary form-source]." In other words, what such persons see is real.

We will discuss the Prāsaṅgika response after another example, one that is particularly evocative. It concerns a certain trio consisting of a human, a god, and a hungry ghost. (Gods and goddesses live long, blissful lives in sublime surroundings; hungry ghosts live in continual desperation in hot, dry, filthy places.) Asaṅga's commentator, Asvabhāva,[1] suggested that if these three were to stand together, viewing a flowing fluid, all would see something different. Some gods would perceive nothing but space; other gods, who evidently in their previous lives possessed the karmic predispositions to "ripen" upon death into a new lifetime full of sensual delights, would see a stream of nectar, perhaps with a delicious fragrance wafting upwards. The hungry ghost, always surrounded by a disgusting and frustrating environment, would observe a slow-moving stream of blood and pus. The human, of course, would see a river of water. It is notable that there is no suggestion that any Buddhist school would reject this scenario.

How can we explain this situation? There are three possible solutions:

1. Only *one* of the beings has correct perception; the other two suffer from elaborate hallucinations.
2. All of the beings have deluded perception such that *none* of them sees what is really there.
3. Somehow, *all* of the beings have correct perception, entailing that water, nectar, and blood and pus are all actually present in the same place.

The first of these possibilities is the one that surely most of us would choose. We believe in the fundamental correctness of our own human perception. The second interpretation, that all three beings are deluded, is essentially that of the Cittamātrins. They would say that there is no river, blood and pus, nectar, or even space that exists externally to the beings who perceive those objects.

The third interpretation of the example—that all three beings are correct—is the explanation of the Prāsaṅgikas. Their basic assumption is that existence is established by valid cognition and that the six consciousnesses of *all* beings are fundamentally valid. Assuming that all three beings in the example have awarenesses that are neither affected by a deep cause of error—such as a defect in the eye—nor a superficial cause of error—such as fog, dim light, etc.—they respectively establish the existence of water, nectar, and blood and pus. Therefore, all three substances must exist. Yet since it is not possible for water also to *be* blood and pus or to *be* nectar, it cannot be the case that the three substances are also one substance. Rather,

---

[1] In his *Connected Explanation of (Asaṅga's) "Compendium of the Mahāyāna."*

three distinct entities are present in one place, each seen only by beings with the karmic propensities to be able to see them.

To illustrate this position, Jamyang Shayba uses two analogies. First, each being has six types of consciousness that certify their own specific types of objects. Eyes do not hear sounds and ears do not see forms, but this non-hearing and non-seeing do not prove the non-existence of sounds and forms. The fact that an eye consciousness cannot certify a sound does not preclude the existence of the sound, just as the fact that an ear consciousness cannot certify a visible form does not preclude the existence of that form. In the same way, the eye consciousness of a hungry ghost has a different purview than that of a human and does not contradict the human's perception. It certifies the existence of blood and pus but does not preclude the existence of water. What can be sensed by one type of being is out of reach of the senses of another.

The other metaphor Jamyang Shayba uses concerns the partial viewing of an object. When we see an object, we typically see only that part of it that faces us; we do not see its far side or interior. Just so, we do not see the nectar or blood and pus that are hidden from us, only the water that appears. Only the water casts its aspect toward our eye consciousness and forms it in its image. The other substances are, for us, beyond our range.[1]

Jamyang Shayba apparently says that these universes interpenetrate, that the totality of saṃsāra is immeasurably richer than we are capable of apprehending.[2] This is itself taken as a very powerful indication that phenomena lack any kind of enduring substantial existence. For the Gelukba interpreters, the interpenetration of phenomena (in this sense) precludes that they could have true existence. An important aspect of our ignorance is that we misconceive of phenomena as though they exist independently of our karma, whereas our karma actually is the cause of their very existence.

The Same Person Can be Seen as Friend or Foe

Along the same lines as the previous example, Dharmakīrti pointed to the fact that when one person is simultaneously seen by a friend and an enemy, the friend sees

[1]Another metaphor that might be helpful is that of color-blindness. The perception of two different people in one place will be considerably different if one can see colors and the other cannot.

[2]This is contested in the Gelukba monasteries, according to Kensur Yeshay Tupden.

the person as attractive whereas the enemy sees the person as repulsive. Or as Nāgārjuna says in his *Essay on the Mind of Enlightenment* (verse 20), an ascetic, a lover, and a wild dog respectively see a woman as a corpse, the beloved, and a source of food. How can one person be both attractive and repulsive? Rather, beauty and ugliness must be in the "eye of the beholder"; that is, they must be mental representations rather than external objects.

However, this is a rather weak argument, for it has to do only with an intangible quality of the observed object rather than its basic entity. That is, it would be easy enough to concede that beauty or ugliness is a mere superimposition without conceding that the beautiful or ugly *person* is a mere projection or superimposition.

Things Can Appear to Mind Without Having External Reality

Both Asaṅga and Vasubandhu show that consciousness can be generated in the absence of external objects. They refer to dreams, illusions, faults in the sense powers, the experiences of yogis, and the experiences of beings in the hells; all involve the generation of consciousnesses, apparently without external objects. Let us explore these examples in more detail.

Dreams. As we all know, dreams can be so vivid that when we awake, we can scarcely believe that what we experienced did not actually occur. Dream-objects are capable of producing effects in dreamers, such as a pleasant or unpleasant feeling, and even physical effects such as perspiration or talking out loud.

Mirror images. Although mirror images are nothing but reflections, they can provoke a reaction equivalent to that produced by what they reflect.

Optical illusions. Along the same lines as the dream example is that of a person with amblyopia, an eye condition that, like cataracts, causes the appearance of squiggly lines in the air that can be mistaken for hairs, insects in one's food, and so forth. Similarly, Asaṅga refers to a person who sees a "double moon," i.e., a double image of the moon, voluntarily or not. As in the case of dreaming, there is a consciousness generated without an external object (that is, at least the "second" moon is not an external object).

Yogic perception. We have already referred to yogis who practice a type of meditation in which all that appears to their minds is water or earth, the water "totality" or earth "totality." The water or earth is called an object for one with "meditative power," these being phenomena that appear only to the mental consciousness and then only to the mental consciousness of the person who has performed the meditation.

Guardians of the hells. Vasubandhu writes about the guards, tormenters, creatures, etc., of the Buddhist hells.[1] As he points out, it is not fitting that these beings be sentient beings themselves who have been born in the hells, since the hells exist as places of suffering and these beings do not suffer from the hells' intense heat or cold or other discomfitures. Hence, he argues, their appearance is not based on an external reality; rather, they are mere projections of the consciousnesses of the hell beings. Others who explain this phenomenon are forced to say that the guards are appearances of external elements generated by the karma of beings born in the hells but are not real sentient beings.

In response to these examples, Prāsaṅgikas argue that the fact that a dream horse, a mirage, or a mirror image can be an object of consciousness does not necessarily demonstrate that external objects are not needed for the production of awareness, only that the observed objects of consciousnesses are not necessarily objects that exist the way they appear. Candrakīrti implies that even forms such as dream images, reflections, and echoes are external objects even though they are deceptive and immaterial, serving as the observed objects of the awarenesses that perceive them. Even though phenomena such as reflections are deceptive, they arise in dependence on causes and conditions and are capable of serving as a cause for consciousnesses that are produced in the aspect of those objects. The appearance of imaginary "falling hairs" to a person with amblyopia is similar. Although the hairs, like the reflection, do not exist in the way they appear, the false appearance of hairs nevertheless functions as an external object by serving as a cause for the eye consciousness that apprehends them.

But beyond this, Prāsaṅgikas argue that these examples demonstrate only that external objects have no true or ultimate existence, something with which they have no quarrel, for the false appearance of these objects precludes their being truly existent. Instead, they criticize Cittamātrins for not being sufficiently radical—for failing to extend their reasoning similarly to consciousness, which also lacks true existence.

External objects are also asserted to exist in the conventions of the world, and the acceptance of ordinary worldly awareness is a frequent theme in Mādhyamika

---

[1]There are eight hot and eight cold hells, and in several of these there are guards who inflict torture on those born there as hell beings. As is the case with every other type of rebirth, birth as a hell being is temporary.

school writings. Candrakīrti, for instance, says in his *Entrance to the Middle Way*, "We assert that worldly [people], abiding in their own views, are valid."[1] In his *Clear Words* he says, "...the Buddhas help beings who are trainees and who do not know suchness with reasoning as it is renowned to them."[2]

"Indivisible Particles"

This chapter has focused upon the presentation and refutation of the Cittamātra view of the world's reality but there is another perspective that arises frequently in our texts. According to the Vaibhāṣikas and perhaps some Sautrāntikas,[3] the basic elements that comprise gross objects are so-called "indivisible particles." These tiny or "subtle" particles are for them the principal units of impermanent physical entities, the "building blocks" for gross objects. Hypothetically, these particles are indivisible because they are too minute to be physically subdivided. They are too small to have directions, so that we could not say they have sides to the north, south, east, or west.

There is, however, controversy over whether or not indivisible particles touch one another or have interstices.[4] The difficulty of maintaining that particles can touch each other is that it would seem to imply that they have parts, since certainly if a particle touched a particle below it, the part that touched the bottommost particle would not also be touching a particle above it. On the other hand, it is difficult to explain the cohesiveness of conglomerations of particles if they do not touch.

The Cittamātra school makes the refutation of indivisible particles part of its case for the rejection of external objects. The principle source is Vasubandhu, who makes two points. First, he says that if we imagine several particles in an array, surely a different part of the central particle would touch (or come close to touching) a particle to its west than would touch (or come close to touching) a

---

[1] *Entrance* (6.22), 5b.2–3.

[2] Translated by Hopkins, *Meditation*, 526.

[3] Another author, Gönchok Jikmay Wangbo, does not mention *any* Sautrāntikas that do not assert indivisible atoms.

[4] Losang Gönchok (99.4) makes the general statement that Vaibhāṣikas assert that particles do not touch but according to other Gelukba authorities this is apparently a position only of the Kashmiri Vaibhāṣikas (Hopkins, *Meditation*, 337–8).

particle to its east. That being the case, it is argued, subtle particles are not "directionless" after all. Second, he argues that if one side of a particle were also its opposite side—that is, if there were no "sides" at all, the particle being without directions—it would be impossible to construct gross forms out of them. All other particles would touch the same place; effectively, there would be just one particle, for no matter how many particles were put together, the aggregate could not get any larger. Hence, the notion of directionally indivisible particles is not viable.

Prāsaṅgikas agree with Cittamātrins that there are no directionally indivisible atoms or particles.[1] In fact, the Cittamātra school's rejection of indivisible particles is said to make them superior to the lower schools, even though they mistakenly deny the existence of external objects.[2] The indivisible particles described by the philosophers of the Vaibhāṣika and Sautrāntika schools are truly existent particles—things able to withstand analysis, things that exist from their own side and are not just imputations. It is better to assert, as the Cittamātra school does, that there are no external objects than to speak of truly existent indivisible particles. However, Prāsaṅgikas do not agree that the rejection of directionally indivisible particles amounts to a rejection of external objects.

[1]However, according to Losang Gönchok (145.4–6.1), Daktsang is said maintain that both the Mādhyamika and Cittamātra schools actually accept indivisible particles.

[2]Ngawang Belden, *Annotations*, 109a.7-b.1.

What Are The Two Truths?

In all of the Buddhist schools, real things are called either ultimate truths or conventional truths. We might not be surprised to learn that Buddhist philosophers consider some things more real than others, which is what "ultimate" and "conventional" imply, but the use of the word "truth" is very curious. We might expect that it refers to propositions, but it does not. It refers to the objects themselves. We might expect that this implies that some objects are just what they seem to be, whereas others are somehow less real. However, that is not the case either.

If we recall the tremendous emphasis of Buddhism on the primacy of mind, it will not be surprising that, generally speaking, objects are divided into these categories mostly because of the kinds of minds that apprehend them. Ultimate truths are those that are the objects of ultimate valid cognition; conventional truths are those that are the objects of conventional valid cognition. Ultimate valid cognition is a "purer" type of mind, either because it is unmediated (for the Sautrāntikas, for whom sense cognition is ultimate) or because it yields liberating insight (for the Mahāyānists, for whom either inference or a direct personal understanding of emptiness is ultimate).

There are other ways to divide phenomena, such as into the permanent or impermanent, the specifically or generally characterized, or the three natures. The division into two truths are used by all the schools as another way to show how the mind works.

Before reviewing the specific tenets of the schools, it is important to understand that the two truths are not in opposition. Indeed, the word "truth" indicates that *both* are valid. Indeed, for the Mahāyāna schools, they are intimately related. Every particular thing in our experience has two truths. A ball is a conventional truth because it is something that is known by conventional valid cognition; the ball's emptiness (however that is defined by the school) is an ultimate truth because it is something that is known by ultimate valid cognition.

Hīnayāna Perspectives

The Vaibhāṣika and Sautrāntika schools have a markedly different perspective on the two truths from the Mahāyāna schools. For the Mahāyāna schools, ultimate truths are the real way that phenomena exist, i.e., their emptiness of something superimposed by our ignorance. Depending on which school we look at, the emptiness is: (1) of naturally being the basis of names, (2) of being a different entity from consciousness, (3) of truly existing, or (4) of inherently existing. For the Hīnayāna schools, on the other hand, ultimate truths are *certain kinds of things themselves.*

For Vaibhāṣikas and Sautrāntikas Following Scripture, *ultimate truths* are the kinds of things for which any part is recognizable as that thing. Sky, for instance, is an ultimate truth because whether we see the whole dome of the sky above us or only a sliver glimpsed between tall buildings, it is recognizably sky. Categories, i.e, universals, are like that as well. To use Jamyang Shayba's example, if we smash a pot, we no longer have a pot, just its shards. But the pot was material *form* before we smashed it, and we recognize it as material *form* afterwards, too. Finally, since these Hīnayānists believe that everything is built out of so-called "indivisible" substance particles, atoms so small that they cannot be further divided, those tiny particles are ultimate truths as well.

Conventional truths for them are simply anything that does not meet the standard of ultimate truth. If we can break something down, even if just in our imaginations, it is a conventional truth. For instance, water has qualities such as taste, odor, and touch.[1] If these were removed, we would not recognize it as water. But sky and form lack particular characteristics that would allow us to analyze them in that way, so they are ultimate truths.

For Sautrāntikas Following Reasoning, *ultimate* truths are things that are able to perform functions, particularly the function of acting as a cause. All things act as causes, if not of their own next moment, then of something else. For example, the last moment of a pot is the cause of its shards and the last moment of a bolt of lightning is the cause of an illumination in the sky. For them, all impermanent phenomena are ultimate truths.

---

[1]This example is Newland's in *Appearance,* 18–9.

Conventional truths are synonymous with permanent phenomena. "Permanent" generally means not changing moment by moment, so this refers to all phenomena that are mere negations or are mental images. For example, space, defined as the mere absence of obstructive contact, is permanent; so are our mental constructs, or "generic images," of things.[1]

These are involved in the process of thinking. When I see an apple, its "aspect" (color and shape, in this case) is "cast" to my eye and I know it. But when I *think* "apple," I have had to match the particular color and shape in front of me with my pre-existing concept of apple, what Sautrāntikas call a "meaning-generality," i.e., a generic image, as we have discussed earlier. We have such concepts or images for everything we are capable of recognizing; they are built out of our life experience. For instance, when I see an apple, I recognize it because of my previous experiences with many kinds of apples. I have a personal definition of apple that, consciously or not, I apply to the particular thing in front of me.

With the Sautrāntikas Following Reasoning, we are getting closer to the concerns that guide the Mahāyāna schools in their division of things into the two truths. That is because what really matters to them is the kind of *mind* to which the two truths appear. Ultimate truths appear to direct perception. Direct perception is the ultimate type of consciousness because there is no mediation by a generic image between the object and the consciousness that apprehends it. But *thought* about an object requires a mixing with generic images. Therefore, it lacks the purity and richness of direct perception and, by comparison, is not ultimate.

Mahāyāna Perspectives

The relationship of the two truths in the Mahāyāna schools is both simpler and more complex than in the Hīnayāna schools. The Mahāyāna schools agree that *conventional truths are all existents except for emptinesses; ultimate truths are emptinesses.* They also all agree that the two truths abide together; for example, my apple is a conventional truth, my apple's emptiness an ultimate truth. An ultimate truth is simply the final nature of any conventional truth. They also agree that what we have translated as "conventional truth" (*saṃvṛti-satya*), which is literally "truth

---

[1]Generalities are classified as permanent, meaning that they do not disintegrate moment by moment. However, our generic images obviously change over time, being the amalgam of our experiences.

for a concealer," is best understood as "truth for an ignorant consciousness," a consciousness that conceals the true nature of things.

The complexity arises from the different ways that these schools define emptiness. It also stems from a disagreement over whether "conventional" can include things that are only imagined but do not actually exist.

For Cittamātrins, *ultimate* truths are the emptinesses of things. They are a person's emptiness of being substantially existent or self-sufficient; for phenomena other than persons, they are their emptiness of naturally being the basis of names or the emptiness of object and subject being different entities.

Conventional truths are those things that are empty, i.e., all other existing things. These are further divided into "other-powered natures," or impermanent things, and "existent imputations," or permanent phenomena other than emptinesses. As before, these are phenomena such as space, cessations, or general categories, that do not change moment to moment; they are imputations because they only appear to the mind through imputation. (In order to recognize space, for instance, I must ascertain mentally that there are no obstructions in a place; I *infer* that space is present.)

With Mādhyamikas, the explanation gets more complex. *Ultimate* truths are emptinesses of inherent, ultimate, true, etc., existence (all of these terms are equivalent). Again, there are other types of emptiness, inasmuch as there are different kinds of misconceptions, but ultimate truths are the most subtle of the emptinesses.

However, Dzongkaba ascertained that there is a significant difference in view between the two types of Mādhyamikas, the Svātantrikas and the Prāsaṅgikas, regarding conventional truths. Svātantrikas assert that conventional truths should be the things that appear to ordinary people who have accurate ways of perceiving them. The problem, say Prāsaṅgikas, is that what appears to us are things that do not exist. That is, what appears to us are things that seem to exist inherently—things that seem as though they do not depend even on the awarenesses to which they appear.

Svātantrikas understand that since things do *not* truly exist, this appearance is false. However, since it is what ordinarily appears and *seems* true for an ignorant consciousness, it is counted as conventional truth, which is also called "truth for a concealer."[1]

[1]To explain a little more deeply, Svātantrikas maintain that a thing can be said to exist if and only if it appears to a non-mistaken consciousness. For example, an apple does not exist by itself but by being experienced by my eye, nose, body, or tongue, assuming that I have no defects in these senses. However, the apple is not a *mere imputation* made in dependence on the aspects I

As we have seen before, Svātantrikas are supposed to be distinguished by their use of syllogisms. Because of their position on conventional truths, these syllogisms are called *svātantra* ("autonomous," synonymous with "inherently existent"). The Svātantrikas say that the terms used in a syllogism are established in a manner common to the Svātantrika and whoever the other person might be. Prāsaṅgikas, looking at what Svātantrikas say about conventional truths, reason that since the person to whom the Svātantrika poses a syllogistic argument naturally assumes the inherent existence of the terms of the syllogism, it follows that the syllogism itself is thought to be inherently existent.[1]

Prāsaṅgikas use a different standard. For Prāsaṅgikas, a *conventional* truth is simply something that can be established by conventional valid cognition. For instance, my eye consciousness can establish the existence of an apple on my desk. It may be true that the apple appears to be a *truly existent* apple but that is not what my eye consciousness is certifying; it is merely seeing the apple. In the same way, although a mirror reflection might appear to be a face, only the *reflection* is ascertained by my eye. Therefore, just an apple, not a truly existent apple—or just a reflection, not a face—is the conventional truth.[2]

---

experience (skin, smoothness, fragrance, flavor, etc.) but actually has its own objective status (to use Newland's term), its own "inherent existence" without which it would not be able to appear to my senses in the first place. Prāsaṅgikas disagree with that assertion.

[1]Jamyang Shayba (*Great Exposition of the Middle Way*, 424.2) glosses "autonomous syllogism" as that a syllogism in which "the three modes exist from their own side." The three modes of a sign are (1) the presence of the reason in the subject, (2) the forward entailment and (3) the reverse entailment. For example, in the syllogism "The subject, a pot, is impermanent because of being a product," the first mode—the presence of the reason in the subject—is the applicability of the reason (product) to the subject (pot), i.e., that pot is a product; the forward entailment, roughly speaking, is that whatever is a product is necessarily impermanent; and the reverse entailment, roughly speaking, is that whatever is not impermanent is necessarily not a product. These modes of the sign are said by Svātantrikas to exist from their own side because they say that conventionally, phenomena *do* inherently or autonomously exist. Therefore, the phenomena used in their syllogisms, and the relationships between them, exist inherently or autonomously.

[2]It may be a bit confusing but it should be noted that to be a *conventional truth* is not the same thing as *existing conventionally.* That is because conventional truths obviously do not include everything that exists, since there are also ultimate truths. On the other hand, everything that exists, exists conventionally. Nothing exists ultimately, not even ultimate truths. (Even emptiness is empty!) Kensur Yeshey Tupden (Klein, *Path*, 48) explained that a consciousness directly realizing emptiness, which is not involved in analysis, is a *conventional* consciousness whose object is a *conventionally existent* phenomenon (although it is, of course, an ultimate truth).

A classic example is that a coiled rope in a darkened corner may appear to be a coiled snake, ready to strike. Despite this appearance, the rope is not in any way a snake. It is only because of an error in perception that it seems to be so. We would not say that a snake exists just because we happened to imagine one.

An *ultimate* truth, according to Prāsaṅgikas, is the emptiness of inherent existence of a conventional truth. It is perfectly compatible with the conventional truth of which it is the true nature.

The following table presents briefly these complex views of the four schools and their branches. (When reading it, keep in mind that "phenomena" refers to things that actually exist.)

School	Conventional Truths	Ultimate Truths
Vaibhāṣikas	Phenomena that are not ultimate truths	Irreducible atoms and phenomena that are recognizable even if broken down
Sautrāntikas Following Reasoning	Permanent phenomena	Impermanent phenomena
Cittamātrins	All phenomena other than emptinesses	Emptinesses (thoroughly established natures)
Svātantrika-Mādhyamikas	All phenomena other than emptinesses *and* non-existent things that appear to ordinary persons as though they exist	Emptinesses
Prāsaṅgika-Mādhyamikas	All phenomena other than emptinesses	Emptinesses

What Did Buddha Mean?

The Mahāyāna schools agree that the Buddha taught tenets that apparently contradict each other. To convince the Hīnayānists who doubt the Mahāyāna because of its apparent contradictions with previously canonized scriptures, Mahāyānists have generally argued that the Blessed One, from the depths of his compassion, taught a broad range of doctrines to captivate diverse types of people.

They do not agree, however, on exactly what the Buddha *meant* when he did this. What, in the end, was his own view? Both the Cittamātrins and Mādhyamikas believe that the Buddha's own viewpoints are reflected in the proper understanding of the sūtras on which they themselves rely. Therefore, they criticize the sources or methods of the other. Mādhyamikas say that the scriptures upon which Cittamātrins rely either have been misunderstood by them or have not been understood to be merely provisional teachings for those incapable of grasping the more profound doctrine of the emptiness of inherent existence.

Before looking at the controversy over the sūtras in which the Buddha taught mind only, we should understand that all of the Mahāyāna schools accept the teaching in the *Sūtra Unraveling the Thought* that the Buddha "turned the wheel of doctrine" three times, although they disagree about some details. The sūtra states that in successive time periods the Buddha taught about the nature of reality in three different ways.

- The *first turning* of the wheel of doctrine is what we generally recognize as the Hīnayāna teachings. The sūtras in this wheel teach that there is no self of persons. Generally speaking, they do not say anything about the selflessness of phenomena and, in particular, do not say anything about the absence of inherent existence. The Prāsaṅgikas, however, maintain that some do teach the absence of inherent existence, arguing that otherwise no Hīnayānist could be liberated from saṃsāra whereas it is clear that some have become Arhats.

- The *second turning* of the wheel is that of the Perfection of Wisdom sūtras, on which the Mādhyamika school depends. These sūtras teach explicitly that everything lacks true existence.
- The *third turning* is that of the "mind only" teaching: the *Sūtra Unraveling the Thought*, the *Sūtra on the Ten Grounds*, the *Descent to Laṅkā Sūtra*, and the *Mahāyāna Abhidharma Sūtra*. These sūtras distinguish between the true existence of most things and the non-true existence of imputational natures.

The Cittamātra and Mādhyamika schools alike characterize the sūtras accorded primacy by the other as authentic but "requiring interpretation," whereas their own authoritative sūtras are labeled "definitive."[1] This might seem to mean that the definitive sūtras are superior to the others but that is not necessarily the case. The Cittamātrins recognize the superiority of the Perfection of Wisdom sūtras despite the fact that they require interpretation. Their "yardstick" is whether the teaching in the sūtra is literally acceptable. Because the Perfection of Wisdom sūtras teach that things lack existence by their own character (which exceeds the measure of selflessness that Cittamātrins use), they cannot be understood literally.[2]

Similarly, Svātantrikas would need to interpret Perfection of Wisdom sūtras because Svātantrikas make a special distinction about statements that things do not have inherent existence. They maintain that while phenomena *ultimately* do not exist inherently, *conventionally* they do exist inherently.

Prāsaṅgikas understand "sūtra" to mean an individual statement by the Buddha, not necessarily whole collections of statements made into a text, as we usually use the term. Hence, a single text could contain both definitive sūtras and those that require interpretation. Definitive sūtras are statements that teach ultimate truths and, therefore, need no further comment to understand properly the mode of being of the things being discussed; other sūtras require interpretation. Thus, within the texts called the Perfection of Wisdom sūtras, which generally teach about ultimate truths, there are passages that are not "actual" Perfection of Wisdom sūtras.

---

[1]The question of definitive and interpretable sūtras is actually quite a bit more complex than this, since *sūtra* can mean a *portion* of a larger text; hence, there are parts of scriptures that the other school finds generally authoritative that might be definitive rather than requiring interpretation, and vice versa. Janggya discusses this problem in his *Presentation*, which is translated and annotated in Cozort, *Unique Tenets*, 487–91.

[2]They say that when the Buddha taught about emptiness, he meant only that *objects* are empty, not minds.

In all cases, the schools get at the final thought of Buddha by logical analysis. Even if there were no sūtras like the *Sūtra Unraveling the Thought* or *The Teaching of Akṣayamati* that give a scriptural basis for the division of sūtras, no school would accept as definitive anything that does not stand up to reasoning, for of course, the Buddha's own final view, the definitive view, could not be logically subordinate to any other.[1] The Buddha's own dictum was that his doctrine be subjected to reasoning in the way in which a goldsmith analyzes a gold nugget. It should be burned, rubbed, and scratched until all qualms are laid to rest.

This principle is the main thrust of what are called the "four reliances."

1 One should *rely on truth, not person.* What is important is the truth, not the source. Buddha may have said something but it may not be logical as it stands and may require interpretation.
2 One should *rely on meaning, not word.* We should search for the underlying intention rather than being hung up on the literal statement.
3 One should *rely on the definitive, not the interpretable.* We should rely on sūtras that do not require interpretation. Of course, once we have interpreted them, this qualification no longer applies.
4 One should *rely on wisdom, not dualistic consciousness.* Only wisdom is reliable when it comes to ultimate truths.

How to Interpret Scripture: Cittamātrins

Once it is determined that a scripture is not definitive, how should we go about interpreting it? The schools agree on three criteria for interpretation.

1 *The basis in Buddha's thought:* What does the Buddha know? What was Buddha *really* thinking to himself when he made a certain statement?
2 *Buddha's purpose:* What did Buddha intend to accomplish by a certain statement? (Of course, his overall purpose is always the same—to help his listeners.)
3 *The damage to the literal teaching:* In what way would this teaching, understood literally, be illogical?

---

[1]For a discussion of the criterion of truth as established by reasoning in the classification of Buddhist scriptures, see Cabezon, "Concepts of Truth...," 7–23.

Since Cittamātrins think that there are no external objects, they must explain why the Buddha did not say so in the first and second turnings of the wheel of doctrine.

When the Buddha first turned the wheel of doctrine, he taught that there are external objects. Cittamātrins claim that the Buddha's *basis* in this case is that Buddha himself knew that no external objects exist but he was aware that to ordinary beings, there *seem* to be external objects. They claim that his *purpose* was that he knew that his particular listeners would benefit from hearing that all phenomena truly exist but that a permanent, indivisible self does not. They claim that the *damage to the literal teaching* is that since it can be shown that objects are not external, it cannot be literally true that all phenomena truly exist.

When the Buddha next turned the wheel of doctrine, he taught that nothing is truly existent. Regarding these sūtras (the Perfection of Wisdom sūtras), the Cittamātrins explain things in terms of their division of phenomena into three natures.

1. *Other-powered* natures are impermanent phenomena, i.e., things that have causes *other* than themselves.
2. *Imputational natures* are things that we must impute by thought; some exist, such as space (which is permanent and understood through a process of elimination), and some, such as the falsely conceived self or the appearance of external objects, do not exist.
3. *Thoroughly established* natures are emptinesses.

Cittamātrins say that other-powered natures and thoroughly established natures truly exist but that imputational natures do not.

Therefore, in these sūtras, the Buddha's *basis* is that he knew that imputational natures lack true existence, that other-powered natures lack self-production, and that thoroughly established phenomena are the lack of a self of phenomena. His *purpose* was to help those who would benefit from this type of teaching, namely people who needed a strong dose of anti-substantialism. The *damage to the literal teaching* is that it is not possible for anything other than a few imputational natures to exist without having something of their own character to which we can point.

How to Interpret Scripture: Mādhyamikas

For Mādhyamikas, definitive sūtras are those that teach ultimate truths. Other sūtras require interpretation in order to be understood properly. The sūtras of the first wheel were taught to those who could not yet understand the emptiness of inherent existence. That things lack inherent existence can be established by any number of reasonings that examine our false conceptions.

The sūtras of the third turning of the wheel of doctrine, those that teach mind only, are a different sort of problem. Although they require interpretation, some Mādhyamikas say that they literally teach mind only and others say they do not.

Bhāvaviveka, the original Svātantrika, does not deny the authenticity of so-called Cittamātra scriptures. His criticism of Cittamātra is to deny that the Buddha literally taught in *any* of those scriptures that there are no external objects. He implies that the basic thrust of the philosophy of Cittamātra is based on a misunderstanding. According to Bhāvaviveka, when, in scriptures such as the *Sūtra on the Ten Grounds*, Buddha said that the "three realms" (the Form Realm, Formless Realm, and Desire Realm which comprise the whole of saṃsāra) are "mind only," he did not mean that there are no external objects. He meant only that mind, in the sense of intentions to act or in the sense of karmic latencies with the mind, is the creator of saṃsāra.[1] Thus, in Bhāvaviveka's view, these sūtras are not even literal.

In saying this, he goes far beyond Candrakīrti, the *de facto* founder of Prāsaṅgika, who is willing to say that in most cases, Buddha actually *did* mean to say that there are no external objects (although that was not the Buddha's own final view). The Buddha taught mind only just provisionally and for certain persons—those not yet capable of understanding the absence of inherent existence. As he says in his *Entrance to the Middle Way*:

> These sūtras teaching no external objects of perception, that is,
> Teaching that the mind appears as the variety of objects,
> Turn away from forms those who are extremely attached to forms.
> These also require interpretation.[2]

In this way, the Buddha is like a doctor who acts for the good of his patients; the *Descent to Laṅkā Sūtra* states:

> Just as a doctor distributes
> Medicines to the ill,

---

[1]The context in which this famous statement appears in the *Sūtra on the Ten Grounds* suggests that Bhāvaviveka and Candrakīrti are correct. It is followed by a statement that the twelve links of dependent-arising depend on the mind, and since that mind is that of ignorance, it conditions the rest of the process (Honda, 189).

[2]*Entrance* (6.94), 8b.6–8. The translation is from Hopkins, *Meditation,* 614.

So Buddha teaches
Mind only to sentient beings.[1]

Of course, the Cittamātrins understand this sūtra to teach that "mind only" is real medicine. For Prāsaṅgikas, it is a placebo—something that cures a minor problem despite the fact that it lacks the potency necessary to cure the major one. In order finally to be cured of the sickness of saṃsāra, it is necessary to identify the conception of inherent existence and apply the strong medicine of Nāgārjuna's reasonings.

[1]Peking edition 775, vol. 29, 34.3.5 (chapter 2). It is cited in Janggya, *Presentation*, 482.20–3.1.

What Is Valid Cognition?

Since our problem, saṃsāra, is a matter of making an error in judgment, Buddhism is very concerned with how to distinguish faulty cognition from reliable, valid cognition.[1] This has been a major topic in Buddhist philosophy since the very beginning, as it has been in many of the non-Buddhist schools.

All of the Buddhist schools identify at least six types of consciousness. Unlike the Western model of mind, in which we think of consciousness as singular and as fed by the senses, in Buddhism each of the senses is itself conscious and is capable of a kind of recognition. Our eyes, ears, nose, tongue, or body in general have consciousness and can know things that are familiar to them even before the mental consciousness, the sixth one, applies its conceptual labels.

The Cittamātrins Following Scripture add two more types of consciousness: the afflicted mentality and the mind-basis-of-all. The *afflicted mentality* is ignorance; in this case, it is the conception that the mind-basis-of-all, which is the "person" in this system, is a self-sufficient, substantial entity. The *mind-basis-of-all* is a very odd sort of entity that neither thinks nor perceives but is a kind of neutral, continuous medium to hold the karmic predispositions.

Asaṅga felt that if there were no mind-basis-of-all, there would be no continuously operating consciousness to be a basis for the infusion of karmic latencies, to appropriate a new body at the time of rebirth, or to be present during "mindless" states such as the meditative equipoise of cessation. As we have seen, other schools have been able to account for these functions without adding to the basic list of six consciousnesses.

---

[1]Much of the discussion of direct perception that follows is based on Napper and Lati Rinbochay, *Mind in Tibetan Buddhism.*

What is "Valid"?

Except for Asaṅga's system and for that of the Vaibhāṣikas, Buddhist philosophers explain consciousness very similarly, taking their cues from the works of Dharmakīrti. This seventh-century writer used the term *pramāṇa* for valid cognition. His followers, whether they be otherwise classed as Cittamātrins or Sautrāntikas, have sometimes been called Pramāṇavādins ("Proponents of Valid Cognition") because of the centrality of this concept for them. In general, for a consciousness to be *pramāṇa* it must be "incontrovertible" regarding what it sees, hears, or thinks; it cannot be overturned.

Many of our awarenesses cannot meet that standard. *Correct assumptions* are cases when we choose correctly but without the conviction that reason might bring. *Unobservant awareness* occurs when we see or hear something but are too distracted to really notice it. *Doubt* is when we are not sure of where we stand. *Wrong consciousnesses* are common. We might experience some sort of a distortion, such as a mirage or a problem with our eyes, etc., or we might have faulty reasoning.

Valid cognition is of two main types: direct perception and inference. The main types of each are shown in the chart below.

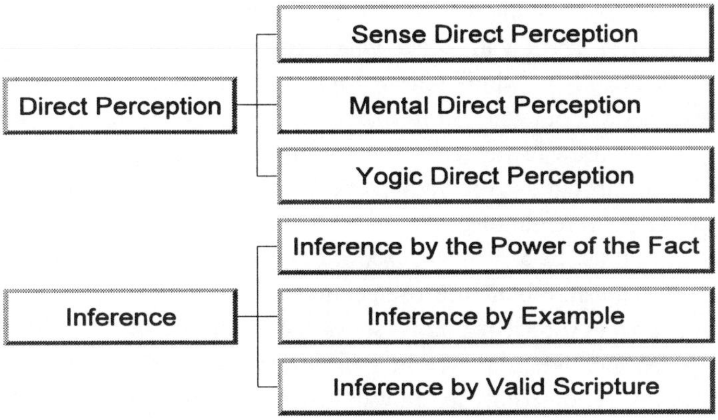

Types of Direct Perception

Direct perception is knowledge that does not involve conceptuality. Thought, as we have previously discussed, is indirect because it employs generic images. When I recognize the thing before me as a table, I do so by mixing my sense perception of the top and legs with my idea of "table" gained from many exposures to tables. Direct perception, on the other hand, is unmediated. It has two types: sense direct perception and mental direct perception.

Sense direct perception is of the five well-known types: eye, ear, nose, tongue, and touch. But we should note that it requires three conditions:

1 the observed object
2 a sense power
3 a preceding moment of consciousness

The *observed object* is whatever form, sound, odor, taste, or tactile sensation is presented to awareness.

The *sense powers* are thought to be invisible, clear material forms that are located in the organs of perception. So, it is not precisely the case that my eyeball sees a flower; rather, the eye sense power transforms into the shape and color of the flower. This is called "taking on the aspect" of the object and it is the common tenet of all schools except Vaibhāṣika, which asserts that sense direct perception happens "nakedly." My "wind" (energy) flows out through my open eyes and knows the object without any transformation. In the case of a body consciousness, which is how we know tactile sensations and internal sensations, the body sense power is spread throughout the body (with the exception of the hair, nails, etc., which experience no sensations).

That there must be a *preceding moment of consciousness* not only makes the point that consciousness is an unbroken continuum—we are never without some sort of mind, even in special meditative states that are supposedly "mindless"—but also that perception takes time. We are well aware within our own experience that if we are exposed to something for only an instant we will not be able to notice it, getting at best a subliminal perception that we cannot remember. For sense direct perception to occur, it must be preceded by many moments ("moments" being fractions of a second) of attention.

Mental direct perception is a special type of knowing, very valued in Buddhism, wherein we know something without using the senses or conceptuality. Normally, this type of knowing is very, very brief; just before sense direct perception induces conceptuality, where we will attach a concept to what has been observed, there is a flash of mental direct perception. Otherwise, for ordinary persons, mental direct perception is what we would call extrasensory perception, which is rather rare.[1] Some of us occasionally, and others of us frequently, are able to know things that are beyond the limits of our senses. The Buddhist tradition recognizes many types of clairvoyance, clairaudience, etc. but does not consider instances other than those induced by meditation to be particularly significant.

Yogic direct perception is, in fact, a kind of mental direct perception but it is set forth separately because it is important and because it is produced in a special way, through the power of meditation. It designates the type of consciousness that can bring about liberation and omniscience. This consciousness is one that combines impeccable strength of concentration, the state of "calm abiding," with the inferential understanding of selflessness, the state of "special insight." It is, therefore, only found amongst Superiors, those who have directly understood selflessness (however it is defined in the various schools).

Types of Inference

An inference is an understanding based on reasoning. For instance, if we know that smoke and fire are related such that whenever we see smoke, we know that there must be fire, when we see smoke in a particular place, we are able to infer that fire exists there, too.

There are actually "three modes" in such a process. The first mode is the *presence of the reason in the subject.* If we say, "In a smoke-filled room, fire exists, because smoke exists," the *reason* is "smoke," and it is present in the subject, "smoke-filled room."

The second mode is the *forward entailment,* the logical relationship of the third element and the second, stated in that order. In our example, it would be, "Wherever there is smoke, there is fire."

The third mode is the other side of that coin, called the *reverse entailment.* Here, it is, "If there is no fire, there is no smoke." When we understand the three modes, we make an inference and have valid cognition.

---

[1]Jamyang Shayba actually classifies these as mental consciousnesses and direct cognition but not as mental direct perception.

There are three main types of inference. The main one is **inference by the power of the fact**, i.e., inference based on the statement of valid reasons. The example of fire and smoke would be such an inference.

Inference comprehending through an analogy is to know something by way of an example. We might be said to comprehend a building through studying a scale model of it, for instance.

Finally, **scriptural inference** is to accept what a scripture teaches, having ascertained that it is not contradicted by direct perception, inference, or other scriptures. For instance, the Buddha taught about the subtle workings of karma, which is not something that we who are without omniscience can establish or disprove by direct perception or inference. It is a "very hidden phenomenon." Although in general the Buddha's statements are to be analyzed carefully, in some cases one simply trusts him on the basis of having analyzed his major teachings and having found them persuasive.[1]

Does the Mind Know Itself?

Those who follow Dharmakīrti—the Sautrāntikas Following Reasoning, the Cittamātrins Following Reasoning and the Yogācāra-Svātantrikas[2]—contend that our subjective consciousness is also an *object* of consciousness. That is, the mind is itself known at the same time that it knows its object. Otherwise, they argue, we could not remember not only the things we experience but our experiencing itself. That we *can* remember our own seeing, hearing, etc., is broadly accepted.

Self-consciousness is part of the "mind only" concept, for it is said to occur simultaneously with the mind that it observes (just as the Cittamātrins, etc., say that

---

[1]This typology of inference is the one that Losang Gönchok uses in the Prāsaṅgika school section but there are other lists of inferences, too. All include these types. Some of the non-Buddhist schools put a great deal of emphasis on inference, also. The Sāṃkhya school propounded two main types, inferences made for oneself and those made for others; the latter were divided into proof statements and consequences (roughly similar to the main logical forms used by the Svātantrika and Prāsaṅgika schools in Buddhism). The Vaiśeṣika and Naiyāyika schools used the same divisions but added that reliance on valid scriptures is a type of valid cognition.

[2]The root text does not specify which Cittamātrins accept self-consciousness, but Losang Gönchok attributes it only to those who Follow Reasoning. He is probably following the *Great Exposition of the Middle Way*, where Jamyang Shayba points out that Asaṅga never mentions self-consciousness. But Losang Gönchok might have gone the other way as well, since Jamyang Shayba also states that some Cittamātrins Following Scripture diverge from Asaṅga on this point.

mind and object occur simultaneously, produced by the same karmic seed). Those who say self-consciousness exists say that mind is like a lamp: at the same time it illuminates other things, it illuminates itself.

Those who dispute self-consciousness use a different metaphor. Mind is like a measuring weight: it cannot measure itself at the same time it measures something else. Or, say the Prāsaṅgikas, it *is* like a lamp; but since the very nature of a lamp is illumination, it does not *act upon itself* to illuminate itself.

But how, other than self-consciousness, can we account for memory of the subjective aspect of experience? Except for the Prāsaṅgikas, other schools account for memory of consciousness itself by the mind's ability to perform "introspection" (looking inside), which observes a mental state (but a moment *after* it occurs, as with any other object).

Prāsaṅgikas deny that self-consciousness is necessary for several other reasons. The most intriguing is that my memories are times when I train my mind upon a past object. This is quite unlike our "mechanical" model of memory, in which we imagine that memory retrieves stored records of past events and displays them on the screen of consciousness. Rather, we are making contact again with a past object and subject. Śāntideva, the ninth-century author of the famous *Engaging in the Bodhisattva Deeds*, even says that memory can reach the subjective aspect of experience even if that awareness was not *noticed* at the time, just by remembering the object. For instance, as long as I can remember Niagara Falls, I can remember my *seeing* of Niagara Falls through association.

Other Controversies

There are many other small differences between the schools on the subject of valid cognition. What follows are brief summaries of four issues on which Losang Gönchok dwells.

Valid Cognition Can be "Mistaken." Prāsaṅgikas are usually keen to uphold the conventions of the world and thus are inclined to classify as valid the cognitions that the world would agree are valid. However, as Jamyang Shayba says, "Until Buddhahood is attained, one has no non-mistaken consciousnesses except for a

Superior's exalted wisdom of meditative equipoise."[1] Because things appear to exist inherently, there is a falseness to every appearance outside of meditation.

However, a consciousness does not have to be non-mistaken in order to be correct about the existence of its object. For instance, when we see mountains in the distance, they appear to be blue because of the haze. Although we might be mistaken about the color, we can still be correct regarding the mountains themselves.

Although this seems to be a minor point, it is a way of refuting the Svātantrika claim that things truly exist on a conventional level, as they appear, because otherwise the consciousnesses that realize things would not be valid. Prāsaṅgikas are saying, to the contrary, that a consciousness can be valid about the *existence* of its object without being correct about the *way* the object exists.

Direct Perception Can be Conceptual. Prāsaṅgikas also are alone in regarding our inferential cognitions as leading very quickly to a kind of direct cognition. They say that once we have had a real inference, which again means an incontrovertible understanding, we no longer depend on the reason that produced our inference. Our understanding is "direct," in that sense; it is still indirect in another sense, because conceptuality always involves a generic image, but it is powerful. Therefore, we can have a mental direct perception that is not merely the "flash" at the end of sense direct perception but which goes on for some time after an inference is made. This mental direct perception is memory, and memory is always conceptual.[2]

Do Objects Cast a True Aspect to Consciousness? True and False Aspectarians, who can be found among the Sautrāntikas and Cittamātrins, agree that the appearance of coarse objects as external is distorted by ignorance.[3] They disagree over whether the coarse appearances of wholes exists as they appear. For example, a patch of blue is actually many tiny parts that are blue; is the appearance of a "patch" true or false? Among True Aspectarians are those who contend that in

---

[1] *Great Exposition of Tenets* 37a.2–3 (in DSK edition), a commentary on a passage in Candrakīrti's *Clear Words.*

[2] This point is made by Dzongkaba in *Illumination of the Thought,* which is cited by Jamyang Shayba.

[3] There are several explanations of the differences between True and False Aspectarians and between types of each but here we are following Jamyang Shayba. Gönchok Jikmay Wangbo gives three versions and much more attention to the topic in his much shorter text (see Hopkins and Sopa, *Cutting*).

relation to a multifarious multicolored object there are as many eye consciousnesses as there are colors (or other aspects) of the object and those who say there is only one.[1]

Pramāṇa Does Not Mean "New." Of less consequence is that there is a difference between Prāsaṅgikas and others over whether *pramāṇa*, the term we have simply said means valid cognition, actually means "prime cognition," i.e., means only a *new* knower which is also incontrovertible. Dharmakīrti and his followers understand the prefix *pra* to mean "new"; Prāsaṅgikas regard it simply as meaning "foremost," or best.

[1]The three divisions are (1) the Proponents of Equal Number of Subjects and Objects, who hold the position that there are as many eye consciousnesses as there are colors (or other aspects) of the object; (2) "Half-Eggists" who speak of only one consciousness but who note that because of self-consciousness, both subject and object are observed simultaneously and are, therefore, one substantial entity; and (3) "Non-Pluralists" who speak of only one consciousness that perceives one multicolored object. Among False Aspectarians, Gönchok Jikmay Wangpo (but no one else, apparently) asserts that there are some Tainted False Aspectarians who either say that the mind is polluted by ignorance or that even Buddhas suffer from false appearances. Most Buddhists would say that neither is possible.

What Are Arhats and Buddhas?

All of the Buddhist schools agree that the elimination of ignorance will bring liberation from saṃsāra. We have already discussed their views of ignorance; what remains is to review their depictions of liberation, Buddhahood, and the states that lead to it.

First, let us distinguish between the attainment of insight—a first, direct cognition of selflessness, however that might be defined—and the attainment of liberation. The Buddhist schools agree that "enlightenment" is not a once-and-for-all experience. We are not immediately liberated upon first gaining insight. The tenacious grip of our previous misconceptions is gradually loosened only by repeated meditation, as we eliminate the afflictions of desire, hatred, etc., which are born from ignorance and bind us in saṃsāra.

There are four degrees of liberation:

1 **Stream Enterer** is the name of the first, since those who have experienced liberating insight have entered into the metaphoric river of wisdom that will carry them out of saṃsāra. Their status has changed permanently. They will definitely be fully liberated Arhats in not more than seven lifetimes, possibly even in this lifetime. None of their rebirths will be lower than the human level (i.e., they will not be born as a hell being, as a hungry ghost, or as an animal).

2 **Once Returners** will achieve that goal in not more than one more lifetime in the Desire Realm (our own realm, which has six types of rebirth).

3 **Never Returners** will be liberated with no more births in the Desire Realm, although they may be born in through meditation in the Form Realm (the realm of higher gods) once.

4 **Arhats** are those who are fully enlightened and liberated (although as we will see, there is some controversy over the permanence of their status).

Each of these four grades can be divided into Approachers and Abiders in the Fruit, respectively, those who are presently absorbed in realization of emptiness, resulting in the abandonment of a portion of the afflictions, and those who enjoy the fruit of that abandonment subsequently. They may also be further distinguished according to where they take whatever rebirths remain. That is why sometimes there are said to be eight or even twenty divisions.

The schools mostly agree that an Arhat is a person whose liberation is incontrovertible.[1] However, the Vaibhāṣikas distinguish six different types of Arhats, five of whom can "fall back." That is, although they have experienced the elimination of the coarse afflictions that can cause suffering, they may not have eliminated the *subtle* afflictions and, therefore, can still commit unethical acts, commit suicide, etc., and thereby lose the status of Arhat.

Is Buddhahood Inevitable?

One of the main ways to distinguish Mahāyāna and Hīnayāna is whether the state of Buddhahood is a realistic goal for a Buddhist practitioner. For the Hīnayāna, Buddhas are extremely rare beings. Motivated by compassion, they have practiced for an amazing length of time (three incalculable eons), have the physical properties of thirty-two major and eighty minor marks, are perfect teachers, and establish a new religion of Buddhism when the world is ready for it. That is why the Buddha did not teach people to seek Buddhahood but rather to seek their own liberation. For the Mahāyāna, Buddhahood is a goal for everyone (although there is some disagreement over whether it will *actually* be reached universally).

The difference between the Mahāyāna and the Hīnayāna can also be expressed by discussing the three "vehicles"—those of the Hearers, Solitary Realizers, and Bodhisattvas. We have already differentiated these, pointing out that the vehicles cannot be correlated to philosophical views or levels of enlightenment but only to circumstance and motivation. That is, Hearers and Solitary Realizers have different

---

[1]Historically, the Arhat was a very early subject of debate in Buddhism. Here the Sarvastivāda (Vaibhāṣika) view is represented; it was opposed by the Vibhajjivāda, the precursor of today's Theravāda school. Unusually, Jamyang Shayba says nothing on this topic; it is found only in Losang Gönchok.

circumstances because the latter do not have teachers; and Bodhisattvas differ from the others by their altruistic intention to attain Buddhahood.

According to the Hīnayāna schools, each of these vehicles is "final." A particular person becomes either a Hearer Arhat, a Solitary Realizer Arhat, or a Buddha (the "Bodhisattva Arhat"). Most of the Mahāyāna schools, by contrast, say that there is only *one* final vehicle, that of the Bodhisattva. Although a person may practice as a Hearer or Solitary Realizer and become an Arhat, such a person will be exhorted by the Buddhas to develop *bodhicitta* and practice as a Bodhisattva until attaining Buddhahood. There are three practice vehicles but only one of them is regarded as a *final* vehicle.[1]

The anomalous Mahāyāna school is Asaṅga's, that of the Cittamātrins Following Sūtra. Asaṅga, in his *Compendium of Abhidharma*, doubts that all beings are destined for Buddhahood. In fact, he sets forth five possibilities. In addition to the three vehicles as final ends, there are those who switch to the Bodhisattva vehicle from one of the others, and those without a lineage for liberation. Therefore, there are two ways that Asaṅga's school differs from the other Mahāyāna schools: it does not assert that the other Arhats necessarily switch into the Bodhisattva vehicle and it holds that there are some beings who are never liberated.

The claim that liberation is not universal is the one that is most problematic. Asaṅga believed that there are persons whose "roots of virtue" have been severed.[2] The roots of virtue are our favorable karmic predispositions, those whose fruition can result in favorable rebirth or mere happy experiences. If our roots of virtue have been cut, we are never born in circumstances where we can create the causes for happiness. We are thrown into a vicious cycle. In lifetime after lifetime we perform non-virtuous deeds and dig ourselves a hole that just gets deeper and deeper.

It is a sad and hopeless state of affairs. What could cause the severance of our roots of virtue? The answer is anger, especially if it is directed against a Bodhisattva by someone who is not one. This emotion has a particularly powerful effect, one that all Buddhist schools recognize.[3] The other Mahāyāna schools also admit that

---

[1]Svātantrikas differ from Prāsaṅgikas in their description of the Bodhisattva path. According to the Svātantrikas, the two sets of obstructions, those to liberation and omniscience, are removed simultaneously, whereas the Prāsaṅgikas say they are removed serially.

[2]He makes a distinction between "roots" and "seeds" of virtue and non-virtue such that it might be possible for someone to have lost "roots" but not "seeds" and, therefore, retain the possibility of future regeneration of the roots of virtue. However, he contends that some of those whose "roots" of virtue are eradicated also have no "seeds" of virtue.

[3]For an extensive analysis, see Cozort, "Cutting the Roots of Virtue."

anger can cut the roots of virtue but do not conclude that there are those whose fates are forever sealed. According to Mādhyamika, in contrast, our mind's emptiness of inherent existence is a "natural lineage" that is the "Buddha nature" of each of us. The fact that the mind has no fixed nature means that change is always possible. Hence, there is no one who will fail, eventually, to attain Buddhahood.

Nirvāṇa With and Without "Remainder"

Nirvāṇa is neither a place nor a mental state. It is a *fact* about us. A nirvāṇa is the absence of afflictions in someone whose cultivation of wisdom has resulted in the destruction of ignorance, desire, hatred, etc. That mere absence is the nirvāṇa.

On that, all Buddhist schools agree. However, they disagree over the use of the term "remainder" used in conjunction with nirvāṇa. Other than Prāsaṅgika, it is said that after a person attains nirvāṇa, he or she subsequently can be said to have a "nirvāṇa *with* remainder," the "remainder" being the body and mind. Death cuts the remainder. However, the nirvāṇa *without* remainder is a single moment, occurring just at the time of death but not after. After death there is no person to whom the nirvāṇa can belong!

The Hīnayāna schools do not recognize any existence after death for an Arhat. The Mahāyāna schools do, and all except Asaṅga's say that Arhats manifest in different forms, no longer helplessly reborn according to karma, and continue to cultivate wisdom and merit until they have become Buddhas. Because Asaṅga and his followers say that there are Arhats who do not go on to Buddhahood, they must explain that those Arhats are born in the pure lands of Buddhas and abide there forever in meditative absorption.

The Prāsaṅgika school uses the term "remainder" in a completely different manner. For them, "remainder" has to do with whether or not to an Arhat things still appear to have true existence. To explain this, we have to recall what was said previously about the obstructions to liberation and obstructions to omniscience. What prevents our liberation is our *conceptions* of inherent existence. Things *appear* to us as though they exist from their own side, independently, and we assent to this appearance by *conceiving* of them in this way. Meditation that analyzes the way things exist will destroy this false *conception*, and we can be liberated from it and from the saṃsāra it causes.

However, because of the way we have been conditioned, which in Buddhism is a process without beginning, things still *appear* to exist inherently. The liberated person is someone who no longer *assents* to this appearance, who is always doubtful of the evidence of the senses and resists *conceiving* of them in the wrong way. He or she is like someone who wears sunglasses, well aware that the green tint pervading all visible objects is just the effect of the lenses. It takes a very long time for the appearance of inherent existence itself to fade. Those "taints" of appearances are the obstructions to omniscience.

From this perspective, then, an Arhat experiences a nirvāṇa with remainder most of the time, since most of the time things appear falsely. But then, when does a nirvāṇa *without* remainder occur? It occurs only when that person is meditating on emptiness because at that time only emptiness appears to the mind. For non-Buddhas, it is impossible for both emptiness and other things to appear to the mind simultaneously. (Another way of putting this is to say that the two truths cannot appear simultaneously to a non-Buddha's mind.)

So, both Prāsaṅgikas and others could identify an Arhat's usual state, the time when he or she is not absorbed in meditation on emptiness, as a nirvāṇa with remainder, but they would mean very different things by it. Prāsaṅgikas would mean that things falsely appear to the mind; others would mean that the Arhat is alive. Similarly, both Prāsaṅgikas and others would identify the nirvāṇa of an Arhat at the time of death as being a nirvāṇa without remainder but they would mean something different by it. Prāsaṅgikas would mean that at that time there is no false appearance to the mind (because, for a short time, only a vacuity appears to the mind), whereas others would mean that the body and mind are abandoned.

Other than the purpose of again pressing home their contention about the empty nature of things, why do Prāsaṅgikas change this terminology? Jamyang Shayba here gives two arguments. First, it makes no sense to say that there is any person who experiences a nirvāṇa without remainder if that means that the aggregates are abandoned. There is no person once the aggregates are destroyed. Second, the language that suggests that Arhats "extinguish" their aggregates really just refers to their emptiness. Like all things, our bodies and minds are "primordially extinguished" into emptiness because they are, and always have been, empty of inherent existence.[1]

[1]In his *Great Exposition,* Jamyang Shayba quotes sūtras and the works of Candrakīrti and Dzongkaba to discuss this point.

Bodies of the Buddha

The Buddhist schools commonly distinguish between two "bodies" of the Buddha, the Truth Body and the Form Body. The Truth Body is not a physical body but the Buddha's enlightened consciousness; the Form Body is his physical form.[1]

The Mahāyāna schools elaborate this scheme considerably. The Truth Body, which for them is an omniscient consciousness, can be further distinguished as the Wisdom Body (the consciousness itself) and the Nature Body (its emptiness). (Further distinctions can be made about the Nature Body because while the mind, like everything else, has always been empty, there are also absences which have come into existence as the obstructions to liberation and the obstructions to omniscience have been removed.)

The Form Body is the manifestation in form of the Truth Body. That is, whether a Buddha appears in the Emanation Body (which can take many forms in addition to the human form in which the twelve "deeds" of a Buddha's career are displayed), or as the Enjoyment Body (which can take many forms and resides in a pure land), it is a case of the Buddha's *mind* taking on these forms. Thus, a Buddha is essentially wisdom, not form.

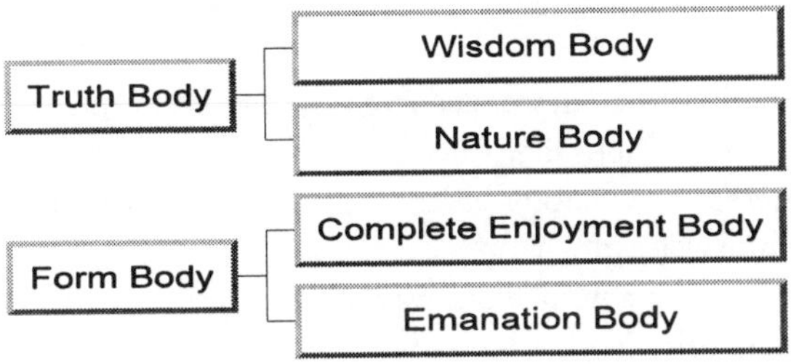

[1]Vaibhāṣikas specify that this body is not the Buddha that is one of the three refuges. The Buddha's form aggregate is the body that he got from his parents, one that was impelled by karma. Although this body is the Buddha, and although once he is enlightened it causes him no more suffering, it is not the Buddha Jewel, which is only his wisdom. Other schools do not make such a distinction. For the Mahāyāna schools, that is because all of a Buddha's appearances in form are manifestations of his wisdom; therefore, there is no "problem" of a body that is impelled by karma.

There is disagreement over whether the mind's emptiness should be identified as the meaning of "Tathāgatha essence" or "Buddha nature." (In sūtras such as the *Tathāgatha Essence,* the Buddha taught that a permanent, fully developed Buddha exists in each being. No Buddhist school, according to Gelukba interpretation, takes this literally.) For Mādhyamikas, it is appropriate to identify the mind's emptiness as our Buddha nature because it is what enables the mind's transformation into an omniscient awareness. But Cittamātrins say that it is a seed or potential for spiritual attainment that has always abided naturally in the mind-basis-of-all. All beings are, therefore, predisposed to attain higher states (although, as we have seen, some Cittamātrins say that not all will be able to attain them, in fact, because their "roots of virtue" may have been cut).

Who Was the Buddha?

The Hīnayāna and Mahāyāna schools have differing pictures of the nature of the man whose earthly career founded the Buddhist tradition. These differences are summarized by their view of the "twelve deeds" of the Buddha. Although both agree on the basic list, Hīnayānists see the deeds as those of a man who becomes enlightened, Mahāyānists as those of an already enlightened being who "displays" the correct way to seek enlightenment. What are these twelve "deeds"?

1 The Buddha-to-be descended from the Joyous Pure Land where he had lived in his previous life.
2 He entered the womb of his mother-to-be, who dreamt of being circled by a white elephant.
3 He was born in a miraculous way. He emerged from his mother's side as she stood, gripping the limb of a tree.
4 He excelled at youthful sports and mastered many arts.
5 He lived in a household with many consorts.
6 He renounced saṃsāra, leaving his wife, child, and father in the palace.
7 He performed acts of asceticism in order to purify himself. He practiced with five ascetics he encountered in the forest.
8 Having understood his mission, he meditated under the tree of enlightenment.
9 He conquered the array of demons who appeared to him.
10 He became a Buddha.
11 He began to teach.
12 He attained his *parinirvāṇa* (death).

According to Hīnayānists, the first nine deeds are performed by the Bodhisattva (the aspirant to Buddhahood), the last three by the Buddha. The Hīnayāna perspective on the Buddha is that he was a human being who had to make the difficult decision to leave his family and responsibilities to follow a spiritual path, who struggled mightily on his own (as a Solitary Realizer, in fact), and on one great night traversed the four degrees of liberation and became omniscient as well.

The Mahāyāna says that all twelve deeds are performed by the Buddha; that is, that he was already fully enlightened before taking birth. The Mahāyāna understands the Buddha to have lived a life that was itself a teaching. From his experience as a young man confronting the "four signs" (a sick man; an old man; a corpse; a monk), we understand the pervasiveness of suffering and the promise of the spiritual path. From his willingness to leave his comfortable, privileged life, we understand that happiness does not come from material possessions. From the persistence of his great quest over six difficult years, we understand the power of compassion as a motivation; and so forth. But like Kṛṣṇa, like Christ, he is depicted as an already perfect being who descends into the field of mortality to lead others through his example.

The Clear Crystal Mirror
by Losang Gönchok

A Commentary on Jamyang Shayba Ngawang Dzöndrü's *Presentation of Tenets: Roar of the Five-Faced [Lion] Eradicating Error, Precious Lamp Illuminating the Genuine Path to Omniscience*

On the Translation

For the most part, we have tried to translate this text in an accurate, literal fashion. However, in an effort to make it more accessible, we have taken a few liberties:

- Jamyang Shayba's root text, which is in boldfaced type, is broken into smaller units than in *The Clear Crystal Mirror.* Losang Gönchok often cites many lines of the root text before beginning his commentary, with the effect of separating the two unnecessarily.
- The root text is not translated as verse. (It was written in meter so that it could be memorized.) With all of the bracketed material that must be inserted to make it comprehensible, it cannot be made to "scan."
- Headings, sub-headings, etc., have been inserted liberally. The Tibetan has no breaks even for paragraphs. Our introduction of these elements is a way of converting Jamyang Shayba's internal outline (e.g., "there are two parts...the first of these has three parts...") into meaningful sections. However, we have not used all of the sub-divisions, and we have often truncated the headings and sub-headings.
- Some of the summary lines at the end of chapters have been dropped. We retained the ones that communicate something about the tenets of the school that has just been discussed.
- We have omitted a few obscure or digressive passages.
- Sanskrit or Tibetan equivalents of translation terms, book titles, or personal names are not in the text but can be found in the name-list, glossaries, and bibliography we have provided.
- Our reference to the 1999 Gomang edition of Jamyang Shayba's *Great Exposition of Tenets* is referred to in the notes simply as "Gomang."
- Bracketed numbers inserted in the text correspond to the arabic numbers found to the left of each folio side in the Tibetan manuscript. Because we have broken the root text into smaller units, sometimes the text begins a few lines after the point indicated.

Introduction

As the reliable supreme rarity of this degenerate time,[2]
Guru Vajradhāra, Lord of all lineages,[1]
Bestow [on me] the rank of fearlessness, like the King of Subduers, and
Until enlightenment stay inseparably in my heart.

Homage to the chief of the Śākyas, Lord who has the three bodies,[2] [3]
Praised as the bravest of the thousand Buddhas of this fortunate era;
[Homage to] his [heart] sons, Nāgārjuna and Asaṅga, and the Protector
Maitreya,
Together with their lineages.[3]

Homage to the second Conqueror, the Mañjunātha Dzongkaba,
To Gyeltsap Chögyi Nyima and [4] Kaydrupjay,
To all the lineage holders, to those who clarify [Dzongkaba's] teaching,
And to the omniscient Jamyang Shaybay Dorjay.[4]

---

[1]Vajradhāra is the personification of the Truth Body (*dharmakāya*), the omniscience of the Buddha.

[2]Śākyamuni (sage of the Śākyas, a clan) is the "nickname" of the historical Buddha. In the Mahāyāna schools, Buddhas are said to have three bodies.

[3]Maitreya will be the next historical Buddha; Nāgārjuna and Asaṅga are the founders of the two principal Mahāyāna schools.

[4]Dzongkaba was the founder of the Gelukba monastic order and Gyeltsap and Kaydrup were his two principal disciples. The next stanza also praises great Gelukba teachers.

I bow to the excellent supreme emanations, the Three Exalted Bodies:[1]
The greatly compassionate Jambel Gyatso, protector of the Teaching;
Paṇchen Rinpoche, emanation of Amitāyus;
And Jikmay [Gyatso], dance that melds the ocean of the Three Bodies.

Regarding the exalted wisdom of all the Conquerors, which descends in whatever measure,
And the assembly of spiritual friends who sustain us through [appearing to be] ordinary beings:
By remembering your kindness and good qualities, I humbly ask you,
Please protect me always through virtue and goodness.

General Discussion of Tenets

With regard to [5] the explicit text of the root verses of the omniscient lama Jamyang Shayba's *Tenets*, I will interpret the words however I can discern with my own mind.

[Jamyang Shayba] begins his text by worshiping the King of Subduers[2] [and the white and yellow Mañjughoṣas, Sarasvatī, and Dzongkaba],[3] then discusses the causes for his composition and the greatness of the text, and finally gives advice to listen:

Relying on skillful captains on the ship of reasoning through hundreds of tiring activities, I crossed to the end of the ocean of tenets and found this jewel

---

[1]Buddhas have Three Bodies: the Truth Body which is the omniscient consciousness itself, and two types of Form Bodies, which are really the Truth Body taking form. That the three scholars, undoubtedly teachers of Losang Gönchok, are referred to in this manner is the greatest possible compliment and reflects the idea that one should see one's lamas as Buddhas. Jamyang Shayba will also be referred to as "omniscient" below.

[2]Buddha, who has subdued the "demons" of lust, anger, and ignorance in his own mind.

[3]White and yellow Mañjughoṣas (the Bodhisattva or Buddha of wisdom) are praised for clearing away ignorance, teaching doctrine to trainees, and bestowing the ability to answer others' questions (Gomang 27.19–22). Sarasvatī is praised because she is Jamyang Shayba's special deity (Gomang 28.2–5). Dzongkaba is praised for bringing together in one person the practices of sūtra and tantra (Gomang 28.6–8).

of good explanations that previously did not exist. O you with discrimination: happily retain this as a lamp clarifying the path to omniscience.

Jamyang Shayba entered onto the Great Chariots'[1] ship of reasoning [6] and relied on its captains—scholars possessing the transmission[2] of proper explanation. He relied on hundreds of arduous activities, getting hold of the teaching, repeating it, thinking about it, and meditating on it. That is how he crossed to the far end of the ocean of tenets and found a great jewel of good explanation containing many new explanations not developed earlier by any master of tenets. Those trainees who have discrimination should hold this explanation as a lamp for seeing clearly the entire path proceeding right through to omniscience.[3]

The etymology of "tenet" (*grub mtha', siddhānta)* is that it refers to something that is classified as existing for one's own mind as correct, [7] having refuted other superimposed factors.[4] *Siddhi* [or *siddha*] is explained as being used for *grub pa* (establishment or existent) and *anta* is explained as being for *mtha'* (end or conclusion).

General Teaching on the Difference Between the Outer and the Inner[5]

The two, Outsiders [i.e., non-Buddhists] and Buddhists, [are distinguished] by way of teaching, teacher, and view.

The two, Outsiders' and Insiders' tenets, are differentiated in three ways: in terms of teachings, teachers, and view.

The [Buddhist] teaching is distinguished by way of views that have the [four] seals, meditation that is the antidote to cyclic existence, behavior that has

---

[1]The "Great Chariots" are the founders of the great Mahāyāna systems, Nāgārjuna (Mādhyamika) and Asaṅga (Cittamātra).

[2]These are scholars who have received the oral tradition on the texts of the Great Chariots.

[3]In other words, tenets study can be as valuable as the much more common approach called the "Stages of the Path" (*lam rim*).

[4]In other words, a tenet is a conclusion reached by eliminating other possibilities.

[5]In this "general" section, the view of the Prāsaṅgika-Mādhyamika school is the default "Buddhist" view.

abandoned the two extremes, and fruits of separation that are analytical cessations [such that the afflictions do not return].

The Buddhist teaching is superior in four ways: view, meditation, behavior, and fruit.

1 The "four seals"[1] that distinguish the [Buddhist] *view* are as follows: all composed phenomena are impermanent, [8] all contaminated things are miserable, all phenomena are selfless, and nirvāṇa is peace.
2 Buddhist *meditation* serves as an antidote to all cyclic existence within the three realms.[2]
3 Buddhist *behavior* is free from the two extremes, having abandoned both the extreme of overindulgence of desire, which is a case of being desirous and wanting good and great quantities of food and clothing, and the extreme of being too tired and worn out in body and mind.[3]
4 The *fruits* are the true cessations, which are abandonments such that the obstruction that is removed does not arise again[4] [and which comes about] through analyzing individually the non-existence of the referent object of the conception of self.

These four [view, meditation, behavior, and fruit] are the distinguishing features of Buddhist doctrine. [9]

Because the opposite of a teacher who has both eliminated [all] faults [and has completed all good qualities] are the [teachers of] others [non-Buddhists], those who assert that [Buddhist and non-Buddhist] are not [differentiated] by refuge and that there is one teacher [for both Buddhist and non-Buddhist] are mistaken.

---

[1]The "four seals" are tenets that are so-called because they "stamp" a doctrine as Buddhist.

[2]Buddhist systems actually have much in common with non-Buddhist systems. Nevertheless, non-Buddhist meditation is not an antidote to saṃsāra (the continuation of rebirth due to the power of karma), since it does not involve realization of selflessness; therefore, it is inferior to Buddhist meditation.

[3]Buddhists and non-Buddhists alike generally agree that attachment to worldly goods is problematic but many schools valorize asceticism. The Jains (Nirgranthas) and others claim to be non-violent but they harm themselves by asceticism. The Buddhist ideal may seem ascetic in comparison to modern life in the West but it does not involve starvation, self-mutilation, etc.

[4]A true cessation is a nirvāṇa. When ignorance is rooted out by wisdom, it does not return.

Our teacher has abandoned all faults and completed all good qualities.[1] Teachings and teachers that are opposite to those two [i.e., that cannot match them] are regarded as the teachings and teacher of others, i.e., Outsiders. Daktsang and others who propound that Buddhist and non-Buddhist are not differentiated by way of [where they] go for refuge[2] and that the teacher of Buddhists and non-Buddhists is the same[3] are very mistaken.

The two, Outer [non-Buddhist] and Inner [Buddhist], [respectively] establish and refute the referent object of the view of self. [10]

There are two types of proponents of tenets: Outsiders who [attempt to] prove the existence of the referent object of the view of a permanent, unitary independent self, and Buddhists who refute [such a self as] non-existent.[4]

The first [are divided] into Proponents of Annihilation and Proponents of Permanence by way of [what they assert about] the manifest and hidden.

---

[1]The "faults" are the obstructions to liberation and the obstructions to omniscience. The obstructions to liberation are primarily the afflictions of ignorance, desire, and aversion (the three poisons), although ignorance is the affliction that is the basis of all other afflictions. The obstructions to omniscience are predispositions for the *appearance* of inherent existence that prevent the simultaneous cognition of the two truths (phenomena and their emptiness). The "good qualities" are twelve types of extraordinary abilities such as the capacity to visit simultaneously many "Buddha-lands," know many eons of past and future, teach many people in an instant, and emanate many bodies.

[2]A Buddhist is a person who goes for refuge to the Three Jewels of the Buddha, his Doctrine (*dharma*), and his Spiritual Community, finding them to be a haven from the terrors of saṃsāra. The *actual* refuge is the Doctrine—in particular, true paths and true cessations, especially cessations (since nirvāṇa is the true refuge from saṃsāra). Non-Buddhists may take refuge in Dharma but what they take as Dharma is not what Buddhists understand by Dharma.

[3]Jamyang Shayba is accusing Daktsang of holding something he surely did not mean. At the beginning of his own book on tenets, Daktsang says, "Buddha taught the systems of tenets that are to be explained," and then goes on later to discuss both non-Buddhist and Buddhist tenets. He surely did not mean that Buddha is also the teacher of the non-Buddhists. Jamyang Shayba imputes many ridiculous positions to Daktsang, who had the temerity to criticize Dzongkaba.

[4]This is the grossest, coarsest false conception of a self, as found in the Hindu Upaniṣads: an individual soul (*ātman*) that is identical with Brahman—infinite being, consciousness, and bliss (*sat-cit-ananda*). Therefore, this soul/self is (1) permanent (not changing moment to moment, eternal); (2) partless (indivisible, unitary); and (3) independent (uncaused, does not produce effect).

Among the first of those [i.e., Outsiders], there are Proponents of Annihilation, who propound that beyond mere manifest appearances there is nothing,[1] and Proponents of a View of Permanence, who make superimpositions with respect to hidden phenomena.[2]

Those who assert and refute truly existent things are respectively Proponents of True Existence and Proponents of Non-Entityness [No True Existence].

Also, among the second—Insiders—there are two: [11] Proponents of True Existence, who assert the existence of truly existent things and Proponents of No-Entityness, who refute [the true establishment of things].[3]

[Within Proponents of True Existence] those who adhere to external and internal [truly existent objects] are [respectively] Proponents of [Truly Existent External] Objects and Proponents of Mind Only.

Also, with respect to the former, there are three: the two, Vaibhāṣikas and Sautrāntikas, [both being] Proponents of [Truly Existent External] Objects, who adhere to the true establishment of external objects; and Cittamātrins, who adhere to the true existence of the internal mind.[4]

---

[1]Proponents of Annihilation believe only what they see, hear, etc. They do not believe in inference and, therefore, do not believe in karma or rebirth.

[2]Proponents of Permanence are those who say something does exist that in fact does not exist, such as a permanent self. Hidden phenomena are those that are not directly perceivable but must be established by inference.

[3]All non-Prāsaṅgikas are Proponents of True Existence, asserting that phenomena truly exist, not being merely designated in dependence upon some basis. Synonyms for true existence include inherent existence, true establishment, ultimate existence, etc.

[4]Cittamātrins say that there are no external objects (i.e., they say that minds and objects occur simultaneously due to a single cause and that objects only appear to be separate from minds). Since external objects do not exist, they do not truly exist; only the mind does. Vaibhāṣikas and Sautrāntikas recognize external objects. For them, both mind and object truly exist.

General Differences Between Buddhist Schools

Most [Insider systems] draw the Teacher [Buddha], etc., to their own school and many respect [Nāgārjuna, etc.].

The four tenet systems draw to their own sects the teacher Buddha and the Superiors Maitreya, Mañjughoṣa, the supreme pair [Śāriputra and Maudgalyāyana],[1] etc., and there are many Hearer schools who respect Nāgārjuna, Asaṅga, etc.[2]

Each [asserts] that their own systems are free from extremes. The higher [systems] refute the conceptual superimpositions [of the lower]. [12]

Those of our own and others' sects assert that their own systems are free from the extremes of permanence and annihilation.[3] The upper refute the conceptual superimpositions of the lower.

The views of the lower are also pedestals [for understanding] the views of the upper systems.

Understanding the views of the lower systems is also a pedestal or method of coming to understand the views of the higher systems.[4]

The other systems have fallen to extremes; the [only] system free from extremes is the honorable Nāgārjuna's.

---

[1]Maitreya is a Bodhisattva (or Buddha, depending on account) who will become the next Buddha to manifest as a teacher and re-found the Buddhist religion after it has become extinct. Mañjughoṣa is another name for Mañjuśrī, the Bodhisattva personifying wisdom. There were Bodhisattvas of these names in Buddha's retinue. Śāriputra and Maudgalyāyana were Buddha's two greatest Hearer disciples, i.e., the greatest of those disciples who heard and practiced the Buddha's teachings without developing the altruistic Bodhisattva attitude. All schools would like to claim that these luminaries agree with them.

[2]There are Hearers who, although they are Hīnayānists by tenet (i.e., are Sautrāntikas or Vaibhāṣikas) are Mahāyānists by path because of their altruistic motivation. Therefore, they respect Mahāyānists such as Nāgārjuna.

[3]Each system has its own interpretation of the "middle way" between the extremes of annihilation (denying too much) or the extreme of permanence (denying too little). We have discussed this in the introduction.

[4]Because the views of the higher schools are quite subtle and require the refutation of grosser views, familiarizing oneself with the views of a lower school can enable one to grasp the full meaning of the views of a higher school.

However, the others have fallen to coarse and subtle extremes of permanence and annihilation. Freedom from all extremes exists only in the Prāsaṅgika-Mādhyamika system commented on by the glorious protector—the Superior Nāgārjuna. [13]

Part One
Non-Buddhist Systems

Introduction to the Non-Buddhist Tenets

At a time when [human] lifespan was incalculable, Kapila composed the texts of the Sāṃkhyas.

At the time at the beginning of this eon when humans were able to live an incalculable number of years,[1] the sage called Kapila of the Brahmin lineage arose and composed the texts of the Sāṃkhyas.

Because of various superimpositions about distinctions of the self, many systems of Forders split off.

With respect to Kapila's discrimination of a permanent, partless, independent self, many different systems arose through imposing superimpositions, whereby many Forder systems split off.

Some explain that the teachers, etc., were different from the beginning.

It appears that some among those explained that the teachers, texts, etc. were different from the beginning.[2] [14]

In some [texts] it is asserted that the teacher of all is [the Jain] sage Arhat.

---

[1]In most non-Buddhist and Buddhist systems, it is understood that the universe goes again and again through a cycle of creation, endurance, destruction, and vacuity. At the beginning of an eon, the human lifespan is immeasurable but then gradually declines. This statement amounts to an assertion that Sāṃkhya is the oldest philosophy.

[2]This is the idea that Sāṃkhya is the original source of *all* the non-Buddhist systems. This is stated by Candrakīrti and others and denied by Bhāvaviveka and others. Jamyang Shayba will later say that he does not know which is true.

According to some texts, Nirgranthas assert that the teacher of all the Forders was the sage Arhat.[1]

Two types of sacrifice arose here in stages.

Pure sacrifice and impure sacrifice of cows arose one after the other.[2]

The Sāṃkhyas are earlier.

With respect to the chronology of the tenets of the Forders of this eon, Sāṃkhya is earlier than the others.

Other Schools, Outsiders, Ford Makers, etc., are synonyms.

Other Schools, Outsiders, Ford Makers, etc. are synonyms. The Sanskrit original of *mu steg* (Forder) is *tīrthika. Tīrthi* means riverbank, bathing (*khrus*), and platform. *Tīryati* means entering the water or swimming. *Sathi* means path or platform. *Ka* means making or propounding. Therefore, if it is explained through contextual etymology, adding on separate letters, [15] [they are called Tīrthikas because] they propound entering the water as the path, or they propound making a ford for entering the water. Therefore, the commentary on the *Vinayavastu* explains [*tīrthi*] as entering into the water.[3]

Although [Outsiders' schools] are explained as twenty-five, here twelve houses [systems] are clear.

Twenty-five divisions of those Outsiders also occurs in sūtra and in Avalokitavrara's *Commentary to (Bhāvaviveka's) "Lamp for (Nāgārjuna's) 'Wisdom.'"* Also, [that there are twenty-five] is explained in both Dzongkaba's *Ocean of Reasoning, Explanation of (Nāgārjuna's) "Treatise on the Middle Way"* and in Kaydrup's *Opening the Eyes of the Fortunate.* With respect to the statement here [in Jamyang

---

[1]"Arhat" may refer to the first Jina (foundational Jain teacher), Ṛṣabha, since all of the Jinas (twenty-four in each era) are called Arhat. This reports a tradition that he composed all of the books of *all* philosophies!

[2]Pure sacrifice would be that which does not involve killing an animal. This passage asserts that the non-Buddhist tradition gradually degenerated into animal sacrifices. (Religious historians would consider the opposite more likely.)

[3]What may not be clear in this explanation is that "ford" is a metaphor: these systems consider themselves a raft for passing over the river of saṃsāra. However, it is also true that ritual bathing is a long-standing custom.

Shayba's text], twelve different houses are treated since their modes of assertion are clear.[1]

Whether Sāṃkhyas and Kāpilas are taken to be one [16] or explained to be separate, they have mutual positions. Therefore, when explained briefly they are counted as one, and when explained extensively they are counted separately.

Regarding the statement in the *Descent to Laṅkā Sūtra* [that there are twenty-two], some say that the way to add three onto the twenty-two [by considering one to be split into three][2] is by their denial of [the existence of] objects, aggregates, etc. There are the one already included and (1) the one that denies them upon having generated a meditative absorption free from attachment in the sense of the fault of taking an object-possessor [consciousness] of attachment [as having] its own entity; (2) the one that denies them in dependence on another dissimilar antidote; and (3) the one that [asserts that] stopping mental application to any kind of object or stopping conceptuality is nirvāṇa. It should be analyzed whether or not three should be newly added on.

[Buddha] says in the *Descent to Laṅkā Sūtra,* [17] "Therefore, although they do indeed come to have minds that have 'passed from sorrow,' since Mahāmati has seen that [their 'cessation'] will disintegrate, they have not [actually] passed from sorrow." This applies to all twenty-five [sub-divisions]. Thus, [Buddha] explains that their [alleged] "nirvāṇa" [attained] through those systems of release is unable [to serve as an actual nirvāṇa]. In this explanation, in answer to a question by Mahāmati regarding the Forders' methods for release, [Buddha] teaches merely their mode of assertion regarding release.[3]

That they are limited to five is a mistake. Unlike our schools, their number is not limited.

The statements by the Foremost One [Dzongkaba] and his spiritual sons that the source for those who propound that there are no causes [or effects] depends on one from among those twenty-five [i.e., the Ayata] that appears to fit together with the [enumeration of them as] eighteen. Daktsang's statement that the enumeration

---

[1]In other words, there are many, many non-Buddhist systems, but Jamyang Shayba will discuss only twelve whose tenets are relatively clear. The fundamental reason the others are not "clear," he admits, is that their books were not translated into Tibetan. He calls them "houses" because there are twelve, like the astrological houses.

[2]Of course, as Ngawang Belden points out, this only adds up to twenty-four, not twenty-five!

[3]The non-Buddhists also speak of nirvāṇa but theirs is not a real nirvāṇa; instead, they achieve a temporary cessation of desire, or temporarily stop thought, etc.

of Outsiders' tenets is definite as five is mistaken.[1] [18] Since they are not like our schools, their number is not limited.

One Proponent of Annihilation and eleven Proponents of Permanence are widely known.

There is one Proponent of Annihilation and eleven Proponents of Permanence in the context of their individual modes of assertion that are well known. There appear to be *twelve* proponents of permanence but the authoritative texts on which they depend are for some, the same, and for others, diverse. Therefore, it appears to be thought that since there are dissimilar features that are the same for both [i.e., tenets that the two schools share that others do not], they are two divisions [of one school] and their specification of tenets is very similar, whereby their general enumeration should be as one.

[1] Daktsang asserts that all Forders are included in five: Lokāyatas, Sāṃkhyas, Vaiṣṇavas, Aiśvaras, and Nirgranthas.

The Ayata School

The first from among the explanations of the twelve Forder sects is the expression of the assertions of the Ayatas.

Bṛhaspati, Lokacakṣu, [19] **and Jukdop are the teachers.**

Devaguru [also known as] Bṛhaspati, the sage Lokacakṣu who was the author of a hundred thousand texts, and Jukdop, Lokacakṣu's student, are their teachers.[1]

They are Hedonists, Proponents of Annihilation, Nihilists, Barhaspatyas, Ayatas, etc.

With respect to names, they are called Hedonists, Proponents of Annihilation, Nihilists, Bṛhaspatyas, Those Flung Afar, Proponents of Entityness, and Proponents of Nature.[2] [20] The etymology of Ayata—Those Gone Afar—is that they have gone far away from the correct view.

It is mistaken to call them Propounders of Nature as Cause.

The translator Daktsang is mistaken in calling them Proponents of Nature as Cause [because that is a name of the Sāṃkhyas, not Ayatas].

---

[1]The principal author of the school is Jayarāśi (flourished 650), who wrote the *Lion of Annihilation of Principles (Tattopaplavasiṃha)*, referring often to the lost sūtras of Bṛhaspati. Jukdop and Lokacakṣu are not mentioned in Lokāyata scholarship.

[2]They are most commonly called Lokāyatas ("concerned with the world") or Cārvākas ("followers of Cārvāka"). An etymology of Ayata more probable than the one given by Losang Gönchok is "concerned with"; they follow ordinary worldly common sense and reject what they cannot see or hear. They are called "Proponents of Entityness" because they believe that qualities inhere in things without being caused.

Because it is explained that some assert and some do not assert cause and effect, gods, etc., it is a mistake [to say that Proponents of Annihilation say] that former and future lives are totally non-existent and that there are only three migrations, etc.

Among Proponents of Annihilation, some assert that there is no existence at all of cause and effect [of actions], other migrations such as gods, and former and later births. [There are others] who assert cause and effect that appears here and who assert six migrations, [saying] humans are merely born as humans and gods are merely born as gods.[1] Therefore, Daktsang is mistaken in saying that [Ayatas] only assert former and future lives as utterly non-existent and that there are merely the three migrations—humans, animals, and non-manifest beings.

[These tenets were made] through [inept] logic, through meditative absorption, through being pained by desire, and through a boast to help.] [21]

Regarding their motivation for explaining that [karma and rebirth, etc.] are non-existent:

- [Their tenets] were born from facsimiles of logical reasoning.
- [They are] based on clairvoyance in meditative absorption [in which they see the coarse but] they could not see the subtle [such as karma and rebirth].
- Because they suffered from desire they wanted to fornicate [and did not want to admit this would have negative karmic consequences].
- Devaguru boasted that he helped.[2]

Therefore, Daktsang is mistaken in saying that [their tenets were created] *only* through being pained by desire.

Since [a maker of thorns, etc.] is not seen and since [happiness] does not follow [virtue], there is no cause and effect [of actions].

The chief of the Proponents of Annihilation says the following: [22] "No one sees who makes the eyes in a peacock's tail-feathers or [the sharpness of] thorns."[3]

---

[1]These are the divisions of "meditators" and "dialecticians." The meditators are those with a limited belief in karma and rebirth because of their clairvoyance.

[2]This is obscure.

[3]They mistrust inference, believing only in the evidence of their senses. Therefore, they do not speculate on the way things have been caused. The things to which he is referring are just inherent in the objects.

[At death,] the self that is merely body and mind disintegrates. Therefore, former and later lifetimes do not exist.

Also, since some people act virtuously and [yet] are tortured by suffering, happiness does not follow virtue. Thus, there is no cause and effect of actions. Merely something within the scope of the senses that has a nature of body and mind is regarded as the self; therefore, since at the time of death body and mind disintegrate, former and later lifetimes do not exist.

The minds [of different beings] depend on their different bodies. Therefore, they are not one continuum.

With respect to births as former and later persons, such as a god in a former life and a human in this life, these minds depend on merely different earlier and later bodies.[1] Therefore, it is not suitable to identify them as one continuum.

Mind is produced from the elements. Therefore, the phenomena of nirvāṇa do not exist.

Because mind is produced from the elements, it is impossible to familiarize the mind [sufficiently], due to which the phenomena of nirvāṇa—Arhats who have abandoned the afflictions, and All-Knowers—do not exist.[2] [23]

[Only] direct perception is valid cognition. Inference is not valid cognition [because of being] mistaken.

Only direct perceptions are valid consciousnesses. Inferential consciousnesses are not valid cognitions because they are mistaken consciousnesses.[3]

Refutation of the Ayata Assertions

Because of being a mind, it is established that [another mind] precedes it.

---

[1]There is a connection between former, present, and future lives but there is no "continuum" of either body or mind. At death, both mind and body cease. The new mind is produced by the new body.

[2]Because the mind is produced from the body, it has its limits: it cannot be perfected. Therefore, eliminating desire, hatred, etc., is not possible, nor is omniscience.

[3]As before, this is saying that we should trust only our senses, not try prove the reality of karma and rebirth by reasoning.

The subject, a knower [i.e., a mind] just after conception, is preceded by a mind that is its substantial cause because of being a knower; for example, this present mind.[1] The subject, the final mind of death of a common being, is able to generate the mind that is its impelled object [24] because of being a knower having desire, such as a prior main consciousness.

Because of movement [to activities immediately after birth] and memory [of former lives] also, [the existence of former lives is established].

Moreover, since a calf who has just been born seeks the milk of the teat and since with respect to animals, etc., the mind moves to activities of eating grass and engaging in desire without being taught, one can understand that this is done due to the conditioning of previous lifetimes. Also, memories of former lifetimes exist, and matter cannot act as a substantial cause to produce consciousness.

Familiarization [with something increases] clear appearance and [the production and abiding of things] is concomitant [with the existence and non-existence of assisters for establishing them]; therefore, omniscience and cause and effect are established.

When one familiarizes the mind [with something], clear appearance increases. Therefore, the existence of omniscience is established.[2] [25] Because the production and abiding of these things is concomitant with the existence or non-existence of assisters for establishing them in this way, the existence of cause and effect is established.[3]

---

[1]This is in the form of a debate, where the convention is to use *chos can* ("the subject") to mark off the subject to which one will predicate something. Here four arguments are presented for the existence of rebirth. First, it is argued that a mind cannot have a merely physical cause but must be preceded by a moment of mind. Even the first moment of mind of a being who has just been conceived in the womb must be linked to a previous moment of mind. Second, because of the power of desire or other afflictions, one's final moment of mind at death is able to produce another moment of mind in the individual who succeeds one in the rebirth sequence (which probably will be the "intermediate state being"). Third, we must be conditioned by experiences of previous lifetimes because we may be moved to act without having been taught, such as the calf that immediately seeks its mother's teat. Fourth, we sometimes experience memories of former lives.

[2]That is, why should there be a limit to knowledge, if our experience tells us that increasing knowledge is merely a matter of applying the mind?

[3]"Assisters" are causes. The sharpness of thorns, etc., is caused by the same ripening karmic predisposition that caused the thorn.

Because the non-existence of former lives is not seen directly [by you Ayatas] and because you refute inference, [your denial of former and later lives and of cause and effect is] also [mistaken].

It follows that you Ayatas are incorrect not to assert former lifetimes because (1) the non-existence of those is not seen by your direct perception, and (2) you refute that inferential consciousnesses are valid consciousnesses. Therefore, [your thesis] is not established by valid cognition.[1]

Because everything is not produced from everything, it is not correct that there is causeless production.[2]

[1]This attempts to turn their reasoning back on them. If you believe only what is established by your senses, then you have no basis for asserting that karma and rebirth do not exist, since your senses are not competent to judge what is not open to the senses. And you cannot use reasoning to establish their non-existence, since you do not accept the reliability of reasoning.

[2]If things had no causes, everything could be produced from everything; a tree could grow from a can.

The Sāṃkhya School

Kapila, Arhat, Maheśvara, and Patañjali are their teachers.

[26] The sage Kapila, the sage Arhat [according to the Jainas], Maheśvara, and the teacher Patañjali are held to be their teachers.

[Their names are] Enumerators, Proponents of Nature as Cause, Kāpilas, etc.

Their names are Enumerators, Proponents of Nature as the Cause, Kāpilas, Principlists, etc.[1]

They are divided into non-theistic Kāpilas [who assert that the previously existing] is manifested and theistic Sāṃkhyas, the system of Patañjali, [who assert that cause and effect are one nature but different] expressions.

With respect to the entities of the divisions, the two are the non-theistic Kāpilas, who assert that what exists previously is merely manifested, and the system of the teacher Patañjali, that of the theistic Sāṃkhyas, who assert that although the two—cause and effect—are one nature, they are made by Maheśvara into different expressions.[2] [27]

---

[1]Spirit (*puruṣa*) and Nature (*prakṛti*) are the two eternal principles and most important concepts in Sāṃkhya. However, Jamyang Shayba and Losang Gönchok use several synonyms for each of these terms interchangeably, which may confuse the reader. Accordingly, we have mostly translated *ātman* ("self") and *puruṣa* ("person") as Spirit; and *prakṛti* ("nature"), *mūlaprakṛti* ("fundamental nature"), *kanthā* ("matter"), *pradhāna* ("principal"), *sāmānya* ("generality"), and *sāmānyapradhāna* ("general principal") as Nature.

[2]Non-theists explain that effects inhere in causes. For instance, a tree already exists in its seed, although the tree is not yet manifest. This is based upon the grand scheme of Sāṃkhya cosmogony in which at the beginning of each eon, Nature, which contains within it all things in their unmanifest state, itself gradually unfolds until all phenomena are made manifest. All things exist from the beginning. Theists, on the other hand, say that god, Īśvara ("Lord") or Maheśvara

Direct valid cognition is the two [types of] engagement of the senses.

For the Kapilas, direct valid cognition is the engagement of the sense [powers]—ear, etc. There are two [ways of asserting this engagement by the sense powers: engagement] with and without the condition [of the engagement of the sense power and the person appearing mixed].

[Inference] for oneself is [through] the seven relations. [Inferences] for others are that with aspect and the clarifying.

There are two types of inference. Inference for one's own purpose is inference through the seven relations. Inference for another's purpose are of two types: that having an [external] aspect, i.e., a proof statement, and that which makes clear [your own assertion], i.e., a consequence.[1]

The seven relations are:

1 Wealth and the owner of wealth
2 Nature and transformation
3 Cause and effect
4 Continuum and possessor of the continuum
5 Branch and branch-possessor
6 Those who work together
7 Harmer and object harmed [28]

Īśvarakṛṣṇa's tantra, the *Thirty*, etc., are [valid] scriptures.

Their valid scriptures are Īśvarakṛṣṇa's tantra, *The Thirty Textual Systems, The Fifty Characteristics,* etc.

The Spirit is consciousness and does not have qualities, is not active, is not an agent, is a permanent thing, and is the enjoyer [of pleasure and pain].

They assert the existence of the Spirit, an entity of consciousness that possesses the five features of self. It:

("Great Lord"), causes Nature to evolve in an orderly fashion. Otherwise, they say, good would not be rewarded. He does not actually interfere directly, for the Spirit is a mere witness to Nature, but "acts" through drawing Nature to him.

[1]One uses reasoning to convince oneself or to convince others. There are seven types of possible relationships between things that can be investigated, as delineated in the next paragraph. Reasoning for another involves using either a proof statement or drawing out the consequences of their statement or your own.

1 does not have the character of the qualities of activity, darkness, etc.[1]
2 is not active.
3 is not an agent [of virtue and non-virtue].
4 is a permanent thing.
5 is the experiencer of pleasure and pain.[2]

[The unreleased self] abides in proximity to Nature, but [the released self] does not abide there.

When divided, [30] there are two, the unrelated self that abides in proximity to Nature and the released self that does not abide there.[3]

Consciousness, Knower, Person, Self, etc. [are synonyms of Spirit].

The synonyms of Spirit are said to be Consciousness, Knower, Person, Self, Experiencer, the Sentient, Knower of the Field, etc.

[The other] twenty-four [objects of knowledge] are Nature.

From among the twenty-five objects of knowledge, the other twenty-four are asserted as Nature.

Nature is asserted to be the agent [of manifestation], permanent, partless, pervading all objects, non-manifest, and the three qualities in balance. [It is called] the mode of subsistence, etc.

The so-called Generality, Principal, or Root Nature is:

- the manifester
- asserted to be an object of knowledge
- permanent because it is not produced
- a partless singularity

---

[1]All things are comprised of the three general qualities (*guṇa*): *sattva*, which has qualities such as illumination, lightness, knowledge, etc.; *rajas*, which has qualities such as activity, passion, etc.; and *tamas*, which has qualities such as darkness, heaviness, obscuration, etc. In India, all things could be described as either pure *sattva*, pure *rajas*, or pure *tamas*, or a combination of two or more, just as in China, all things could be described as pure *yin* or *yang* or a combination thereof. The qualities will be referred to as mental potency, activity, and darkness.

[2]The Spirit is an eternal, uncreated, and unmanifest spiritual reality; it itself does not act but merely witnesses what is reflected to it through mental processes, which along with all other phenomena are considered part of Nature. Spirit is "pure" consciousness.

[3]Until one has become liberated from saṃsāra through the yogas practiced by this system, the Spirit is associated with Nature through rebirth.

- just an object [of use by the Spirit]
- that which pervades all environments and beings
- non-manifest, since it is not manifest for anyone [31]
- the three qualities of activity, darkness, and lightness in balance[1]
- called the mode of subsistence or ultimate truth

The subconscious awareness, which [evolves] from [Nature], is like a mirror; when the two mix, comprehension occurs.

The subconscious awareness [32] [is produced] from Nature. Since the subconscious awareness is like a mirror, it is contradictory for there to be a mixture or meeting of an external object and the internal Spirit or of subconscious awareness and Spirit.[2]

[Synonyms of] the qualities are mental potency, activity, and darkness, or pleasure, pain, etc.

The synonyms of the three qualities are mental potency, activity, and darkness, or, pleasure, pain, bewilderment, etc.

---

[1]Nature itself is not manifest (like a black hole, it exists invisibly) but is known through what evolves from it, namely the whole manifest cosmos as summarized in twenty-three categories. When all three of the qualities are in balance, there is no manifestation from it. For instance, when the cosmos is in a state of vacuity, after a period of dissolution and before a period of creation, the qualities are in balance, and there is no evolution from Nature. At the appropriate time, there is a shift in the balance so that one predominates, and then Nature begins to unfold. Our ordinary self is all Nature; our bodies and mental states are all part of it and, therefore, are "matter."

[2]The first evolute from Nature is the subconscious awareness *(buddhi, blo)*, also known as the Great One *(mahat)*, which is the most subtle level of ordinary consciousness. We have translated both *buddhi* and *mahat* as "subconscious awareness" to avoid confusion. This awareness mediates between our ordinary minds and the Spirit. It reflects what we know consciously, through the senses and thought, to the pure consciousness, or Spirit. On the other hand, the Spirit shines its light on the subconscious awareness, and this reflected light enables us to perceive the world. But this "exchange" is like a two-way mirror: although Spirit can "see" through the subconscious awareness, we cannot "see" Spirit through it. Any comprehension we have of the world occurs through this "mirror," but since all of the knowing is indirect, as when we see things in a mirror, there is no real "mixing" or "meeting" of the two.

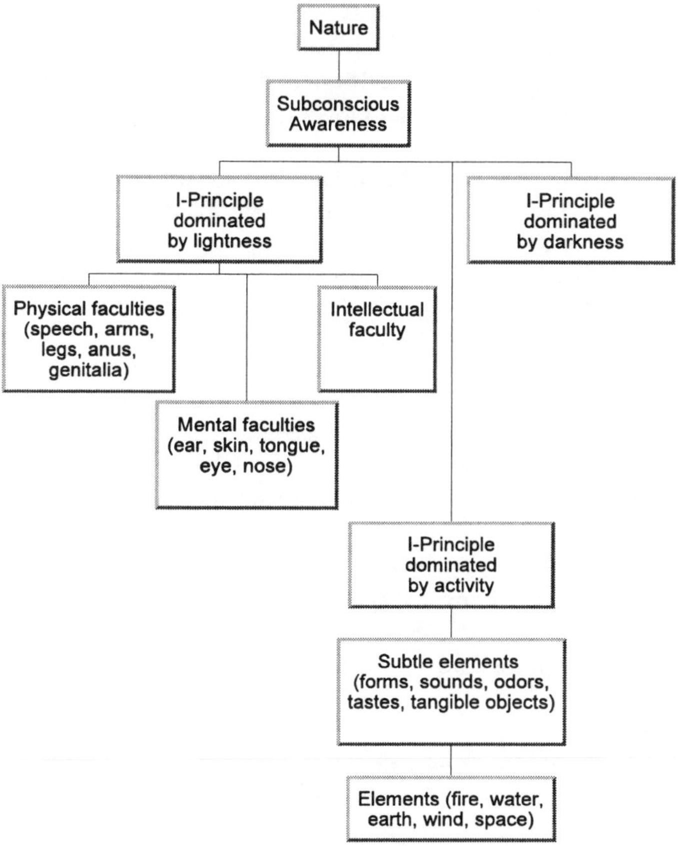

From the subconscious awareness, the three I-principles are produced.

The three I-principles—the I-principle dominated by activity, the I-principle dominated by darkness, and the I-principle dominated by mental potency—are produced from the subconscious awareness.[1]

---

[1]From the subconscious awareness evolves the I-principle, or self-awareness (*ahaṃkara*). All evolution occurs through shifts in the predominance of the basic strands or qualities (*guṇa*) from which all things are made, so there can be an I-principle emerging with knowledge, passion, obscuration, etc.

From the first [I-principle], the five subtle objects are produced. From those five, the five elements [are produced]. From the second [I-principle], the five action faculties, five mental faculties, and the intellectual faculty [are produced]. The third [I-principle] moves the [other] two.

- From the first of those [the I-principle dominated by activity] evolve:
  - The five subtle objects—forms, sounds, odors, tastes, and tangible objects. The five elements—earth, water, fire, wind, and space—evolve from those.
- From the second [I-principle, that dominated by mental potency,] evolve eleven [faculties]:
  - The five mental faculties—the faculties of eye, ear, nose, tongue, and body [33]
  - The five physical faculties—speech, arms, legs, anus, and genitalia
  - The intellectual faculty.
- The third [I-principle, that dominated by darkness,] moves the other two.[1]

Because there are four possibilities [between Nature and evolute] that the twenty-five [objects of knowledge] are included in Nature and the Spirit is very mistaken.

There are four possibilities [between Nature and evolute]:

1 Nature is just Nature.
2 the sixteen—the eleven faculties and five elements—are just evolutes.
3 the seven—the subconscious awareness, the I-principle, and the five objects—are both.
4 that which is neither is the Spirit.[2]

Because of this, Daktsang's saying that all twenty-five objects of knowledge are included in Nature and Spirit is very mistaken.

---

[1]Perhaps the most counter-intuitive aspect of this philosophy is its assertion that physical objects actually evolve (or perhaps more accurately reflecting the Sāṃkhya perspective, *de*volve) from subtle mental states. Nature, which is not in itself ever even manifest, gradually takes form and acquires coarseness through the shifts in its qualities. We might contrast this with the generally accepted scientific view of evolution, in which consciousness is seen as the final evolute from gross matter rather than its cause.

[2]This seems to mean that since the seven initial evolutes from Nature are themselves the basis of further evolution, they are both evolutes and Nature themselves.

Nature and Spirit are truly existent things and the others are false.

It is asserted that Nature and Spirit are true things and that the other twenty-three [34] are established as false.[1]

The mode of production [of produced things] is that effects exist previously and become manifest.

With respect to the production of things that have production, there are differences. Although both systems of Sāṃkhya assert that effects exist previously, non-theistic Sāṃkhyas assert that the non-manifest becomes manifest, whereas for the theistic Sāṃkhyas [effects] also evolve due to the condition [of Maheśvara acting on them].[2]

Disintegration is by dissolution or pacification.

With respect to the mode of disintegration, they dissolve into Nature in the order in which they are generated or become pacified in their respective natures.[3]

Varieties [of environments and beings] do not [arise] just from Nature because [it] has no mind.

The theistic Sāṃkhyas do not say [35] that these varieties of environments and beings arise from just Nature because Nature does not have a mind.[4]

[If] there were no supervisor, [nothing] would begin.

If there were no supervisor, [no one] would begin undertakings.

The Spirit [is not the supervisor] because it is ignorant.

---

[1]That is, only Spirit and Nature themselves are ultimately real, as the process leading to liberation reveals.

[2]Whether or not they are theists, Sāṃkhyas say that the effect exists even before it is produced, abiding in its cause. However, theistic Saṃkhyas say that Maheśvara must act if the effect is to emerge.

[3]At the end of a world-cycle, or due to the success of the yogas used by this system, all that has evolved from Nature devolves back into it.

[4]Nature *itself* cannot know anything; its evolutes, the subconscious awareness and the coarser levels of ordinary consciousness, do the knowing. The theists argue that evolution must be caused by something sentient.

Even the Spirit is not the supervisor because at that time it does not know anything.[1]

Through the three qualities [of activity, lightness, and darkness] that abide in the entity of Nature, there is production, abiding, and disintegration [of beings and environments].

The way causes—Nature and Īśvara—continuously produce effects is: they are made to produce, maintain, and destroy [things] by means of those three qualities of activity, darkness, and lightness that abide in the entity of Nature.

The causes exist, and because of the seriality [of the qualities], effects [arise serially].

Because there is a seriality to the qualities that are causes, it is said that effects—the production, maintenance, and disintegration of beings and environments—arise serially.[2]

Through the paths of the concentrations and absorptions, clairvoyance, viewing Nature, etc., [36] there are two liberations, of [the Spirit abiding] alone and of Nature from the Spirit.

Through the paths of the eight concentrations and formless absorptions, clairvoyance, viewing Nature and the Spirit and meditating on them as different, and the path that is a meditation on the emptiness of other—the emptiness of those two of each other—there are the two, liberation through the Spirit abiding separately and liberation of Nature from the Spirit.[3]

[Also] there are fifty characteristics, three bondages, three liberations, etc.

Moreover, there are fifty characteristics:

- nine pleasures
- eight accomplishments
- twenty-eight forces

---

[1]When Nature is not manifest, the Spirit cannot know anything because it witnesses the activity of Nature. Therefore, it will be argued, an external force must cause evolution.

[2]It is the predominance of action (*rajas*) that enables creation; of lightness (*sattva*) that enables maintenance; and of darkness (*tamas*) that enables destruction.

[3]The end result of the path is a state called "isolation" (*kaivalya*) in which the Spirit shines alone because Nature has devolved and become unmanifest. Thus, the two eternal principles are "liberated" from one another.

- five perversions
- three [bondages]—bondage of nature, bondage of transformation, and bondage of wealth
- three liberations from those [37]
- release through knowing the twenty-five [objects of knowledge], etc.[1]

The Refutation of the Sāṃkhyas

If what existed were produced again, [production] would be senseless and endless.

If what already existed previously were produced again, production would be senseless. If what was already produced were produced again, [production] would be endless.[2]

The producers being permanent and not deteriorating, and the effects disappearing, is contradictory.

While the fundamental Nature, which is the cause producing suffering, is permanent and abides without deteriorating, it is contradictory that the effect, which is that produced by that, i.e., saṃsāra, is overcome.[3]

Because [the subconscious awareness] is matter, it does not experience [pleasure and pain], and because [the Spirit] is pervasive, it is contradictory that it is partless.

Because the subconscious awareness is matter, it does not experience pleasure and pain, and because the Spirit is partless, [38] it is contradictory that it exists through pervading everywhere.[4]

---

[1]These seem to refer to gradations of insight toward realizing the distinction between Nature and Spirit. The bondage of Nature may be evolution; the bondage of Transformation may be rebirth; the bondage of Wealth may be attachments to material things.

[2]The Sāṃkhyas held that effects existed prior to their production, abiding in their causes; hence, here it is argued that if that were the case, production would be unnecessary or would be endless.

[3]It is argued that since the cause of saṃsāra, Nature, is endless, it must be impossible to end saṃsāra, too.

[4]The "experiencer" is the Spirit, so the subconscious awareness does not experience itself. Also, it is argued that if the Spirit were partless, it could not exist everywhere, since it would then have north, south, east, and west parts.

Because [the Spirit] is permanent, it is not consciousness. How could the permanent be bound and liberated?

If the Spirit is permanent, it must not be consciousness, and one could not identify that which is permanent as bound in saṃsāra and liberated from that.[1]

[1] If it is permanent (which is assumed to mean unchanging), it could not really be consciousness, which is always changing, nor would it make sense to say that it was caught in saṃsāra and could be liberated from it, which would also imply change.

The Brahmaṇa, Vaiyākaraṇa, Vedānta, and Guhyaka Schools

There are four systems [that similarly fall to an extreme of permanence].[1]

The Assertions of the Brahmaṇas

Brahmā, etc., are the teachers. Brahmaṇas, Vaidakas, etc. [are their names].

[39] Brahmā, Prajāpati, etc., are their teachers, and their names are Brahmaṇas and Vaidakas.[2]

Brahmā, born from a lotus or an egg, has seven names [in the seven] ages.

There are explanations that Brahmā was born from a lotus at the navel of Viṣṇu, born from an egg that was emanated by the mind of Īśvara, etc.[3] Brahmā has seven names, designated chronologically: Self-Arisen, Brahmā, Prajāpati, One

---

[1]According to Losang Chögyi Nyima, the last three are divisions of the first.

[2]Brahmā and Prajāpati are the same person, the creator god. Vaidakas are followers of the Vedas, the wisdom texts that define Hindu orthodoxy.

[3]Brahmā is the Hindu creator god. There are a variety of myths about how he is born. He emerges from a lotus growing from the navel of Viṣṇu as the latter sleeps on the primordial ocean. Another myth is that he emerges from an egg that is emanated by the mind of Īśvara (Viṣṇu), the egg being the container of all material existence. Despite the designation of the Brahmaṇas as a school, the worship of Brahmā was never strong in India. With Śiva as the destroyer and Viṣṇu as the preserver, Brahmā is a member of the Hindu trinity that symbolizes all aspects of godhood.

Whose Place of Birth Was a Lotus, Four-Faced, Patriarch, and Golden Womb.[1] [40]

From his four faces and four parts of his body, the four Vedas and four castes of humans were produced; [therefore] he is the creator of the world.

The four Vedas—Yajur Veda, Ṛig Veda, Sāma Veda, and Atharva Veda—arose from the four faces of [Brahmā], and he produced the four castes of humans: the royal caste (Kṣatriya) from the shoulders of his body; the priestly caste (Brāhmaṇa) from his mouth; the merchant caste (Vaiśya) from his thighs; and the commoner caste (Śūdra) from his heel. He is asserted to be the creator of the world, the producer of the eight mothers of the world: the mother of the sun, who produced the gods; the mother of the sacrificing women who produced the demi-gods; the mother of the Nāgas; etc.

The Vedas are self-arisen.

The Vedas are self-produced without having been made by anyone.[2]

The horse sacrifice is supreme.

The *aśvamedha*, that is, horse sacrifice, is said to be the supreme means of achieving the rank of Brahmā and high status.[3] [41]

The Assertions of the Vaiyākaraṇas

Sadāśiva is their teacher, Vaiyākaraṇa and Śabdakāra, their names.

Brahmā and Sadāśiva are the teachers, and Vaiyākaraṇa and Śabdakāra are their names.

---

[1]These are all epithets. He is self-arisen because he and others *believe* that he is immortal; he is Prajapāti because he is Lord of All Beings; he is born in a lotus; he has four faces; he is called "grandfather," or "patriarch," because he is the first person to exist in a world age; and golden womb may refer to the egg myth or to his role as generator of things.

[2]The Vedas are the words of the gods as heard by the sages (*ṛṣis*), so are created in that sense; on the other hand, they are eternal and beginningless. Brahmā spoke them from his four faces but he did not invent them.

[3]In ancient India, the horse sacrifice was a special ceremony of kings and a cause for rebirth in the heaven of Brahmā.

They propound a Sound Brahmā that serves as the basis for the varieties. The syllable, *oṃ* or long *auṃ*, is the nature of all things, partless and permanent. [Terms] are truly affixed [to objects]. The varieties appear through pollution by obscuration.

The Sound Brahmā that serves as the basis for generating all the various things is the creator, is permanent in the sense of not being produced or disintegrating, and is able to bear analysis by reasoning.[1] [42] These proponents of a self assert that [the Sound Brahmā], the entity of which is the long syllable *oṃ* (or *auṃ*), is:

- the nature of all things
- partless in terms of direction and time
- permanent in the sense of being free from production and disintegration
- truly affixed to objects by the power of the things themselves
- the basis of the appearance of the apprehender and apprehended as various at the time of pollution through ignorance

External and internal burnt offerings are the path. The bliss of emission is liberation.

The two, external burnt offerings—the sacrifice of cows—and internal burnt offerings—the emission of the constituent—are asserted as the supreme of paths. The orgasmic bliss of the emission of the constituent into a woman is said to be liberation.[2]

Valid cognition is only the Vedas. Some [also assert] the two, [direct perception and inferential cognition].

The Vaiyākaraṇa mostly assert that the valid source of cognition is only the Vedas but some also assert that there are two, direct perception and inferential cognition.[3]

---

[1]This is an idea found in several of the principle Upaniṣads. The syllable *oṃ* is the creator itself; that is, creation occurs through vibration.

[2]This seems to be the tantric principle that sexual bliss can be used to empower a consciousness that is focused on the appearance of deities. Since the Vaiyākaraṇa were concerned mainly with language (they are the "Grammarians"), it is unlikely that these practices were part of their system.

[3]That is, not all knowledge is contained in the Vedas. Direct perception is cognition without conceptuality, such as happens with sense perception and intuition, whereas inference involves reasoning.

The Assertions of the Vedāntins

Brahmā, etc., are the teachers. [43] **Vedāntavādin, etc. [are their names].**

Their teacher is Brahmā, etc., and their names are Vedāntavādin and Parabrahmāvādin.

Only the Person—pervasive, subtle, consciousness, permanent, sun-colored, and beyond darkness—creates beings and environments, binds [migrators], etc.

It is asserted that the Self—a Person pervading everywhere, subtle, the entity of which is consciousness and permanent—only this sun-colored Person, who is beyond darkness, produces and destroys beings and environments, binds and releases migrators, and creates the varieties of bliss and suffering.

When [the Person] is seen as the color of gold, [the yogi] dissolves as part of [the Person] and is released.

In dependence on a concentration, one meditates on the Self. Through that, one sees it directly. [44] As a sign of liberation from [suffering], one sees the Person as the color of gold. When [the yogi] dissolves as part [of the Self], that is said to be liberation.[1]

The Assertions of the Guhyakas

Brahmā, etc., are the teachers, and Vedaguhyaka [is their name].

Brahmā, etc., are their teachers, and they are called Vedaguhyaka.

***Drop of Ambrosia* (*amṛtanāda*) is their scripture. The Self that is consciousness, knower, and permanent is asserted to be partless, without entityness, and to be truly established.**

---

[1]Liberation in Vedānta is dissolution into the infinite Brahman, due to eliminating the illusion that one is separate from It. It is "sun-colored" in the sense that it is beyond the darkness of saṃsāra and that it contains all colors. The consciousness of one who is not going to be reborn leaves the skull through a tiny aperture at the top of the head and travels along a sun-ray.

The Self that is consciousness and a knower is permanent and partless, lacking the entityness[1] of objects of apprehension, and is asserted to be truly established.

The Refutation of Those Four Systems

There are not four castes. [45]

The four castes are non-existent because all are generated from the one body of Brahmā.[2]

All brothers and sisters are doing it.

If all four castes engage in the mutual copulation of brother and sister, that is a mode of behavior of barbarians. Therefore, your system of religious practice would be corrupt.[3]

If harming is religious practice, what are the causes of [birth in] hells? [The Self is not great, but small. It is not single, but many.]

If, due to your assertion of the sacrifice of cows as religious practice, what are the causes of being born in hells? It follows that the Self that has the color of the sun is not great because of being small. It follows that it is not single because of being many.[4] [46]

---

[1]Regarding "lacking entityness," Jamyang Shayba's root text says *ngo bo nyid med pa* and we have translated it accordingly. Ngawang Belden (347.2) says the text should read *ngo bo gnyis med pa* ("without a second entity") since an object of knowledge that is a different entity from it does not exist. Losang Gönchok explains that the self does not have objects of apprehension; as in the explanation of Sāṃkhya, the self does not have contact with objects directly but rather witnesses through coarser ordinary consciousnesses.

[2]In other words, if they all have the same father, they could not be differentiated.

[3]If everyone has the same father, we all must be brothers and sisters.

[4]The self is not necessarily great because it is also small, being one with the varieties of phenomena; and as the self of all beings, it is pluralistic.

The Vaiṣṇava and Mīmāṃsā Schools

The Assertions of the Vaiṣṇavas

Their teachers are Vāsudeva, Candra, and Taker of Virgins. [46.5]

Their teachers are Vāsudeva, i.e., Viṣṇu, Guru Candra, and the Taker of Virgins.

[Their system is called] Vaiṣṇava, Cāndrika, and Proponents of the Doctrine of the *Gītā*.

With respect to the names of their system, [47] they are called Vaiṣṇavas, Cāndrikas, and Proponents of the Doctrine of the *Gītā*.[1]

[Their texts are] *Branches Helping Investigation, Fifth Night,* etc.

Their texts are *Branches Helping Investigation, Fifth Night, Words Revealing the Activities of War,* etc.

Viṣṇu dwells in Doors City surrounded by many women.

Viṣṇu lives in Doors City in the great ocean surrounded by many women.

"I am the supreme, the sun, etc.; I act through the body of Brahmins."

[Viṣṇu] says, "I am all supreme things among the stable and the moving, the sun, moon, etc. Through abiding in the body of Brahmins, I am the sacrificer and the enjoyer."[2]

---

[1]The *Bhagavad Gītā* is India's most loved text and a foundation of Vaiṣṇavism.

[2]Viṣṇu himself does not act but by omnipresence is in a sense both actor and enjoyer.

If, from between the two entities, the peaceful is meditated upon, liberation is attained. [48]

There are two entities of Viṣṇu. From among these, if one meditates on the peaceful entity that is beyond existence and non-existence, it is asserted that one will attain enlightenment.[1]

Concerning the non-peaceful, the ten incarnations of the fish, tortoise, boar, man-lion, dwarf, two Rāmas, Kṛṣṇa, Buddha, and Kālki took out, helped up, suppressed, killed, deceived, killed the Ten-necked, severed the lineage, aided, purified sins, and will tame sentient beings.

With respect to Viṣṇu's non-peaceful entity:

1 in the form of a fish, he brought out the four Vedas that had fallen into the ocean.
2 in the form of a tortoise he remains, supporting the world.
3 in the form of a wild boar, he suppressed the Brahmā world and below.
4 in [the form] of a man-lion, [49] he killed the demi-god Hiranyakaśīpu.
5 in [the form of] a dwarf, he deceived the demi-god Baliko.
6 from among the two Rāmas or Rāmanas, as the first, the Rāmana who is the son of Dasaratha, he killed the ten-necked king of the demons [Rāvana].
7 in [the form of] the Rāmana who is the son of Jamanāgni [i.e., Paraṣu-rāma], he severed the royal lineage of Ārjuna.
8 in [the form of] Kṛṣṇa, he served the aims of all sentient beings through drawing the Ganges, etc.
9 by emanating as Śākyamuni Buddha, he purified [his] sins [of killing demons as Rāma].
10 in [the form of] Kālki, the son of the Brahmin Kuliko, he will tame many sentient beings in the future.

These are asserted to be the ten incarnations [of Viṣṇu].

They assert that creators, self, activities, time, natures, qualities, emptiness of degeneration, cause and effect [, etc., are the base]. [50]

They assert that the phenomena of the base are:

---

[1]His higher reality is *nirguṇa* (without qualities, i.e., formless); but to maintain the cosmos he is also *saguṇa,* descending *(avatāra)* in various forms. It is by meditating on the "peaceful," *nirguṇa* aspect that one can gain enlightenment.

- objects of knowledge such as Viṣṇu
- permanent subtle particles, etc., which are the creators of beings and environments
- the permanent, partless self
- virtuous and non-virtuous actions
- time, which is a permanent thing
- the natures of earth, etc.
- the qualities of activity, darkness, and mental potency
- emptinesses, i.e., the degeneration of things
- cause and effect, etc.[1]

Through cultivation of wind [yoga] and the syllable, etc., there is liberation. They [also] assert a [temporary] end to saṃsāra.

With respect to the path, they assert that liberation is obtained when one cultivates the wind yoga that possesses six branches, the syllable *oṃ,* and the emptiness that is the dissolution [of things], etc. Therefore, they also assert that saṃsāra has a temporary end.[2]

The Assertions of the Mīmāṃsakas

Their teacher is Jaimini. [51] **[Their names are] Mīmāṃsakas and Jaiminis.**

Viṣṇu and Jaimini are their teachers. [52] Their names are the Mīmāṃsakas and Jaiminis.

The Self is awareness, consciousness, knower, permanent, a substantial existent, etc.

[Unlike the Sāṃkhyas] they assert a Self that is awareness, consciousness, knower, permanent, a substantial existent that is separate [or isolatable] from the body, has enumeration [or states] that are the experiencers of individual times of pleasure and [pain], and although its states are impermanent, its entity is not

---

[1]Viṣṇu is the "prime mover": he sets in motion particles, which are the direct creators. "Emptiness" refers to the dissolution of things back into their source, i.e., Viṣṇu.

[2]Liberation consists in birth in Viṣṇu's heaven. It is temporary, although it is a very long and pleasant life as a god.

divisible into parts, etc. The term, "etc.," [in the root text] includes the proofs that the Self exists because of the existence of recognition and memory.[1]

Stains are in the nature of the person, [thus,] omniscience does not exist.

Since stains are [in] the nature of the Person who is the consciousness and knower, they say that an omniscient consciousness in which [all] faults have been removed does not exist.

High status is asserted as liberation but [is not irreversible].

They assert a liberation, the heaven of Brahmā, for instance, that is a release from bad migrations. They also say that Jaimini is omniscient.[2]

They assert that the forty-eight powers of deeds are causes [of becoming a Brahmin].

The forty-eight powers of deeds [53] are causes of becoming a Brahmin.[3]

The four horns, three feet, two heads, seven hands, three bonds, chief of the herd, and roar are features of the Vedas.

The rites of the Vedas are hidden by various terms:

- the four Vedas are the four "horns."
- the three times or three fires are the three "feet."
- the performer and his wife, for instance, are the two "heads."
- seven lines of poetry, ranging from six to twelve syllables, are the seven "hands."
- the "three bonds" are the three, heart, neck, and head.
- the "chief of the herd" is *oṃ*.
- the "roar" is vocalization.

They assert offerings through the three [benediction, etc.] or seven [divisions of] seven, with butter.

---

[1]Without a Self, there could be no memories as there would be no continuous entity to link them.

[2]Jaimini is the author of the *Mīmāṃsaka Sūtra*. Most Mīmāṃsakas do not assert the existence of God and, therefore, do not identify any beginning to the universe or any paradise into which a person might be liberated. Liberation, then, is mere dissolution at death without subsequent rebirth.

[3]According to Jamyang Shayba, a Brahmin boy is produced through the "internal offering" of copulation, with the forty-eight powers of ritual acts as "nourishers."

Offerings are made through the senseless rites of the three—benediction, etc.—or the seven divisions of seven—the seven foods, etc.—and expressions such as "You are to be satiated with butter, Svāhā!" etc.

There are six valid cognitions, called direct perception, inferential cognition, comprehension through an example, [valid knowledge] arisen from sound, understanding the meaning and [observing] that a thing does not exist.

They assert six valid cognitions:

1 direct perception
2 inferential cognition [54]
3 comprehension through an analogy
4 valid cognition arisen from sound
5 valid cognition from understanding the meaning—for instance, understanding from the hotness of fire its capacity to burn
6 valid cognition of the non-existence of a thing and the realization that a meaning exists that is not produced by any of the [other] five valid cognitions—for example, knowing that yogurt does not exist in milk.[1]

One asserts that knowing [what is seen], possibility, non-observation, renown, thinking, etc. [, are also valid sources of knowledge].

One of them says that:

- seeing by way of concomitance and obverse concomitance is the logical valid source of knowledge.
- knowing that the non-observed does not exist is the valid source of knowledge of non-observation.
- realizing that since one thousand exists, one hundred exists is the valid source of knowledge of that which possesses occurrence.
- realizing a fact from an old transmission of stories is the valid source of knowledge of renown.
- [thinking,] "Such occurs from thinking such occurs," is the valid source of knowledge of thinking. [55]

---

[1]Only the last two are unique to this system. Valid cognition from sound refers to the authority of the Vedas. Valid cognition that understands non-existence is, for instance, to understand that since John is not here, he must be somewhere else.

Refutation of These Two Systems

Because [Viṣṇu] pervades all, his fleeing is contradictory. The ten incarnations [also] are false.

Because Viṣṇu pervades everything, "to run away upon becoming afraid of the black powerful one" is contradictory. If Viṣṇu is single, partless, and all-pervasive, to kill another, to support [this world], to suppress [the nether-world], etc., are unsuitable. Also the ten incarnations are false because of contradictions concerning the human body at that time, numbering, history, etc.[1]

Since abandonment [of faults] and realizations [that are antidotes] can be brought to completion, omniscience that has abandoned all faults is established.

With respect to the incorrect assertion that the extinction of all faults [56] does not exist, since the root of all faults is the conception of self and the antidote to the conception of self is the wisdom that realizes selflessness, if one seeks out that [antidote] and familiarizes with it, it is possible to bring to complete fullness the two, the abandonment that is the extinction of [all] faults and the realization that is the antidote ever increasing. Therefore, it is established that there is a state of omniscience that is the extinction of all faults.

[1] If Viṣṇu is omnipresent and partless, none of the stories about him make any sense, whether it be the story that he ran and hid under a throne when a demon approached, or any of the incarnation stories. Losang Gönchok also claims, without specifying, that there are many contradictions in the stories having to do with history, enumeration, etc.

The Śaiva, Vaiśeṣika, and Naiyāyika Schools

The Assertions of the Śaivas or Aiśvaras

Śiva, the sage Akṣipāda, etc., are their teachers. [57]

The god Īśvara and the sages Prasadika or Akṣipāda, etc., are the teachers.[1]

They are called Aiśvaras, Followers of the Origin of Existence, etc.

The proponents of this system are called Aiśvaras, Followers of the Origin of Existence, and Śaivas.

When divided, there are three [types].

When divided, in general there are the three: the theistic Sāṃkhyas, Vyañjakas, and Those Who Do Not Pierce Their Ears.

The tantras *Renowned Sound* and of Bhurkuṃkūṭa are the valid scriptures. Other valid sources of knowledge [will be explained at the] appropriate [time].

---

[1]Īśvara means "Lord" and is here applied to Śiva. Sometimes he is called Maheśvara ("great Lord").

The tantra of the *Renowned Sound* and the tantra of Bhurkuṃkūṭa are the valid scriptures. Other valid sources of knowledge will mostly [be explained] in the approp-·ate context.

Maheśvara has eight qualities.

Maheśvara possesses the eight qualities of being subtle, light, [58] the object of worship, the owner, the controller, the one who goes everywhere, the one who possesses all desires, and abiding joyfully and happily.

He lives on Mount Kailāśa.

With respect to the place of abode, he lives on Mount Kailāśa surrounded by one thousand attendants, Uma, etc.[1]

Because [things] remain [different and separate], etc., and because of confusion, he is established as the agent of production and disintegration.[59]

Because the shape of things in the environment, etc., are different and abide separately, etc., and because the pleasure and pain of beings in the environment [sometimes] arise confusedly from ill deeds and virtue, it is established that the agent of production and disintegration of the world of the environment and the beings in the environment is Īśvara.[2]

[They assert] a Creator, Self, etc. [in the way the Vaiṣṇavas do. The five sense powers and the mental sense power] are the six paths [for consciousness to engage the six objects].

They assert the agent, Self, actions, time, nature, qualities, etc., in accordance with the assertions of the Vaiṣṇavas. In addition to that, [they assert] the six paths—eye, ear, nose, tongue, body, and mind—[by which consciousness] engages in the six objects.

There are five principles of the constituents, mantra, desire, Self, and Śiva.

The five principles are:

1 the principle of constituents, which is the mixture of the five—space, wind, fire, water, and earth—with the constituent of the sixth, heightened consciousness [60]

---

[1]Uma, also named Parvatī, is Śiva's wife.

[2]Because one can see that there are forces of chaos in the world, and because virtue is not always rewarded nor non-virtue punished, there must be a greater power who can sort things out.

2 the principle of mantra, which has the essence of the series of vowels and the series of consonants
3 the principle of desire, which is the sixty-four arts of joyous behavior
4 the principle of the Self, that is to say, the permanent Self
5 the principle of Śiva, which pervades all

[Śiva] brings together [the six paths at birth through] abiding in the three [doors] and disperses them [at death], and is [the twelve astrological houses that are called the] twelve knots.

The principles of Śiva are asserted to be the agent of bringing together the six paths at the time of birth through abiding in the three doors [of body, speech, and mind] and dispersing the six paths at the time of death, respectively, and as the twelve astrological houses that abide in the bodies of all, i.e., the twelve knots.[1]

They propound the pristine wisdom of the fourth state to be the rank of liberation.

Achieving pristine wisdom at the time of orgasm, which is the fourth state, is propounded as the rank of liberation.[2]

Wind yoga, initiation [at the phallus] of Maheśvara, and the bliss of emission [of the essential constituent into a woman] are the path.

Yoga—the pot-possessing wind-yoga and the wind-yoga of the six branches, initiation taken at the tip of the phallus of Īśvara, [61] and the bliss of emission of the essential constituent into a woman are asserted to be the path.[3]

Since their verbal conventions [and the meanings] are contradictory, they are not the Vaiśeṣikas, etc.

In that case, not only because the verbal conventions are contradictory but also because the meaning does not accord, Aiśvaras as mentioned in the *Kālacakra Tantra* are not the Vaiśeṣikas, etc., who are widely renowned in India.[4] [62]

---

[1]This refers to how the twelve astrological houses can be found in the body.

[2]This is again the tantric notion that the bliss of sexual union can be used to gain enlightenment.

[3]The reference to initiation probably means that the tantric couple imagines themselves as Śiva and consort. The sexual yoga can include anointing and decorating of the genitals.

[4]The Aiśvaras of Śambhala, the mythical land where the Kālacakra tantric teachings originated, are not to be confused with the worshipers of Śiva found among the Vaiśeṣikas, Sāṃkhyas, etc.

The Assertions of the Vaiśeṣikas and Naiyāyikas

Their teachers are Uluka, Kaṇāda, and Akṣipāda.

With respect to their teachers, the sage Uluka and the sage Kaṇāda are the teachers of Vaiśeṣikas. Akṣipāda is the teacher of the Naiyāyikas.

[Their names] are Kāṇādas, Akṣipādas, Ulukaputrīyas, Āgamamātrins.

Their names are Kāṇādas, Akṣipādas, Aulukyas, Ulukaputrīyas and Āgamamātrins.

Their divisions are Vaiśeṣikas and Naiyāyikas.

The entities of the divisions are the two, Vaiśeṣikas and Naiyāyikas.

The six categories are comprehended by the four valid sources of knowledge.

The six categories are asserted to be comprehended through the four [valid cognitions]—direct perception, inference for one's own sake, inference for the sake of another, and valid scripture.

Direct perception is the meeting of sense power, [mind,] and object, of which there are six.

The first, direct perception, [63] is the meeting or relation of sense power, mind, and object.

The Vaiśeṣikas [assert that] the relations [or meetings] are matter.

The assertion of the Vaiśeṣikas is that the six, the four relations of joining and the two relations of including, are mindless matter.[1]

The Naiyāyikas [assert that] the conceptual consciousness [produced from] a meeting that apprehends a specificity [is a direct perception].

The assertion of the Naiyāyikas is that the consciousness produced from the meeting of sense power and object, that is to say, a conceptual consciousness that without aspect apprehends a feature of the object, is a direct valid cognizer.[2]

[Both systems assert] the three inferences.

---

[1]These will be explained in the next section.

[2]As we will see, Buddhist systems in general deny that conceptual consciousnesses can have direct cognition. (Prāsaṅgikas are the exception.)

Both systems [assert] three inferences that are generated by each of the three modes of the sign and the inference that realizes the meaning from seeing directly the relation of the completion of the three modes.[1]

[The Naiyāyikas assert] that [inference] having remainder is correct, etc.

The Naiyāyikas assert the three inferences [for oneself]:

1 from the sign of that which has a preceder
2 that which has a remainder
3 that which has general perception[2] [64]

The sign that has a remainder is asserted to be correct, and the Vaiśeṣikas assert the five inferences of:

1 inferring a cause from an effect
2 inferring an effect from a cause
3 inferring that which possesses relation from a relation
4 inferring that which possesses inherence from [the fact of] inherence
5 inferring that which possesses contradiction from contradiction

Daktsang's assertion that the inference of smoke from fire is a [reasoning] having a remainder is not correct. If fire is considered as [fire in] general, since it is seen in the discordant class [i.e., in places where there is no smoke], the reverse entailment is not established. When fire is considered as a particular [type of fire], since these four [inferences for oneself] are inferences upon remembering relationships that have already been ascertained, they are called "signs possessing the former" and are not those having remainder.

According to Dharmakīrti's *Commentary on (Dignāga's) "Compendium of Valid Cognition,"* [an inference] having a remainder that has doubt towards the discordant class, that they accept as a correct sign, [65] is [actually] an indefinite sign.

---

[1]In reasoning, there are three "modes" in a statement such as "It follows that the subject, a pot, is impermanent, because of being a product." The first is that the reason applies to the subject (that pots are products); the second is the forward entailment that whatever is a product is necessarily impermanent; the third is the reverse entailment that whatever is not impermanent is necessarily not a product.

[2]For example: if I have previously observed that B follows A, I can infer that this will occur again; if I bite into a fruit and find it to be sour, I can infer that the other fruits on the tree are sour, too; if I see the moon disappear behind a mountain, I can infer that the sun will disappear behind it also. Inference for oneself needs only involve the three modes whereas inference for others should include five steps including an example and a conclusion.

Moreover, the meaning [in Jamyang Shayba's root text] of saying, "Inference is the three, three. Remainder is correct," is as follows. The three inferences for each mode of sign [are what Naiyāyikas assert are the three inferences for oneself], and the three inferences that are produced by them [are what the Vaiśeṣikas assert are the three inferences for oneself]. For all of these, having a remainder of doubt is asserted to be a correct sign.

The sixteen categories of logic included by the word "et cetera" [in the root text] are:

1 valid source of knowledge
2 object of comprehension
3 doubt
4 qualm
5 example
6 tenet
7 branch
8 logic
9 delineation
10 debate
11 expression
12 eradication of opposition
13 facsimile of a reason
14 cancellation of a word
15 self-refutation
16 place of annihilation

That which possesses the five [branches of a proof statement] is [inference] for others. Comprehension is through similarity.

They assert the five-branched proof statement to be comprehension of something through an example. [66] They assert it to be a proof for the sake of generating an inference in another through emphasizing mainly an example that possesses a likeness.

[Among valid sources of knowledge risen] from terms, the tantras by Śiva and the *Lokacakṣu Sūtra* are valid scriptures.

Valid sources of knowledge arisen from sound are of two types—consciousnesses and scriptures. Of these, the scriptural valid sources of knowledge are the tantras: *Śiva's Beautiful Composition* by Śiva, the *Sūtra Clarifying Distinctions* composed by Uluka [also called the *Lokacakṣu Sūtra*], and the *View of Knowledge* composed by Akṣipāda.

With respect to the [Vaiśeṣikas' and Naiyāyikas'] mode of asserting the base, the six categories—substance, quality, activity, generality, particularity, and inherence—are truly [established] functioning things, or bases. [67]

The six categories—substance, quality, activity, generality, particularity, and inherence—are asserted to be truly established functioning things and the basal subjects.

The four elements, mind, space, direction, self, and time are the nine substances.

Moreover, the four elements—earth, water, fire, and wind—and mind, space, direction, self, and time are the nine substances. [68]

Five substances are non-pervasive; four are pervasive. The four [elements] have four [qualities], etc.

The first five are non-pervasive substances and the latter four are pervasive substances. Earth and particles of earth have the four qualities of odor, taste, form, and touch. Water and water particles have three [of the four qualities of earth] minus odor. Fire and fire particles have two—form and touch. Thus, there are four [types].

The others are permanent. Quality has two classes. Activity is impermanent.

From among the six categories, activities are impermanent. Qualities have both permanent and impermanent classes. The other four—substance, generality, particularity, and inherence—are permanent.

They assert a Self that is the experiencer, the agent, a non-product, permanent, not consciousness, pervasive, and without activity.

Moreover, with respect to the mode of Identifying the self, both the Vaiśeṣikas and Naiyāyikas assert the Self to be:

- a substantial existent that is different from body, sense powers, and mind
- the experiencer [of pleasure and pain]
- the agent [of virtuous and non-virtuous actions] [69]
- non-product
- a permanent phenomenon
- [matter,] not consciousness
- all-pervasive
- a partless singularity
- without activity

It is [respectively] pervasive and tiny.

The Vaiśeṣikas say that two selves exist: the gross all-pervasive self and the subtle Self that abides inside. These are respectively external and internal. It is as follows: They say that the all-pervasive self is mindless and is physical matter of two types: (1) the inner Self, abiding inside, the Person that is the cause of apprehending I, and (2) the external self that has an entity that is a composite of the body and the sense powers and that aids the inner self. [70] The Naiyāyikas assert that a portion of the pervasive Self, [the size of] a mere particle, because it possesses mind, is not all-pervasive.

Mind is awareness, a permanent functioning thing, conceptual and an object possessor.

Mind is a permanent functioning thing and is an awareness that is an object-possessor involved in conceptuality.

Qualities possess four [attributes] and are twenty-four or also twenty-five.

The second category, qualities, possess four features. They:

1 depend on substance.
2 do not possess other qualities.
3 are not a cause of inherence or disjunction.
4 do not depend on a sign.

When they are divided, there are the following twenty-four:

1	form	13	pleasure
2	taste	14	pain [71]
3	smell	15	desire
4	touch	16	hatred
5	sound	17	striving
6	number	18	heaviness
7	dimension	19	moisture
8	separateness (and conjunction)	20	heat
9	disjunction	21	oiliness
10	otherness	22	momentum
11	non-otherness	23	merit
12	awareness	24	demerit

There is also an explanation of twenty-five.

Activity is fivefold. Part and whole are different substantial entities.

The third category, "activity," is the five:

1 lifting up [the feet]
2 putting down [the feet]
3 extension
4 contraction
5 going

They assert as different substantial entities such things as part and whole, quality and qualificand, and definition and definiendum.

Generality is factually other than the [other] three [categories] and has eight attributes.

They assert that the fourth category, generality, is factually other than the three—substance, quality, and activity. The three—generality, particularity, and inherence—possess the eight attributes: [72]

1 non-production
2 pervasiveness
3 permanence
4 partlessness
5 absence of activity
6 dependence on substance
7 dependence on qualities
8 dependence on activity

That which [provides for] difference is particularity.

The fifth category, particularity, is the differentiator from other substantial entities. It has the five features explained previously.

Inherence [involves] two relations.

The sixth category, called inherence, also has the eight qualities [explained] earlier. It is other than the five categories, substance, etc. The relation that causes realization—"this has this"—is inherence. Inherence is twofold: the relation of conjunction—the relation between support and supported that [occupy] different places—and the relation of inherence—the relation of [support and supported] not [occupying] different places.

Beings and environments are [created] by tiny particles and Maheśvara. [73]

Beings and environments are created by permanent tiny particles and through the supervision of Maheśvara.

Bathing, etc., are religious practice.

Bathing, initiation, fasting, pure behavior, sacrifice, giving, etc., are religious practice; the opposite of those is not.

Saṃsāra is the inherence of the qualities in the Self.

Saṃsāra is taken as the inherence of the nine qualities of the Self in the Self.

Liberation is inexpressible—the Self separated from inherence with the qualities.

Liberation is asserted as the ultimate inexpressibility of the categories, the Self that is separated from inherence with the qualities, or the exhaustion of conceptuality, like a butter lamp going out.[1] [74]

Since the realization of suchness is a cause of liberation, [calling] it liberation is mistaken.

Daktsang's explanation that the realization of suchness is liberation is mistaken because they assert that it is a *cause* of attaining liberation.

Refutation of Those Three Schools

Maheśvara would be the cause of pleasure and pain, and he would perform sins.

It follows with respect to the subject, Maheśvara, that he is the cause producing the pleasure and pain of migrators because he *creates* the pleasure and pain of migrators. If this is accepted, then it [absurdly] follows that Maheśvara is not the cause of migrators because of being the cause of just their pleasure and pain. [Whatever is the cause of just the pleasure and pain of migrators is] necessarily [not the cause of migrators] because the cause of migrators [75] and the cause of just their pleasure and pain must be different, and since he is partless, it is not suitable that he is the producer of those two. Furthermore, all the sins of immediate retribution would be performed by Maheśvara.

If [his creation] depends on his wish, he would not have [independent] capacity.

If Maheśvara's production of beings and environments were dependent on Maheśvara's wish, it would be contradictory with his being permanent without capacity.

Pervading all and being partless are contradictory.

If he pervades all, it is contradictory that he is partless.

---

[1]There are different descriptions of liberation. As we have seen with other schools, one problem is the misidentification of the Self with the qualities that are impermanent. Apparently, attaining a state of non-conceptuality is also regarded as liberation.

Because he is permanent, [things] would always be produced or never be produced at all.

Because he is permanent, if he produces one effect, he must [absurdly] produce it constantly because it must be that his being the direct cause would never cease. Or, if [effects] must be produced by Īśvara, it [absurdly] follows that effects are utterly not produced because Īśvara does not have that capacity [76] due to being permanent. It is easy to extend the refutation through analyzing their assertion that generality and particularity, definition and definiendum, etc., are different substantial entities, and through analyzing the eight attributes that were explained before.[1]

---

[1]Buddhists argue that things that are different substantial entities cannot have any relationship, such as in the case of generality and particularity. For example, it would be absurd to say that the color red and a particular instance of red were different substantial entities.

The Nirgrantha School

Jinatā, Ṛṣabha, and Dongri are the teachers.

The twenty-five—Mahavīra, the sage Arhat, Ṛṣabha, Vardhamāna, etc.—are their teachers.[1] [77]

Kṣapanas, Arahatas, Nirgranthas, and Parivrajakas [are their names].

Their names are Kṣapanas, Arahatas, Nirgranthas, and Parivrajakas.[2]

The living being, called person and migrator, is the permanent self the size of one's body.

The living being (*jiva*) is the permanent Self that is the size of one's body and the entity of consciousness. Its synonyms are person, migrator, nourisher, etc.

Conceptual and non-conceptual perceivers comprehend generalities and instances.

There are two types of direct perceivers: those free from conceptuality that comprehend generalities and those that are conceptual that comprehend instances.[3]

The three modes are incorrect; inference has one mode.

---

[1]There are twenty-four Jinas or Tīrthaṅkaras (liberated spiritual teachers) of the present cycle of the universe; Ṛṣabha was the first, Mahavīra the last.

[2]Here their principal name is Nirgantha (either "book-less," i.e., not reliant upon the Vedas, or "bond-less," i.e., liberated) but they are best known as Jainas ("followers of the Jinas" [the spiritual Victors, the liberated teachers]).

[3]Ngawang Belden thinks that this may be reversed; it should be put that "the conceptual comprehends generalities and the non-conceptual comprehends instances." See Hopkins, *Maps.*

The three modes exist but since there are many illogicalities, [78] they propound that inference has one mode.[1]

The treatise of Bhāratatāraka, etc., are their texts.

They assert that the treatise of Bhāratatāraka and the *Various Calculations* of Arhat are valid scriptures.[2]

Life, lifeless, contamination, abandonment, restraint, bonds, liberation, going, and coming are the nine [categories]; or [alternately,] life, contamination, restraint, wearing down, bonds, activity, sin, merit, and liberation are the nine.

In the system of Arhat of Śambhala, [all objects of knowledge are included within] nine categories:

1 living beings
2 the lifeless
3 virtuous and non-virtuous contaminants
4 restraints, which will be explained below
5 abandonment of faulty deeds
6 the knots or bonds of views, which will be explained [79]
7 liberation
8 going from this life to the next
9 coming from the former life to this life

In the system of Arhat of India, there are nine:

1 life
2 contamination
3 restraints
4 wearing down
5 bonds
6 activities
7 sin
8 merit
9 liberation

With respect to all [phenomena], their substantial entities are permanent, and their states are impermanent.

---

[1]Jains say that it is not necessary to go beyond a simple reason when stating a proposition. For instance, stating "There is fire on the hill because there is smoke there" would be sufficient, without giving an example or stating the forward and reverse entailments.

[2]These are obscure. The Jain literature is vast. "Bhārata" may refer to the son of the first Jina of our age, who was the first *cakra-vārtin* ("universal monarch").

Also with respect to all of those, the substantial entity is permanent and their states are impermanent.[1]

There are three times, six substances, and six or nine life-possessors.

The assertions of the Kṣapana of Kālapa are:

- the three times, which are substantially existent entities, are: past, future, and present.
- the six substances are: living beings, persons, time, space, merit, and sins.
- the six life-possessors are: earth, water, fire, wind, trees, and fruit. [80]

The Kṣapana of India adduce nine life-possessors:

1	earth	6	worms
2	water	7	ants
3	fire	8	bees
4	wind	9	humans
5	trees		

It is not the case that these two [systems] do not assert life-possessors other than these.

The five restraints, the five modes of conduct, the five exalted wisdoms, and the thirteen behaviors are asserted to be the path.

The topics of the path are:

- the five restraints: restraint of behavior, restraint of speech, restraint of seeking your own livelihood, restraint of not wastefully discarding alms, and restraint of [holding] closely [the screen for filtering insects][2]
- the five modes of conduct: not harming, [81] speaking the truth, taking only what is given, giving away everything, and holding the screen
- the five exalted wisdoms: intelligence, hearing, boundaries, mentally searching, and divination

[1]Jains says that existing things have a substratum or substance that supports their unique qualities, which are variable in mode depending on conditions. An apple, for instance, has a certain underlying substance and particular qualities such as shape and fragrance but the qualities may change over time.

[2]Jains are well known for the care they take not to harm living beings, including insects. They may filter their water, use whisks, and wear cloth masks (to avoid inhaling insects).

- the thirteen behaviors: the former [i.e., the five restraints and the five modes of conduct] together with the secrecy of body, the secrecy of speech, and meditation on the path of liberation with the mind

Liberation is form.

Liberation is a form, and it exists like a white umbrella, four million five hundred thousand *yojanas* above the three realms.[1]

They assert five migrators, five bodies, those who possess one power, etc., three hundred and sixty bonds, and [four] activities, i.e., lifespan, etc.

They assert:

- there are five migrators: hell beings, animals, gods, humans, and liberated migrators. [82]
- there are five bodies: the bodies of those who make use of morsels of food [i.e., coarse food], the body of light, the natural body, the body of spontaneous birth, and the body of the limit.
- earth, etc., possess the single sense power for tangible objects.
- worms, etc., with tastes, have two [the tangible object sense power and the tongue sense power].
- ants, etc., with the nose [sense power], have three.
- bees, etc., with the eye [sense power], have four.
- humans, etc., adding the ear sense power to the former ones, have five sense powers.
- the bonds are the three hundred sixty views of bad proponents.
- the four activities are those that determine later experience, name, family, and lifespan.

Because [Buddha] did not compose [astrological treatises] and remained silent [in response to fourteen questions], and because [trees] sleep, it is established that omniscience does not exist and that trees, etc., possess mind.

[1]The liberated soul rises to the summit of the universe, which as a dome-like shape, there to reside perpetually in perfect quiescence. This is being contrasted with Buddhist liberation, which is a liberation from defilements and not only involves no particular place but in the Mahāyāna will lead to embodiment for the sake of others.

Since [Buddha] did not compose treatises on astrology, etc., remained silent on fourteen questions, and did not know the origin of saṃsāra, omniscience does not exist.[1]

Because leaves sleep [at night, this] proves that trees possess mind.[2]

[There are] many facsimiles [of schools of Outsiders' tenets here in Tibet] [83] **but there is little need [to know them. Therefore,] I will not elaborate [on that topic] here.**

Even though there are many facsimiles of schools of tenets that are included amongst outsiders in Tibet, since there is little need to refute them, I will not elaborate here.[3]

Refutation of this System

[If you analyze] whether the substance and its states are mutually one entity or not, [the differences] fall apart.

Through analyzing whether the two, substance and its states, [84] are mutually one entity or not, the examples that are posited mostly fall apart. Since this system asserts that the nature of the substance and of its states is partless and singular, at the time of the disintegration of the state the nature of the state must be cancelled, whereby the substance also must disintegrate. If the substance does not disintegrate, the nature of the state abides, whereby the disintegration of the state is unfeasible.[4]

Because liberation is a form, the exhaustion of karma is senseless.

Liberation does not pass beyond form and being an entity of a migrator, whereby the exhaustion of karma for the sake of achieving liberation is senseless.[5]

---

[1]The Buddha famously refused to answer questions on the origin and age, etc., of the cosmos, saying that his answers would not be helpful. The Nirgranthas just take this as evidence of his ignorance.

[2]Some leaves curl up at night, as if "asleep," and this is taken as evidence that they are sentient.

[3]Losang Gönchok probably is referring to the Tibetan indigenous religion of Bön.

[4]If the unchanging substratum, or substance, of a thing is one entity with its qualities or states, it cannot be the case that one is permanent and unchanging and the other is not.

[5]The liberated soul continues to have the form it took within the body, i.e., to have its shape. This is being construed as a kind of continued embodiment and therefore, no real liberation at all.

If the living being has size, it is impermanent.

If the living being exists equal to the size of the body, it has size, whereby it must be impermanent.[1]

A single mode is also contradictory.

It is easy to understand the unfeasibility of a sign that has a single mode.[2] [85]

---

[1]The soul is said to be the same size as the body. The argument is that whatever has extension is necessarily impermanent.

[2]It is being argued that a person may not be convinced simply by stating, "there is fire on the mountain because there is smoke there." The other modes (stating that whenever there is smoke, there is fire, and whenever there is no fire there is no smoke) are also necessary.

Part Two
Hīnayāna Systems

Introduction to the Hīnayāna Systems

Regarding the tenets of our own schools, our own schools are limited to the four: Vaibhāṣika, Sautrāntika, Cittamātra, and Mādhyamika, for it is said that here there are not five systems of tenets.

Our own schools—Insiders, Bauddhas—are limited to the four systems of tenets: Vaibhāṣika (Great Exposition), Sautrāntika (Sūtra), Cittamātra (Mind-Only), and Mādhyamika (Middle Way). Many sūtras, tantras, and scholars and adepts say that this teaching of Śākyamuni Buddha does not have five systems of tenets.

These four are [included in] the two: Hīnayāna and Mahāyāna. [86] **Inclusion into three vehicles, asserting three [schools] and dividing them into five are mistaken.**

Identifying the first two of these four as Hīnayāna schools and the latter two as Mahāyāna schools is correct.[1] Some condense [those four] into three, making [Vaibhāṣika and Sautrāntika the school of Hearers], Cittamātra the school of Solitary Realizers, [and Mādhyamika the school of Bodhisattvas].[2] Some divide

---

[1]They are classified as Hīnayāna or Mahāyāna in dependence on the scriptural collections they follow.

[2]Daktsang is one such author. These divisions are mistaken because all three types of beings "on the path" are identified for each school.

A Hearer is one who hears doctrine, practices it, and proclaims it to others, but who has not yet developed *bodhicitta* (the aspiration to enlightenment motivated by altruistic compassion). Such a person may become liberated in a minimum of three lifetimes but will not become a Buddha until he or she switches to the Bodhisattva path.

Solitary Realizers are persons who have no teacher in their last life; they also extend their practice for 100 eons, which is why they get a similitude of a Buddha's body when they become enlightened. There are two types of Solitary Realizers: the *rhinoceros-like* who extend their practice

them into five, separating the Vatsīputrīyas from the Vaibhāṣikas, but they are mistaken.[1]

The two Hearer schools do not assert a basis-of-all, afflicted mind, selflessness of phenomena, the ten grounds, the three bodies, etc.

The two Hearer schools[2] do not assert a basis-of-all, an afflicted mind, the selflessness of phenomena, [87] the ten [Bodhisattva] grounds, the three bodies [of a Buddha], the obstructions to omniscience, etc.[3]

The earlier [Hearer schools] do not accept the Mahāyāna [scriptures] as the word [of Buddha]. It is renowned that the later ones do accept them.

The earlier Hearer schools do not accept the Mahāyāna scriptural collections as being the word [of Buddha] but it is greatly renowned that the later ones do accept [those scriptures] as the word [of Buddha].[4]

---

because they believe they are to become Buddhas, and the *congregating* who, because they had a teacher earlier in their last lives, are not so solitary.

Bodhisattvas have the extraordinary motivation to attain enlightenment for the sake of others and practice for an extraordinary length of time, three periods of countless great eons. Any of these types could be found among any of the proponents of the tenet systems. For instance, a Hīnayānist by tenet could be a Bodhisattva by motivation.

[1]The Vatsīputrīyas are among those whose identification of self is controversial, and some have thought that this should distinguish them from other Vaibhāṣikas.

[2]"Hearer schools" here refers to those who reject the Mahāyāna sūtras as not being the word of Buddha. As explained on the previous page, this is not a proper designation for the Hīnayāna schools, since they include not only Hearers but also Solitary Realizers and Bodhisattvas.

[3]These are unique Mahāyāna tenets that will be explained later.

[4]The Hearer schools objected to the Mahāyāna scriptural collection being the word of the Buddha because they regarded their own canon as complete and because the Mahāyāna sūtras appear to be deprecating—as not truly existent—the Four Truths, the Three Jewels, etc. Proofs that the Mahāyāna sūtras were spoken by Buddha are made in Maitreya's *Ornament for the Mahāyāna Sūtras* and Nāgārjuna's *Precious Garland*, stanzas 367–93. In general, Hīnayānists do not accept that the Mahāyāna sūtras are the Buddha's word. However, Jamyang Shayba says in his *Great Exposition of Tenets* (Gomang 170.15) that within the Vaibhāṣika school there were some who accepted the Mahāyāna, due to similarities between the sūtras of the Mahāsaṃghikas and the Mahāyāna.

The Vaibhāṣika School

Regarding the first of the four systems of tenets, the Vaibhāṣika system, they are called Proponents of the Great Exposition [or Proponents of Particulars] because they mainly propound the *Great Exposition of Particulars (Mahāvibhāṣā)* and because they propound particulars of substantialities.

They are called Vaibhāṣikas because they propound chiefly the treatise called the *Great Exposition of Particulars (Mahāvibhāṣā)*[1] and because they propound many instances of substantial[ly established] phenomena such as the three times.[2]

Vaibhāṣika Sub-schools

There are two modes of the splitting off [of the eighteen sub-schools], etc. [From] the Sarvāstivādins, Mahāsaṃghikas, [88] **Sthaviras, and Saṃmitīyas, [respectively] there are seven, five, three, and three [sub-schools].**

The way the eighteen [sub-schools] split off [may be considered] from whether there are one, two, three, etc., root schools. The way the [eighteen] split off from

---

[1]In Tibetan the text is known by two names, either *Ocean of Great Exposition* (*bye brag bzhad mtsho*) or *Treasury of Great Exposition* (*bye brag bzhad mdzod*) although it was not translated into Tibetan until the twentieth century. It *was* translated into Chinese.

[2]It is not discussed further, but Vaibhāṣikas are unique among Buddhist schools in asserting that not only a present thing but its past and future exist now. Consider a sprout. The seed from which it comes exists now as a past seed; the tree it *will* become exists now as a future tree. The seed, sprout, and tree are all examples of the sprout.

the four root schools—the four: Sarvāstivādins, Mahāsaṃghikas, Sthaviras, and Saṃmitīyas—is as follows.[1]

- Sarvāstivādins have seven: Kāśyapīyas, Mahīśasakas, Dharmaguptakas, Bhadrayānīyas, Tamraśaṭiyas, Śaikṣas, and Vibhajyavādins.
- Mahāsaṃghikas have five: Purvaśailas, Aparaśailas, Haimavatas, [89] Prajñaptavādins, and Lokottaravādins.
- Sthaviras have three: Jetavaniyas, Abhayagirikas, and Mahaviharins
- Saṃmitīyas have three: Kurukullas, Avantakas, and Vatsīputrīyas.

Or, in another way, the Mahāsaṃghikas have eight, and the Sthaviras have ten.

Another [way of the splitting off of eighteen schools is from two root schools]:

- eight Mahāsaṃghika schools: Mahāsaṃghikas, Ekavyaharikas, Lokottaravādins, Prajñaptivādins, Bahuśrutīyas, Caitikas, Pūrvaśailas, Aparaśailas
- ten Sthavira schools: Haimavatas (also called Sthaviras), Sarvāstivādins, Vatsīputrīyas, Dharmottaras, Bhadrayānīyas, [90] Saṃmitīyas, Mahīśasakas, Dharmaguptakas, Kāśyapīyas, Uttarīyas

This is the position of the Sarvāstivādin system. Bhāvaviveka constructed the etymologies of the eighteen schools in terms of this. Therefore, it is important, and earlier [scholars] said it must be taken as our own system in general.

It is contradictory that all of those are Vaibhāṣika schools and that [the Mahāsaṃghikas] are the second school [Sautrāntika]. It is [too] restrictive to include [Sautrāntika in Vaibhāṣika] because the Mahāyāna also [could be] explained [as included].

It is contradictory to assert that all of these [schools] are schools of Vaibhāṣika and that the [Mahāsaṃghikas] are the second of our schools, that is, the Sautrāntikas. If it is thought that [the Sautrāntikas] are merely included [in the Vaibhāṣ-

[1]Not all differences between the Vaibhāṣika sub-schools are based on different interpretations of doctrine. Some groups became known as schools due to the fame of their main teachers, and others were regarded as discrete schools because they lived in an isolated place. Very few texts of any of these schools survive. Some we know about only because their positions are described or attacked in the texts of other schools, and some we know nothing about.

ikas], [that which is being included] is too small, because even the Mahāyāna has been said [erroneously] to have been gathered from the Mahāsaṃghika sūtras.[1] [91]

The five Saṃmitīya schools propound a self that is inexpressible, but [since their position]—that a self that possesses the three [characteristics] does not exist—is similar to all [our schools], they are not other [than Buddhist in terms of view].

The five Saṃmitīya schools—Vatsīputrīyas, Bhadrayānīyas, Kurukullas, Dharmaguptakas, and Uttarīyas—propound an inexpressible self, but since their position—that a self that possesses the three, permanence (being a separate entity from the aggregates), unity (in the sense of being partless), and self-power, does not exist—is similar to all of our schools, they are not regarded as being other [than Buddhist] schools by way of view.[2]

The Vatsīputrīyas, etc., assert the existence of a self or person that is inexpressible as being just [the aggregates] or just different [from the aggregates], permanent or impermanent, etc. But since they are similar to all of our other schools of tenets in asserting that there is no self that possesses the three [characteristics]—permanence, singularity, and self-power—as in the assertions of Outsiders, the five

[1] The Mahāsaṃghika school is proto-Mahāyāna; in many ways, its positions are forerunners of later Mahāyāna ideas. This has led some to speculate that the whole Mahāyāna is derived from the Mahāsaṃghika. Jamyang Shayba maintains that this sort of collapsing of distinctions goes too far.

[2] These schools say that there *is* a substantially existent self able to set itself up but which cannot be identified as either the same as nor different from the five mental and physical aggregates. "Substantially existent" means not merely imputed in dependence on its bases of designation, but truly existent. That it can "set itself up" means that it has pointable existence, that it can be identified as one of the aggregates or as their collection or separate from them.

Nevertheless, they also say (with apparent contradiction) that this self is inexpressible as being either the same as the five aggregates or different from them. (Most other schools identify the person as the mental continuum or as a consciousness.) Their position is actually close to Prāsaṅgika-Mādhyamika, which says that the person is merely imputed in *dependence* on the five aggregates, and hence, is not any of the five aggregates.

Why do they say that the person cannot be said to be either the same as or different from the aggregates? If it were identical to them, it would cease at death; if it were not, it would be separate from them and, therefore, would be eternal and without qualities. Unlike non-Buddhists such as the Sāṃkhyas, they will not say that the self is unchanging and separate from the aggregates. This view was regarded by other Buddhist schools as heretical but it was very popular. According to the seventh-century Chinese pilgrim Xuanzang, it was the view of 66,000 of 254,000 monks at that time.

Saṃmitīya schools are not different from our own schools, because they propound that all phenomena are selfless. [95][1]

Some scholar's saying that they do not assert selflessness is incorrect because they assert that the Supramundane Victor [Buddha] said that all phenomena are selfless, and they propound [their tenets] without contradicting that. At the time [this scholar] expressed their mode of assertion, having explained that [Buddha] propounds that all phenomena are selfless, he also said that they do not assert selflessness; this is an explicit contradiction of his own words.

Therefore, when they say that the self that is the object of observation in the conception of self exists in an inexpressible manner, they refer to the person that is the object of observation of the [mis]conception of self.[2] The self that is like the one asserted by the Outsider Forders, inasmuch as it exists as a different substantial entity from the aggregates, [96] is the object of the mode of apprehension of the conception of self and *is* the self that is to be refuted. For example, it is like the fact that the Svātantrika-Mādhyamikas speak of the conventionally established existence of the self or of all phenomena not being substantial entities in the sense of being self-sufficient persons; when they do that, they assert an object of observation of the conception of self that is the *person.* They assert substantial establishment in the sense of self-sufficiency of that [person] as the self that is to be refuted and as the object of the mode of apprehension of the conception of self. Candrakīrti's *Entrance to (Nāgārjuna's) "Treatise on the Middle Way"* (6.146) says:

> Some assert substantially existent persons,
> Inexpressible as the same or other, permanent or impermanent.
> They assert it as an object of knowledge of the six consciousnesses,
> And also as the basis of the conception of I. [97]

Also, Dzongkaba's *Illumination of the Thought* says, "The 'basis of the conception of I' is that which is observed." Since they said that, the object of the mode of apprehension of the conception of I that takes that self as its object of observation is the self that is to be refuted, whereby the existence of the object of the mode of

---

[1]91.4–94.2, which contains a long digression on this issue, has been omitted.

[2]The "inexpressible self" propounded by several Vaibhāṣika sub-schools is wrongly *conceived* by ignorance to be a substantially existent entity that is *different* from the aggregates. However, these schools take care to stipulate that the self *cannot* be said to be different from the aggregates (or it would be "expressible"). Some people think that they are propounding a substantially existent self-sufficient person that is separate from the aggregates, like the non-Buddhist "Forders." Candrakīrti and Dzongkaba point out that the "inexpressible self" is merely the *basis* for the misconception of I, not itself a person of the sort propounded like the non-Buddhists.

apprehension of the conception of I is not asserted by any of the proponents of our schools of tenets.

Therefore, the explanation by many great [scholars] of our own and other [schools] that the Saṃmitīya are other [i.e., non-Buddhist] schools by way of view is a lamentable mistake. Therefore, hold without error the essential meaning of their position on the selflessness of persons. [98]

The Vaibhāṣika School's Positions

[They assert] two truths, aggregates, constituents, sources, five migrations, foods, contaminated phenomena, non-contaminated phenomena, caused phenomena, and three uncaused phenomena.

As will be explained, [the presentation of the basis made by the Vaibhāṣika school is in terms of the following]:

- conventional and ultimate truths
- the five aggregates: forms, feelings, discriminations, compositional factors, and consciousnesses
- twelve sources: eye, ear, nose, tongue, body, mind, form, sound, odor, taste, tangible object, and phenomena
- eighteen constituents: the six consciousnesses are added on to [the twelve sources]
- five migrators:[1] hell beings, [99] hungry ghosts, animals, gods, and humans
- four foods: food that is morsels, the food of touch, the food of intention, and the food of consciousness
- contaminated phenomena
- non-contaminated phenomena[2]
- caused phenomena

[1]Usually there are said to be six types of migrators, with gods and demi-gods (*asura*) counted separately.

[2]Non-contaminated phenomena are (1) true paths, e.g., ethics, meditation, and wisdom, and (2) non-products such as space. Analytic cessations are absences cause by meditation, as when wisdom causes a portion of the afflictions to cease, whereas non-analytic cessations are any other kind of mere negation.

- uncaused phenomena: individual analytical cessations, non-analytical cessations, and space.[1]

Space is illumination or darkness.

Space has the nature of illumination or darkness.[2]

Subtle particles do not have parts and do not touch.

They assert that subtle particles do not have parts and that when they aggregate they do not touch each other, whereby there is empty intermediate [space].[3]

Direct perception and inference are valid cognition. The paths are five. [The seven branches of] enlightenment, etc., [are the thirty-seven harmonies with enlightenment]. They also assert the six perfections. [100]

The phenomena of the path are:

- two [types of] valid cognition: direct perception and inference
- five [paths]: accumulation, preparation, seeing, meditation, and no more learning
- thirty-seven harmonies with enlightenment:
  - four mindful establishments[4]
  - four thorough abandonments[5]

---

[1]These are phenomena that, being mere negations or mere absences, are not caused.

[2]The "space-constituent" included in a list of sixty-two constituents is said to have an essence of either illumination or darkness. Perhaps this means that although space is not matter, and is a mere negation of obstructive contact, it nevertheless can be light or dark depending on the presence of an outside source.

[3]This is the position of the Kashmiri Vaibhāṣikas. By saying that the tiny particles that aggregate together to make larger objects do not touch, they avoid a problem connected with asserting directionally partless particles. If such particles touched, a particle touching the west side of another particle would be touching its east side, etc. (This is discussed further in the Sautrāntika chapter.)

[4]The four establishments in mindfulness are: mindfulness of body, feelings, thoughts, and other phenomena.

[5]The four thorough abandonments are: getting rid of afflictions; non-generation of future afflictions; increase of pure phenomena such as compassion, cessations; and generation of new pure phenomena.

- four legs of manifestation[1]
- five faculties[2]
- five powers[3]
- seven branches of enlightenment[4]
- eight-branched superior path
- six perfections of giving, etc.[5]

There are twenty aspirants to virtue, and eight Approachers to and [Abiders in] the fruit.

The paths which are the basis are, in terms of a Hīnayāna person, the twenty aspirants to virtue: [6]

1. Approachers to Stream Enterer with sharp faculties
2. Approachers to Stream Enterer with dull faculties
3. Abiders in the Fruit of Stream Enterer with sharp faculties
4. Abiders in the Fruit of Stream Enterer with dull faculties [101]
5. Stream Enterers who will be reborn from [a god lineage into a god lineage][7]

---

[1]The four legs of manifestation are prerequisites for magical manifestation—aspiration, effort, thought, and analysis.

[2]The five faculties are: faith, effort, mindfulness, meditative stabilization, and wisdom of the level of the lower levels of the path of preparation, forbearance and supreme mundane qualities.

[3]The five powers are: faith, effort, mindfulness, meditative stabilization, and wisdom of the higher levels of the path of preparation, which are called heat and peak.

[4]The seven branches are: mindfulness, discrimination of phenomena, effort, joy, pliancy, meditative stabilization, and equanimity.

[5]The six perfections are: giving, ethics, patience, effort, meditation, and wisdom. These are usually associated with the Mahāyāna.

[6]Ordinary Hīnayāna persons are those who practice with at least the motivation to have a happier rebirth. The other categories have to do with the four degrees of enlightenment: Stream Enterer, Once Returner, Never Returner, and Arhat. All are called Superiors because they have realized selflessness directly.

[7]Saṃsāra is comprised of three realms of rebirth: Desire, Form and Formless. The Desire Realm has six types of rebirth: hell being, hungry ghosts, animals, humans, demi-gods, and gods. The Form Realm is comprised of four main areas, each of which has a number of lands (for a total of seventeen); beings born there are all classified as gods. The Formless Realm, which is above the Form Realm, has four areas: Limitless Space; Limitless Consciousness; Nothingness; and Peak of Saṃsāra. Beings there are classified as gods and have no bodies. "Gods," like all other beings, are

6 Stream Enterers who will be reborn [from a human lineage into a human lineage][1]
7 [Special Abiders in the Fruit of] Once Returner with one lifetime intervening [who will take rebirth once as a god of the Desire Realm before being liberated]
8–11 four [Never Returners who] are liberated while being elevated to a rebirth in the Form Realm[2]
12–14 three [Never Returners who] fly up to the highest land [in the Form Realm]
15 [Never Returners who] go to the Peak of Saṃsāra[3]
16 [Never Returners who] go to the Formless Realm
17 [Never Returners who attain] peace in this life [when the path of seeing is attained, having conquered desires included within the levels of form][4]
18 [Never Returner with the manifest corpus of the eight meditative liberations, that are attained and not degenerated][5]
19 Approacher to Arhat
20 Solitary Realizer

Regarding Stream Enterer, Once Returner, Never Returner, and Arhat, there are the four Abiders in the Fruit and the Four Approachers to the Fruit, making eight Approachers and Abiders:

---

mortal and subject to rebirth.

[1]To be reborn in a human lineage is a higher level than to be reborn in a god lineage because, in terms of spiritual practice, it is advantageous to be a human, who has a better balance of pleasure and suffering.

[2]Never Returners no longer are born in the Desire Realm, although they may be reborn elsewhere. This category comprises four types of Never Returners who attain nirvāṇa (1) in the intermediate state (between death and rebirth) on the *way* to the Form Realm, (2) upon rebirth once in the Form Realm, (3) with great exertion upon rebirth once in the Form Realm, or (4) without great exertion upon rebirth once in the Form Realm. (This is based on Paṇchen Sönam Drakba's *General Meaning of (Maitreya's) "Ornament for Clear Realization,"* Hopkins unpublished translation.)

[3]The highest of the Formless absorptions, this is the most subtle type of rebirth in saṃsāra.

[4]The path of seeing is the first direct cognition of selflessness.

[5]Losang Gönchok omitted this type, apparently by mistake. But comparing his list to Jamyang Shayba's in *Great Exposition of Tenets,* he omits the first type, which Jamyang Shayba calls the "eighth Superior," and adds the nineteenth type, "Approacher to Arhat."

1 Approachers to the Fruit of Stream Enterer
2 Abiders in the Fruit of Stream Enterer
3 Approachers to the Fruit of Once Returner
4 Abiders in the Fruit of Once Returner
5 Approachers to the Fruit of Never Returner
6 Abiders in the Fruit of Never Returner
7 Approachers to the Fruit of Arhat
8 Abiders in the Fruit of Arhat

Or, there are the two Approachers of sharp and dull faculties and the Abiders in the Fruit of those—the two, those of faith and belief, and the two, those who see and those who attain—making a general enumeration of four. [102]

When considered in detail, [the twenty aspirants to virtue] are:[1]

Stream Enterers
1 seven who take birth [in the Desire Realm]
2 those reborn from a god lineage [into a god lineage]
3 those reborn [from a human lineage] into a human lineage

Once Returners
4 [Special Abider in the Fruit of Once Returner] with one lifetime intervening [who will take rebirth once as a god of the Desire Realm before being liberated]

Never Returners
There are eight types of Never Returners who [take rebirth] in the Form Realm:
5 those who attain liberation in the intermediate state [on the way to the Form Realm]
6 those who attain liberation as soon as they are born
7 those who attain liberation with great exertion
8 those who attain liberation without great exertion
9 those who in their final lifetime go to the highest [heaven in the Form Realm and thereafter are liberated in the intermediate state]

---

[1]There are various lists of the twenty aspirants, and this is another, although it appears to have only seventeen members! The previous list has six types that are related to Stream Enterer, one for Once Returner, eleven with Never Returner, and two with Arhat. Some of these are clarified by reference to Paṇchen Sönam Drakba's *General Meaning of (Maitreya's) "Ornament for Clear Realization,"* which Jamyang Shayba cites in *Great Exposition of Tenets.*

10 those who rise half of the way [taking rebirth only three times: in the Form Realm in the heaven of Brahmā, in any of the pure lower places, and in the highest land where he attains nirvāṇa]
11 those who transmigrate in all stations [taking rebirth in sixteen of the Form levels—but not the heaven of Brahmā—and then attain nirvāṇa in the highest land]
12 those who go to the finality of the Peak of Saṃsāra[1]

[There is also one type that takes rebirth in the Formless Realm:]
13 those [who go to the] Formless Realm who have abandoned attachment to the Form Realm

Approacher to Arhat
14 Approachers to [Hearer] Arhat who have abandoned the eight afflictions of the Desire Realm
15 Approachers to [Solitary Realizer] Arhat who have abandoned the eight afflictions of the Desire Realm [103]

Approacher to Arhat[2]
16 [Approachers to Bodhisattva Arhat who attain] peace [in this lifetime] when the path of seeing is attained, [having conquered desires included within the levels of form]
17 [Approachers to Bodhisattva Arhat who attain liberation] with the cessation of the body

I have explained the mere enumeration of the twenty aspirants to virtue. Although this was done as in Vasubandhu's *Treasury of Abhidharma*, since concordant phenomena of illustration are not needed here, I wonder whether it was appropriate.

There are six types of Hearer Arhats:[3]

1 those who have the quality of degeneration
2 those who have the quality of killing self
3 those who have the quality of thorough maintenance
4 those who have the quality of not being disturbed from abiding

[1]Peak of Saṃsāra is actually in the Formless Realm.

[2]These last two are uncertain. They do not appear in the other lists to which we have referred.

[3]According to Vaibhāṣika, five of the six types of Arhats can "fall back" from attainment of liberation for bad behavior, attempting suicide, etc. Other schools deny this possibility.

5 those who have the quality of being suitable for realization
6 those who have the quality of immovability

There are two types of Solitary Realizers, the Rhinoceros-like and the Congregating, but simultaneous [abandonment] is not asserted.[1]

The twelve deeds of the Buddha are:

1 descent from the Joyous Pure Land [104]
2 entering the womb
3 birth
4 youthful sports and mastery of the arts
5 living in the household together with consorts,
6 renunciation
7 asceticism
8 meditation under the tree of enlightenment
9 conquest of the array of demons
10 becoming a Buddha
11 turning the wheel of doctrine
12 nirvāṇa (*parinirvāṇa*, death)

The twelve deeds [of Buddha] have two parts. [Our teacher is explained to be a complete,] perfect Buddha.

Regarding these twelve deeds, there are] two parts, the first five [that are in] the category of [deeds done while he was] a householder, and the remaining ones [that are in] the category of having come out [from that].[2] Alternatively, the latter three are taken as the deeds of a Buddha [and the former nine are taken as the deeds of a Bodhisattva]. Our teacher, for instance, is explained to be a completely perfect Buddha.

Severing the material and mental continuum [at the time] of all three [nirvāṇas] without remainder is the fruit.

---

[1]In other words, instead of simultaneously abandoning all of the eighty-one levels of afflictions, one *serially* abandons them in nine steps. First one gets free of desire, etc. for the Desire Realm, then the Form Realm, then the Formless Realm.

[2]The "twelve deeds" are interpreted differently by Hīnayāna and Mahāyāna. According to the former, the first nine are by the Bodhisattva (the aspirant to Buddhahood), the last three by the Buddha, whereas the Mahāyāna says that all twelve are performed by the Buddha—that is, that he was already enlightened fully before taking birth.

Cutting the material and mental continuum on the occasion of the three [nirvāṇas] without remainder is asserted as the fruit.[1]

Phenomena such that awareness of them is [and is not] cancelled when they are broken up or mentally separated [105] **are, respectively, conventional truths and ultimate truths.**

When a pot, for instance, is actually broken up or when that phenomenon is [mentally] broken down by an awareness, the awareness that apprehends [it] as being a pot is cancelled, whereby [a pot] is asserted to be a conventional truth. However, even though form, for instance, is broken up or broken down [mentally], the awareness that apprehends [it] as being form is not cancelled, whereby [it] is asserted to be an ultimate truth. [106]

Because [there must be] three [scriptural collections], the seven Abhidharma treatises are the word [of Buddha].

Because there must be three scriptural collections, the seven Abhidharma treatises are the word [of Buddha].[2]

Scriptures are [non-associated] compositional factors.

The entities of the scriptures, the word of Buddha and the treatises, are asserted to be non-associated compositional factors.[3]

Direct perceivers are sense, mental, and yogic. Self-consciousness does not exist.

---

[1]Nirvāṇa with remainder is the nirvāṇa (absence of afflictions) in the continuum of a person who still has a "remainder" of aggregates (i.e., is still alive). A nirvāṇa without remainder is that which occurs upon that person's death. Since there are three final vehicles (of Hearer Arhat, Solitary Realizer Arhat, and Buddha Arhat), there are three types of nirvāṇa without remainder.

[2]The Abhidharma ("higher knowledge" or "manifest phenomena") literature is the analysis and systematizing of the Buddha's teachings. The Abhidharma collection of the major Hīnayāna schools is comprised of seven treatises, although schools differ on identification of their authors. Only Vaibhāṣikas accept these as the word of Buddha; accordingly, they also deny that the treatises fall outside of the three collections of Sūtra (discourses), Abhidharma, and Vinaya (discipline).

[3]Non-associated compositional factors are impermanent phenomena that are neither consciousness nor matter, such as a person. Vaibhāṣikas say that the Buddha's word is "generic images of words." As we shall see, other Buddhist schools consider the scriptures to be matter, since they are collections of words.

They assert three direct perceivers—sense direct perceivers, mental direct perceivers, and yogic direct perceivers—but self-consciousness does not exist.[1]

[There is] simultaneous cause and effect.
Cause and effect exist simultaneously.[2]

Non-revelatory form is form.
Non-revelatory form is fully qualified form.[3]

Sense consciousnesses [know objects] without [taking on] their aspect.
Sense consciousnesses apprehend objects nakedly and without aspect.[4] They assert valid cognition that is physical sense powers.[5] [107]

The five categories [of phenomena] are things and are substantially existent.
The five categories of objects of knowledge are:

1 appearing forms
2 main minds[6]

---

[1]Some schools (the followers of Dharmakīrti and Dignāga in the Sautrāntika and Cittamātra schools) assert that consciousness itself is known. For example, when an eye consciousness knows a table, it too is known (by a self-consciousness), such that later it is possible to remember not only the object seen but the consciousness that saw it.

[2]Vaibhāṣika is the only Buddhist school to say this. Their principal example is a main mind and its mental factors, which they argue are cause and effect but must be simultaneous. Other Buddhist schools do not say that a mind and its mental factors are cause and effect.

[3]Non-revelatory forms are forms generated by oneself that others cannot perceive, e.g., deeds of body and speech, such as silent vows or keeping ethics, that no one sees. Only Vaibhāṣikas consider these to be form.

[4]They say that sense consciousnesses cognize objects without any intermediary and without "taking on the aspect" of that which is perceived. Other schools say that there are sense powers inside the physical sense bases (such as the eye, ear, nose, etc.) that are transformed into the aspect (shape, color, etc.) of the object. They are matter and, therefore, not themselves sentient.

[5]The sense power itself apprehends things, not just the consciousnesses that use the sense powers. They argue that since the eye consciousness, for instance, is not matter, it should be unobstructed by walls, etc.; therefore, matter must be involved in the process of cognition, limiting what can be perceived.

[6]These are the eye, ear, nose, tongue, body, and mental consciousnesses.

3 accompanying mental factors[1]
4 non-associated compositional factors[2]
5 uncaused phenomena

They are asserted to be functioning things and to be substantially established.[3]

The form aggregates [of a Buddha] are not Buddha. [Buddha is] the attributes of non-learning [in the continuum of that Buddha].

The form aggregate of a Buddha is not Buddha.[4] Therefore, the phenomena of non-learning in the continuum of that Buddha—[true] cessations and [true] paths—are regarded [as Buddha].

[The individual schools have] many unique [positions. To know them] look in the texts of Bhāvaviveka etc.

Since there are many unique modes of assertion of the individual schools, [Jamyang Shayba] says that one should know them in dependence upon texts such as Bhāvaviveka's *Blaze of Reasoning.* [108]

---

[1]Main minds are accompanied by mental factors such as feelings, discriminations, etc. There are fifty-one altogether.

[2]As explained earlier, non-associated compositional factors are impermanent phenomena that are neither consciousness nor matter, such as the person.

[3]The first four categories are the five aggregates, and the last is non-products. All phenomena are contained in these categories. All are functioning things. Even space acts as a cause, because it causes the non-obstruction of a cup when the cup is moved. Other schools deny that uncaused phenomena are functioning things or are substantially established.

[4]The Buddha's form aggregate is the body he got from his parents, one impelled by karma and, therefore, is not itself a Buddha.

The Sautrāntika School

Due to propounding that the sets of sūtras are valid, they are called Proponents of Sūtra (Sautrāntikas).

Due to holding the sets of sūtras to be valid and propounding their own tenets in accordance with that, they are called Proponents of Sūtra (Sautrāntikas).[1]

When they are divided [by way of] entity, there are Followers of Scripture and Followers of Reasoning.

When Sautrāntikas are differentiated, [109] i.e., when they are divided by way of entity, there are the two: the Sautrāntika Followers of Scripture and the Sautrāntika Followers of Reasoning.[2]

[When they are divided] by way of aspect, there are three.

[When differentiated] by way of aspect, there are three: [Those Propounding] an Equal Number of Objects and Subjects, the Non-Pluralists, and the Sequential [Non-Pluralists].[3]

---

[1] 108.3–.5 is obscure, and omitted here, but is concerned with whether or not the sūtras accepted by the Sautrāntikas could contain Mahāyāna sūtras.

[2] "Entity" refers to the main Sautrāntika view, as opposed to "aspect," which refers to how they regard the specific issue of how many consciousnesses are involved in the perception of variegated objects. Losang Gönchok differentiates them by their definitions of the two truths and otherwise regards them as being the same. Gönchok Jikmay Wangbo points out that they also differ over their identification of the person and over the existence of self-consciousness.

[3] The first say that many aspects of an object are cast toward subjects and that either there are an equal number of consciousnesses (e.g., many eye consciousnesses) *or* that one consciousness is generated in many different aspects. Non-Pluralists say that many aspects appear simultaneously and a single consciousness is generated in all those aspects. Sequential Non-Pluralists assert that those aspects *seem* simultaneous, but actually just appear rapidly and sequentially. See Klein,

The General Assertions of the Sautrāntikas

The two truths are, [respectively, those phenomena that] are and are not truly able to perform functions.

The two truths are asserted by the Followers of Scripture in accordance with the Vaibhāṣikas. The Followers of Reasoning assert that an ultimate truth is a phenomenon that ultimately is able to perform a function and that a conventional truth is a phenomenon that is *unable* to perform a function ultimately.[1]

The aggregates, constituents, sources, caused phenomena, and uncaused phenomena are the bases.

The bases [from within a division of tenets into bases, paths, and fruits] are:

- the five aggregates
- the eighteen constituents [110]
- the twelve sources
- caused phenomena
- uncaused phenomena

The [thirty-seven] harmonies with enlightenment, the [eight] liberations, the [nine] serial [absorptions], mercy, etc., are the path.

The phenomena of the path are:

- the thirty-seven harmonies of enlightenment
- the eight [meditative] liberations[2]
- the liberation of the embodied looking at a form
- the liberation of the formless looking at a form

Knowledge, 141.

[1]To perform a function primarily means to act as a cause. All functioning things act as causes, if not of their own next moment, then of something else. For example, a moment of pot can cause the next moment of pot, but even the last moment of a pot is a cause, since it is the cause of potshards; a moment of lightning can cause another moment, but the last moment of lightning is the cause of illumination in the sky. On the other hand, permanent phenomena, which are not functioning things, cannot act as causes. For instance, space and other absences do not cause anything.

[2]These are limited liberations in the sense that they only free beings from the manifest activity of specific afflictions.

- the liberation of beautiful form[1]
- the four actual bases of the formless absorptions, and the equipoise of cessation[2]
- the eight consisting of the actual four concentrations and the four formless absorptions
- the nine serial absorptions [adding] the equipoise of cessation [to the eight absorptions]
- mercy
- great compassion
- the six perfections
- and so on.[3] [111]

The two, [the Hearer] Approachers and Abiders and Solitary Realizers, and perfect Buddhas [are the fruits of practicing the paths].

The persons who practice the paths are: regarding Hearers, the eight Approachers and Abiders in the Fruit; regarding Solitary Realizers, the two, the Rhinoceros-like and the Congregating; and completely perfect Buddhas.

Sautrāntika Assertions That Differ from Those of the Vaibhāṣikas

Things are momentary.

[112] Things are necessarily momentary.[4]

---

[1]The liberations associated with forms are ways that yogis consider themselves: as having a body, as not having a body, and as having an attractive body. They then cultivate the meditative absorptions of the Form Realm. These meditations are pre-requisites for producing physical manifestations.

[2]The four absorptions of the Form Realm and the four absorptions of the Formless Realm are levels of meditation associated with the Form and Formless Realms (i.e., that are causes of rebirth in the heavens of those places). Equipoise of cessation is a state beyond the meditative states of the four concentrations and four absorptions that involves cessation of feelings and discernment associated with the last absorption, the "Peak of Saṃsāra." In it, there is no manifest operation of the six consciousness (but there is some sort of operative subtle mind, just as in deep sleep).

[3]Mercy, great compassion, and the six perfections were practiced by Śākyamuni while he was a Bodhisattva in training to become a Buddha. It is interesting that these are listed as aspects of the path of a Hīnayāna school.

[4]In other words, changing very rapidly.

The seven [Abhidharma] treatises are not taken as [Buddha's] word.

The seven Abhidharma treatises are asserted to have been written by Śāriputra, etc., without being [Buddha's] word.

Abhidharma is the explanations of the specific and general [characteristics of phenomena] from within [the scriptural collections that also include] the sets of discourses and disciplines.

The scriptural collection of abhidharma is taken as words that explain the specific and general characteristics [of phenomena] that exist in the scriptural collections of the sets of discourses and discipline.

Scripture is words, [thus] form.

Since scripture, i.e., [Buddha's] word and treatises, are garlands of words, they are form aggregates.[1]

Tiny particles [are asserted by some to have] parts, [by others to be] partless.

Some [followers of the Sautrāntika school] assert that tiny particles have parts and some assert that they are partless. Among those who assert that [tiny particles] are partless, in the case of one particle being surrounded by many, some assert that there is [space between them and thus] no contact, while others assert that there is no space between [yet they still do not touch].[2] Although [tiny particles] are neither aggregates of particles nor substantial particles, they are asserted to be a collection of the eight particle substances.[3] [113]

---

[1]Vaibhāṣikas assert that Buddha's word is "generic images of words"—not matter. Sautrāntikas say that it is matter, or form (terms generally synonymous except for forms for the mental consciousness).

[2]If the particles have no contact, there is no problem that when we tough the "west" side of a particle we also absurdly touch the "east."

[3]The tiny particles of which we are speaking are comprised of at least eight substances, each of which could itself be called a "particle," but unlike the conglomerate particles, they do not exist on their own. The eight substances are earth, water, air, fire, form, smell, taste, and touch. (A particle may have more substances than these if it is part of the body, or part of the sense faculty, etc.)

The larger issue is whether the tiny particles belong or do not belong to the wholes in which they are perceived. For instance, we perceive a mass of water, such as a lake, as a whole. The "collection" view holds that each atom contributes to the perception of a unity, but does not actually share it. The "aggregate" view sees both the subtle aspect of individuality and the coarse aspect of aggregation being present. For an excellent discussion, see Dreyfus, *Reasoning* 100.

Non-revelatory [form] is not form.

Non-revelatory form is not form.[1]

Physical [sense powers] are not valid cognition.

Physical sense powers are not valid cognition.[2]

Non-products are non-things.

Whatever is a non-product is necessarily imputedly existent and a non-thing.

[Non-associated] compositional factors are not material; they are imputed.

Non-associated compositional factors are not matter, being mere imputations to states.[3] [114]

Sense consciousnesses are aspected. The three systems [of asserting aspects are] an Equal Number of Apprehended Objects and Apprehending Subjects, an Equal Number Apprehended Serially, and the Varieties as One Aspect. [These] are the systems of [most of] the schools of Scripture and Reasoning.

[Sautrāntikas] assert that sense consciousnesses are aspected. There are three assertions about the aspect. [Some] Followers of Reasoning assert an equal number of subjects and objects, and [some others assert] non-pluralism. One Follower of Scripture asserts that the varieties arise successively.[4]

Cause and effect are not simultaneous.

Cause and effect must not be simultaneous.[5]

[Arhats] do not fall from their abandonments and realization.

Arhats do not fall from their abandonments and realizations.

A body consciousness [generated through the power of meditation] is suitable as a branch [of the first three concentrations].

---

[1]In other words, non-revelatory form, such as a vow, is not *actual* form, just *called* form.

[2]The sense powers themselves are matter, and matter and consciousness are mutually exclusive.

[3]These are phenomena that are neither matter nor consciousness (hence, "not associated" with either), such as general categories.

[4]These differences were explained at the beginning of the chapter.

[5]A cause precedes its effect. They are unlike the Vaibhāṣikas, in other words, who say that an effect exists at the time of the cause.

The bliss that is a branch of the first two concentrations is suitable to be [considered a] body consciousness, [and hence, a body consciousness generated by the power of meditation is suitable as a branch of a concentration].

Direct perceptions are the four: sense, mental, yogic, and self-consciousness.

Directly perceiving consciousnesses are asserted as four: sense direct perceivers, mental direct perceivers, yogic direct perceivers, and self-knowing directly perceiving consciousnesses.[1] [115]

[Since] the appearing object of direct perception [must be] an impermanent phenomenon, selflessness is realized implicitly.

Since the appearing object of direct perception must be an impermanent phenomenon, selflessness is realized implicitly.[2]

Bodhisattva Superiors are [necessarily] in meditative equipoise.

Bodhisattva Superiors are necessarily in meditative equipoise.[3]

The two, Truth and Form [Bodies], are Buddha.

Both the Truth and Form Bodies are asserted to be Buddha.

This has been the ninth chapter of the commentary on those who propound the [scriptural collections] of sets of discourses as valid through refuting the permanent self and [those who propound the three times, etc., as] substantialities.

---

[1]Sense direct perceivers, such as eye consciousnesses, are non-mistaken, non-conceptual knowers. Mental direct perception is ordinarily just one moment of recognition that occurs at the end of a continuum of sense perception. Special types of mental direct perception include five types of clairvoyance (magical emanation, divine eye, divine ear, memory of former lives, knowing other's minds), self-consciousness, and yogic direct perception. Self-consciousness is that aspect of sense direct perception that is its knowing of itself (non-dualistically) at the same time an external object is perceived. Yogic direct perception is mental direct perception produced from a meditative stabilization that is a union of calm abiding and special insight; so, its object has to do with selflessness—either the Four Noble Truths or emptiness.

[2]They say selflessness is realized *directly*, but since selflessness is permanent (being a mere negative that does not disintegrate momentarily), it is not realized *explicitly*. Explicitly, one realizes the impermanent aggregates; implicitly, one realizes selflessness (i.e., one realizes that there is no self in or with those aggregates).

[3]According to Sautrāntika, there was only one Bodhisattva Superior of this era, and he became a Buddha in one sitting; therefore, he went from Stream Enterer to Arhat in one night). Buddhas are always in meditative equipoise.

Part Three
Mahāyāna Systems

Introduction to the Mahāyāna Systems

Because the Proponents of [Truly Existent External] Objects are posited in accordance with the meaning of the first wheel, and the two, Mādhyamika and Cittamātra, in accordance with the system of the middle and final [wheels], [all] four tenet systems are the thought of the Subduer. They are asserted as [differing in terms of] superiority and inferiority. [116]

All four tenet systems are the pure thought of the Subduer. This is because, from among the three serial turnings of the wheel of doctrine[1] by the Conqueror, there is a presentation of the two schools [Vaibhāṣika and Sautrāntika] that propound [truly existent external] objects and propound [tenets] in accordance with the meaning of the first wheel and of the Mādhyamika and Cittamātra [tenet systems] that propound [their tenets] in accordance with the middle and last [wheels]. However, there is a great difference of superiority and inferiority, whereby the lower are refuted by the higher. Also, when those of the lower systems have their continuums ripened, they discard those [uncommon] tenets and are caused to enter into the higher. Since this is a matter of skillful means like the way a doctor cures an illness, it is asserted that there is no contradiction. [117]

---

[1]The three turnings of the wheel of doctrine are three collections of discourses of the Buddha that apparently contradict one another but which were deliberately taught by the Buddha in order to serve the needs of people with different capacities and dispositions. The Hīnayāna schools depend upon the sūtras of the first wheel, the Mādhyamika upon the second, and the Cittamātra upon the third.

In particular, the Mahāyāna is included within sūtra and mantra. Scholars [of sūtra and mantra] comment on [them] in the systems of Mādhyamika and Cittamātra.

In particular, the scriptural collections of the Mahāyāna are included in two [types], sūtra and mantra. Scholars who are followers of each of those comment [on sūtra and mantra] in the individual modes of Mādhyamika and Cittamātra.

The two charioteers prophesied by the Conqueror newly opened the systems of Mādhyamika and Cittamātra through the kindness of Mañjughoṣa and Maitreyanātha in accordance with the *Teachings of Akṣayamati Sūtra* and the *Sūtra Unraveling the Thought.*

There are two great charioteers prophesied by the Conqueror, the Glorious Protector. The Superior Nāgārjuna, through the kindness of the foremost venerable Mañjuśrī whom he took as his teacher, [118] newly opened up the way for the tenet systems of Mādhyamika in accordance with the *Teachings of Akṣayamati Sūtra.*[1] The master, the Superior Asaṅga, newly opened up the way of the tenet system of Cittamātra through the kindness of the foremost venerable Maitreya in accordance with the *Sūtra Unraveling the Thought.*

The renown that there are four [charioteers] is not correct. [Here] it is asserted that three are suitable.

The renown that there are four charioteers opening the way is incorrect.[2] However, in the *Ornament for Clear Realization,* [Maitreya] newly opened a system of explanation that did not exist before, indicating very clearly the hidden meaning of the Perfection of Wisdom sūtras, the complete and full stages of clear realization. Therefore, even though the foremost venerable Maitreya did not differentiate the definitive and the interpretable or open the way for a tenet system, he did open the way for the chariot of commentary on the proper meanings of the clear realizations, the secret meaning of the Mother [Perfection of Wisdom sūtras]. [119] Since there is no harm [to this sort of position], the foremost great being Dzongkaba asserts that three [openers of chariot ways] are suitable.

Mostly, the path of the vast [deeds] is similar. [The path] of the profound [view] is not.

---

[1]This text is the key to Mādhyamika hermeneutics (interpretation of scripture) because it says how sūtras of the other two wheels are to be interpreted.

[2]The four would be Nāgārjuna, Asaṅga, Vasubandhu, and Dignāga, but the latter two are not suitable to be called openers of a chariot-way.

The class of the paths of the vast [deeds] of the two Mahāyāna systems is mostly concordant, but regarding the paths of the profound [view], there is utterly no similarity.[1]

[1] The Mahāyāna schools share paths such as the six perfections, but their tenets are quite different.

The Cittamātra School

Since they propound that the three realms are cognition itself and mind only, they are called Proponents of Cognition (Vijñaptivādins) and Proponents of Mind Only (Cittamātrins).

Since they propound the mere assertion that all compounded phenomena are [included] in the substantial entities of the nine cognitions[1] and assert that all objects of knowledge are [included] in the nature of the nine cognitions, and since they propound that the three realms are mere cognition and mere mind, they are called Vijñaptivādins and Cittamātrins. [120]

Their divisions are Followers of Scripture and Followers of Reasoning or [in another way True] Aspectarians and False [Aspectarians].

Their divisions by way of entity are two types: some are Followers of Scripture due to propounding mainly Asaṅga's Five Treatises on the Grounds, and some are Followers of Reasoning due to holding Dignāga's *Compendium of Valid Cognition* and Dharmakīrti's Seven Treatises as chief. When divided by way [of how they assert] aspects, there are the two True Aspectarians and False Aspectarians.[2]

---

[1]The nine cognitions are categories of impermanent phenomena. They are cognitions of the five senses; cognitions of the afflicted mentality; cognitions of the mental consciousness; cognitions of the six objects—forms, sounds, odors, tastes, tangible objects, and phenomena; cognitions making use of those six consciousnesses; cognitions of time; cognitions of enumeration; cognitions of location; and cognitions of four conventions—the seen, the heard, the known, and the understood.

[2]These are the same divisions as in the Sautrāntika school. True and False Aspectarians agree that the appearance of coarse objects as external is distorted by ignorance. They disagree over whether the coarse appearances of wholes exists as they appear. For example, a patch of blue is actually many tiny parts that are blue; is the appearance of a "patch" true or false?

Interpretation of Scripture

[The wheel] of good discrimination is definitive. The other two [wheels] are interpretable.

[From among the three wheels of doctrine] explained in the *Sūtra Unraveling the Thought*, [Cittamātrins] accept the final wheel—that of good differentiation—as definitive. They assert that the other two [wheels of doctrine], the first and middle [wheels] as explained in that [sūtra], require interpretation.[1]

[Sūtras requiring] interpretation and definitive [sūtras] are differentiated by the four reliances, the four reasonings, the four thoughts, and the four indirect intentions.

QUESTION: How do the Mādhyamika and Cittamātra [schools] distinguish the interpretable and the definitive regarding the word of the Conqueror [Śākyamuni]?

ANSWER: The speech [of Buddha] is differentiated, "This is a meaning requiring interpretation, and this is a definitive meaning," [by means of] having analyzed well by way of these modes of individual analysis:

The four reliances[2]

1 do not rely on the person; [121] rely on the doctrine
2 do not rely on the word; rely on the meaning
3 do not rely on the meaning that is to be interpreted; rely on the definitive meaning
4 do not rely on a [dualistic] consciousness; rely on an exalted wisdom consciousness

[1]In the second and third wheels of doctrine, Buddha made contradictory statements regarding the imagined nature that phenomena lack. The Cittamātra school considers Buddha's final thought to be contained in the third wheel, the wheel of good differentiation, which it considers to be definitive in the sense that it can be taken literally, while the other two wheels of doctrine require interpretation in the sense that they cannot be taken literally.

[2]The four reliances are: (1) *doctrine, not person*: truth is important, the source is not; (2) *meaning, not word*: intention supercedes what is actually said; (3) *definitive, not interpretable*: rely on sūtras that do not require interpretation; (4) *wisdom, not dualistic consciousness*: wisdom is a consciousness directly realizing emptiness and, therefore, is not dualistic.

The four [reasonings][1]
1 the reasoning of dependence
2 the reasoning of performing functions
3 the reasoning of proving feasibility
4 the reasoning of nature

The four [thoughts][2]
1 the thought of similarity
2 the thought of another meaning
3 the thought of another time
4 the thought of the person's aptitude

The indirect four [intentions][3]
1 the intention of [causing someone] to enter
2 the intention of nature
3 the intention of the antidote
4 the intention of transformation [122]

The first [turning of the wheel of doctrine] requires interpretation because of scripture and because external objects do not exist.

The Cittamātra Followers of Scripture propound [how the first wheel requires interpretation] in this way. The *Sūtra on the Ten Grounds* and the *Sūtra Unraveling the Thought* prove the first turn of the wheel indicated here [in the *Sūtra Unraveling the Thought*] requires interpretation, and [123] reasonings prove that external objects do not exist.

---

[1]The *four reasonings* are: (1) dependence: to analyze how things arise in dependence on causes and conditions; (2) performing functions: to analyze the feasibility of phenomena performing their own functions; (3) feasibility: to analyze to see whether or not something is contradictory to valid cognition; (4) nature: to depend on worldly renown that fire is hot, etc.

[2]The *four thoughts* (of Buddha when he spoke certain passages) are: (1) similarity: the similarity of something to the Truth Body (wisdom consciousness of a Buddha); (2) another meaning: Buddha was thinking of something else when he said, for instance, "all phenomena are without entities," because that is not literally true; (3) another time: Buddha was thinking of another time; (4) person's aptitude: Buddha adjusted his teaching to a person's dispositions.

[3]The *four intentions* (of Buddha) are: (1) causing someone to enter: preaching a doctrine that persuades them to enter Buddhism; (2) nature: thinking of the three natures, Buddha said all phenomena were without entity; (3) antidote; (4) transformation.

Thinking of the appearance of [external] objects, [Buddha spoke of external objects] for the sake of [trainees] entering [the path].

The *basis* in [Buddha's] thought [for teaching in the first wheel that external objects exist when in fact they do not] is that the appearance of external objects does exist. [Buddha's] *purpose* was that he taught [the existence of external objects] for the purpose of causing the intended trainees for whom he spoke this to enter into realization of the selflessness of persons.[1]

The middle [wheel], the Mahāyāna sūtras on the profound, are not literal because [Buddha] was thinking of the non-nature [appropriate to each] of the three natures.

The middle turning of the wheel indicated here [in the *Sūtra Unraveling the Thought*], the Mahāyāna sūtras on the profound, the Perfection of Wisdom, is not literal. Because [when Buddha] said that all phenomena are natureless, [in terms] of the three natures—imputational natures, other-powered natures, and thoroughly established natures[2]—[he was thinking of]:

1. the *character-non-nature* of the first [i.e., that imputational natures are not established by way of their own characteristic nature];
2. the *production-non-nature* of the second [i.e., that other-powered natures are not produced under their own power];

---

[1]The three ways to interpret scripture are by examining: (1) *the basis in Buddha's thought*: What was Buddha *really* thinking of when he said this? (2) *Buddha's propose*: What did Buddha intend to accomplish by saying this? (3) *the damage to the literal teaching*: What faults would be accepted if this passage were considered literally? For instance, with regard to the Buddha's teaching in the first wheel sūtras that there are external objects, the *basis* is that Buddha was thinking of the fact that to ordinary beings, there seem to be external objects (though not to himself); the *purpose* is to help his hearers understand selflessness and, therefore, he told his hearers that all phenomena truly exist but that a permanent, partless self does not; and the *damage to the literal teaching* is that since it can be shown [by Cittamātrins] that objects are not external, it cannot literally be true that all phenomena truly exist.

[2]The three natures are: (1) *other-powered natures*, which are impermanent phenomena themselves, produced by causes other than themselves; (2) *imputational natures*, which are natures that exist for thought but are not ultimately existent; and (3) *thoroughly established natures*, which are emptinesses. All phenomena are one of these. Imputational natures include both existents and non-existents. Existent imputational natures include generalities like "existent," "same," etc., whose instances include both permanent and impermanent phenomena, as well as non-products such as space. Non-existent imputational natures include external objects or a substantially existent self.

3 the *ultimate-non-nature* of the third [i.e., that thoroughly established natures lack a self of phenomena]. [124]

Therefore, [the middle wheel] is not suitable to be literal because in that case [Buddha] would have spoken deprecatingly of all three natures.[1]

Because [the three natures] are not produced, etc., in the way [that they lack their own independent nature, Buddha said that phenomena] are unproduced, etc.

Because [the three natures] are unproduced and unceasing, etc., in just the way that they are natureless, [Buddha] said [in the Perfection of Wisdom sūtras] that they are unproduced and unceasing, etc.[2]

[Buddha spoke of attaining] forbearance regarding the doctrine of non-production by way of [becoming accustomed to] the eight, [the non-production of imputational natures by way of their] own [nature, the non-production of] other[-powered phenomena from themselves], etc.

The basis in Buddha's thought concerning non-production when he said, "One attains forbearance regarding the doctrine of non-production," was of these eight [types of non-production].[3]

---

[1]With regard to the interpretation of the middle wheel sūtras, the *basis in Buddha's thought* was that Buddha was thinking that imputational natures are not truly established; that other-powered phenomena are not produced from themselves, i.e., are depend-arisings; and that thoroughly established phenomena are the lack of a self of phenomena. That is why he could say that phenomena lack their own entity (meaning inherent existence) without contradicting his own thought. The *purpose* was to help those who could understand this teaching. The *damage to the literal teaching* was that it would "deprecate" the three natures to say that phenomena lack entityness, for Cittamātrins feel that if something exists, it truly exists; therefore, other-powered and thoroughly established natures truly exist.

[2]In the *Sūtra Unraveling the Thought,* Buddha says about character-non-natures, "Concerning that, thinking of just character-non-natures [that is, thinking of mere imputational factors that are not established by way of their own character], I taught that all phenomena are unproduced, unceasing, quiescent from the start, naturally thoroughly passed beyond sorrow." Hopkins, *Emptiness in Mind-Only,* 97.

[3]Through understanding these eight types of non-production one understands selflessness, i.e., attains a forbearance in terms of the selflessness of phenomena.

- non-production of a beginning of saṃsāra
- non-production in the sense that what has already been produced is produced again
- non-production of sentient beings who did not exist previously
- non-production of imputational natures by way of their own character
- non-production of other-powered natures by self-production
- non-production of change regarding thoroughly established natures
- non-production of the afflictions [in arhats] who [have attained] knowledge of the extinction
- non-production of enhancement regarding the Truth Body [125]

The term, "etc." [in the root text] was used to include the basis in his thought when [Buddha] said that there is one final vehicle.[1]

In the *Sūtra Unraveling the Thought*, when [Buddha] summarized the meaning established [by what had gone before], Paramārthasamudgata asked questions to the Blessed One [Buddha] regarding the meaning of the mode of apprehending an illustration of the interpretable and the definitive and asked about the meaning of the middle wheel, stating some words from among the first two wheels about which he had qualms. In reply, [Buddha] taught a brief indication, an extensive explanation, and identifications together with examples.

When he offered the teaching of the meaning established [by those], including a mode of differentiating the interpretable and the definitive, [126] he explained in general the turning of the wheel of the doctrine of the Four Noble Truths in the first wheel [of the doctrine], and he praised it. [Also, he said] that the likes [of those teachings in the first wheel that Paramārthasamudgata] had put into his question are surpassable, are opportune [in the sense of providing an opportunity for someone to debate against them], are of interpretable meaning, etc.

The middle wheel can be understood through that [same reasoning].

That which he was speaking now, [the *Sūtra Unraveling the Thought* itself, was given] as an illustration of the final wheel. It is the third wheel, is unsurpassable,

[1] "One final vehicle" means that whether one is currently a Hearer, a Solitary Realizer, or a Bodhisattva, one will eventually practice the Bodhisattva path and become a Buddha. As we will see under "The General System of the Cittamātra School," the Cittamātrins Following Scripture (i.e., those who follow Asaṅga) say that there are five lineages, so, in fact, many beings will not become Buddhas. Here it is asserted that when Buddha said there is only one final vehicle, he was thinking about non-production, i.e., selflessness. Losang Gönchok does not explain this further, so we are left to speculate about why these two things are connected. Ours is that Buddha was thinking that Hearers, Solitary Realizers, and Bodhisattvas alike must realize the coarse selflessness of the person.

does not afford opportunity [for valid dispute], and is definitive. It appears that this is what [Buddha] offered in answer.

[According to the master Dharmakīrti, in consideration of the non-existence of] apprehended object and apprehending subject [as different substantial entities, Buddha taught that all phenomena are without entity. Buddha also] explained in [the Perfection of Wisdom sūtras] that [all phenomena] are natureless in consideration that object and agent of cause and effect and that the factors of definition and definiendum, etc., [are not established by way of] their own characteristic nature, or are not truly established.

The glorious Dharmakīrti's *Commentary on (Dignāga's) "Compendium on Valid Cognition"* says that the Cittamātra school's *unique* way to comment on [how Buddha's] statement in the Perfection of Wisdom sūtras that [all phenomena] are without entityness [requires interpretation] is as follows. Buddha was thinking of the non-existence of specifically characterized [127] phenomena,[1] which [exist] in accordance with the appearance of apprehended object and apprehending subject as different substantial entities, etc.[2]

The mode of interpreting the Mother [Perfection of Wisdom] sūtras as requiring interpretation that is *common* to Sautrāntika and Cittamātra [holds] that [Buddha] said such thinking that the factors of object and agent of cause and effect, definition and definiendum, etc., are not established by way of their own nature, or truly existent.[3]

---

[1]Jamyang Shayba, in his *Great Exposition of Tenets*, treats "apprehended object and apprehending subject" as does Losang Gönchok, but without using the term from the root text "specifically characterized phenomena." Not only that, he repeats the word "specifically characterized phenomena" at the start of the next passage but again does not use it in his commentary (Gomang 253.19).

[2]Dharmakīrti explains two ways to interpret middle wheel sūtras, such as Buddha's statement that "all phenomena are without entityness," which to Cittamātrins makes no literal sense, as phenomena do indeed have their own entity. The first explanation is one found only in Cittamātra; the next will be common both to Cittamātra and Sautrāntika. When he said that phenomena have no entityness, Buddha was thinking (his basis) that subject and object appear to be different substantial entities but are not.

[3]This interpretation is that when Buddha said that phenomena lack their own entityness he was thinking about definitions and definiendums being agent and object regarding each other. A pot is defined as being "bulbous, flat-based, and able to hold water." If they were truly established as agent and object, they would not have the relationship of being one entity (but conceptually different, i.e., different "isolates"). (Gomang, 253.20.)

The General System of the Cittamātra School

The former [school, the Cittamātra Followers of Scripture, asserts that] because the basic constituent is definite as capacities and is truly established, the lineages of the three vehicles are definite. Although those whose lineage is severed [try] to enter [into the teaching] by way of hearing, etc., they utterly fail to generate discouragement [regarding saṃsāra], renunciation, etc.

The former system, the [Cittamātra] Followers of Scripture, [128] asserts that:

- Because the basic constituent, or lineage, is a definite capacity for generating its respective enlightenment, and because it is truly established, those definite in the lineage of the three, Hearers, Solitary Realizers, and Mahāyānists, do not change [to another vehicle].[1]
- Those whose lineage is indefinite change according to conditions.
- Those whose lineage is utterly severed, although they might [try to] enter the teaching through hearing, thinking, and meditating, utterly fail to generate discouragement regarding saṃsāra, an attitude of renunciation, great compassion, etc.

The latter [system, Followers of Reasoning asserts that] one vehicle is established because [stains] are impermanent, a method [for abandoning them] exists, those who know them exist, there are teachers, and an interest [in liberation] occurs.

The latter system, the Followers of Reasoning, asserts that:

- Since the defilements in the continuum of one whose lineage is "cut off" can be eliminated, they are impermanent.[2] [129]
- A means for abandoning those exists.
- There are those who know that method.
- Through knowing it, there are skilled teachers.

---

[1]There are three final vehicles—Hearers, Solitary Realizers, and Bodhisattvas. In other words, Hearers and Solitary Realizers do not necessarily go on to become Bodhisattvas and Buddhas. Also, there are five lineages—the three vehicles, one whose lineage is indefinite, and one who fails. This is the only Mahāyāna school to say that there are some who cannot be liberated.

[2]In other words, no one's lineage is forever cut off, because there are no defilements that cannot be removed. Therefore, everyone can eventually become liberated, find their way into the Mahāyāna, and become a Buddha.

- When [the method for removing stains] is taught when [persons] are tormented by suffering, they will generate an interest [in liberation], whereby it is established that they are able to abandon their defilements.
- Through this reasoning, it is established that there is one final vehicle.

How the Two Extremes Are Abandoned

That imputational natures are truly established is a superimposition. That the other two are not truly established is a deprecation. The opposite is the path of the middle way.

The Cittamātra system asserts that conceiving imputational natures to be truly established is a superimposition, and conceiving other-powered natures and thoroughly established natures to be not truly established is a deprecation. [130] The opposites of those, realizing that imputational natures are not truly established and that the other two are truly established, is asserted to be the path of the middle way that is free from the two extremes.[1]

If all things were truly established, why it is explained that even agents exist conventionally? There are two ways in which two truths exist. The first is the [true] existence and non-[true] existence that the Mādhyamikas and Cittamātrins debate.

QUESTION: If all things are truly established, what is the meaning of the explanation in many texts of this system that agents, persons, etc., are conventionally existent? [131]

ANSWER: Regarding statements that [phenomena] exist as the two truths, there are different contexts in terms of modes of identifying [the meaning of existing conventionally and ultimately]. Therefore, the first [mode of identifying two truths] is as before; it is that [interpretation of] true or non-true existence about which Mādhyamikas and Cittamātrins debate.[2]

---

[1]The "middle way" propounded by Cittamātra is: the extreme of permanence is avoided because imputational natures are *not* truly established and the extreme of annihilation is avoided because other phenomena *are* truly established.

[2]They disagree about true existence. For Cittamātra, ultimate truths are things that are truly existent (= other-powered natures and thoroughly established natures) whereas conventional truths are those that are not truly existent (= imputational natures). For Mādhyamikas, nothing has true existence.

The second, being or not being a conventional basis that is suitable to give rise to thorough afflictions, is just said to be conventional and ultimate existence [respectively].

The second [mode] is: a conventional basis that is suitable to give rise to thorough afflictions is conventionally existent and what is not that is said to exist ultimately.[1] Thus, there is no contradiction [in agents, etc., being truly established and yet also being said to exist conventionally].

Because there are also two [modes of identifying] substantial and imputational phenomena, that things are falsely established is mistaken.

Not only that, [the Cittamātra school] regards an existent that is self-sufficiently apprehendable to be substantially existent, while an existent that is not self-sufficiently apprehendable is an imputed existent.[2] Also, according to this interpretation, since whatever is either a substantial existent or an imputed existent in this [interpretation] must exist, how could [all] conceptions of a substantial existent be a conception of a self of persons?[3] [132] Furthermore, the view of the transitory collection that accompanies an afflicted mind would [absurdly] not be a wrong consciousness.[4] Dzongkaba's *Illumination of the Thought, Explanation of (Candrakīrti's) "Entrance to the Middle Way"* says:

> Propounding that the person is not a substantial entity in the sense of being self-sufficient is an assertion from the point of view of the self-isolate

---

[1]In this second way, conventional truths are those phenomena that can give rise to afflictions. For example, a gem could give rise to desire; a war, to anger. Everything except selflessness can give rise to afflictions; therefore, only selflessnesses are ultimate truths.

[2]That something is "self-sufficiently apprehendable" means that it can be apprehended without seeing another phenomenon of a different type. For example, a table can be recognized upon merely seeing one. A person, on the other hand, cannot be so apprehended, since what we see is a body, what we hear is a voice, etc., and on that basis we conclude that we are in the presence of a person. Therefore, this is a way to distinguish what must be imputed from what is not.

[3]This involves a fine distinction between two uses of the term "self" in "self-sufficient self" (meaning the non-existent self that is to be refuted) and "self-sufficiently apprehendable" (meaning substantially existent or truly existent, which for Cittamātra is perfectly suitable). All substantial existents are "self-sufficiently apprehendable" but are not "self-sufficient."

[4]The afflicted mentality is the seventh consciousness, which looks at the mind-basis-of-all and wrongly conceives it to be a self-sufficient substantial entity. If it were permissible that substantial existence be *self-sufficient*, then, when the afflicted mind looked at the mind-basis-of-all and conceived it to be self-sufficient, it would not be wrong.

of the person, but the consciousness that is the illustration of the person is not asserted in that manner.[1]

This statement must refer to just this substantial existent [that is spoken of] in Asaṅga's *Compendium of Ascertainments.* If there is no difference between this and substantial entity that is the self of persons, then there would be many [types of] damage, such as that the great charioteers, the master Bhāvaviveka, etc., would have to assert that the consciousness that takes birth is a self of persons.[2] [133]

Since there are many different contexts, such as enumerated substantial and imputed phenomena, etc., there must be two or more modes of identifying substantial and imputed phenomena, and therefore, someone's position that things are falsely established is mistaken.[3] [134]

The Three Natures

Factors of superimposition are imputational natures.

Factors of superimposition that are not the mode of subsistence are imputational natures.[4]

There are the two types, completely nihil and enumerated. Respectively, non-existents and unproduced conventionalities are posited as them.

---

[1]The "self-isolate" is the person itself. The "illustration-isolate" is that which is designated *as* a person, namely the mind-basis-of-all. The person that can be posited is not self-sufficient but it is self-sufficiently *apprehendable.*

[2]If one had to say that "self-sufficiently apprehendable" meant "self-sufficiently," then the mind-basis-of-all (the consciousness that takes birth) would be self-sufficient and, therefore, *refuted* (as being a self of persons).

[3]There is more than one way of identifying substantial and imputedly existent phenomena; e.g., one can say substantial existents are "self-sufficiently apprehendable," hence, not falsely existent, but rather truly existent.

[4]"Not the mode of subsistence" means not truly existent, i.e., merely imputed. These superimpositions do not have their own way of subsisting, i.e., existing.

When those are divided, there are two: imputational natures of completely nihil character and enumerated imputational natures. Those are, respectively, posited as non-existents—the two selves, etc.—and unproduced conventionalities.[1]

The bases of mistaken [appearance] and mistaken [consciousnesses] are other-powered natures.

The [two] bases of mistaken [dualistic perception] are compounded phenomena in general and erroneous conceptual consciousnesses.[2]

The pure and impure are, respectively, [for instance,] non-conceptual exalted wisdom consciousnesses and afflictions.

When those are divided, there are the two: pure other-powered phenomena, [such as] a Superior's non-conceptual wisdom consciousnesses, and impure other-powered phenomena, [such as] the afflictions.[3]

The emptinesses of the superimpositions of the two selves are thoroughly established natures.

The emptinesses of the superimpositions of either of the two selves of persons or phenomena are thoroughly established natures.

There are twenty with respect to each of the two selflessnesses, etc.

When divided, there are twenty with respect to each of the two, the selflessness of persons and the selflessness of phenomena. [135] The explanation of the division of the selflessness of persons into twenty is in Dzongkaba's *Golden Rosary*.[4]

Terminologically, there are objective, attainment, and practical ultimates.

---

[1]Imputational natures are distinguished into those whose character is nihil, that is, that have no defining characteristics, i.e., are non-existent; and enumerated imputational natures, i.e., those "counted" as existents, even though they are just imputed, such as space.

[2]Other-powered natures are just impermanent phenomena. They are the basis of wrong views.

[3]That is, the class of pure other-powered phenomena is very, very small.

[4]Since there are four false conceptions connected with each of the five aggregates, there are a total of twenty ways, observing the aggregates, to falsely conceive a substantially existent self. It is uncertain what the twenty are regarding the selflessness of phenomena.

Terminologically,[1] there are three: emptinesses are "object-ultimates"; nirvāṇas are "attainment-ultimates"; and paths are "practice-ultimates."

If the conception of a self of persons were necessarily either a conception of I or mine, then the view that conceives the person in another's continuum as a self-sufficient substantial existent would [absurdly] be a view of the transitory. It would also contradict the statement in Gyeltsap's *Explanation of (Dharmakīrti's) "Commentary on (Dignāga's) 'Compendium of Valid Cognition'"* that there is a conception of self but not a view of the transitory, etc.[2]

Differences Between Asaṅga and Vasubandhu

The [coarse] factors of the formation, abiding, destruction, etc., of the animate and inanimate are similarly [explained by Asaṅga and Vasubandhu].[3]

[136] The higher and lower [i.e., Vaibhāṣika and Cittamātra treatises on] Abhidharma [Vasubandhu's *Treasury of Abhidharma* and Asaṅga's *Compendium of Abhidharma*], etc., explain that there are, respectively, twenty intermediate eons each of formation, abiding, destruction, and vacuity regarding the animate and inanimate world, these eighty being one great aeon. Moreover, the coarse factors of Mount Meru along with four continents being piled up on top of spheres of wind, water, and earth, and encircled by surrounding mountains, are similar in Vasubandhu's *Treasury of Abhidharma* and Asaṅga's Treatises on the Levels, etc., and are also explained in other places.[4]

---

[1]The term "terminologically" is used when all the divisions are not actual members. Here, only the object-ultimate and the attainment-ultimate are actual thoroughly established natures and actual ultimates. Paths are consciousnesses.

[2]The view of transitory is the view of the aggregates as a self in *one's own continuum.* Therefore, one's conception of another's self is *not* a view of the transitory.

[3]Asaṅga and Vasubandhu were the half-brothers whose works are foundational for the Cittamātrins Following Scripture. Vasubandhu's *Treasury* is used by Tibetans as the source for Vaibhāṣika tenets, his own commentary on that, for Sautrāntika. Asaṅga converted him to the Mahāyāna, and his later works support Cittamātra.

[4]Mount Meru is the mountain at the center of the Desire Realm. Four continents are arrayed around Mount Meru (we are on the southern continent, Jambudvīpa). There are also eight sub-continents.

However, the thirty-six [levels] of the Desire Realm and the eighteen [levels] of the Form Realm, the shape of Mount [Meru], etc., are not [similar].

There are thirty-six Desire Realm migrations: eight hot hells, eight cold hells, hungry ghosts, demi-gods, humans of the twelve continents, and six types of Desire Realm gods.[1] [137]

In the Form Realm there are three lands each in the first, second, and third concentrations, and in the fourth concentration there are three lands of common beings and five lands of Superiors. In addition to those there is the Heavily Adorned Highest Pure Land, [making] eighteen types of lands [in the Form Realm].

The shapes and measures, etc., of Mount Meru, etc., in the texts on Abhidharma and, for instance, in the *Kālacakra Tantra*, are not similar.[2]

They are dissimilar regarding whether actions [definite to issue forth fruitions] can be purified, and how to divide the aggregates, virtues, etc.

Also, there are many differences with Vasubandhu's *Treasury of Abhidharma* such as that [in the Mahāyāna,] even actions that are definite [to give their fruition] are purified by disclosure and restraint,[3] and how to divide the aggregates, constituents, and sources.

There is much commentary [by Jamyang Shayba] on the point of the ten differences of strength with regard to virtue and non-virtue. [138] Therefore, since it would be difficult to state that in a condensed form, I will not write about it.

---

[1]All Buddhist cosmologies say that there are three "realms": Desire (where beings have sexual desire); Form (where all beings are types of gods and live in heavens dispersed among four "concentrations"—a reference to the meditative states that cause rebirth there); and Formless (where all beings are gods but have no bodies).

[2]For instance, according to *Kālacakra*, the universe is conical or pyramidal, whereas the *Treasury of Abhidharma* describes it as cylindrical.

[3]One division of karma is into actions that are definite to ripen in a certain lifetime and actions that are "indefinite." According to the Mahāyāna schools, one can "purify" (nullify) karma by confession and by making a promise not to repeat the action (unless it is quite serious and involves anger).

The Two Truths

Objects of knowledge are divided into the two truths, which are one entity and different isolates.

Regarding the presentation of the two truths, when objects of knowledge are divided there are the two: conventional truths and ultimate truths. These two are differentiated by way of being one entity and different isolates.[1]

A conventional truth is an object of observation suitable to produce thorough afflictions.

The definition of a conventional truth is: an object of observation that is suitable to produce thorough afflictions.

Its synonyms are conventional truth, etc.

Synonyms are conventional truth, basal phenomenon, [139] etc.

When divided, there are three types.

When divided terminologically, there are the three: "imputational conventionalities," "mental conventionalities," and "expressional conventionalities."[2]

An ultimate truth is a final object of observation of a path of purification.

The definition of an ultimate truth is: a final object of observation of a pure path of purification.[3]

Its synonyms are reality, suchness, etc.

Synonyms are reality, suchness (*tattva*), limit of reality, the signless, etc.

Its divisions have already [been explained].

---

[1]An "isolate" is a double reverse. For example, the isolate of table is non-non-table. This is the way conceptual thought is said to operate. To recognize something as a table is to eliminate all that is non-table; in this way, "table" is isolated. Just so, we can distinguish conceptually the two truths with respect to something, but they remain one entity.

[2]Of these three, "expressional conventionalities" are actually *not* conventionalities but rather thoroughly established phenomena, which are ultimate truths. Perhaps they are called expressional because the *expression* of ultimate truth is a conventionality. "Imputational conventionalities" are existent imputational natures; "mental conventionalities" are consciousnesses.

[3]That is, an ultimate truth such as the emptiness of subject and object being different entities is what is understood by an exalted wisdom consciousness.

The divisions [of ultimate truth] have already been explained elsewhere as the two selflessnesses and the sixteen [selflessnesses], etc.

Valid Cognition

By the force of there being manifest and hidden phenomena, regarding valid cognition there are the two: direct [valid cognition] and inferential [valid cognition].

Within valid cognition, due to their [objects of comprehension] being manifest phenomena and hidden phenomena,[1] there are the two: direct valid cognition and inferential valid cognition. [140]

There are four types of directly perceiving consciousnesses.

In the system of the [Cittamātrins] Following Reasoning, four directly perceiving consciousnesses are asserted:

- sense directly perceiving consciousnesses
- mental directly perceiving consciousnesses
- yogic directly perceiving consciousnesses
- self-knowing directly perceiving consciousnesses.

In the system of the [Cittamātrins] Following Scripture, four directly perceiving consciousnesses are asserted:

- sense directly perceiving consciousnesses
- mental directly perceiving consciousnesses
- directly perceiving consciousnesses of worldly persons
- pure directly perceiving consciousnesses[2]

The sense directly perceiving consciousnesses of [beings] lower [than a Buddha] are mistaken.

---

[1]A phenomenon is "hidden" if it can be realized by inference (which does not understand directly, but in its "hidden" manner). Since all phenomena can be realized by inference, this class includes everything existent. Manifest phenomena are those that can be directly perceived, such as the objects of the senses.

[2]These categories are not mutually exclusive.

Except for a Buddha, whatever is a sense consciousness of someone lower [than a Buddha] is necessarily mistaken.[1]

Establishing Selflessness

Because an awareness [that knows that a bulbous object is called "pot"] does not exist prior [to learning the name "pot," that the name "pot" exists in] the nature of that [bulbous object] is contradictory. [141]

Regarding the mode of proving selflessness, if a bulbous thing were established by way of its own mode of subsistence as a basis of the convention "pot," it would necessarily not depend on linguistic instruction. Therefore, because the awareness that [it is called "pot"] does not exist prior to designating it [i.e., learning the name "pot"], that [the name] exists independently of the nature of that [object] is contradictory.[2]

Because that [bulbous object has] many names, one object [would have] many essences, [but that is] contradictory.

Because [one object] has many names, that one object would [absurdly] be many different essences that are mutually unrelated. This is a contradiction [because we know there is only one object].[3]

There is no limitation that a name is used for [only] one object. Therefore, [various] essences [would be] mixed, [but that is] contradictory.

It would [absurdly] not be definite that a name could be used for just one [type of] object. Therefore, when a name is used for two, etc., [types of] objects that are contradictory, the essence of those contradictory objects would [absurdly] be mixed, or one. This is contradictory [with the fact that there is more than one].[4] [142]

---

[1]This is because to non-Buddhas, apprehended object and apprehending subject appear to be separate substantial entities.

[2]Things do not naturally exist as the basis of names. A bulbous thing is not naturally a "pot" or one would know "pot" innately, without instruction.

[3]If one were naturally the basis of a name, then for John Jones, "John" and "Jones" would indicate unrelated different essences.

[4]If a bulbous thing inherently existed as a basis for "pot," then two pots would have to be absolutely identical to be named pot.

Because when one investigates by way of the four investigations [whether or not names inhere in objects, whether objects are naturally the bases of names, etc., one sees that they do not exist] in that way, those [objects] do not have [a mode of existing separately from consciousness].

The four investigations are:[1]

1 the investigation of names
2 the investigation of objects
3 the investigation of imputing entities
4 the investigation of imputing attributes

Further, if names were affixed to those objects by way of their own entityness or if those objects were established by way of their own characteristic as bases of the affixing of those names, when one analyzed as before, [revealing] the necessity of [the name] being independent of any instruction in language, etc., then because of not existing [in that way], these bases do not have a mode of being factually other than the mind.[2]

Because [perceiving consciousness and perceived] are necessarily observed [by valid cognition] together [i.e., simultaneously], they are not separate [entities].

Because of being necessarily observed [by valid cognition] together, those two, blue and the eye consciousness apprehending blue, are not established as separate substantial entities in the way they appear.[3] If, through having refuted that those are *separate* substantial entities, one were to establish that they were *one* substantial entity, then:

[1]The four investigations are: (1) investigation of names, which concerns whether names are mere imputations or emerge from the side of the object; (2) investigation of objects, which concerns whether they naturally exist as the basis of names; (3) investigation of imputing entities, which concerns whether there is a substantially existing relationship between the word and the object; and (4) investigation of imputing attributes, which concerns whether objects naturally exist as the basis of the designation of qualities (such as color, shape, impermanence, etc.).

[2]That is, realizing the emptiness of names is also a way to realize the non-difference of entity of subject and object.

[3]This is Dharmakīrti's main reasoning refuting external objects. His premise is that if two things are necessarily observed simultaneously, they are one entity. He maintains that an eye consciousness apprehending blue and a self-consciousness apprehending that eye consciousness occur simultaneously. No schools other than those that use his works agree that there is anything like a self-consciousness and, therefore, would not accept this reasoning.

1 the emptiness of object and subject of being separate substantial entities would [absurdly] not be a non-affirming negative[1] [143]
2 the uninterrupted path[2] that realizes that non-affirming negative would not occur
3 it would contradict [the fact] that the exalted wisdom of meditative equipoise has no appearance [of anything other than this non-affirming negative]
4 [it would contradict] the explanation in the *Sūtra Unraveling the Thought* that thoroughly established phenomena are non-affirming negatives.

Furthermore, "substantial entity" in the statement, "different substantial entities that are to be refuted by definite simultaneous observation," either refers to a substantial entity in the sense of the self of phenomena being taken as a substantial entity or refers to a substantial entity in the sense of [functioning] things being explained as substantial entities. If it is the latter, then [definite simultaneous observation] would not be feasible as a reason that proves the selflessness of

---

[1]A non-affirming negative is something that is a mere absence, not implying anything positive. For instance, "non-existence of a round square" does not imply the existence of a square, just that there is no such thing as a round one. But "treeless plain" both negates something (trees) and posits something (plain) and, therefore, is an *affirming* negative. In this instance, speaking of a patch of blue and an eye consciousness that apprehends it, it is argued that they are merely established as *non-different* (a non-affirming negative), not as *one* (a positive phenomenon). We *could* infer oneness of entity from this, but that needs an additional step. The significance of this is that because it is always said that an exalted wisdom consciousness realizes an emptiness, a non-affirming negative, it would contradict scripture and the foundational literature of the Cittamātra school to equate the non-affirming negative with the positive phenomenon. When a Superior—someone who has directly realized emptiness—is in one-pointed meditative equipoise on emptiness, *only* emptiness (a non-affirming negative) appears, not the phenomenon that is the basis of the emptiness. It is notable that this is an issue on which Jamyang Shayba and Janggya, another major author of tenets texts, disagree; Janggya thinks that anyone who understands an absence of difference in entity also implicitly understands a sameness in entity, since two things *are* either the same entity or different entities, after all.

[2]An uninterrupted path is a consciousness that, while directly realizing emptiness, serves as an actual antidote to its corresponding object of abandonment. That is, it is an instance of wisdom eliminating afflictions. It is "uninterrupted" in the sense that it will turn into a "path of release" (a consciousness that has abandoned that corresponding level of misconception) in that very meditative session without interruption.

phenomena.[1] If it is like the first [meaning], it is not suitable to consider as a dichotomy (1) different substantial entities [of subject and object], that is, the self of phenomena, and (2) [subject and object being] one substantial entity that exists conventionally.[2]

Furthermore, regarding the subject, an uninterrupted path of a Mahāyāna path of seeing,[3] [144] it [absurdly] follows that it *establishes* blue and the apprehender of blue as *one* substantial entity because it *refutes* that they are *different* substantial entities. If this is accepted, there would be a degeneration of the position that thoroughly established phenomena are non-affirming negatives. I think that it would be permissible to assume that [these great teachers'] thought [when they spoke about subject and object being proved to be *one* substantial entity by the *refutation* of a *difference* in entity] was that although external objects are refuted, it is necessary to prove to some whose faculties are dull that [subject and object] exist conventionally.[4]

When a tiny particle is encircled [by other particles], if the eastern side does not face the western direction, it is seen to have parts, [but if it does] face [west] there is no gross [form].

When one tiny particle is encircled by four tiny particles in the four directions, if that part of the central particle that is touching the [particle on the] eastern side does not face or touch the particle on the western side, [145] that central particle would have parts; if it *does* face or touch [both the eastern and western particles] that eastern particle would have to touch the western particle, whereby those tiny particles would be in one place, whereby gross form would be impossible.

Although there *are* tiny particles, what contradiction is there that they are not [the type asserted] by Vaibhāṣikas [and others]?

---

[1]It would be absurd to say on the one hand that this reasoning showed that things have an emptiness of being different substantial entities from the consciousnesses that apprehend them and at the same time say that both are substantial entities.

[2]Dichotomies are "explicit contradictories with contradictory abandonments" i.e., phenomena that have no intersection. It is not possible to say that the two formulations—(1) subject and object being different substantial entities and (2) subject and object being one substantial entity conventionally—are dichotomous.

[3]In general, the Mahāyāna path of seeing is a meditative consciousness directly realizing emptiness conjoined with the force of great compassion.

[4]That is, it was *said* that this proves they are one entity because some people needed to hear that.

In this context [of Cittamātra], since it is asserted that tiny particles exist but *do* have parts, they are not the partless particles [asserted by], for instance, the Vaibhāṣikas, Sautrāntikas, and Vaiśeṣikas.[1] What is the contradiction? There is no contradiction.

Because many have refuted [partless particles], that Mādhyamikas and Cittamātrins assert those is mistaken.

Because many sūtras and textual systems of the great charioteers, on occasions of proving the sign [that is the reasoning on] the lack of being one or many, have refuted their object of negation through demonstrating that all phenomena have parts, [146] Daktsang the Translator's explanation that in the Mādhyamika's and Cittamātrin's own systems such partless particles are asserted is mistaken.

Refutation of External Objects

Because [no external objects] exist in the perspective of meditative equipoise, because regarding one thing there are many mental consciousnesses, because the pleasant and unpleasant [arise together], because appearances [are controlled by] yogis, etc., and because [the appearance of external objects] is similar to dreams, etc., [external] objects do not exist, and that they are just mind is true.

[Cittamātrins assert that there are no external objects] because:

- Objects such as forms, etc., do not appear to the uncontaminated exalted wisdom consciousnesses of Superiors.[2]
- When the three gods, humans, and hungry ghosts, see a thing, for instance, water, a plurality of mental awarenesses arise for which nectar, water, or pus appears in accordance with their own karma.[3]

[1]Cittamātrins maintain that physical objects are indeed built out of tiny particles—not physically divisible—but since they can be *mentally* divided into directions, they are not "partless."

[2]In meditative equipoise on emptiness, only emptiness appears to the exalted wisdom consciousness. The argument assumes that if something existed, surely it would appear to the highest type of consciousness.

[3]The idea is that since it is not possible for one thing to be three different substances, in the instance in which different types of beings experience different perceptions in the same place, there must not be external objects present. Rather, these beings must be experiencing only the

- When one person [147] is simultaneously seen by enemies and friends, the pleasant and unpleasant arise together.[1]
- Earth appears as water in accordance with whatever is imagined in yogic appearance, i.e., the appearances for a yogi or in yoga.[2]
- [The appearance of objects] is similar to dream [objects], etc.[3]

Since external objects do not exist, the abiding of all phenomena as the nature of the internal mind is true.[4]

Since objects are not [by their own nature established] as referents of conceptual consciousnesses, their appearance as that to non-conceptual consciousnesses is mistaken, whereby it is refuted that those [objects] and [consciousnesses] are different substantial entities.

When those objects, i.e., all phenomena, are seen as being without their own measure of subsistence as being the referents of conceptual consciousnesses, then, through knowing that even to a non-conceptual sense consciousness there are appearances [of objects] as existing by way of their own nature as referents of conceptual consciousnesses, one understands that those [appearances] are false. [148] Thereby, it comes to be refuted that the two, those [consciousnesses] and those objects, are different substantial entities.[5]

In accordance with the statement, "An apprehender without an apprehended object is not seen," it should be known how, when an object's establishment as an

---

projections of their own karma.

[1]It is argued that since one person can be seen as friend and enemy by two different observers, the appearance of that person must not be an external object.

[2]Yogis doing certain meditative practices validly see water where others would see earth. This, it is argued, must indicate that there are no external objects.

[3]It is argued that it is perfectly possible to have vivid experiences in the absence of external objects, as in the case of dreams and waking visions.

[4]If objects are not a different entity from mind, they must be one entity with mind (i.e., must arise simultaneously with mind). An object and the mind apprehending it are caused by the ripening of a single karmic predisposition.

[5]As mentioned earlier, the fact that objects are not naturally the basis of names (and, therefore, the referents of conceptual consciousnesses) also points to their being the same entity as consciousness.

external object is taken as one's object of negation, the subject's being a mind that realizes an external object must also be taken as the object of negation.[1]

Because it is the basis [of all faults], eliminating this [conception of a self of phenomena] reverses thorough conceptuality, i.e., the one hundred [eight conceptions of subject and object], etc.

Because it is the basis of all faults, when one eliminates the conception of a self of phenomena, it is said that one reverses thorough conceptuality, i.e., the one hundred eight conceptions of subject and object, twenty-two thorough obscurations, eleven assumptions of bad states, sixteen conceptions of self, etc.[2] [149]

True and False Aspectarians

The appearances as gross objects to operative consciousnesses is the basis of debate. True and False Aspectarians debate whether or not [those appearances] are true, whether or not they exist, and whether they are unpolluted or polluted by obscuration.

These appearances [of objects] as [gross] colors, shapes, etc., and continuums, etc., to operative consciousnesses is the basis of debate between the True Aspectarians and False Aspectarians. The mode of debate is that those two debate whether or not [the appearance of gross objects] is true in accordance with how it appears, whether or not it exists in accordance with that appearance, or whether or not that appearance is affected by pollution by ignorance.[3]

They do not [debate] whether [these appearances] are true or false [as do] Mādhyamikas and Cittamātrins, or [whether or not] they are things, etc.

Therefore, they do not debate whether or not [objects] exist truly or falsely as in the Mādhyamika-Cittamātra debate [150] or whether or not they are things, etc.

---

[1]It is not merely the case that there are no external objects; there are also no consciousnesses that apprehend external objects. Both of these are being negated.

[2]The twenty-two "thorough obscurations" is a special category of minor faults that are abandoned along with the obstructions to omniscience. For example, some Arhats (liberated beings) still do things like "jump like monkeys" due to previous conditioning, even though they are free of desire, ignorance, etc.

[3]They debate whether a patch of blue exists as a gross object as it appears (i.e., whether or not the perception of anything larger than a tiny particle is necessarily false).

Regarding True Aspectarians, there are three: Half-Eggists, Proponents of an Equal Number of Subjects and Objects, and Non-Pluralists.

When True Aspectarians are divided, there are three: Half-Eggists, Proponents of an Equal Number of Subjects and Objects, and Non-Pluralists.

Respectively, the Brahmin [Śaṃkarananda] asserts that apprehended object and apprehending subject [are different substantial entities] within being consciousness.

Respectively, [the Half-Eggist] the Brahmin Śaṃkarananda asserts that the two, apprehended objects and apprehending subjects that are the nature of consciousnesses, are different substantial entities in terms of the time of their establishment.[1] [151]

Śākyabuddhi asserts aspects equal in number to apprehended objects.

[The Proponent of an Equal Number of Subjects and Objects] Śākyabuddhi asserts that the aspects of the various apprehended objects and concordant types of consciousnesses arise simultaneously.[2]

The honorable Dharmakīrti asserts that the various [aspects are in the entity of] one consciousness.

[The Non-Pluralist] the honorable Dharmakīrti asserts that the aspects of consciousness to which the various [appearances] of the blue and yellow of a mottle, etc., appear are in the entity of one consciousness.

Regarding False Aspectarians, there are two; it is reputed[3] that there are those [False Aspectarians who assert that even] the Conqueror has the taints of dualistic appearance and those [who assert] that he does not, whereby they are renowned as Tainted and Untainted [False Aspectarians].

---

[1]"Half-eggists" are half like Sautrāntika, half like Cittamātra. They say that an object produces a subject, but that both are of the nature of mind. The meaning of this is unclear, but perhaps it is that a karmic seed produces the appearance of an object, and the object produces the subject in the sense of being one of its causes. In any case, they do not propound an equal number of subjects and objects like the first type of True Aspectarians.

[2]That is, there are as many consciousnesses as there are aspects. For instance, something that is part blue, part yellow, has two aspects and would be seen by two eye consciousnesses.

[3]*grags* is usually translated positively as "renowned," but here it is translated as "reputed" in accordance with Jamyang Shayba's disapproval of this position.

Regarding the False Aspectarians, there are two: Tainted False Aspectarians and Untainted False Aspectarians. It was reputed by earlier [Tibetan scholars] that Tainted False Aspectarians assert that even the Conqueror [Buddha] has the taints of dualistic appearance, and Untainted False Aspectarians assert that he does not have those. The word "reputed" [in the root text] appears to be a word indicating disapproval. What then are [the two types of False Aspectarians]? [152] In our own system, those who assert that the entity of the consciousness that has the apprehended object aspect is polluted by stains are Tainted False Aspectarians, and those who assert that, since stains are adventitious, the entity of the mind is not polluted even though the aspect of the consciousness is mistaken are regarded as Untainted [False Aspectarians].[1]

That the False Aspectarians [present] valid cognition and effects in which external objects are taken as the object is not correct. If external objects are established, how could they be Cittamātrins?

The translator Daktsang says that the two types of False Aspectarians assert a presentation of valid cognition and effects in which external objects are taken as the object [153] and as the object of comprehension. This is very mistaken. If they assert external objects, how could they be Cittamātrins? They must not [assert external objects].

If it is said that this is in terms of a conceptual consciousness, it would be similar for the True Aspectarians. [Therefore, the assertion] is mistaken.

If it is said that this is due to [external objects' being the object of comprehension] in terms of a conceptual consciousness that [mis]conceives external objects to exist, then there is no reason to apply this to only the False Aspectarians. It must be similar with the True Aspectarians. Therefore, this assertion is mistaken.

Saying that all phenomena are mind is a coarse incorrectness. There would be many faults, etc., such as that faults and good qualities and saṃsāra and nirvāṇa would be one.

---

[1]The Tainted False Aspectarians hold the unique position that the nature of the mind itself can be tainted by ignorance. All other Buddhists contend that all the latencies established by ignorance and the afflictions motivated by ignorance are adventitious and removable. It seems to them that if the mind could be stained, it would be difficult or impossible to remove the afflictions. Jamyang Shayba and Losang Gönchok acknowledge that some past Tibetan scholars have stated that there are Tainted False Aspectarians who think that even after becoming a Buddha, one can have mistaken appearances, but they obviously think that no one in India has ever really propounded this.

Moreover, Daktsang's saying that all phenomena are mind is also incorrect. It is the sign of a very coarse awareness that is the system of analysis of a fool. It is as follows: Then it [absurdly] follows that all faults and good qualities are one [154] because when all faults and good qualities appear to one consciousness, that one consciousness must be all faults and good qualities. If that is accepted, the two, saṃsāra and nirvāṇa, would [absurdly] be one. Furthermore, there are many faults such as that one would eat consciousness and drink consciousness.[1]

Mind-Only

What is the meaning of mind-only? The appearances to a human in a dream are not propounded to be the mind but are not [external objects] that are other than the mind and not it. In the same way those that appear and are renowned [in the world] are not substantial entities that are other than the mind.

Then if someone asks, "In your own system what is the meaning of the statement in sūtra that all phenomena are mind-only?" [we reply that] just as, for example, when a mountain, a home, etc., appear to a human while dreaming a dream, [155] one does not propound that the mountains, etc., that appear *are* the mind that perceives them, but they are also not external mountains, etc., that are not appearances of the mind. So, forms, sounds, etc., that appear and are renowned [in the world], are not the mind but they also are not substantial entities separate from the mind.

Mind-Basis-Of-All and Afflicted Mentality

The [mind-]basis-of-all is a non-defiled and neutral mind. It is subtle, hidden, and that which possesses all seeds.

Regarding the [mind-] basis-of-all, its entity is non-defiled, and it is neither virtuous nor non-virtuous. Therefore, it is non-defiled and neutral. [156] It is a

---

[1]Whether or not Daktsang actually held such a position, this is a possible misunderstanding of the Cittamātra rejection of external objects. To say that subject and object are one entity is not to say that they are the same. They have the same cause, and they occur simultaneously, but they are not equivalent.

mind, but its mode of perception is difficult to ascertain, and it is difficultd by those of weak mind to recognize it. Therefore, it is subtle and hidden. It serves as the basis of all seeds that are deposited by virtue, etc.[1]

The afflicted mind possesses the quality [of being a mind that], observing that [mind-basis-of-all], thinks "I."

The afflicted mind is an awareness possessing many qualifications that, having observed that [mind-] basis-of-all, thinks "I" and "mine."

The followers of the Brothers [Asaṅga] and Vasubandhu assert eight collections of consciousnesses.

The Cittamātra Followers of Asaṅga and his brother [Vasubandhu] assert eight collections of consciousnesses, that is to say, the six operative consciousnesses, the mind-basis-of-all, and the afflicted mind.

Because of not explaining [a mind-basis-of-all on suitable occasions] and because two conceptual consciousnesses do not [occur] simultaneously, the systems of the Followers of Dharmakīrti's Seven Treatises [on Valid Cognition] assert six collections of consciousnesses, not eight.

The Cittamātra followers of Dignāga's *Compendium of Valid Cognition* and Dharmakīrti's Seven Treatises on Valid Cognition assert just six collections of consciousnesses and not eight collections of consciousnesses because:

- [Dignāga and Dharmakīrti] did *not* explain [that there are more than six types of consciousness] on many occasions when they should have spoken if they did assert a mind-basis-of-all. [157]
- [Dharmakīrti] said that two conceptual consciousnesses do not arise simultaneously.[2]
- [Dharmakīrti] explained that conceptual consciousnesses are understood to operate serially.

---

[1]Only the Cittamātrins Following Scripture and the Yogācāra-Svātantrika-Mādhyamikas propound the existence of this type of consciousness. It is really nothing other than a continuously existing basis for the infusion of karmic seeds. It must itself be neutral and undefiled in order to hold the seeds.

[2]Those who assert an afflicted mentality say that it continuously operates; hence, two mental consciousnesses would exist simultaneously whenever the mental consciousness thought about something. Dharmakīrti denies that there can be more than one mental consciousness at a time.

The Path

Because one needs skill in methods of cultivating mental contemplation and objects of observation, [one must become skilled in] the seven actual mental contemplations and the other forty—the four objects of observation, and the thirty-two signs, etc.

Because one must become skilled in the methods of cultivating the path (the places, times, behavior, etc.), how to apply the mind, and the [process of] objects of observation that are antidotes, let us explain them. [158]

Those actual mental contemplations must be posited from the point of having attained pliancy. Regarding actual mental contemplations for achieving special insight through having achieved and made firm the calm abiding [that comes after] the nine abidings of mind, there are the seven mental contemplations:[1]

1 the mental contemplation of individual knowledge of the character
2 the mental contemplation that is arisen from belief
3 the mental contemplation of thorough isolation
4 the mental contemplation of either withdrawal or joy
5 the mental contemplation of analysis
6 the mental contemplation of final training
7 the mental contemplation of the fruit of final training

In detail, there are the forty [mental contemplations] ranging from [the mental contemplation] of phenomena to the mental contemplation serving all, and four objects of observation or signs—object of observation, cause, object of abandonment, [159] and antidote. When those are worked out in detail, there are the thirty-two signs: the signs of one's own mind, etc.

When these are condensed there are the two[, objects of observation and signs,] or the nine [abidings of] mind, [the eight antidotes that are the means of] abandoning the five [faults], etc.

When condensed, there are the two—the basic objects of observation and signs—or the nine abidings of mind: [2]

1 setting the mind inside
2 continuous setting

---

[1]The seven mental contemplations are how one achieves an actual absorption, ranging from the first concentration to the meditative absorption of the Peak of Saṃsāra.

[2]These are nine stages of attaining tranquil abiding (*śamatha*), i.e., mental stabilization.

3 resetting
4 close setting
5 disciplining
6 pacifying
7 thorough pacifying
8 making one-pointed
9 setting in equipoise

And the five faults:

1 laziness
2 forgetting the precept
3 laxity and excitement
4 non-application
5 [over-] application

Also, there are the eight applications [i.e., antidotes] that are the means of abandoning those [faults]; [160] the four mental engagements; the six powers; the four objects of observation, etc. One should become skilled in these.

The twelve [sets of good qualities] and the four [features], etc., are the features of the grounds and perfections.

As will be explained regarding each ground, there is a significant increase of the number of the twelve sets of one hundred good qualities. Also, each of the perfections has the qualities of the four features:

1 vanquishing of the discordant type
2 fulfilling the wishes of others
3 ripening sentient beings
4 being conjoined with non-conceptual exalted wisdom, etc.[1]

[On the Buddha ground] there are the twelve sets of one hundred [good qualities] when the eye, etc., are transformed; the four and five exalted Bodies [of a Buddha], etc., and the ten and two exalted activities, etc.

---

[1]The "good qualities" are twelve types of extraordinary abilities such as the capacity to visit simultaneously many "Buddha-lands," know many eons past and future, teach many people in an instant, and emanate many bodies. First-ground Bodhisattvas (those who have just realized emptiness for the first time) have these qualities one hundred-fold (i.e., they can visit one hundred Buddha lands, emanate one hundred bodies, etc.). Second-ground Bodhisattvas have them one thousand-fold, third-ground Bodhisattvas have them one hundred thousand-fold, and so on.

When on the Buddha ground the eye, etc., are transformed, [161] one attains one thousand two hundred good qualities, i.e., twelve sets of one hundred regarding each.[1] There are the three Bodies:[2]

1 Nature Body
2 Enjoyment Body
3 Emanation Body

[Adding] the Wisdom Truth Body to those makes four Bodies. Also, there are the five Bodies:

1 Truth Body
2 Enjoyment Body
3 Artisan Emanation Body
4 Construction Emanation Body
5 Emanation Body of Great Enlightenment[3]

[Also, on the Buddha ground there are the] five exalted wisdoms:

1 mirror-like exalted wisdom
2 exalted wisdom of equality
3 exalted wisdom of individual realization
4 exalted wisdom of achieving activities
5 exalted wisdom of the expanse of reality[4]

---

[1]At Buddhahood, all the parts of one's body become omniscient.

[2]The Emanation Body is a Buddha's appearance in ordinary form such as Śākyamuni, or as an object (for this, see the next note). The Enjoyment Body is a special Form Body with which a Buddha teaches in a pure land. The tantric deities are this sort of form. The Truth Body is a Buddha's omniscient consciousness, and it can be further distinguished into a Wisdom Body which is the continuous exalted wisdom of meditative equipoise, and the Nature Body, which is its emptiness of obstructions to liberation and omniscience.

[3]The last three are types of emanation bodies. The *Artisan* Body is the Buddha's appearing as musicians, sculptors etc. The *Birth* or *Construction* Body occurs when the Buddha is born as the host in heavens of the Form and Formless Realms, teaching the gods there. The *Great Enlightenment* occurs when the Buddha appears as a Dharma teacher, e.g., as when he manifested as Śākyamuni.

[4]Wisdom is wisdom, but it can be described in at least these five ways: it accurately reflects reality, like a mirror; it sees all things as equally devoid of inherent existence, and so forth. The eight consciousnesses transform into these wisdoms. The mind-basis-of-all transforms into the mirror-

According to Maitreya's *Ornament for the Mahāyāna Sūtras* there are ten exalted activities. When condensed, there are the two [exalted activities] of setting [sentient beings] in high status and in definite goodness. They assert the twenty-seven exalted activities, etc., that are set forth in Maitreya's *Ornament for Clear Realization.* [162]

[Know] the explanations in the two *Differentiations,* [Maitreya's] *Ornament for the Mahāyāna Sūtras,* the *Sūtra Unraveling the Thought,* etc.

Regarding the bases, paths, etc., that are not explained here, [Jamyang Shayba] says that one should know the explanations in Maitreya's *Discrimination of Phenomena and the Nature of Phenomena,* his *Discrimination of the Middle and the Extremes,* his *Ornament for the Mahāyāna Sūtras,* the *Sūtra Unraveling the Thought,* and the root text and commentary to Asaṅga's *Summary of the Mahāyāna,* etc.

This has been the tenth chapter, the commentary on the section of the Proponents of Cognition (Vijñaptika), those who prove the selflessness of phenomena through refuting external objects, etc., the coarse self of phenomena.[1]

---

like wisdom; the afflicted mentality into the wisdom of equality; the mental consciousness into the wisdom of individual realization; and the five sense consciousnesses into the wisdom of achieving activities.

[1]This summation is from a Mādhyamika viewpoint, since the Cittamātrins would not agree that the misconception of self they refute is only a coarse misconception.

Introduction to the Mādhyamika Schools

[Next, Jamyang Shayba sets forth his] explanation of the fourth system of [Buddhist] proponents of tenets, the Mādhyamika school.

Because they propound a middle free from the extremes, and because they propound non-nature, they are called Mādhyamikas (Proponents of the Middle) and Proponents of Non-Nature.

They are called Mādhyamikas (Proponents of the Middle) [because] they propound a middle that is free from the extremes of permanence and annihilation,[1] [163] and Proponents of Non-Nature [because] they assert from the depths that there is no nature in the sense of true establishment.[2]

The divisions are two: the Prāsaṅgika school (Consequence school) and the Svātantrika school (Autonomy school). Others have merely the name.

The divisions are definitely only two: the Prāsaṅgika school (Consequence school) and the Svātantrika school (Autonomy school). Those other than these who claim to be Mādhyamikas, apart from the mere name, do not fit the meaning.[3]

---

[1]For the Mādhyamika schools, the extreme of permanence is the concept that phenomena ultimately exist, and the extreme of annihilation is that phenomena do not exist at all—even conventionally.

[2]Saying "all phenomena are natureless" does not mean that phenomena do not have any kind of nature whatsoever. Rather, phenomena lack the "nature" that innate ignorance assumes they have and imputes to them. It is a deliberately provocative statement, designed to induce analysis by meditators.

[3]All Buddhist tenet systems claim to be proponents of the middle free from the two extremes. To take this as their name is to assert that they are the *true* middle way school.

Both are Mādhyamikas in that they similarly assert, as the middle, dependently arisen phenomena, refuting the extreme of non-existence wherein [phenomena] do not exist even conventionally, and the extreme of permanence wherein things are truly [established].

Both the Prāsaṅgika school and the Svātantrika school[1] [164] are similar in that, through refuting the extreme of non-existence in which [phenomena] do not exist even conventionally and the extreme of permanence that is the true establishment of things or substantial existence, they assert, as the Mādhyamika, phenomena that are dependent-arisings like magicians' illusions.[2] Therefore, both must be asserted to be Mādhyamikas, for the Svātantrika school also knows how to identify by way of valid cognition a middle that is free from the extremes of annihilation and permanence such as cannot be figured out by the Cittamātra school and below. Thus, because they are not other than our own four schools of tenets, they must not be the other three.

The system that is free from all subtle extremes is the Prāsaṅgika.

However, that which is free from all subtle extremes of permanence and annihilation is only the system of the Prāsaṅgika school.

Regarding chronology, four hundred years after the Chief of the Subduers [Buddha, passed away], Nāgārjuna brought the Mahāyāna, commenting on it as Mādhyamika and opening the way. [165]

The general chronology of Mahāyāna tenets is that they arose in the year the Teacher displayed[3] the mode of becoming a Buddha.[4] Having vanished in the intervening period, the way that it spread again in India is that after four hundred years had passed from when the Chief of the Subduers taught, the glorious protector Nāgārjuna brought the word of the Mahāyāna—the Perfection of

[1]Although the terms *prāsaṅga* and *svātantra* were used in India, adapting them to apply to discrete schools of thought was a Tibetan innovation.

[2]A magician's illusion is a standard example for something that exists, but not in the way it appears. It does not indicate complete non-existence. A reflection of a face in a mirror may not be a face, but it is a reflection of a face.

[3]When and where Śākyamuni became a Buddha is a point of controversy. The Hīnayāna traditions hold that Siddhārtha, not yet a Buddha, became enlightened during one night in India. The Mahāyāna traditions say that Śākyamuni became Buddha in a highest pure land and thereafter merely "displayed" how to become a Buddha.

[4]This traditional view has Buddha teaching the Mahāyāna secretly to suitable trainees at the same time he taught the Hīnayāna openly.

Wisdom sūtras, etc.—from the country of the Nāgas,[1] etc., commenting on them in the manner of Mādhyamika and opening the chariot way.[2]

Nine hundred years [after Buddha,] Asaṅga opened the way for Cittamātra.

When nine hundred years had passed after the Teacher, the master Superior Asaṅga opened the way for Cittamātra. [166] It appears that there are two ways of counting nine hundred years. It is renowned that in India one *bgrod pa* is regarded as a year; thus, it is permissible to apply this to the year of his birth. When done by coarse calculation, it fits together with the time of his opening the way and spreading it widely.

Buddhapālita commented on the *Treatise on the Middle Way* by way of consequences.[3]

After that, the master Buddhapālita made a vast commentary on Nāgārjuna's *Treatise on the Middle Way*,[4] commenting on the reasoning of [Nāgārjuna's] text in the manner of flinging consequences[5] at the opponent, [167] thus opening the chariot way of Prāsaṅgika-Mādhyamika.[6] As Dzongkaba's *Essence of Eloquence* says:

---

[1]Nāgārjuna is said to have traveled to the underwater land of the Nāgas, who are part-serpent beings who were entrusted with the Perfection of Wisdom sūtras.

[2]Nāgārjuna and his disciple Āryadeva, considered to be "model Mādhyamikas," are seen as reliable by all later Mādhyamikas, who are considered to be "partisan Mādhyamikas."

[3]Tibetan scholars later named Bhāvaviveka's branch Sautrāntika-Svātantrika-Mādhyamika, the Sūtra Autonomy Middle Way school, and Śantarakṣita's branch Yogācāra-Svātantrika-Mādhyamika, the Yogic Deed Autonomy Middle Way school.

[4]Nāgārjuna's *Treatise on the Middle* (also called *Treatise on the Middle Way*) is the most important Mādhyamika school text. Tibetans studied it through analyzing the interaction among three Indian commentaries on it written by Buddhapālita, Bhāvaviveka, and Candrakīrti; Tibetans wrote treatises analyzing those Indian commentaries. In brief, Bhāvaviveka criticized Buddhapālita, who was in turn defended by Candrakīrti. This interaction also serves as the basis for the Tibetan tradition of distinguishing two divisions of Mādhyamika schools: the Svātantrika school (following Bhāvaviveka) and the Prāsaṅgika school (following Buddhapālita and Candrakīrti).

[5]The Prāsaṅgika school gets its name from its tenet that consequences alone can be sufficient to overcome wrong views and to generate the correct view in an opponent. Restating the idea as a syllogism is not always necessary to produce an insight in another.

[6]Jamyang Shayba takes the unusual position that Buddhapālita is the founder of Prāsaṅgika. Most other scholars identify Candrakīrti as the founder of the Prāsaṅgika school. In any event, both Buddhapālita and Candrakīrti are seen as presenting a view of emptiness different from Bhāvaviveka.

Seeing the path taught by Buddhapālita,
Who would not take as chief the good system of Nāgārjuna?

It is clear that he made a system in which one is able to generate an inference through a mere consequence. He vastly set forth (1) the mode of refuting other systems through taking establishment by way of one's own entity as the object of negation and (2) the mode of providing his own system.

Also, the self of persons that is to be refuted is taken as establishment by way of [the object's] own entity. He established through the example of [the image] of a deity the teaching of phenomena by way of just what is renowned [to the world]. [168]. Also, he took the conception of true existence as an afflictive [obstruction].[1] Also, through the example of the birth of a child and planting a tree, he refuted otherness that is established by its own character, etc.[2] Thus, he clarified the distinguishing features of the Prāsaṅgikas.[3]

Bhāvaviveka apprehended faults [in that commentary] and opened the way for the Svātantrika-Mādhyamika school.

However, because most reasons meet back to the object of negation,[4] they could not be posited for the mind of Bhāvyakara,[5] that is, the master Bhāvaviveka, due to which he held some fallacies that derive from his own [stance] of autonomy and opened the chariot way of Svātantrika-Mādhyamika.

---

[1]This is unique to Prāsaṅgika, because for Svātantrika, the conception of true existence is an obstruction to omniscience, not an afflictive obstruction, i.e., not an obstruction to liberation.

[2]Buddhapālita refuted inherently existent production from other by pointing out that although an embryo is different from a child, and a seed from a tree, if they were inherently other they would be completely unrelated, and therefore, one could not be the cause of the other. Therefore, there is no inherently existent production from other.

[3]Losang Gönchok is defending Jamyang Shayba's position that Buddhapālita, and not Candrakīrti, founded the Prāsaṅgika school. Neither Jamyang Shayba nor Losang Gönchok is saying Buddhapālita and Candrakīrti have different views of emptiness.

[4]Svātantrikas and Prāsaṅgikas identify differently the object of negation, i.e., the false conception of self that is to be eliminated. Bhāvaviveka's school makes a distinction between whether things inherently exist ultimately or conventionally. It says that conventionally, phenomena do inherently exist, whereas ultimately, they do not. For Prāsaṅgika, phenomena are not even conventionally inherently existent.

[5]*legs ldan 'byed.* The name Jamyang Shayba uses in his root text is Bhavya. He is also known as Bhāvyakara. Western writers tend to use the name Bhāvaviveka most frequently.

Candrakīrti refuted Bhāvaviveka and established [Nāgārjuna's system] as unshared [with the Svātantrika school].

Regarding this, the great master Candrakīrti showed that those faults [Bhāvaviveka attributed] did not apply to [Buddhapālita], and having refuted well with many scriptures and reasonings the mode of autonomous syllogisms, [169] own character, etc., of the system of Bhāvaviveka, he established with clear terminology and vast logic, in accordance with the explanation by Buddhapālita, that this is the excellent tenet system that must be held as unshared with other Mādhyamikas and is the complete thought of the Conqueror [Buddha].

In brief, the honorable Candrakīrti clearly used the language, "This system is unique,"[1] and through making vast refutations [of other systems] and proofs [of his own system], and through seeing as literal the affixing of the qualification "ultimate" [by Bhāvaviveka] to the object of negation, Candrakīrti thought that this was clearly explained formerly [by Buddhapālita].[2] [170]. One should hold that seeking ascertainment that Buddhapālita opened the way of the Prāsaṅgika chariot is the actual meaning.

After that, Śantarakṣita opened the way for the second Svātantrika school [i.e., the Yogācāra-Svātantrika-Mādhyamika school].

After that, the master Śantarakṣita opened the chariot way of the second Svātantrika school, the Yogācāra-Svātantrika-Mādhyamika (Yogic Autonomy Middle Way) school. Bhāvaviveka opened the chariot way of Sautrāntika-Mādhyamika, along with Svātantrika in general. It is not necessary that it be opened separately.

---

[1]Candrakīrti's *Entrance to (Nāgārjuna's) "Treatise on the Middle Way."* Tibetan Gelukba authors writing from the fifteenth century on make clear distinctions between a Svātantrika- Mādhyamika school and a Prāsaṅgika-Mādhyamika school. They emphasize a difference between the two schools in terms of the view of emptiness. However, no Indian Mādhyamika author seems to have even noticed Candrakīrti's claim of uniqueness in terms of a view of emptiness, much less refuted it. For example, Dzongkaba writes in the *Essence of Eloquence* that Bhāvaviveka's commentator Avalokitavrata considered Bhāvaviveka and Buddhapālita as similar in terms of phenomena existing conventionally as only like illusions, without an ultimately inherent nature, even though—in Dzongkaba's view—they actually did differ about these points.

[2]Bhāvaviveka said, "Ultimately, the internal sources are not produced from self because of existing." For the debate over whether he should have said "ultimately," see Hopkins, *Meditation*, 499–530.

Refutation of Error In General

Those who have fallen to these extremes—propounding not taking anything [to mind], other-emptiness, or a permanent self, not asserting the two truths, [claiming that the Prāsaṅgikas have] no system, or that there is nothing established by valid cognition, etc.—although they claim to be Mādhyamikas, are not. [171]

Here in Tibet, the Chinese abbot Hashang and his many Tibetan followers propounded that all conventionalities do not exist at all, like the horns of a rabbit.[1]

The Jonangba, Dölboba Shayrap Gyeltsen, together with his followers said that an other-emptiness is best through [holding] that thoroughly established natures are empty in the manner of being neither other-powered natures nor imputational natures and propounded that a permanent self exists.[2]

Paṇchen Śākya Chokden propounded that conventionalities are not established by valid cognition and that ultimates are truly existent and substantially existent in the sense of being independent.[3]

---

[1]This hashang (*hva shang*, abbot) was named "Mahāyāna," and really ought to be referred to as Abbot Mahāyāna. He represented the Ch'an school in the ninth-century debate at Samye in Tibet. Kamalaśīla, a disciple of Śantarakṣita (identified with the Yogācāra-Svātantrika-Mādhyamika school), defended the view of gradual enlightenment against Abbot Mahāyāna, who held the view of sudden enlightenment. The Tibetan tradition holds that Kamalaśīla won. Hashang is famous for arguing that in meditation, one should not take anything at all to mind (whereas Prāsaṅgikas hold that one must directly oppose one's misconceptions in meditation in order to overcome them). Here, the commentary of Losang Gönchok does not even mention this point, which Jamyang Shayba makes in the root verse, but rather makes Hashang out to be a Nihilist.

[2]Gelukbas accuse Dölboba Shayrap Gyeltsen of asserting a permanent self. Hopkins concludes that, based on Dölboba's reading of sūtras on the *Tathāgatagarbha* (matrix-of-one-gone-thus), Maitreya's *Sublime Continuum of the Mahāyāna,* and the *Kālacakra Tantra,* Dölboba asserts that the matrix-of-one-gone-thus is endowed with Buddha qualities "in the sense that these *ultimate* qualities presently reside in sentient beings' continuums, but that sentient beings are not Buddhas since they have yet to develop a Buddha's compounded qualities." Hopkins, *Maps of the Profound,* commentary accompanying the current stanza. For a treatment of Dölboba's views on this subject, see Hopkins, *Reflections on Reality,* chapters 16–17d.

[3]This fifteenth-century author was thinking that conventionalities are not established by valid cognition because they are not found under analysis, i.e., by a reasoning consciousness searching for the ultimate. When one ponders whether a table inherently exists, one searches for an independent (or substantially existent or inherently existent or truly existent) table. He was also thinking that since this ultimate reasoning consciousness *finds* an ultimate truth, an emptiness,

A certain great bearer of the teaching asserted that ultimate truths are not objects of knowledge [i.e., they do not actually exist].[1]

Tangsakba,[2] etc., asserted that all phenomena do not exist conventionally. [172] Also, some of his followers said that the two truths exist conventionally but that that does not function as existing.

Jangdzön[3] and Ganggyamar, etc., assert that Mādhyamikas do not have their own position or own system.[4]

A certain [scholar] asserts that there is no establishment by valid cognition and asserts that both the name and the meaning of valid cognition is not correct.[5]

---

that emptiness truly exists, etc. But the Prāsaṅgika position will be that a reasoning consciousness does not really *"find"* an ultimate truth, since such was not being sought. Ultimate truth is a "non-finding."

[1]Some scholars thought that if an ultimate truth existed, it would have to be found by a reasoning consciousness, and thus, it would be able to bear analysis and, accordingly, would ultimately exist. Since that contradicts the root Mādhyamika tenet that nothing ultimate exists, the only conclusion open to them was that ultimate truths are not objects of knowledge. Gelukbas critique their argument by saying that their premise—that in order to exist, ultimate truths must be findable by reasoning consciousnesses—is incorrect. For a excellent discussion of contrasting views on whether or not existents are the basis of the division of the two truths, see Newland, *The Two Truths,* chapter 2.

[2]Hopkins says (in *Maps*) that this is likely to be the eleventh-century Gadamba *thang sag pa ye shes 'byung gnas.* See *Blue Annals,* 344ff.

[3]Hopkins (*Maps*) thinks this is *stod lung rgya dmar ba byang chub grags,* who flourished in the eleventh century.

[4]Nāgārjuna says in his *Refutation of Objections* "If I had any thesis, then I would have that fault. Because I have no thesis, I am only faultless." Taken literally and out of context, he does seems to be saying that he does not have any theses. Setting aside the obvious point that the statement itself is a thesis, examination of the context makes it clear that Nāgārjuna is talking about the ontological status of theses, not whether or not he has any at all. Understood this way, Nāgārjuna is saying: "If I had any [inherently existent] thesis, then I would have that fault [of contradicting my own thesis that nothing inherently exists]. Because I have no [inherently existent] thesis, I am only faultless." The Gelukba tradition explains that this means that there are no *inherently existent* theses, no theses the three modes of which are inherently established (which boils down to meaning that the subject and predicate of a thesis statement are not inherently established).

[5]The bases of this mistake can be found in statements the *King of Meditative Stabilizations Sūtra* (9.23), such as "The eye, ear, and nose [consciousnesses] are not valid cognitions" and Candrakīrti's statement in his *Entrance to Nāgārjuna's "Treatise on the Middle Way"* (6.31a), "in all respects worldly [consciousnesses] are not valid cognitions." The point of these passages is that the innate worldly awareness is not valid regarding *suchness,* i.e., emptiness; it is not that these consciousness are not valid cognizers regarding conventional truths. See Napper, *Dependent-*

The systems of all these [scholars] are boasted to be Mādhyamika, but because they fall to very unsuitable extremes of permanence and annihilation, they are not even a mere portion of Mādhyamika.

Refutation of Daktsang

Regarding refuting his accumulated mass of contradictions in detail, the translator Daktsang Shayrap Rinchen cast many unsuitable refutations at the foremost great being [Dzongkaba]. [173] Therefore, the Great Fifth [Dalai Lama, His Holiness Ngawang Losang Gyatso], the All-Seeing Lord of Conquerors, made a general exhortation in his *Sacred Word of Mañjuśrī* of the need for the followers of [Dzongkaba] to make a reply of refutation. Then the all-knowing [First Paṇchen Lama,] Paṇchen Losang Chögyi Gyeltsen, made a mere actual reply of refutation. Then this omniscient Lama [Jamyang Shayba] indicated that all of Daktsang's own system is nothing more than a mass of contradictions and made a detailed refutation of it, as follows.

In particular, [Daktsang] boasts that [his system] is the system of Candrakīrti. Thoroughly taking the Omniscient Ones as the foe, you have many contradictions and mistakes. [174]

In distinction from the former faulty proponents [of tenets, that is to say, those just mentioned], the translator Daktsang Shayrap claimed that his own [system] was the system of Candrakīrti and thoroughly took as foes those Indians and Tibetans who are asserted as having omniscience. In the positing of your system, you who hold [those Indians and Tibetans as foes], there are a great many such contradictions and mistakes.

[Asserting] knowledge of all without knowledge of the varieties is contradictory.

The omniscient Buddha is understood in accordance with the statement in Candrakīrti's *Entrance to (Nāgārjuna's) "Treatise on the Middle Way"*:

> The exalted wisdom of omniscience
> Is asserted as possessing the character of direct perception.

Saying that he does not realize even one of the varieties of phenomena:

Arising, chapter 4, for Dzongkaba's explanation of these passages.

- is contradictory with reasoning, due to establishment by a sign of the power of the fact that Buddhas have abandoned the obstructions to omniscience [175]
- is contradictory with scriptures such as [those that speak of] the ten powers
- is contradictory with your own words, since, having asserted omniscience, you say that [Buddha] knows none of the various phenomena

All three [contradictions] are complete.

The ten powers, etc., not existing is the bad system of the Kṣapaṇa and Mīmāṃsaka. That it is Mādhyamika is mistaken.

The explanation from your bad identification of words that the powers, etc., exist only in the perspective of the trainees, whereby Buddhas do not have mind, etc., is very mistaken. You are holding as the system of the Mādhyamikas that bad system of the Forders wherein it is asserted by the two, the Kṣapaṇa Jains and the Mīmāṃsaka Jaiminis, that when defilements are extinguished the mind must be obliterated.[1] [176]

That the ultimate is a dependent-arising and is able to set itself up is very contradictory.

The position that the ultimate that is the non-existence of true production is a dependent-arising and is able to set itself up in the Mādhyamika system is very contradictory. This is because whatever is able to set itself up does not depend on another and dependent-arisings depend on another.

Asserting actions and their effects and the utter non-existence of their fruition is contradictory.

The assertion of actions and their effects and the assertion that the fruitions of those [actions]—the fire and molten bronze of hell beings and the water, pus, ambrosia, etc., of others—are utterly non-existent like falling hairs in space are contradictory.[2]

---

[1]They are saying that there is no omniscience (and other powers) because the elimination of defilements results in a cessation of mind, and Daktsang's position is thought to be the same.

[2]This is perhaps the idea that the objects experienced by other types of beings such as hell beings and gods are not real, but just projections of their karma. In that case, the karma is not really coming to fruition.

[If] non-disintegrated actions produce effects, [causes and effects are] simultaneous. This is mistaken. [177]

If actions produce their effects without having disintegrated, then cause and effect would have to be simultaneous. Therefore, [this position] is mistaken.[1]

Actions not disintegrating for eons and the middle way are contradictory.

If actions exist without disintegrating for eons, you are propounding that caused phenomena are permanent, whereby you abide in a coarse extreme of permanence. This is contradictory with asserting a middle way that is free from extremes.[2]

Not asserting the profound and the vast in one's own system is contradictory with the middle way.

By saying, "Worldly conventionalities exist," it is being said that Prāsaṅgikas do not assert [these] in their own system. Then, since it is said in the Mother, [the Perfection of Wisdom sūtras, that all these things] from forms to exalted knowers [of all aspects exist] conventionally, if you do not assert all of those, you do not assert the profound and the vast in your own system. [178] Therefore, it is contradictory that this view of annihilation be the middle way that is free from extremes.[3]

That the unanalyzed is the basis of the division and that analyzed objects are the divisions [of the two truths] is contradictory.

It is easy to realize that it is contradictory that objects of knowledge that are not investigated and not analyzed are the basis of the division and [on the other hand that] analyzed objects are the divisions of the two truths.[4]

---

[1]If an action could produce an effect before it itself ceased, the effect would occur along with the action. Rather, an action in one moment produces an effect in some subsequent moment.

[2]Although karma may not have its fruition for a very long time, it is not the case that it exists without disintegrating. Like all impermanent phenomena, it disintegrates moment to moment, while causing another moment of similar type until its fruition. Even in Prāsaṅgika, which as we shall see talks about "disintegratedness" of actions as causing effects, the having-disintegrated of the action itself disintegrates moment to moment.

[3]Daktsang is being accused of not asserting the existence of worldly conventions, which is then taken to be a view of annihilation.

[4]If the two truths are things found upon analysis, and yet one of the two truths is that which is *not* found upon analysis, there is a contradiction.

That [something that is] not emptiness is a path of liberation and that two doors to peace do not exist is contradictory.

It is contradictory to assert that the awareness realizing the voidness of [conceptual] elaborations, which is *not* emptiness, is a path of liberation and that a second door to peace does not exist, because the awareness that realizes emptiness is the path of liberation.

It is contradictory that not meditating on anything is meditating on emptiness.

The position that not meditating on anything in the mind is meditation on emptiness [179] is contradictory with the high speech [of Buddha] and all pure quintessential instructions.

It is contradictory to assert production from other merely due to their being other and not to assert production from self merely due to asserting a self.

It is contradictory to assert that if there is production from what is merely conventionally other than oneself or one's continuum, one must assert production from other, and [on the other hand] not to assert that, since the mere I, for instance, is conventionally the self, production from that is production from self. Although it is said that if a cause and something are inherently established others, production from it is production from other, it is not said that production from *conventionally* established other is production from other.[1]

A mistake regarding the stages of the path is that: although one must train in all topics for many eons, [180] **at the time of the fruit one does not know even one of the varieties.**

It is contradictory that there are stages of progressing on the path in that although at the time of the cause one must train in all the topics of objects of knowledge for many eons, at the time of the effect—the time of Buddhahood—one does not know even one of the phenomena of the varieties.[2]

That [nirvāṇa] without remainder is utterly without form or knowledge that there are Four Bodies [of a Buddha] are contradictory.

---

[1]Part of what Nāgārjuna refutes is that something is produced from what is other than it, which Gelukbas understand as meaning something that is *inherently* other. If we are talking about things that are merely conventionally other and not *inherently* other, we are not talking about "production from other" as it was discussed by Nāgārjuna.

[2]Daktsang is accused of holding that Buddhas do not know the varieties of objects, i.e., that they are not really omniscient.

If there is no mind on the ground of a Buddha who has attained a non-abiding nirvāṇa, then form must have vanished. If form and consciousness are utterly non-existent, it is contradictory to assert the existence of the Four Bodies [of a Buddha]—the two Form Bodies and the Wisdom Truth Body, etc.[1]

Asserting direct perception and inference and not asserting valid cognition is contradictory. [181]

It is contradictory to assert direct perception and inferential valid cognition and not assert valid cognition.

That there are proofs but that there are no things that are validly established is contradictory.

It is easy to realize that it is contradictory that there are proofs but there are no things that are established by valid cognition, etc.[2]

That [Buddhas] attain the unshared powers and that complete Buddhas have suffering is contradictory.

Your assertion that a complete Buddha, who has attained the eighteen unshared qualities of a Buddha of the Perfection Vehicle, the six powers, etc., has material saṃsāra or very subtle true sufferings in his continuum is contradicted by your own words, whereby it is refuted.

It is contradictory that [the Cittamātrins, etc., both] prove and refute the referent object of the view of the transitory. [182]

If, through refuting the imputational natures that are only imputed by proponents of tenets, one harms the innate mode of apprehension, both would be [innate] views of the transitory since the innate mode of apprehension must exist in the artificial mode of apprehension. Thus, when the Cittamātra system, etc., refutes a permanent, single, self-powered self and proves the existence of a self that is established from its own side, one would have to say that they are proving and refuting the referent object of the view of the transitory, and this is contradictory.[3]

---

[1]If Daktsang regards nirvāṇa without remainder as being like the non-Prāsaṅgika understanding of the term, then absurdly there is no mind or body at the time of Buddhahood.

[2]In other words, what does valid cognition mean if even a valid proof does not qualify as one?

[3]A view of the transitory is to view the mind and body—the aggregates—as a real I and mine, as a self and, therefore, its referent object is that self. This seems to mean: If, when you get rid of a mere artificial idea about the self, you also harm the innate conception, it has to be the case that both conceptions are actually really innate. In that case, you could not really refute one concept and accept another, since they would be at equal levels of subtlety. The Cittamātra coarse

It is contradictory that the two views of the coarse and subtle selflessnesses have one object.

If those two bad views have one object with a concordant mode of apprehension, it is contradictory that coarse and subtle levels exist within the selflessness that is a non-existent in accordance with what is conceived by those. [183]

It is contradictory to assert that a mind-basis-of-all exists and to assert external objects.

If a mind-basis-of-all exists, then in accordance with what is set forth in sūtra, all beings and environments must be established as only the essence of those minds that are cases of the ripening of predispositions that are with the mind-basis-of-all. Therefore, the existence of external objects that are other than the mind would be contradictory.[1]

That ultimates are established by a reasoning [consciousness] and that meditative equipoise is without an object is contradictory.

Asserting that ultimate truths are established by a reasoning consciousness and also asserting that the exalted wisdom of meditative equipoise does not have an object is contradictory.

That [non-Superiors] do not have yogic direct perception and that selflessness is directly realized is contradictory.

Having propounded that yogic direct perception [184] does not exist for non-Superiors, it is contradictory to assert that for common beings there is actualization of that selflessness that is the conventional mode of subsistence from the point of view of directly realizing subtle impermanence.[2]

That there are three roots of saṃsāra and one door of peace is contradictory.

It is contradictory that, having asserted three roots of saṃsāra—(1) the gross root of saṃsāra, afflicted ignorance, (2) the subtle root of saṃsāra, the levels of the predispositions of ignorance, and (3) the very subtle root of saṃsāra, the predisposi-

---

conception of a self of persons is: a permanent, partless, independent person. The subtle concept is: a self-sufficient person. The first is artificial, the second, innate. It would be inappropriate that harming the artificial concept would also harm the innate conception.

[1]The very function of a mind-basis-of-all is to enable experience without the stimulus of external objects.

[2]If common beings—those who have not yet been liberated, i.e., become Arhats—do not have yogic direct perception, they could not have direct realization of selflessness and, therefore, could never become Arhats.

tions for the emission [of the essential constituent][1]—there exists no more than one door of peace. If different roots of saṃsāra exist, it is necessary also to identify different doors to peace that are the realizations of the objects of the mode of apprehension of those roots of saṃsāra as non-existent.[2] [185]

That those treatises that refute those [Outsiders] are the system of those [Outsiders] is contradictory.

It is contradictory to assert that those treatises, such as Dignāga's *Compendium of Valid Cognition*, Dharmakīrti's *Commentary on (Dignāga's) "Compendium of Valid Cognition,"* etc., that refute individually the systems of Outsiders [i.e., non-Buddhists] are [themselves] Outsider systems.

That conventionalities are devoid of correctness but that [all presentations] are feasible and suitable is contradictory.

Your explanation that all conventionalities are devoid of correctness is contradictory with your statement that all the presentations in the Mādhyamikas' own system are feasible and that the Four [Noble] Truths, etc., are suitable.

[Your assertion that] all bases do not exist is contradictory with [your assertion] of substratum and basis of imputation.

Your assertion that all bases are conventionally non-existent and devoid of any foundation [186] is contradictory with all [your other] explanations of substratum, basis of designation, illustration, etc., in other places.

Complete Buddhahood is contradictory with having to enter [from the Mantra] path of accumulation.

That the Buddhahood that is explained in the Perfection Vehicle is complete Buddhahood and your explanation that [such a Buddha] enters from the Mantra path of accumulation is contradictory.[3]

---

[1]This refers to the esoteric Highest Yoga Tantra practice.

[2]"Objects of the mode of apprehension" are the objects that are *conceived* to exist. In a conception of the person as substantially existent, the "object of the mode of apprehension" would be a substantially existent person. One would need to realize the non-existence of this supposedly substantially existent person. Jamyang Shayba is saying that if there were three different root causes of cyclic existence, then there would have to be three different realizations of each of those objects of modes of apprehension as non-existent.

[3]It is contradictory to say both that one can become a Buddha without entering the Mantra (tantric, i.e., esoteric Mahāyāna) vehicle and to assert that it is necessary to enter it. Gelukbas say that one must enter the Mantra vehicle to become a Buddha.

Having exhausted all obstructions to omniscience and having predispositions for emission is contradictory.

It is contradictory that a [Buddha] has exhausted all obstructions to omniscience but that there exist in his continuum predispositions for the emission of the constituent. That is because the term "the predispositions of emission" [or the desire that brings about emission] is set forth in Kulika Puṇḍarika's *Great Commentary on the "Kālacakra Tantra"* as ignorance, i.e., the predispositions and seeds of the afflictions that bring about emission of the essential constituent, [187] whereby if one has abandoned the obstructions to omniscience, one has necessarily also abandoned those.[1]

[Texts] entitled "unpredictable" and bad [essays on] meditation are the causes of your mistake.

There are many ways to apply the statements in the high speech about non-observation, not taking to mind, non-conceptuality, etc. [Daktsang] did not know the identifications [of these] in the quintessential instructions of the great charioteers predicted by the Conqueror. [Thus,] it appears that the many bad Tibetan books on meditation that accord with the system of the Chinese Hashang [i.e., abbot, whose name was Mahāyāna] and the meditations of [texts] titled "unpredictability," "transcending the mind," etc., and hoping for goods, respect, and fame, etc., are [Daktsang's] mistakes and the causes of his propounding mistakes.

In this way, regarding each of the twenty-seven contradictions, contradictions with scriptures, reasoning, and his own words appear very clearly, [188] but because it would be too much, I have not written more than a little bit.

---

[1]Sexual desire is something that a Buddha has eliminated.

The Svātantrika School

Because autonomous sign and own-powered sign have one [meaning], Svātantrikas (Autonomists) are those who state a sign proving a thesis through the three modes and the subjects being own-powered as appearing in common [to both parties].

Because "autonomous signs," signs that are established by way of their own power, and signs that are established from their own side have one import,[1] a Svātantrika (Autonomist) is someone who asserts that one is to state signs providing theses by way of the three modes—the presence of the reason in the subject, the forward entailment, and the reverse entailment[2]—and the subject [all] being established by way of their own power in accordance with a common appearance to the awarenesses of both parties.[3] [189]

---

[1]An autonomous sign is a reason in a syllogism or consequence in which the phenomena and the relationships between them exist inherently or autonomously. This is considered to be a principal difference between Svātantrikas and Prāsaṅgikas. The latter do not accept that anything exists in this way ultimately *or* conventionally.

[2]For instance, in the syllogism, "pot is impermanent because of being a product," the presence of the reason in the subject that "product," is a property of "pot"; the forward entailment is that whatever is a product is necessarily impermanent, and the reverse entailment is that whatever is not impermanent is necessarily not a product.

[3]The topic called "commonly appearing subjects" highlights the differences between the Svātantrika and Prāsaṅgika schools regarding what is certified as existing by a conventional valid consciousness such as an eye consciousness. For Prāsaṅgika, even though a conventional phenomenon appears to exist *inherently* to the valid consciousness that certifies the existence of it—such as with an eye consciousness looking at a pot—that eye consciousness is not competent to certify an object's mode of existence, and thus it cannot certify the inherent existence of the pot. Only a reasoning consciousness analyzing the ultimate is competent for that certification. Svātantrikas hold that a valid consciousness certifies whatever appears to it, and hence they think

There are the two: Sautrāntika-Svātantrika-Mādhyamika and Yogācāra-Svātantrika-Mādhyamika. The former establish external objects. The latter refute them.

When divided, there are two: Sautrāntika-Svātantrika-Mādhyamika and Yogācāra-Svātantrika-Mādhyamika. The former of these two prove that external objects exist, and the latter refutes [that external objects exist].

The Sautrāntika-Svātantrika-Mādhyamika School

Refutation of Cittamātra

They assert that the three natures are established by way of their own character. However, thinking of non-true existence, [Buddha] said, "This and that do not exist."

Both [Svātantrika schools] assert the three natures that are established by way of their own character.[1] However, thinking of the non-existence of a nature that has the character of true establishment, etc., [as presented] in the *Sūtra Unraveling the Thought,* [190] [Buddha] said [in the Perfection of Wisdom sūtras] that this and that do not exist.[2]

---

inherently existent objects exist conventionally. For this reason, the three modes of a syllogism do not have "common appearance" for Prāsaṅgikas and non-Prāsaṅgikas in the sense that the parties do not agree regarding the extent of certification for the validly cognizing consciousness that certifies the three modes. For more on the topic of commonly appearing subjects, see Hopkins, *Meditation,* 505–515.

[1]A controversy exists between the Cittamātra and Svātantrika schools about what Buddha meant in *Sūtra Unraveling the Thought* when he called imputational natures character-non-natures. For Cittamātra, the three natures are: (1) *other-powered natures,* impermanent phenomena themselves, produced by causes other than themselves; (2) *imputational natures,* natures that exist for thought but are not ultimately existent; and (3) *thoroughly established natures,* emptinesses.

[2]Svātantrikas agree with Cittamātrins that Buddha's statements in the Perfection of Wisdom sūtras that phenomena ranging from forms through omniscient consciousnesses are natureless was based on the three non-natures, which Losang Gönchok will soon distinguish. They understand those non-natures differently from Cittamātrins. Cittamātrins think that when Buddha taught there that phenomena lack true existence, he meant that imputational natures lack true existence; that other-powered natures lack ultimate production; and that truly established natures lack of a self of phenomena. Still, only imputational natures lack true existence. However, Svātantrikas

The bases of emptiness, the factors of superimposed true existence, and the emptiness of that are, respectively, other-powered natures, imputational natures and thoroughly established natures. This is [respectively] because of not being independent, because of being imputed, and because of being the mode of subsistence [of phenomena].

[Regarding the three natures in our own system,]

- Things, the bases of the emptiness of true establishment, are *other-powered natures* because they are not produced by way of their own power.
- The factor of true establishment that is imputed to those phenomena is the *imputational nature* [of phenomena] because of being a mere superimposition.
- Other-powered natures' emptiness of the true establishment that is imputed to them is the *thoroughly established nature* [of phenomena] because of being the final mode of subsistence [of those phenomena]. [191]

Those are the mere three natures. In accordance with [Jamyang Shayba's] commentary, when they are applied to the three *non-natures*, they are as follows:

- Other-powered natures are *production* non-natures. This is because functioning things—the bases of emptiness—are produced in dependence upon another, and are not produced ultimately by way of their own power.
- Imputational natures are *character* non-natures. This is because the factor of true establishment that is imputed to forms, etc., is a superimposition that does not accord with the actual fact and because it is ultimately without being that which has an imputational character.
- Thoroughly established natures are *ultimate* non-natures. This is because reality that is the emptiness of true establishment is thoroughly established without being a superimposition, is the mode of subsistence, is the object of an ultimate reasoning consciousness, and is without an entityness of true establishment. [192]

In the same way that all phenomena—other-powered phenomena, etc.—are ultimately without [their] imputed entityness, they are asserted to be non-produced and non-ceasing.

---

deny that anything has true existence.

The collectors [of Mahāyāna and Hīnayāna scriptures] are not the same [because Hīnayānists] do not realize [the meditative stabilizations and] meanings of the Mahāyāna. Because there is [a purpose for the Mahāyāna scriptures being set forth separately,] the selflessness of phenomena was not taught in the Hīnayāna sūtras.

Regarding Sautrāntika-Svātantrika-Mādhyamika, because the collectors of the word of the Mahāyāna and Hīnayāna are not the same[1] and because there are meditative stabilizations and profound meanings of the Mahāyāna even the names of which are not realized, that is to say, cannot be realized, by Hīnayānists,[2] the selflessness of phenomena is not taught in the Hīnayāna sūtras.[3] [193] However, Haribhadra asserts that the Perfection of Wisdom sūtras were collected by Ananda.[4]

Just as the fear [generated upon misapprehending] a coiled rope as a *snake* is eliminated by an awareness that apprehends it as a *vine*, so by realizing the selflessness [of the person] one destroys obscuration, [even though the selflessness of the person] is not the [final] mode of subsistence.

When fear is generated through misapprehending a coiled rope as a snake, through generating an awareness that apprehends [it] as a *vine*, that fear is eliminated even though it is not shown to be a *rope*. Just so, when Hearers overcome the afflictions—obscuration, etc.—through realizing the selflessness of persons, that is sufficient [for them to be released from cyclic existence]. They do not need to realize emptiness, the mode of subsistence.[5]

---

[1]The collectors of the Hīnayāna were Upāli, Kāshyapa, and Ānanda; the collectors of the Mahāyāna were Maitreya, Mañjughoṣa, and Vajrapāūi.

[2]For instance, the three pure Bodhisattva grounds, whereby Bodhisattvas remove the obstructions to omniscience, were not taught to Hearers.

[3]The selflessness of phenomena for Svātantrika in general is the emptiness of true existence. (For the Yogācāra-Svātantrikas, the emptiness of a difference in entity of subject and object is also a kind of selflessness of phenomena, albeit one that is not as subtle.) Svātantrikas say that Hearers can be liberated by realizing just the selflessness of persons, i.e., realizing that the person is not self-sufficiently substantially existent. (Prāsaṅgikas, as we shall see, think that all persons attain liberation the same way, by realizing the emptiness of inherent existence of all things.)

[4]Ananda was the Buddha's personal attendant. The tradition maintains that Ananda reliably remembered all of the Buddha's teachings and recited them at a council held after the Buddha's *parinirvāṇa*. This is an assertion that the Mahāyāna scriptures were not just a separate transmission from the absolutely public teachings but were originally part of the scriptures transmitted by Ananda.

[5]If one sees a rope but thinks it is a snake, one will be afraid, whereas if one thinks it is vine one will not be afraid. By analogy, as long as we are ignorant about the self (mistaking a rope for a

[Buddha] said that ultimately external objects do not exist. Saying that solely the mind is the [194] abode, body, etc., refers to the aspects [of those being generated in consciousness].

[Buddha] said in sūtra that external objects do not exist *ultimately,* but he did not say that external objects do not exist in general. Also, the statement that solely the mind is the abode, body, resources, etc., refers to the dawning of the aspects of those [in consciousness].[1]

Because the term "mind-only" refutes an agent, the non-existence of the apprehended is not the meaning of the sūtra.

Therefore, because the term "only" in the statement, "All phenomena are mind-only," refutes that a permanent self is the agent, Sautrāntika-Svātantrika-Mādhyamikas assert that it is not the meaning of any sūtra that external objects, the apprehended, do not exist.[2]

Sense consciousnesses possess the aspect [of the object]. The apprehended and the apprehender are cause and effect; [thus, they are established] in sequentially.

The sense consciousnesses [195] possess the aspect of the object. Since, for instance, the blue that is apprehended and the eye consciousness apprehending blue are cause and effect, Sautrāntika-Svātantrika-Mādhyamikas assert that they are established in sequentially.[3]

An aggregation of separate [phenomena]—an army, etc.—are imputedly existent. [Individual particles and] a composite of particles of concordant type

---

snake), we will continue to have attachment and aversion. By eliminating a false view of self that empowers attachment, pride, jealousy, etc., Hearers can overcome those afflictions even though they do not understand the final nature of phenomena (because they still "mistake the rope for a vine").

[1]That statement does not mean that the physical reality around us is actually mind; it means that they are known to exist by their *appearance* to mind.

[2]Sautrāntika-Svātantrika-Mādhyamikas holds that when Buddha said phenomena were mind-only, he was refuting that the agent who performs actions and experiences their effects is other than mind. He never meant that external objects do not exist.

[3]When an eye consciousness knows an apple, what happens is that the apple that exists in moment A causes the eye consciousness to take on its shape and color, its "aspect," in moment B. That is, objects cause consciousnesses, and a cause always precedes its effect.

are substantially existent. Even individual [particles] are suitable as the observed object condition.

[The Cittamātra school also says external objects do not exist because subtle particles could not be noticed by sense consciousnesses, and their aggregation does not substantially exist. Sautrāntika-Svātantrika-Mādhyamikas agree that subtle particles are too subtle to be noticed and also agree with Cittamātrins'] assertion that the aggregation of *discordant* types of particles of earth or many different bases, such as an army or a forest, is *imputedly* existent [and thus not suitable to appear to a sense consciousness]. However, a composite of *concordant* types of particles in one base, such as a pot, is a *substantial* existent. [Bhāvaviveka] asserts that when one sees coarse forms, individual tiny particles in the collections of those forms are suitable to be the observed object condition of that sense consciousness.[1] [196]

If external objects did not exist, there would be no production of the appearance of a double moon in dependence on a single moon. That would be deprecation.

[The Cittamātra school also says that all appearances of external objects are false, just as with the appearance of one moon as two to a wrong sense consciousness. Sautrāntika-Svātantrika-Mādhyamikas counter by holding that] the perception of two moons appearing, etc., must exist in dependence upon a single moon existing as the basis of the appearance.[2] Because of this, if external objects did not exist, those apprehenders (i.e., consciousnesses) would not be produced. Therefore, they assert that if someone claims that external objects do not exist, what is directly perceived would necessarily be deprecated.

Because there is no appearance of an object, there is no self-consciousness [experiencing] an object-possessor.

Without the dawning of the appearance of an object, the dawning of a mode of appearance of a separate consciousness that is an object-possessor does not occur; [therefore,] self-consciousnesses for which there is such a dawning [of appearance through perceiving only the consciousness] do not exist.[3]

---

[1]Although it is true that single tiny particles are too small to be causes of consciousness, aggregations of concordant types are suitable; on that basis, Bhāvaviveka will say that the external particles are causes of consciousness.

[2]The mere fact that one can suffer from an optical illusion or a problem with the eyes does not establish that there are no external objects; indeed, the perception of a double moon could not occur without an external object—a real single moon—being its basis.

[3]If there are no external objects, consciousness and object are already one entity. The idea of self-consciousness is that in addition to the consciousness that observes its object there is another

The Sautrāntika-Svātantrika-Mādhyamika's Own System

IDENTIFICATION OF THE OBJECT OF NEGATION

If something were truly established, it would have to exist for the perspective of a reasoning [consciousness] because [that which is sought] is true establishment. [197]

If something were truly established, it would have to be existent in the perspective of a reasoning consciousness analyzing the ultimate because that reasoning consciousness investigates of whether or not something is truly established; what it is seeking is true establishment.[1]

That which exists for that [reasoning consciousness] is not necessarily truly established, like reality. Although objects are found by a reasoning consciousness, what is able to bear analysis by that [consciousness] must truly be truly established because [that reasoning consciousness] analyzes for true establishment. Bearing analysis by a reasoning consciousness is true establishment, the object of negation here.

However, if something exists in the perspective of a reasoning consciousness, it need not be truly established, like the reality that is found by that [consciousness] without being truly established. For that reason, although objects found by a reasoning consciousness exist, [198] if something is able to bear analysis by that [reasoning consciousness], it would have to be truly established.[2]

---

consciousness that observes the consciousness, but that is obviously unnecessary here.

[1]If something "truly existed" it would have to be findable when sought by a reasoning consciousness. There are two ways one conceives phenomena to be truly established. Jamyang Shayba says we might or might not have an "artificial" conception (one taught) that conceives that phenomena are able to bear analysis by a rational consciousness analyzing the ultimate. But we definitely have an "innate" conception that phenomena have a mode of abiding not established as posited by the force of conventional valid cognition; in other words, they seem to exist from their own side without having to be posited this way. *Great Exposition of Tenets,* Gomang 501.22–502.2.

[2]A wisdom consciousness analyzing the ultimate searches for a truly established object. It does not find it, but instead "finds" the absence of true establishment, i.e., emptiness. This does not mean that emptiness *itself* truly exists, for emptiness itself is not able to bear analysis by a reasoning consciousness when it is analyzed to determine if it is truly established.

Reasonings Refuting the Object of Negation

Because it is easy [to prove] a similar example possession the sign and predicate of the probandum, [Bhāvaviveka] mostly stated signs of negative phenomena, i.e., observations of a contradictory object. For example, his statement, "Because it is a sense power, the eye does not ultimately see forms, as is the case with an ear sense power" and so forth.

Because they are easy to prove, if one indicates a similar example that is both the sign and the predicate of the probandum, most statements of syllogisms are statements of signs that are observations of contradictory objects.[1] For example, a statement such as, "The subject, the eye, does not ultimately see forms because of being a sense power, as is the case with, for example, the nose sense power."[2] [199]

The Two Truths

Objects of knowledge [are exhaustively divided into] the truths.

Objects of knowledge are definitely enumerated as the two: conventional truths and ultimate truths [or highest object truths].[3]

[In the term "highest object truth,"] "highest" is a non-contaminated awareness. "Object" is that which is found by that [awareness]. Because they are not deceptive, they are truths (*satya*).

"Highest" in the term "highest object truth" refers to a non-contaminated awareness—an exalted wisdom consciousness—realizing non-true existence.[4]

---

[1]Bhāvavevika accepts the three types of reasons used by Dharmakīrti (effect, nature, and non-observation). The point here is that the *main* reasonings used for realizing the absence of true existence use reasons that employ the observation of a contradictory object. In the example, the sign uses the object, nose sense power, which is contradicted by the eye sense power.

[2]Bhāvaviveka argues that if the eyes were ultimately established as seeing forms, there would be no way to distinguish between the eye sense power seeing forms and the ear sense power *not* seeing forms. This is because if something were to ultimately exist, it would not be posited through the force of appearing to an awareness the way it does; it would have to exist through the force of its own objective mode of subsistence. There would be no valid cognition that could differentiate between sense powers seeing and hearing.

[3]All existents (=objects of knowledge) are either conventional truths or ultimate truths and thus, "definitely enumerated" as one or the other. Although use of the word "truth" seems to indicate different types of propositions, it refers to phenomena themselves.

[4]This is the mind of a Superior directly realizing emptiness.

"Object" refers to the object found by that consciousness.[1] Since truths subsist the way they appear, they do not deceive one who perceives them; therefore, they are called truths.[2]

Because they obstruct, they are obscurational [i.e., conventional truths]. Because of being truths for the perspective of an obscurer, they are other.

Furthermore, they are called "obscurational truths" because ignorance [a consciousness conceiving true existence], since it prevents [itself] from [perceiving] the mode of subsistence, is the obscurer, and a truth for just the perspective of [ignorance] is called an obscurational [or conventional] truth.[3]

Although the master Bhāvaviveka [200] explains that the subtle selflessness of persons—the person's emptiness of being substantially existent in the sense of being self-sufficient—is an emptiness and an element of attributes, he does not assert that it is an ultimate truth. This is so because:

- whereas [an ultimate truth] is necessarily definitive, [the subtle selflessness of persons] must be interpreted as other than the selflessness of persons [to determine its final mode of subsistence].[4]
- on many occasions of debating with the lower schools of tenets about whether something ultimately exists or not, etc., [Bhāvaviveka] takes that which is established for the perspective of a reasoning consciousness analyzing the ultimate as the object of negation [rather than taking a substantially existent person as the object of negation].
- [Bhāvaviveka] teaches that [Hearers] abandon the afflictions, even though they have not realized the final mode of subsistence, through the example

---

[1]The reasoning consciousness is looking for true existence. Instead of finding it, the reasoning consciousness finds the absence of true existence. The absence of true existence is an emptiness, thus emptiness is found by the reasoning consciousness looking for true existence.

[2]The object of an exalted wisdom consciousness is the emptiness of true existence of some phenomenon. It exists the way it appears. Svātantrikas also say that conventional truths exist the way they appear to valid consciousnesses not distorted by superficial causes of error, although Prāsaṅgikas would disagree and do not explain that conventional truths exist the way they appear (since they appear to truly exist but do not).

[3]The phenomena included in this class, i.e., all phenomena except for emptinesses, are true only for awarenesses that are still ignorant, conceiving of these things to exist the way they appear.

[4]The person's emptiness of *true existence* is the "final" mode, i.e., the most subtle level, of its mode of being. See the table in the introductory chapter on ignorance.

of overcoming the conception of a rope as a *snake* through apprehending it as a *vine.*[1]

- Kaydrup's *Opening the Eyes of the Fortunate* says that the subtle selflessness of persons is not an ultimate truth and is not established by a reasoning consciousness analyzing the ultimate. [201]

Someone might ask, "Does not this contradict the statement in Kamalaśīla's *Illumination of the Middle Way,* 'The selflessness of phenomena and persons...?'" Regarding this, Dzongkaba's *Essence of Eloquence,* in the chapter on both [schools of the] Svātantrika-Mādhyamikas where it says, "Ultimate regarding persons and phenomena," means the selflessness of phenomena regarding those two, and since there are many such [statements in the texts of the Svātantrika-Mādhyamikas], it should be known in this way.[2]

Although the Foremost Precious One [Dzongkaba] says that Bhāvaviveka asserts that the one stanza *prior* to, "Through extinguishing actions and afflictions one is released," indicates a Hīnayāna release, and the one stanza, "Through extinguishing actions and... etc.," indicates a Mahāyāna release, [202] it is not that all of the earlier [lamas] said that [this stanza] applied to the Hīnayāna.

Because phenomena that are and are not able to perform functions in accordance with the way they appear are conventional truths, obscurational [truths] are divided into the real and the unreal.[3] The first are effective things, and the second are reflections, etc.

When obscurational truths are divided, there are two types:

---

[1]The example of the rope, seen in dim light, being misunderstood as a vine (which is better than its being misunderstood as a snake) is used by Bhāvaviveka to show that even though Hearers do not abandon the conception of true existence, they can be liberated through eliminating the conception of the person as self-sufficiently substantially existent.

[2]Dzongkaba is making it clear that Kamalaśīla, stating that the selflessness of persons and phenomena is an ultimate, was not stating that the selflessness of persons realized by Hearers is an ultimate truth; only the selflessness of phenomena (the lack of true existence of phenomena other than persons, and a person's lack of true existence in the sense of being a possessor of truly existent phenomena) is an ultimate truth.

[3]When *yang* and *log* refer to a consciousness, we translate these contradictory terms as *right* and *wrong*; when they refer to objects, they are *real* and *unreal.*

1 real conventional truths, [such as][1] phenomena that are able to perform functions in accordance with the way they appear [to the awareness to which they clearly appear]
2 unreal conventionalities, [such as] phenomena that are unable to perform functions in accordance with the way they appear.

The first are functioning things that are not superimpositions, and the second are reflections, the two selves, the Nature of Sāṃkhya, etc.[2]

Valid Cognition

There are two [types of valid cognition], direct perception and inferential cognition and, respectively, three or four direct perceivers.

Regarding valid cognizers, there are the two: direct perceivers and inferential cognizers. [203] Regarding direct perceivers, respectively, for the Sautrāntika-Svātantrika-Mādhyamikas there are three—sense direct perceivers, mental direct perceivers, and yogic direct perceivers—and for the Yogācāra-Svātantrika-Mādhyamikas there are four with [the addition of] self-consciousnesses.

The Fruit

Those definite in the [Mahāyāna] lineage simultaneously extinguish the two obstructions and [attain] complete enlightenment.

Those who are definite in the Mahāyāna lineage simultaneously remove the two obstructions—the predispositions of the afflictions and the conception of true

---

[1]"Such as" is added within brackets because the text wrongly implies that all real conventionalities are able to perform functions (mainly, to act as causes). Permanent phenomena (those that do not change moment-to-moment, such as space) are real conventionalities but do not perform functions.

[2]Losang Gonchok has a problem here by saying "when obscurational truths are divided" and then indicating that one of the divisions is "unreal conventionalities" because "unreal conventionalities" includes the nonexistent. Phenomena (i.e., existents) are divided into real and unreal conventional truths respectively in accordance with whether they can or cannot perform a function in accordance with how they appear to conventional valid cognition. "Unreal conventionalities" includes the imagined self of persons and the Sāṃkhya's Principal, which are not conventional *truths* because they are refuted by valid cognition. On the other hand, a reflection, a mirage, or special effects tricks are conventional truths because they exist but are "unreal conventional truths" because they are deceptive.

existence—and attain full Buddhahood. They abandon the afflictive obstructions [and their seeds] through [i.e., up to and including] the eighth ground.[1]

[They attain] the Three Bodies, three secrecies, three hundred unshared [qualities, etc., of a Buddha.]

They attain the qualities of a Buddha—the fruits such as the Three Bodies of Truth, Complete Enjoyment, and Emanation, the three secrecies of body, speech, and mind, [204] the three hundred unshared qualities of a Buddha, and spontaneous activities.

The Path

[The objects of abandonment are] the three poisons—the afflictive obstructions—and the cycles of the conception of true existence—the obstructions to omniscience.

Regarding the objects of abandonment, the three poisons (desire, hatred, and ignorance) are afflictive obstructions, and the nine cycles of the conception of true existence, etc., are obstructions to omniscience.[2]

The paths of Hearers and Solitary Realizers are concordant, but differ by way of time and the fruit [as well as the mode of attaining it].

Although the paths of the two, Hearers and Solitary Realizers, are concordant because they do not have dissimilar types of realizers, their differences can be distinguished by the length of time for achieving the path, whether or not they need to depend on the speech of others to obtain the fruit of Arhat, etc.[3]

---

[1]"Definite in the Mahāyāna lineage" means entering the Mahāyāna from the beginning without first having become an Arhat through completing Hīnayāna paths. Such a person abandons the afflictive emotions and their *seeds* on the eighth ground, and abandons the *predispositions* of the afflictive emotions and the conception of true existence simultaneously at the time of achieving Buddhahood. Prāsaṅgikas, by contrast, say that a person definite in the Mahāyāna lineage practicing the sūtra path (called the "Perfection Vehicle" as opposed to the tantric path, the "Secret Mantra Vehicle") eliminates the conception of true existence (which they identify as the obstruction to liberation) over the first eight "grounds" of ten (the "Bodhisattva grounds") on the path of meditation (the fourth of five "paths" into which the path is distinguished). Only after that does such a person begin to eliminate the obstructions to omniscience, the predispositions for mistaken dualistic appearance.

[2]Prāsaṅgikas, by contrast, consider the conception of true existence to be an afflictive obstruction (=an obstruction to liberation).

[3]A Hearer is one who hears doctrine, practices it, and proclaims it to others, but who has not yet

The Yogācāra-Svātantrika-Mādhyamika School

True and False Aspectarians

In the second Svātantrika-Mādhyamika [system] there are two [divisions]: those who accord with the True Aspectarians and those who accord with the False Aspectarians.

Regarding the second Svātantrika-Mādhyamika system, Yogācāra-Svātantrika-Mādhyamika, there are the two [divisions]: Svātantrika-Mādhyamikas who accord with True Aspectarians and Svātantrika-Mādhyamikas who accord with False Aspectarians.[1]

The first, [the system of] Śantarakṣita, [205] **the father, and his [spiritual] sons, [asserts the gross] aspect as a thing.**

Therefore, the masters Śantarakṣita and Kamalaśīla [are True Aspectarians because they] assert that the aspects of blue, yellow, etc., that are the factors experienced by [for instance, an eye consciousness] apprehending blue are functioning things that are real conventionalities.

The second, [the position that the gross aspect is not a thing,] is the system of] Haribhadra.

The great master Haribhadra, etc., [are False Aspectarians because they] assert that even that which is the nature of the aspect [of, for instance, blue] does not exist as a thing that accords with its appearance [as a gross object]. [206]

Jetāri accords with the Tainted False Aspectarians. Kambala accords with the Untainted False Aspectarians.

---

developed *bodhicitta.* Such a person may become liberated in a minimum of three lifetimes. Solitary Realizers are persons who have no teacher in their last life; they also extend their practice for 100 eons, and that is why they get a similitude of a Buddha's body when they become enlightened. Both of them attain liberation by way of realizing the person's emptiness of being self-sufficiently substantially existent, but their difference is accounted for by the length of time practicing the path.

[1]True and False Aspectarians agree that the appearance of coarse objects as external is distorted by ignorance. They disagree over whether the coarse appearances of wholes exists as they appear. For example, a patch of blue is actually many tiny parts that are blue; is the appearance of a "patch" true or false?

A Svātantrika-Mādhyamika who accords with the Tainted False Aspectarians, who assert that the entity of the mind is polluted by taints, is the master Jetāri. Svātantrika-Mādhyamikas who accord with the Untainted [False Aspectarians], who assert that although the aspect of the mind is mistaken, its entity is not polluted, are Kambala, also called Lawaba, etc.[1]

Interpretation of Scripture

[Svātantrikas assert that] in the system of the *Sūtra Unraveling the Thought,* sūtras such as the *Hundred Thousand Stanza Perfection of Wisdom Sūtra* are definitive. Sūtras that do not affix "ultimately," although similar in being second [wheel sūtras], require interpretation.

[Svātantrikas assert that] in the system of the *Sūtra Unraveling the Thought,* [second wheel] sūtras such as the Mother, the *Hundred Thousand Stanza Perfection of Wisdom Sūtra* [in which the qualification "ultimately" is affixed to the object of negation either explicitly or implicitly] are definitive.[2] [207] Sūtras such as the *Heart of Wisdom* and *Diamond Cutter* that need to affix—but do not affix—the qualification "ultimately" to the object of negation, are similar in being second wheel [sūtras], but they are regarded as sūtras requiring interpretation.[3]

The mode of the three natures is the same. External objects do not exist.

The mode of the three natures is the same as before [as explained by the Sautrāntika-Svātantrika-Mādhyamikas]. [However, Yogācāra-Svātantrika-Mādhyamikas] assert that the non-existence of external objects is the meaning of [some] sūtras.[4] Two meanings—principal and secondary—having been distinguished in

---

[1]Untainted False Aspectarians deny that the mind itself can be polluted by its taints. The afflictions are like clouds passing through a pure sky.

[2]By contrast, Cittamātra holds that the meaning of the *Sūtra Unraveling the Thought* is that the second wheel requires interpretation.

[3]According to the use of "definitive" in the *Sūtra Unraveling the Thought,* which is used by the Cittamātra school, definitive sūtras are those that can be taken literally. Prāsaṅgikas consider those sūtras "definitive" that teach about emptiness, whether or not they are literal. But Svātantrikas regard as definitive only those that are *both* literal *and* teach about emptiness. If a sūtra does not specify "ultimate" (as in, "form does not exist") it is not literal and would not be a definitive sūtra.

[4]Bhāvaviveka denied that sūtras that *apparently* teach that there are no external objects were actually teaching such. This is a major difference between Sautrāntika- and Yogācāra-Svātantrika and, for that matter, with Prāsaṅgika, which also says that the sūtras actually do teach that there are no external objects.

sūtras such as the *Sūtra on the Heavily Adorned*, the *Sūtra Unraveling the Thought*, the *Descent to Laṅkā Sūtra*, and the *Kashyapa Chapter Sūtra*, they are, respectively, regarded as the Mādhyamika and Cittamātra systems.[1]

The Object of Negation

It is agreed that not being posited [through] appearance to a non-defective awareness is the object of negation.

The two Svātantrika-Mādhyamika systems agree that the establishment of any phenomenon without its being posited by the power of appearing to a non-defective consciousness [208] is the principal object of negation to be refuted.[2]

Kamalaśīla's *Illumination of the Middle Way* says, "All false things that [the consciousness conceiving true existence] sees are called 'mere conventionalities.'" "Sees" [means] all the falsities of [wrong] conceptual consciousnesses or the things of conceptual consciousnesses for which [the object of] the mode of apprehension does not exist.[3] They are said to be concealers, i.e., obscuring ignorance. Therefore, do not think that they are valid cognitions. Therefore, "only concealers" in this [context] is the ignorance in the face of which [phenomena] are posited as truths. Later, [in *Illumination of the Middle Way*,] "conventional" in "exists only conventionally" must be taken as valid cognition.

The thought of Jñanagarbha's *Discrimination of the Two Truths* is that the non-appearance of the object of negation—true existence—to sense consciousnesses [209] has the meaning that:

- the sense consciousnesses do not conceive true existence
- true establishment for the perspective of a reasoning consciousness [does not appear to sense consciousnesses]

---

[1]These sūtras have some passages that accord with Mādhyamika, some that accord with Cittamātra. While Sautrāntika-Svātantrika holds that the non-existence of external objects was not taught at all, Prāsaṅgikas say that Buddha taught that tenet for the benefit of certain people not ready for the teaching about non-inherent existence.

[2]In other words, phenomena are validly established only by valid cognitions. These are sense consciousnesses that are not affected by "superficial causes of error," such as a mirage, and conceptual consciousnesses that accurately identify their objects. Therefore, the conception that phenomena truly exist, meaning that they exist independently, is the ignorance that must be eliminated.

[3]An ignorant consciousness conceives of things as truly existent. Therefore, the object of the mode of apprehension of such a consciousness is a truly existent thing. That is a "false conventionality."

- [sense consciousnesses] do not conceive [objects] to exist as they are displayed [by ignorance].[1]

Because of being set forth in the *Descent to Laṅkā Sūtra* and the *Meeting of Father and Son Sūtra*, they mostly state signs that are non-observations of related objects. For example, "because of being free from being either a truly established singularity or plurality, forms, etc., are not truly established, like reflections."

At the time of refutation, they mostly state signs that are non-observations of related objects because these are set forth in the *Descent into Laṅkā Sūtra* [210] and the *Meeting of Father and Son Sūtra*. For example, it is stated, "It follows that the subjects, things such as forms, etc., are not truly existent because of being devoid of being either truly established singularities or truly established pluralities—for example, like a reflection."

If something is truly established, it is definite as [either of] those two, thus the entailments are established. Regarding the property of the subject, [things such as forms] are not singular because of having parts, nor many because [a truly established] oneness does not exist.

If something is truly established, it must definitely [be established as one] of the two modes of establishment, therefore, the entailment that is established. Regarding the mode of establishing [the reason as] a property of the subject, [things] are not truly established singularities because of having parts. They are not truly established pluralities because truly established singularities do not exist.

One needs to think well, investigating how in the Svātantrika system [211] if something is merely posited by an awareness, it does not need to be independent, but if something is *not* merely posited by the power of appearing to a non-defective awareness, it becomes independent. Doing this, one needs to strive at a method of gaining ascertainment regarding this Mādhyamika reasoning.

The diamond slivers, the refutation of production of the existent and the non-existent, the refutation of production of the four alternatives, and the sign of dependent-arising are chief.

Moreover, the diamond slivers, the refutation of production of the existent and non-existent, the refutation of production of the four alternatives, and the sign of dependent-arising are taken as the main proofs of non-true existence.[2]

---

[1]Objects *do* appear to truly exist. However, sense consciousnesses are not conceptual consciousnesses and, therefore, do not *conceive* of true existence.

[2]These are described extensively in the Prāsaṅgika chapter.

The Path

The presentations of the selflessness of persons and the two truths are concordant.

[214.2][1] The selflessness of persons is posited in terms of all phenomena,[2] and both Svātantrika [systems] agree on the presentation of the basis of the division of the two truths, their definitions, divisions, etc. [215]

The subtle and coarse obstructions to omniscience are the conception of true existence and the conception of subject and object [as different entities], etc.

The latter [the Yogācāra-Svātantrikas, unlike the Sautrāntika-Svātantrikas] assert that the main objects of abandonment of the three vehicles are:[3]

- the subtle obstructions to omniscience—the conception of true existence [for Bodhisattvas]
- the coarse obstructions to omniscience—the conception of subject and object as different entities [for Solitary Realizers]
- the obstructions to liberation—the three poisons, etc. [for Hearers]

[Realizers of] the sixteen aspects of the [Four Noble] Truths, the emptiness of the two [subject and object, being different entities], and non-true establishment are the different types of realizers of the Hearer, Solitary Realizer, and Mahāyāna paths.

The paths [i.e., meditative consciousnesses] that realize the sixteen aspects of the Four Noble Truths—impermanence, suffering, etc.—are Hearer types of realizers; the paths that realize the emptiness of the two, subject and object [as being different entities] are Solitary Realizer [types of] realizers; and the [paths] that realize non-true existence are Mahāyāna path types of realizers.

Both [Svātantrika systems] agree on the features of there being meditative equipoise and subsequent attainment on [the paths of] seeing and meditation.

---

[1]211.4–214.2 has been omitted.

[2]The selflessness of persons is posited in terms of all phenomena in the sense that all phenomena are empty of being objects of use of a substantially existent self-sufficient person.

[3]These are, respectively, the conceptions of a subtle self of phenomena, a coarse self of phenomena, and a subtle self of persons. In contrast, Prāsaṅgikas identify the conception of inherent existence as the single object of abandonment for all vehicles, although it distinguishes between the conception of inherent existence as the obstructions to liberation and the taints of the *appearance* of inherent existence as the obstructions to omniscience.

The features of the wisdoms of meditative equipoise and subsequent attainment of the path of seeing and of nine cycles of the path of meditation are set forth concordantly by both Svātantrika-Mādhyamika [systems].[1] [216]

This has been the eleventh chapter, the commentary on the section of Svātantrika, those who, having eliminated the extreme of truly established things, establish the middle way.

---

[1]The path of seeing is the brief moment in which one first directly realizes emptiness. It can be distinguished into meditative equipoise, when only emptiness appears to the mind, and the moments subsequent to equipoise in which other things appear to truly exist but the meditator refuses to assent to the false appearance. The path of meditation follows, and over it one gradually eliminates the innate afflictions. They are distinguished into nine degrees, gross to subtle, ranging from the "big of the big" to the "small of the small," the idea being that it is possible to get rid of gross afflictions more easily than subtle ones (just as when washing a sheet it is easy to get out loose dirt but difficult to scrub out deep stains).

The Prāsaṅgika School

[Next, Jamyang Shayba] sets forth the system of the glorious Prāsaṅgika-Mādhyamika (Middle Way Consequence school)—the utmost peak of all schools of tenets.

Because they do not accept autonomous inferences but mainly state consequences that contradict the positions of the other party, they are called Prāsaṅgikas (Consequentialists).

Because they do not assert autonomous syllogisms[1] but assert that the inference that realizes the probandum is generated by way of merely using mainly whatever correct contradictory consequences contradict the positions of the opponent, [that is to say, correct contradictory consequences that] imply or do not imply the opposite meaning, they are called Prāsaṅgikas (Consequentialists).

They are known as Prāsaṅgikas, Only-Appearance [217] **Mādhyamikas, and Non-Abiding Mādhyamikas.**

---

[1]Jamyang Shayba (*Great Exposition of the Middle Way* 424.2) glosses "autonomous syllogism" as that in which the "three modes exist from their own side." The three modes of a sign are the presence of the reason in the subject, the forward entailment, and the reverse entailment. For example, in the syllogism, "The subject, a pot, is impermanent because of being a product," the first mode—the presence of the reason in the subject—is the applicability of the reason (product) to the subject (pot), i.e., that pot is a product; the forward entailment, roughly speaking, is that whatever is a product is necessarily impermanent; and the reverse entailment, roughly speaking, is that whatever is not impermanent is necessarily not a product. Because the Svātantrikas are said to hold that conventionally, phenomena *do* inherently or autonomously exist, the phenomena used in their syllogisms, and the relationships between them, are said to inherently or autonomously exist. For the Prāsaṅgika school "established inherently" (*rang bzhin gyis grub pa, svabhāvasiddha*), and "autonomous" (*rang rgyud, svatantra*) are equivalent.

Regarding synonyms, they are renowned as Prāsaṅgikas, Only-Appearance Mādhyamikas who assert just these appearances of conditionalities without investigation or analysis,[1] and Thoroughly-Non-Abiding Mādhyamikas, due to not abiding in any extreme of permanence or annihilation.

Their divisions are Model, Partisans, and Non-Partisans.

When [Prāsaṅgikas] are divided, there are the three: the Mādhyamikas of the model texts—the master Nāgārjuna and his spiritual son [Āryadeva]; the Partisan Prāsaṅgika-Mādhyamikas—Buddhapālita, the honorable Candrakīrti, and Śāntideva; and Mādhyamikas such as Aśvaghoṣa and Nāgabodhi who, although they maintain the [Prāsaṅgika] view, are Non-Partisan.[2] [218]

Their books are the profound sūtras, the Collections of Reasonings, the *Four Hundred, Engaging in the Bodhisattva Deeds, Compendium of Sūtra, Compendium of Instructions, Lamp for the Path,* etc.

Their texts are:

- the seventeen Mother and Son [sūtras of the Perfection of Wisdom class] that teach the profound [emptiness], the *Teaching of Akṣayamati Sūtra*, the *King of Meditative Stabilizations Sūtra*, etc.
- Nāgārjuna's Six Collections of Reasoning and his Collections of Praise
- Āryadeva's *Treatise of Four Hundred Stanzas*, etc.
- Buddhapālita's *Commentary on (Nāgārjuna's) "Treatise on the Middle Way"*
- the four great commentaries of Candrakīrti, namely his *Clear Words, Commentary on (Nāgārjuna's) "Treatise on the Middle Way," Commentary on (Nāgārjuna's) "Sixty Stanzas of Reasoning," Commentary on (Āryadeva's) "Four Hundred Stanzas on the Yogic Deeds of Bodhisattvas,"* and his own commentary on his own *Entrance to (Nāgārjuna's) "Treatise on the Middle Way"*
- Śāntideva's *Compendium of Instructions* and *Engaging in the Bodhisattva Deeds*
- Atīśa's *Lamp for the Path to Enlightenment, Introduction to the Two Truths,* [219] *Quintessential Instructions on the Middle Way*, etc.

---

[1]An important Prāsaṅgika tenet is that nothing can withstand analysis (that is, when something's "pointable existence," its essence, is sought, it cannot be found). However, this does not lead to nihilism, since they accept as conventional truths the phenomena that the world accepts (but only as long as they can be established by ordinary valid cognition).

[2]The Partisan Mādhyamikas are clearly not Svātantrikas because of being criticized by Bhāvaviveka or criticizing him. The Non-Partisans are clearly Prāsaṅgikas, but they never criticized the Svātantrikas.

These are valid texts that teach the uncommon tenets [of the Prāsaṅgikas].

On any and all occasions and in all ways [Jamyang Shayba] makes his explanation by way of just that which is held by the word of the three: the father, the Foremost [Dzongkaba], and his spiritual sons [Gyeltsap and Kaydrup].[1]

If you examine [Jamyang Shayba's] own mode of explanation of the commentary, in the text of [Jamyang Shayba s] *Root Verses of "Tenets,"* it seems that [the line], "The great commentaries of Buddhapālita and Candrakīrti," should appear. It does not appear in any edition, and whether or not it has been omitted [by the printers] should be examined. [220]

Interpretation of Scripture

Sūtras teaching the two truths are, respectively, those to be interpreted, because they must be interpreted otherwise, and the definitive, because the mode of subsistence is definite there.

The definition of a sūtra that requires interpretation is: a sūtra that explicitly and mainly teaches conventional truths. It is explained that since the final mode of subsistence must be interpreted as other than that which is taught in that sūtra, they are called interpretable. The definition of a [sūtra] of definitive meaning is: a sūtra that explicitly and mainly teaches ultimate truths. It is explained that since the final mode of subsistence is definite as it is taught by that sūtra, they are called definitive.[2]

There are two ways of interpretation: when even the literal meaning is not suitable and when the literal meaning, though established, is not the final mode of existence.

Regarding the mode of interpreting [a passage] in another way, since, for instance, the statement, "Father and mother are to be killed," is not suitable to be held in accordance with the literal [meaning], it must be interpreted otherwise.[3]

---

[1]In other words, even when Jamyang Shayba does not cite Dzongkaba, Gyeltsap, and Kaydrup, he is following their thought.

[2]Whether or not something requires interpretation does not depend on whether or not something is completely literal, but whether it teaches ultimate truths—emptiness. A sūtra that occasionally teaches ultimate truths is both; the *passages* teaching ultimate truths are definitive whereas other passages require interpretation.

[3]Two types of passages require interpretation: (1) the non-literal, e.g., "father and mother must be killed," (where father and mother refer to "attachment" and "existence," two links of dependent-arising leading to rebirth), and (2) literal passages that must be interpreted because

[221] [However,] if with respect to the literal meaning of, for instance, the teaching, "From wholesome and unwholesome actions happiness and suffering arise," one knows that happiness arises from wholesome actions and suffering arises from unwholesome actions, one comes to have unmistaken adoption of virtue and discarding of non-virtue. Thereby, there exists the great benefit of establishing the roots of the collections of goodness. This is a conventional mode of subsistence that one very much ought to know. Therefore, although such a special meaning that [still] requires interpretation is established, the final mode of subsistence, [direct realization of which] removes suffering from the root, is not that.[1] Therefore, [the passage] must be interpreted in another way. There are these two modes of interpretation.

The first and last wheels require interpretation. The middle are definitive sūtras.

The first and last of the three wheels about which questions [were asked by Paramārthasamudgata] and replies [were made by Buddha] that are explained in the *Sūtra Unraveling the Thought* [222] are sūtras requiring interpretation.[2] The middle [wheel consists of] definitive sūtras. Does this not contradict the statement in Dzongkaba's *Essence of Eloquence* in the context of Prāsaṅgika that the first wheel has two [types of passages, those of] interpretable [meaning and those of] definitive [meaning]?[3] The *Sūtra Unraveling the Thought*, at the point of giving the meaning

---

they do not say that the mode of subsistence of its subject is the emptiness of inherent existence.

[1]In other words, while it is true that happiness comes from virtuous actions, since this passage does not teach the non-inherent existence of virtuous actions, for the Prāsaṅgika school the passage in interpretable.

[2]The "three wheels" are collections of similar teachings by the Buddha, acknowledged to be significantly different from one another and in some ways contradictory. To repeat what we wrote in the introduction: the first turning is what we generally recognize as the Hīnayāna teachings. The sūtras in this wheel teach that there is no selflessness of persons. Generally speaking, they do not say anything about the selflessness of phenomena and, in particular, do not say anything about the absence of inherent existence (although Prāsaṅgikas maintain that some do, arguing that otherwise no Hīnayānist could be liberated from saṃsāra, whereas it is clear that some have achieved liberation). The second turning is that of the Perfection of Wisdom sūtras, on which the Mādhyamika school depends. These sūtras teach literally that everything lacks true existence. The third turning is that of the "mind-only" teaching: the *Sūtra Unraveling the Thought*, the *Sūtra on the Ten Grounds*, the *Descent to Laṅkā Sūtra*, and the *Mahāyāna Abhidharma Sūtra*. These sūtras distinguish between the true existence of most things and the non-true existence of imputed phenomena.

[3]Prāsaṅgikas are unique in saying that some Hīnayāna sūtras have passages that are definitive. The question arises: is not Jamyang Shayba incorrect to just say that first wheel sūtras require

that has been established by what preceded it regarding the first wheel, treats as Hīnayāna sūtras [those referred to in] the statement that [Buddha] taught the aspects of the Four Noble Truths to those [persons] who were entering the Hearer Vehicle correctly, that is to say, to the sages in Varaṇāsi staying at the Deer Park.

[However,] Prāsaṅgikas assert that there is convergence of being a Hīnayāna sūtra and being a sūtra of definitive meaning.[1] Others [such as Bhāvaviveka] do not assert as Hīnayāna sūtras *words* in Hīnayāna sūtras that teach the final definitive meaning. [223] Here [in Jamyang Shayba's root text], since he is thinking about the first [wheel] about which there were questions and replies [in the *Sūtra Unraveling the Thought*], there is no contradiction.

Five sūtra sections of the *Descent to Laṅkā Sūtra,* the *Sūtra Unraveling the Thought,* and the *Sūtra on the Heavily Adorned,* thinking that there is no other creator and thinking of emptiness, teach mind-only, no external objects, a permanent essence, the existence of the basis-of-all, the true existence of other-powered natures and of thoroughly established natures, and three final vehicles. These five teachings are proved to require interpretation.

Five sections of words of the *Descent to Laṅkā Sūtra,* the *Sūtra Unraveling the Thought,* the *Sūtra on the Heavily Adorned,* etc., are regarded in their own class by way of the way in which, thinking of emptiness and the non-existence of another "creator self"—[224] the basis in Buddha's thought—they teach that there are no external objects apart from mere mind, that a stable, permanent essence and basis-of-all exist, that other-powered phenomena and thoroughly established phenomena are truly established, and that there are three final vehicles.[2] These five are proved to require interpretation. The word "teach" (*ston*) [that appears in the root text] should be put together with the instrumental word "five" (*lngas*).

---

interpretation? The answer will be that he was just making a generalization.

[1]Only Prāsaṅgikas maintain that some of the Hīnayāna sūtras teach non-inherent existence. While Bhāvaviveka agrees that there are such teachings in those sūtras, he would not call them "Hīnayāna" any longer.

[2]According to Bhāvaviveka, Buddha did not mean to teach that there are no external objects, etc.; he was just talking about how the mind is the creator of the world and was misunderstood. According to Prāsaṅgika, he *did* mean to teach those things, in order to help those for whom those views would be a step towards the more difficult Prāsaṅgika view. However, when he taught those things, Buddha was always simultaneously in meditative equipoise realizing the emptiness of inherent existence that is the actual way in which all phenomena exist.

The Object of Negation

All of saṃsāra and nirvāṇa, appearing and well known to [the mind]—the varieties [of phenomena] and their mode [emptiness], are regarded by the inborn non-analytical intellect [as existing] according to the conventions of the world. Therefore, "existing objectively [without just being an imputation] there by thought," "substantially existing," "existing by way of its own nature," "existing from its own [i.e., the object's] side," "truly existing," "existing in its own right," etc., are what is negated. [225]

All of that which is included by the modes and the varieties that appear and are renowned [in the world], the phenomena of saṃsāra and nirvāṇa, are regarded as existing in the face of that which is renowned in worldly conventions, that is to say, to the innate valid cognition that does not analyze [to try to find] the object imputed.[1] Therefore:

- establishment here along with the object that is the basis of designation without being merely put there [from the subject's side] by a non-defective conceptual consciousness
- substantial establishment
- establishment by way of its own character
- establishment from its own side
- true establishment
- establishment by way of its own entityness
- establishment by way of its own power

are [hypothetically][2] synonymous in being the object of negation by a sign, that is, that which is to be refuted. [226]

The Mādhyamikas, those free from extremes, present all actions and agents in this [system] of no "existence from its own [the objects's] side" and of "imputation by name and thought there [to the object]." Anything coarser or finer than this is an extreme of permanence or annihilation.

If you know how to identify all doings and doers, such as actions and their effects, here in this context of not existing from their own side and merely being

---

[1]In other words, Prāsaṅgikas accept what worldly valid cognition can establish.

[2]Technically, only existents may be equivalents. The members of this list are not actual equivalents because none of these imagined ways of existing actually occurs. The conception that they exist occurs, and that conception is a mind.

imputed there by names and conceptual consciousnesses, then you are a Mādhyamika who is free from all extremes. [227] If what you do is coarser or more subtle than that, you fall to an extreme of permanence or annihilation.[1]

There are the two selves of persons and [other] phenomena. The non-existence of these two there is asserted as the two selflessnesses.

These Prāsaṅgikas assert that the [imagined] existence of the aforementioned object of negation in terms of the person is the [conception of] a self of persons, and that the [imagined] existence [of that object of negation] in terms of [other] phenomena—the aggregates, etc.—is the [conception of] a self of phenomena.[2] Therefore, the two non-existences of the two selves that are the object of negation in those bases are asserted as the two selflessnesses.

A self of [other] phenomena is refuted by the four: the diamond slivers, etc. A self of persons is refuted by the fivefold and sevenfold [reasonings]. Both also [are refuted] by [the sign of] dependent-arising.

Hence, the self of phenomena is refuted[3] by the four [reasonings] such as the diamond slivers, etc.,[4] and the self of persons is refuted by the fivefold or sevenfold

---

[1]The other Buddhist schools are regarded as falling to the extreme of permanence because they do not deny "enough"; they still, in some way or another, retain the idea of a "pointable" existence.

[2]The *conception* that persons and other phenomena exist in that way exists, but the *referent object* of that conception—inherently existing persons and other phenomena—does not exist. The Prāsaṅgika school holds that the two selflessnesses (the absence of persons and other phenomena existing in that way) are not distinguished and do not differ in terms of the imagined self, or in more technical terms, in terms of *mode of apprehension*. What is this mode of apprehension? It is to conceive that persons and other phenomena exist inherently. In contrast, the other Mahāyāna systems see a difference in coarseness and subtlety between the two conceptions of self and, accordingly, the two selflessnesses.

[3]In this context, "refuted" is understood not in the external sense of persuading somebody else they are wrong but internally by the meditator in the sense of searching for the self and not finding it.

[4]The four reasonings used to gain access to phenomena's lack of inherent existence are (1) the diamond slivers; (2) simultaneous refutation of production of the four extremes and production of the existent, the non-existent, both, and neither; (3) the refutation of production of the four alternatives; and (4) dependent-arising. Diamond slivers—also called reason refuting the four extreme types of production—refutes inherent existence in the context of analyzing production. The simultaneous refutation of production of the four extremes and production of the existent, the non-existent, both, and neither refutes inherent existence in the context of analyzing what is produced by those causes—an inherently existent effect, an utterly non-existent effect, an effect

reasonings.[1] Both selves are refuted by stating the sign of dependent-arising.[2] [228] I think that it would be suitable for "both also" [in the root text to be understood as] either drawing in the [unstated reasoning] of the lack of being singular and plural or as including the [reasonings] that have preceded it.

Extensive Explanation of Reasonings Refuting Inherent Existence

[This section has two parts: reasonings refuting a self of phenomena (other than persons) and reasonings refuting a self of persons, together with an elimination of errors.]

Reasonings Refuting a Self of Phenomena

[This subsection has four parts: (1) the diamond slivers, (2) the (simultaneous) refutation of production of the four extremes and production of the existent, the non-existent, both, and neither, (3) the refutation of production of the four alternative types, and (4) the reasoning of dependent-arising, along with an elimination of error.]

THE DIAMOND SLIVERS

Because production from self, other, both, or without cause does not exist, inherently existent production does not exist.

---

that is both existent and non-existent, or an effect that is neither existent nor non-existent. The refutation of production of the four alternatives refutes inherent existence while analyzing both causes and effects. Finally, the reasoning of dependent-arising refutes inherent existence through analyzing the entities of phenomena. See Hopkins, *Emptiness Yoga,* 192–3.

[1]The fivefold reasoning comes from Nāgārjuna's *Treatise on the Middle Way.* Nāgārjuna's commentator Candrakīrti extended it to seven lines of inquiry. These reasonings refute inherent existence through analyzing the relation between a phenomenon and its basis of designation.

[2]This means that in addition to the other stated reasonings, the reasoning of dependent-arising is also used to refute either the self of persons or the self of phenomena.

The subjects, things that have causes, are not inherently produced because of not being produced from self, other, both, or without cause, for example, like a reflection.[1]

Regarding the mode of establishing the reasons individually, if [things] were produced from themselves [their re-production] would be senseless and endless, that which [already exists in something] is not [produced from] it, causes and effects [229] **would always be seen, it would contradict worldly perception, and all objects and agents [of production] would be one.**

If a sprout were produced by way of its own nature acting as its cause, since prior to the sprout the nature of the sprout would already have been established, the need for production in its own time would be senseless.[2]

If it were produced again even though it was already produced, since all things would necessarily be that way, the later and later continuum of the sprout, becoming a sprout, would be endless. In that case, seeds would also be similar to that, whereby that which is a sprout would be a continuation of a seed because it would become a sprout without discarding the nature of the seed. [230]

Therefore, causes and effects like seeds and sprouts would be seen to be permanent and simultaneous and would contradict worldly perception that sprouts are produced upon the destruction of seeds. Since [if the Sāṃkhya's theory of production were correct, effects such as sprouts] would be their own producers and objects produced, all objects and agents would be established as one.

If things were produced from [what is naturally] other, then darkness would arise from a flame, and all would arise from all, both causes and non-causes.

Also, if that sprout were produced by that which is inherently other than it, since dependence is not suitable in that which is inherently other, [the seed that is its cause], would be an unrelated cause, and if it were produced from one unrelated [cause] it would have to be produced from everything. Therefore, darkness would arise from fire, and everything that is and is not an effect would arise from everything that is and is not a cause.

---

[1]In the most important Mādhyamika text commenting on Buddha's thought, Nāgārjuna's *Treatise on the Middle Way*, Nāgārjuna begins by saying, "There is never production anywhere, of anything, from itself, from others, from both, or without cause." Gelukbas add "inherently" to his terms because conventionally, things *are* produced by other things.

[2]The Indian Sāṃkhya school holds that things *are* produced from themselves in the sense that the effect (such as a sprout) exists unmanifestly within the cause (such as a seed).

Because [cause and effect would be] other, they could not be one continuum; [they would be] like wheat and barley. [231]

Also, seed and sprout would be established as inherently other, due to which it would be unsuitable for them to be one substantial continuum; they would be like wheat and barley [which are different].

Causes and effects would have to be simultaneous, but because it is not so, what production is there of another from another?

Since that which is inherently established is unsuitable to be a newly arisen fabrication or to become another entity, once a seed and sprout are established as different, [232] they must exist simultaneously,[1] and because [simultaneous existence of cause and effect] does not exist, there is no production of another from another at all.

Refuting temporally different others is wrong. [Using] a mass exactly the same, etc., are also wrong. [231]

This production [from] other, accordingly, necessarily refers to production from another thing that is established from its own side, and someone's calling the refutation of the mere earlier seed and later sprout as being other, the "coercion of being identical," etc., is very mistaken.[2]

Because the four extremes are not asserted and because production from other is said to be non-existent even in the world, its assertion here is a dance of the insane.

In general, in the Prāsaṅgika system, production of the four extremes is not asserted, and production [from] other is refuted extensively with special emphasis. It is explained that [production from other] does not exist even in the conventions

[1]The seed and sprout must exist simultaneously, because otherwise, one would exist when the other does not, and that would mean that they were produced; they cannot be produced, because they would then not inherently exist. But if they do exist simultaneously, then they cannot possibly be related as cause and effect. This reasoning is circular because it depends on accepting "otherness" as "lack of relation," and once that is accepted, this further point is unnecessary.

[2]The root text is difficult to understand, but the commentary is clear: Prāsaṅgikas are not talking about mere production from other, but about inherent production. About this reasoning, some would say that this kind of refutation is just a refutation where because of the way terms have carefully been defined, the result is predetermined. Jamyang Shayba thinks that this criticism is unjustified; inherent otherness would have to mean no relation. And "no production from other" must mean that.

of the world. Therefore, Daktsang's saying that production [from] other is asserted in this system [233] is like a dance of the insane.[1]

Because there is no [production] from self and other separately, production from both is refuted.

Because separately there is no production [from] self and no production [from] other, production from both is also refuted.

If things were produced without cause, exertion would be senseless. It would contradict perception. All would be produced from all.

If something were produced without cause, planting seeds for the sake of fruit, striving at buying and selling, etc., would be senseless and would contradict the perception of undeceived worldly valid cognition.

[Also, it would absurdly follow that] in order for something to produce an effect from itself, it would not need to be the cause of that [effect]. Therefore, if something were produced from what is not [its] cause, everything would be produced from everything. [234]

Simultaneous Refutation of Production of the Four Extremes and of the Existent, Non-existent, Both, and Neither

If things are produced from others, consider [whether the effects are] existent, non-existent, both, or neither. What use [are causes] for [something already] existent?

Regarding reasoning that refutes the four extremes, production from other does not exist, [for] one should consider whether something truly existent, truly non-existent, both [truly existent and truly non-existent], or neither [truly existent nor truly non-existent] is produced. Therefore, what already exists does not need production.

The non-existent lacks object and agent. These [reasonings] refute its being both. What [would causes] do for what lacks both?

---

[1]Stong condemnation indeed! But to Gelukbas, it is extremely important to understand that inherent existence (in this case, the production of one inherently existent thing from another) does not have legitimacy in any way, not even in the conventions of the world. It may appear to worldly people that things inherently exist, but there is no valid cognition that can establish such things, just as although a mirage appears to be water, there is no valid cognition that establishes the appearance as actual water.

Since what is non-existent in the sense of never occurring is devoid of [being either] an object or an agent, it cannot be produced. That which is both existent and non-existent is eliminated by the fallacies that arise in both [of the two latter positions], and how could that which is truly established and devoid of both, that is, that is neither, or devoid of, both, be affected by causes? [235] The statement of the first two of these reasons is the reasoning that refutes production of existents or non-existents.

REFUTATION OF PRODUCTION OF THE FOUR ALTERNATIVES

Things are not truly produced by causes. One does not produce one; nor many, one; nor one, many; nor many, many.

The subject, [functioning] things, are not produced by truly existent causes, because ultimately one cause does not produce one effect, ultimately many causes do not produce one effect, ultimately one cause does not produce many effects, [236] and ultimately many causes do not produce many effects.[1]

Because it is established that one produces one, and because the others are suitable, not affixing here a qualification of what is negated is mistaken.

Candrakīrti's proves in *Clear Words, Commentary on (Nāgārjuna's) "Treatise on the Middle Way"* that conventionally one [cause] produces one [effect], and because the other three [alternatives for production] are also suitable [conventionally], in this system refuting [production] in general without affixing a qualification ["ultimately"] to the object of negation is a mistake.

The great Foremost Being [Dzongkaba] only briefly indicates the reasonings here, but he says in his *Great Exposition of the Stages of the Path* that for a more extensive [rendition] one should take whatever is appropriate [in Nāgārjuna's *Treatise on the Middle Way*] on the occasions of the analysis of the sources, the analysis of the constituents, etc. In particular, this latter [reasoning on production of the four alternatives] is indicated by way of the refutation at the end of the first chapter [of Nāgārjuna's *Treatise on the Middle Way*], that the individual and many pieces of woolen cloth [237] are ultimately produced by the individual and many threads. Dzongkaba says in his *Essence of Eloquence* that if one understands the reasonings of the great charioteers, it enhances the mind greatly. Therefore, one should be respectful, remembering the kindness of the Supreme Omniscient Lama [Jamyang Shayba's] stating [the reasons] here.

---

[1]The Indian source for this reasoning is the Svātantrika-Mādhyamika Jñānagarbha's *Discrimination of the Two Truths*. It analyzes single or multiple effects from single or multiple causes.

THE KING OF REASONINGS: THE SIGN OF DEPENDENT-ARISING

Because here there are no phenomena that are not dependent-arisings and because dependent-arising [means] only "existing through meeting," "existing through reliance," and "existing dependently," all phenomena are not able to set themselves up and are not established from their own side. Profound and vast, eradicating the two extremes, this is the king of reasonings. [238]

When one ascertains that in this system, phenomena that are not dependent-arisings do not exist, then "dependent-arising" is [that is, means] that all phenomena are unable to establish themselves and are not established or existent from their own side because:

- they exist through meeting with their own parts or bases of designation;
- they are established or exist through relying on, for instance, the conceptual consciousness that posits them;
- they arise or are established in dependence on, for instance, causes and conditions.

The predicate of the probandum and the sign respectively suggest the profound [emptiness] and the vast [dependent-arising], whereby both extremes of permanence and annihilation are simultaneously eliminated.[1] Therefore, this is explained to be the king of reasonings.

Therefore, [asserting] that the ultimate is "able to establish itself" is [like wanting] to eat space; no one takes "validly established" and "able to establish itself" as synonyms.

Therefore, [to say] the ultimate is able to establish itself is like fancying that space is food and wishing to eat it, [239] whereby there is no one among the four schools who asserts that the meaning of "established by valid cognition" is "able to establish itself."[2]

---

[1]In the syllogism, "Phenomena do not exist inherently because of being dependent-arisings," the predicate of the probandum is "not exist inherently" and the sign or reason proving the thesis is "dependent-arising."

[2]Daktsang is the target of this criticism. Both Daktsang and Dzongkaba agree that objects do not exist as they appear. For Dzongkaba "valid certification of objects" opposes habitual assent to appearances; for Daktsang "valid certification of objects" reinforces habitual assent to appearances. At minimum, the two authors mean different things by the term "valid certification of objects." As a practical matter, each author's whole system needs consideration, rather than focusing solely on differences regarding one point in isolation.

Reasonings Refuting a Self of Persons

THE SEVEN-FOLD REASONING[1]

An own-powered self does not exist because [the person] is not the aggregates, not [an entity] other than [the aggregates], not the base of the aggregates, and does not [ultimately] depend on the aggregates. [The person] does not [ultimately] possess the aggregates, is not the shape [of the aggregates], and is not the collection [of the aggregates], just as [the collection of parts is not] a chariot. Apply [this analysis] to all phenomena.

The subject, the person, does not exist as an own-powered self, because it is not the aggregates that are its basis of designation. If it were, then it [absurdly] follows that:

- it would be impermanent such that its continuum would be utterly annihilated[2]
- the [selves] would be plural
- the assertion of a self would be senseless[3] [240]
- memory of [former] lives would not be feasible[4]
- either there would be many selves, or the aggregates would be one

[The person] also does not exist as a [completely] *different* entity from those [aggregates] that are [its] basis of designation. In that case it would follow that:

- it would not have the character of the aggregates[5]
- it would be permanent.[6]

---

[1]This sevenfold analysis comes from the root text and auto-commentary of Candrakīrti's *Entrance.* It is based on a fivefold reasoning used by Nāgārjuna in the twenty-first chapter of the *Treatise on the Middle Way.*

[2]It must be remembered that the object of negation, the conception of self that we are said to hold innately, is a self that is permanent, partless, etc. Regarding that conception, these are all absurd consequences of equating self with the aggregates of body and mind.

[3]That is, if the self and the aggregates are the same thing, there is no need to use the concept of self.

[4]This is because the self would have no connection to its previous aggregates.

[5]In other words, it would not be produced, disintegrate, etc.

[6]It could only be permanent, because the aggregates include all impermanent phenomena.

- it would be something that is apprehendable separate from the aggregates.
- object and agent would not be feasible.

[The person] is also not established by way of its own entity as the *basis* of the aggregates.

It also does not *depend ultimately* on the aggregates over there. If it did, since they must be different, there would occur the faults expressed regarding difference.

[The person] also does not inherently *possess* the aggregates. [241] Whether it possesses [the aggregates] within one entity or separate entities, those [faults] occur that are expressed regarding sameness and difference.

Because the [person] is not form,[1] the *shape* of the aggregates also is not it.

If the *basis of designation* were the phenomena designated, then object and agent would be one. Therefore, [the person] also is not the *collection* of the aggregates. It is like, for example, a chariot.[2] In accordance with this position, this should be applied to all phenomena. A statement omitting the latter two of these reasonings is the fivefold reasoning.[3]

Elimination of Error Concerning the Refutation of a Self of Persons

Although they assert that on some occasions there is valid establishment [with] the three modes appearing similarly and that there are just [similarly appearing] reasons, because they do not [assert] self-powered valid [establishment], they do not assert autonomous [syllogisms]. That autonomous [syllogisms are asserted] in this system is mistaken. [242]

Although on some occasions of Prāsaṅgikas stating [signs] amongst themselves the validly established common appearance of the three modes and mere correct

---

[1]The person is not the form aggregate because the person is designated in dependence on any of the five aggregates.

[2]The example of a chariot is one that has been used since almost the beginnings of Buddhism and is used by Candrakīrti in the seven-fold reasoning. If we try to determine what exactly is something like a chariot, we find ourselves asking whether "chariot" should be equated with its parts, or whether it is something distinct from them, whether it is the collection, etc. None of the possibilities is without its problems, which can then lead us to understand that a chariot is something just imputed in dependence on experiencing certain parts but which is neither the same as nor different from them.

[3]The fivefold reasoning is used by Nāgārjuna in the twenty-first chapter of the *Treatise on the Middle Way.*

signs are asserted,[1] because there is no autonomous valid cognition, i.e., signs, autonomous signs are utterly not asserted. It is easy to understand that Daktsang is mistaken in saying that there is autonomy in this system.

The Detailed Explanation of the Presentation of the Two Truths of this System

Basis of the Division

The basis of the division is objects of knowledge. When divided, there are the two truths. More are not [needed], and if there were less, they would not [all] be included; [therefore,] the count is limited to those [two].

The basis of the division into two truths is objects of knowledge. When those are divided, they are definitely enumerated by way of entity as the two, conventional truths and ultimate truths, because there is no need for more than those, and if there were less, [all objects of knowledge] would not be included.[2]

Meaning of the Divisions

Because [if the two truths were different entities,] it would be unsuitable for [ultimate truths to be] the mode of subsistence. [243]

---

[1]For a Prāsaṅgika, even though a conventional phenomenon appears to exist inherently to the valid consciousness that certifies the existence of it—such as with an eye consciousness looking at a pot—that eye consciousness is not competent to certify an object's mode of existence, and thus it is not certifying the appearance as inherently existent. Only a reasoning consciousness analyzing the ultimate is competent for that certification. For their part, the Svātantrika school holds that a valid consciousness certifies whatever appears to it, and hence, they think inherently existent things exist conventionally. For this reason, the three modes (*tshul gsum mthun snag ba*) of a syllogism have "common appearance" for two Prāsaṅgikas in the sense that both parties agree that the validly cognizing consciousness that certifies the three modes, etc., does not also certify the inherent existence of it. "Merely" (*tsam*) eliminates that the valid cognition is autonomous (*rang rgyud*). The three modes of a syllogism do not have "common appearance" for a Prāsaṅgika and a non-Prāsaṅgika in the sense that the parties do not agree regarding the extent of certification for the validly cognizing consciousness that certifies the three modes.

[2]It is important to note that "truths" does not refer to propositions but rather to objects themselves. Everything that exists is either a conventional truth or an ultimate truth.

If the truths were different entities:

- it would be unsuitable for ultimate truths to be the mode of subsistence of their own substratum.
- [wisdom] would not outshine the conception of signs.
- cultivation of the paths would be senseless.
- even Buddhas would not have abandoned all defilements.[1]

[If the two truths were one isolate,] everyone would directly [perceive ultimate truths], etc. The two truths are an indivisible entity [but] are distinguished by [different] isolates.

Also, if the mere isolates[2] of those two were one:

- all common beings would directly see ultimate truths. [244]
- when the afflictive obstructions were abandoned, the reality [emptiness] of those would be abandoned.
- reality would be various.
- reality would be defiled.

Therefore, the two truths are indivisible in entity but are distinguished by different isolates.

---

[1]With regard to the first objection, for instance, emptiness could hardly be the nature of a pot if it were a different entity from the pot. With regard to the second, one would absurdly, for instance, realize the emptiness of a pot but not overcome the conception that the pot truly existed. With regard to the third and fourth, if realizing emptiness did not replace the conception of inherent existence, there would be no point in cultivating the paths, since ignorance could not be removed, and hence, there would be no Buddhas—or those called Buddhas would still have defilements.

[2]An isolate, a reverse, (or, Dreyfus translates, a *distinguisher*) is, regarding some phenomenon, the negation of its opposite. For instance, the isolate of table is that which is not non-table. Thought is said to operate in this manner; to recognize something, we eliminate what is *not* it to arrive at it. Things that are the same entity (meaning that whatever is one is necessarily the other) can nevertheless be different isolates. Synonyms, like product and impermanent phenomenon, are one entity and different isolates. Although whatever is a product is impermanent, and vice versa, the two are clearly different: "product" denotes being the effect of a cause and "impermanent" denotes change.

Defining Properties

Definitions: [an ultimate truth is] that with respect to which an awareness—a rational consciousness—comes to distinguish the ultimate and which is found by it.

Regarding definitions, respectively, the definition of an ultimate truth is regarded as:

> an object with respect to which a reasoning consciousness analyzing the ultimate becomes [a reasoning consciousness] analyzing the ultimate and the object found [by it].[1]

[A conventional truth] is that with respect to which a conventional awareness comes to distinguish a conventionality and which is found by it.

The definition of a conventional truth is regarded as:

> an object with respect to which a conventional awareness becomes an analyzer of the conventionality and the object found [by it].[2] [245]

Etymologies

An ultimate truth [is so-called] because of being an object, ultimate, and a truth.

[An ultimate truth] is an *object* due to being an object known, analyzed, and found by an excellent exalted wisdom consciousness. It is *ultimate* due to being the supreme among objects. It is a *truth* due to abiding as it appears. Because of that, it is called an ultimate truth.

An obscurational [i.e., conventional] truth is [so-called] because of being a truth for the perspective of the obscured due to obscuration.

---

[1]This rather tortured definition refers to emptinesses (mainly; Jamyang Shayba also thinks that true cessations, the absence of afflictions upon their destruction, are ultimate truths). A reasoning consciousness analyzing an object (as in the example in the previous section of wondering how to identify the essence of a chariot) searches for but does not find the object of its search, whereby it realizes (i.e., finds) the non-inherent existence of it.

[2]Roughly speaking, this just means that a conventional truth is something that can be established by ordinary valid cognition.

Because of obscuring the mode of subsistence [of phenomena], ignorance is the concealer, and since [obscurational truths] are true for merely the perspective of that [ignorance conceiving true existence], they are called obscurational truths.[1]

Individual Divisions

When ultimate truths are divided, there are two, four, sixteen, etc. [246]

When ultimate truths are divided, there are:

- the two: the selflessnesses of phenomena and persons
- the four: the emptinesses of things; non-things; own-entity; and others' entity.
- the sixteen: the emptinesses of the internal; the external; the internal and external; emptiness; the great; the ultimate; products; non-products; what has passed beyond extremes; what is beginningless and endless; the indestructible; nature; all phenomena; definitions; the unapprehendable; and the entityness of non-things[2]
- the twenty: the combination of the sixteen and four, etc. [247]

[Terminologically divided,] there are two: the awareness of [common] beings [realizing emptiness] along with their objects are metaphorical [ultimates] and the awareness of Superiors [in meditative equipoise] along with their objects are other [i.e., non-metaphorical ultimates].

When divided terminologically, the dualistic consciousnesses of common beings, etc., who realize emptiness, along with their objects, are metaphoric ultimates, and the non-contaminated awarenesses of Superiors who realize emptiness directly, along with their objects, are non-metaphorical ultimates.[3]

---

[1]Literally they are "concealer" truths (*saṃvṛti-satya*). Previously, we have called them "conventional truths," and we still prefer that translation and use it elsewhere although it is not as literal. "Obscurational" is a better translation as long as it is understood that we are referring to all existents or phenomena other than the ultimate truths, not to agents that are actively obscuring as the term seems to suggest. They obscure only in the sense that their appearance is false, that is, that to ordinary persons they appear to exist inherently although they do not.

[2]For more on these sixteen as well as two others, see the list of eighteen emptinesses in Hopkins, *Meditation*, 204–5. This really amounts to a kind of peculiar list of phenomena. For instance, the emptiness of the internal is the emptiness of the five senses and the emptiness of the great is the emptiness of the ten directions.

[3]Common beings are meditators who have not yet realized emptiness *directly*, although they may

[In] the Mādhyamika's own system there are no real and unreal conventionalities, [but] for the perspective of a worldly consciousness, a human, a reflection, etc., are merely real and unreal in the sense of being true and untrue.

In the Prāsaṅgika-Mādhyamika's own system, conventionalities are not distinguished as real[1] and unreal.[2] However, for the perspective of a consciousness of an ordinary worldly being that is not directed toward suchness, since a human, conventional valid cognition to which a human appears, etc., are true in accordance with how they appear, they are real conventionalities. Since a mirror image and the awareness that apprehends it as a face are not true as they appear,[3] those are called unreal conventionalities. This is merely a division for the perspective of that [conventional] consciousness.[4] [248]

In his *Ocean of Reasoning, Explanation of (Nāgārjuna's) "Treatise on the Middle Way,"* Dzongkaba says:

> The objects of apprehension of the two innate conceptions of true existence, for instance, are said to be "apprehended by non-defective senses";[5] they are real or true relative to ordinary worldly thought but do not exist even conventionally.[6]

This refutes those who say that [the ordinary worldly being's] thought [with respect to which the division into real and unreal is made] is [necessarily] valid cognition and also refutes those who say that real [conventionalities must necessarily] exist.[7]

---

have realized it inferentially. With the direct realization of emptiness, one passes from being a common being to being a Superior (*'phags pa, ārya*).

[1]*yang dag.* This is translated as *real* when applied to objects and as *correct* when applied to consciousnesses.

[2]*log pa.* This is translated as *unreal* when applied to objects and as *incorrect* when applied to consciousnesses.

[3]This means that what appears as a face—a reflection of a face in a mirror—does not exist as a *face.* It does exist as a *reflection;* but it is not being perceived as a reflection of a face.

[4]A face being apprehending as a face by an eye consciousness is real in the perspective of the world, even though that eye consciousness assents to the appearance of true existence.

[5]Non-defective means that the senses are free from superficial causes of error, such being fooled by optical illusions or being affected by a physical malady.

[6]Because an eye consciousness correctly apprehending a face as a face is also conceiving that face to exist inherently, the actual face is true in relation to the worldly perspective, but the face as conceived to exist, an inherently existent face, simply does not exist at all.

[7]For more on this complex topic, see Newland, *The Two Truths,* chapter eight.

Differences Between Method and What Arises from Method

Conventional [valid cognition] are assisters that [must] precede [ultimate] reasoning consciousnesses; they are [respectively] the means and that arisen from the means.

There are a great many valid cognitions of faith of conviction distinguishing conventionalities.[1] This is due to the existence of great force of ascertainment regarding actions and their fruits, such as those that ascertain the divisions of the aggregates, etc., and the mode of dependence of dependent-arisings [249] [within taking] valid cognition as their basis. They are indispensable assisters that must precede generating a reasoning consciousness distinguishing the ultimate. Therefore, [regarding] those two, [conventional valid cognition and reasoning consciousnesses distinguishing the ultimate,] the former is the means and the latter is arisen from the means, and after finding the view, they are assisters that are mutually dependent without separation.[2]

Purpose of Teaching the Two Truths and Dispelling Mistakes

The purpose [of teaching the two truths] is to overcome all [wrong] views and for the sake [of knowing what to] discard and adopt. Therefore, [meditation] without elaborations and not on emptiness in a third period is mistaken.

The purpose of teaching the two truths is to overcome all wrong views of permanence and annihilation and for the sake of coming to be able to differentiate subtly what is to be abandoned and adopted regarding actions and their fruits.[3] [250] Therefore, Daktsang's assertion that, as a third stage [of meditation, one meditates] free from elaborations, which is called "neither existence, non-existence

---

[1]The faith of conviction arises from understanding causes and their effects. These are conventional phenomena that are realized by valid cognition. It is not that realization of the ultimate—emptiness—harms apprehension of conventional truths.

[2]In other words, emptiness is not realized in the abstract but in relation to something that exists conventionally and is established by conventional valid cognition. Jamyang Shayba adds in his *Great Exposition of Tenets* that the five aggregates, six constituents, twelve sense spheres, eighteen constituents, etc., must first be established for one's awareness before their mode of subsistence can be understood. An additional point is undoubtedly to emphasize how the two truths reinforce each other (Gomang, 581.3).

[3]Jamyang Shayba's annotator Ngawang Belden sees "discard and adopt" as referring to discarding awarenesses conceiving true existence and adopting awarenesses realizing the absence of true existence.

[nor both or neither]" and is not meditation on the meaning of emptiness, is mistaken.[1]

Order of Overcoming Wrong Views

The stages of the mode of leading trainees on the paths must be done as follows in the root text:

Sūtra and mantra assert that initially, by [causing the student to ascertain] actions and their fruits, etc., non-meritorious [actions] are overcome.

Both sūtra and tantra assert that in the first [stage, the teacher] causes [the student] to ascertain the entities of actions and their fruits and their incontrovertible mode of relation, and, having explained the good qualities of the Three Jewels, [the teacher] causes [the student] to overcome accumulated non-meritorious sinful actions [251] in order that [the student] might be protected from going to bad [migrations].[2]

In the middle, by [teaching] impermanence, etc., the two [conceptions of self] are overcome.

In the intermediate [stage, the teacher] causes [the student] to overcome the two conceptions of self—(1) the conception of a permanent, single, independent [self], and (2) the conception [of the person] as substantially existent in the sense of being self-sufficient, i.e., having a character that does not accord with the aggregates[3]—through teaching impermanence, suffering, etc., whereby one is made into a suitable vessel for realizing subtle selflessness.[4]

---

[1]Jamyang Shayba adds in his *Great Exposition of Tenets* that Daktsang bases his view on what Jamyang Shayba characterizes as a misreading of the explanation in Āryadeva's *Four Hundred* that initially, the non-meritorious is overcome, in the middle, self is overcome, and finally, all views are overcome. Gomang, 583.17. The translation follows Hopkins. Meditation on emptiness is all that is needed to overcome the obstructions to liberation.

[2]These are the practices of a being of small capacity within the scheme of the beings of three capacities in the Stages of the Path (*lam rim*).

[3]A substantially existent self-sufficient person would not have the character of the aggregates in the sense that such a self would not have production, abiding, and disintegration.

[4]In other words, one grows accustomed to this emptiness that is coarser than the emptiness of inherent existence. One is thereby "made into a suitable vessel for realizing subtle selflessness" in the sense that one will thereby become able to understand the more subtle emptiness of inherent existence.

Finally, suchness is actualized. Through these stages, all [wrong] views, along with their defilements, are overcome.

In the final [stage], all artificial and innate [wrong] views, along with their defilements, are conquered by stages of realizing the profound suchness and actualizing capacities for increasing [that realization] higher and higher.[1]

Stages of Meditation on the Profound That Are the Means of Overcoming Wrong Views

There are five stages of meditation [on emptiness]. Look into the statements of the wise. [252]

Regarding the stages of the mode of meditation on the meaning of such profundity, [there are] the quintessential instructions that actually came from the mouth of the Protector Mañjughoṣa [that are contained in] the unique system of the Foremost Second Conqueror, the Father [Dzongkaba], which he gave in the whispered lineage. However, while I have indeed obtained, in the whispered lineage, the mode in which all the non-erroneous systems of sūtra, tantra, and the great chariots appear as instructions [for practice], clear and vast, and in particular, [the instructions on] the generation of the ascertainment of the view by beginners and the knowledge of the way of developing experience [regarding the view], it is said that it is not to be taught commonly. [Hence,] the mere entity [i.e., outline] of the meaning is as follows.

There are five [stages in meditation on emptiness]:[2]

1. the beginners' [253] mode of developing experience regarding the view
2. the mode of cultivating a similitude of calm abiding and special insight
3. the mode of cultivating actual [special insight and calm] abiding
4. the mode of direct realization [of emptiness]
5. the mode of cultivation by way of the stage of completion [of Highest Yoga Tantra]

---

[1]Returning to the explanation in Āryadeva's *Four Hundred* that initially, the non-meritorious is overcome, in the middle, self is overcome, and finally, all views are overcome, Jamyang Shayba explains in his *Great Exposition of Tenets* that the three stages overcome, respectively, the Nihilistic view, the view of a substantially existent self-sufficient self that does not have the character of the aggregates, and the conception of true existence. Gomang, 587.13.

[2]See Hopkins, *Meditation,* 43–115, for a full discussion of these five stages.

Therefore, [Jamyang Shayba] says, "Look into the statements of the wise," i.e., their quintessential instructions.[1]

Subsequent Attainment As Well As Union

Just as [it is difficult to realize] emptiness, it is difficult to [ascertain] the limits for identifying conventionalities. Since whichever of the two truths one falls from, one is ruined and falls to extremes, it is unsuitable to be partisan regarding those two. Cherish their union.

Just as it is difficult to realize emptiness, it is very difficult, having refuted the object of negation on a subtle level, to [ascertain] the limits of identifying conventionalities that are objects and agents posited as name-only. Therefore, because no matter which of the two truths one falls from, one is ruined [254] and falls to extremes—because if one falls from conventionalities, one goes to bad migrations, and if one falls from the ultimate, saṃsāra is not cut off—cherish the harmonious union of those two [existing conventionally and not existing ultimately] from the point of view of ascertaining that it is not suitable to be partial [close to one and far from the other] and that the two serve to assist one another.

The Three Natures in the Prāsaṅgika System

[The Prāsaṅgika identification of] the three natures is similar [to other Mahāyāna schools].

Regarding the manner of [identifying] the three natures, the [Prāsaṅgikas'] mere identifying of the bases of emptiness as empty of imputations is similar [to the explanation on the occasion of the Svātantrika school].

It is asserted that the nature [appearing] in other-powered phenomena is an imputation for the childish but is thoroughly established for Conquerors.

In this context [of Prāsaṅgika], in relation to the bases of emptiness, other-powered phenomena, whose [ultimate] nature is non-artificial and non-dependent,

[1]Dzongkaba's main writings on the Mādhyamika view may be found in the following: *Great Explanation of (Nāgārjuna's) "Treatise on the Middle Way"; Great Explanation of Candrakīrti's "Entrance to (Nāgārjuna's) 'Treatise on the Middle Way'; Essence of Eloquence; Great Exposition of Special Insight*; and *Middling Exposition of Special Insight.*

their appearance to childish beings is asserted to be an imputation, [255] whereas their appearance to Conquerors is asserted to be a thoroughly established phenomenon.[1]

The Unique Tenets of the Prāsaṅgika System

Because they do not assert establishment by way of [the object's] own character even conventionally, there are many distinguishing features such as the eight unique [tenets].

Because establishment by way of [the object's] own character is not asserted even conventionally, there are many [points], as will be explained, such as the eight unique qualities that are the superior features of [Prāsaṅgika] tenets.[2] Moreover, they are as follows.[3]

Distinctions About the Existence of External Objects and the Non-Existence of a Mind-Basis-of-All

[The Prāsaṅgika school] asserts that external objects exist because they are not refuted by an awareness distinguishing conventionalities. They assert that a mind-basis-of-all does not exist because it is not established by awareness distinguishing conventionalities.

Because of not being refuted by an awareness distinguishing conventionalities, external objects exist, for if they did not exist, they would have to lack existence even conventionally. [256] Because of not being established by an awareness distinguishing conventionalities, a mind-basis-of-all is asserted not to exist, for if it

---

[1]This seems to mean that when "childish beings," those who have not realized emptiness, apprehend other-powered phenomena (ordinary things that have causes) what appears to them, along with the aspect of the object, is the false, superimposed appearance of inherent existence. For Conquerors (Buddhas), on the other hand, there is no such appearance; along with the aspect of the object, what appears is emptiness, the thoroughly established phenomenon.

[2]See Cozort, *Unique Tenets*, 283–423, for a complete translation of this topic in Jamyang Shayba's root text and auto-commentary as well as in Ngawang Belden's *Annotations*,

[3]Jamyang Shayba adds this eleven-part topical outline in his *Great Exposition of Tenets*, Gomang 598.5. We have added it to facilitate one's understanding of the changes in topic.

did exist, due to its being a consciousness it would have to be established by [an awareness distinguishing conventionalities].[1]

Distinctions About the Two Selflessnesses

There is no liberation for those who conceive of true existence. That [conception] is an afflictive [obstruction]. The selflessnesses are similarly [subtle].

Sūtras and the Superior [Nāgārjuna] say that liberation does not exist for one who conceives of [truly existent] things.[2] Therefore, the conception of [truly existent] things is established as being an afflictive obstruction that mainly prevents liberation.[3] In that case, Hearer [Arhats] must [also] have eliminated it. Except for the fact that the abandoners, i.e., the paths, [are different], the two selflessnesses are established similarly.

Distinctions About Subsequent Cognitions as Valid Cognitions and About the Conventional

Because there are none unpolluted, all consciousnesses of childish persons are mistaken.

---

[1]In both of these instances, the crucial factor is whether or not conventional valid cognition—ordinary cognition such as an eye consciousness—refutes or affirms existence. No valid conventional cognition (which means just any awareness not involved in an analytical search for an inherently existent object) refutes external objects and, therefore, the Prāsaṅgikas, who treasure worldly conventions, accept them. On the other hand, no such awareness can establish a mind-basis-of-all (which means that it is not logically necessary to accept such a consciousness to explain that karmic seeds can produce appearances).

[2]Unlike some other schools, who posit conceptions grosser than true existence (e.g., a permanent, partless self) as the root of saṃsāra, the Prāsaṅgika school says that this concept is the obstruction to liberation.

[3]According to Prāsaṅgika, one does not realize anything more subtle to eliminate the obstructions to omniscience than one did to eliminate the obstructions to liberation. The selflessness of persons and the selflessness of phenomena are equally subtle. They are differentiated by way of their bases of emptiness: persons and phenomena other than persons. For the other Mahāyāna schools, the selflessness of phenomena is more subtle than the selflessness of persons. The Svātantrika school sees the conception of a self of phenomena only as an obstruction to omniscience. For them, afflictive ignorance—what keeps beings in saṃsāra—is the conception of the person as substantially existent in the sense of being self-sufficient.

All consciousnesses of the childish, i.e., common beings, are established as mistaken consciousnesses. This is because they are not unpolluted by ignorance in their own continuums [257] in the sense that [the object's] own mode of appearance is that it appears to be established from its own side.[1]

Because new realization is unsuitable, subsequent cognizers are established to be valid cognizers.

The proof, in the texts of the Proponents of True Existence, that the first moment of [an eye consciousness] apprehending blue, for instance, is a prime cognizer[2] due to being a new realizer, is a case of analyzing the object imputed [and finding it]. Since that is not suitable here [in Prāsaṅgika], it is established that the later continuation of that [direct cognizer] and subsequent cognizers that are induced by it are prime cognizers.[3]

Distinctions About Mental Direct Perception and Yogic Direct Perception

Because feeling is a mental direct perception, conceptual mental direct perception exists.

---

[1]The mistaken element of all cognitions for non-Buddhas—the single exception being one-pointed meditative equipoise on emptiness—is that objects appear to inherently exist. Since this meditative equipoise occurs only in Superiors, it being the meditative accomplishment that sets Superiors apart from common beings, common beings are never without this mistaken element. To put this another way, the first time a person ever perceives anything without this mistaken element is in the meditative session in which that person becomes a Superior through directly realizing emptiness.

[2]*tshad ma, pramāṇa,* is translated alternately as *valid cognizer* and *prime cognizer* as required by context. In those systems that hold only the first moment of, for instance, an eye consciousness apprehending a patch of blue to be *pramāṇa,* the translation "prime cognizer" is appropriate. In addition to Cozort's treatment of this topic in *Unique Tenets,* Dreyfus has a very interesting discussion of *pramāṇa* in *Recognizing Reality.*

[3]The other schools are said to engage in ultimate analysis. An ordinary awareness would designate a consciousness as prime cognition simply because it is incontrovertible regarding its object. It would not engage in investigation to determine if that consciousness was the first or a subsequent moment of a continuum of perception. To investigate the relationship between the object imputed—the consciousness—and the basis of imputation—the moments of a continuum of consciousness—would be ultimate analysis.

Because Candrakīrti explains in his *Commentary on (Āryadeva's) "Four Hundred"* that an ordinary feeling [258] is mental direct perception,[1] and because in his *Clear Words* Candrakīrti refutes that [mental direct perception] is necessarily non-conceptual, it is asserted that there are conceptual mental direct perceivers.[2]

Because even when one actualizes the sixteen [aspects of the Four Noble Truths], one is not [necessarily] a Superior, it is asserted that there are common beings who actualize the sixteen aspects of the [Four Noble] Truths.

[Some] sūtras, and the reasoning in Śāntideva's *Engaging in the Bodhisattva Deeds*, establish that there are some who, even though they actualize, i.e., directly realize, the sixteen [aspects of the Four Noble Truths]—impermanence, etc.—fall into bad migrations due to having doubt regarding the path. Because those are necessarily not Superiors, it is asserted that there are common beings who actualize the sixteen aspects of the [Four Noble] Truths.[3]

The sixteen aspects of the [Four Noble] Truths are:

1-4 [the four attributes of True Sufferings]: impermanence, suffering, emptiness, and selflessness

5-8 [the four attributes of True Causes]: cause, origin, strong production, and condition

9-12 [the four attributes of True Cessations]: cessation, pacification, [259] auspicious magnitude, and definite emergence

---

[1]Direct perception is that which does not depend on a sign or reason. Sense consciousnesses are direct, but after the first moment of a mental consciousness (e.g., the conceptual understanding of something that has been seen), it too can be direct. Other Buddhist tenet systems from the Sautrāntika school to the Svātantrika school hold that mental direct perception is necessarily non-conceptual (as when the mind stays with an object that no longer is being experienced by the senses). Beyond the mere position that mental direct perceptions can be conceptual is the more subtle point that *feelings* can be instances of them. It is not clear that Candrakīrti, Dzongkaba, or even Jamyang Shayba is saying anything more than that feeling is an *object* of mental direct perception. See Cozort, *Unique Tenets*, 251 *et seq.*

[2]Jamyang Shayba's position is that there are instances of conceptual mental perception, not that *all* instances of mental perception are necessarily conceptual. Dzongkaba says in his *Illumination of the Thought, Explanation of (Candrakīrti's) "Entrance to the Middle Way"* that there are instances of mental direct perception that are memory consciousnesses, and thus necessarily conceptual.

[3]Prāsaṅgikas say that it is necessary to realize the emptiness of inherent existence in order to become a Superior. However, if one realizes the absence of a permanent, partless, independent self—the conception of self that the Hīnayāna schools identify as afflicted ignorance—one can be said to directly realize, or actualize, the Four Noble Truths.

13-16 [the four attributes of True Paths]: path, suitability, achievement, and deliverance.[1]

Also, regarding [the Four Noble Truths] there are gross and subtle [ways to identify them];[2] what common beings directly realize are the gross.[3]

Distinctions About Assertions on the Aspects of the Four Truths and on the Three Times

Because [attaining] special insight regarding emptiness and [attaining] the path of preparation are simultaneous, and because disintegratedness is a thing, [respectively, realizing] the sixteen [aspects of the Four Noble Truths] by direct perception is not [the same as] reaching the path of preparation, and the three times are asserted to be [functioning] things.

Because attaining special insight regarding emptiness and attaining the path of preparation are simultaneous, one does not reach even the path of preparation by merely attaining yogic direct perception directly realizing the sixteen [aspects of the Four Noble Truths], impermanence, etc.[4] [260]

---

[1]For a discussion of these attributes and how they are meditated upon, see Hopkins, *Meditation,* 292–6.

[2]These sixteen aspects of the four truths have both coarse and subtle aspects. The coarse aspects arise from what the Prāsaṅgika school holds to be the coarse selflessness of persons—the person's absence of being substantially existent in the sense of being self-sufficient. The subtle aspects arise from what the Prāsaṅgika school holds to be the subtle selflessness of persons—the person's absence of inherent existence. See Cozort, *Unique Tenets,* 265 *et seq.*

[3]Direct realization of the subtle aspects would necessitate direct realization of emptiness—the absence of inherent existence—whereby the meditator would be a Superior, not a common being, since becoming a Superior is regarded in terms of directly realizing the emptiness of inherent existence.

[4]This is the same point that was made in the previous section: it is possible for a person to realize a kind of absence of self that would enable us to say that he or she had realized the Four Noble Truths, but such a person would not be an Arhat, a liberated person, or even a Superior, because of not having realized the emptiness of inherent existence, the most subtle selflessness. "Emptiness" means the most subtle emptiness—the absence of inherent existence, and it is realized inferentially on "the path of preparation."

The five spiritual paths—a scheme that delineates progress from developing motivation to actually being a Buddha—are set forth differently for Hearers, Solitary Realizers, and Bodhisattvas, and within the latter are set forth differently for those following sūtra than for those

At the time of [i.e., in the context of asserting that phenomena] need not be posited upon analyzing the imputed object, it is permissible to identify disintegratedness [and thus the past] as a [functioning] thing. Also, because [this] reason is similar for future objects, the three times—past, future, and present—are all three asserted to be [functioning] things.[1]

[Distinctions about] Disintegratedness Being a [Functioning] Thing and Effects Being Feasible, as Well as a Dispelling of Objections

Because of being produced, disintegratedness is a [functioning] thing. Although many [eons] pass after an action has ceased, effects issue forth, even though "acquisition," [mental] continuums [in which predispositions are infused], and "non-wastage" do not exist.

Because of being produced by causes, disintegratedness is a [functioning] thing,[2] and since it is able to produce effects directly, although many eons have passed after the cessation of actions that have all [the features of] having been done

---

following tantra. For a Bodhisattva, the initial path would be "accumulation," begun when he or she has *bodhicitta*, a spontaneous altruistic wish to attain enlightenment. "Preparation" is a conceptual understanding of emptiness through a union of calm abiding and special insight. With further development, the meditator can develop this conceptual consciousness realizing emptiness into a non-conceptual consciousness realizing emptiness directly, the path of "seeing." After this moment of initial direct cognition of emptiness, one enters the path of "meditation," which has ten Bodhisattva levels. The further contemplation of emptiness within the perfection of qualities such as generosity and patience serves as an actual antidote to progressively more subtle levels of the innate conception of inherent existence. At the lower half of the eighth ground, the innate conception of inherent existence is entirely removed such that it will never return. From the upper half of the eighth ground through the tenth ground, a meditator abandons the obstructions to omniscience, which cause the appearance of inherently existent objects to sense and mental consciousnesses. When the subtlest of stains are removed, one passes to the path of "no more learning," or Buddhahood.

[1]This will be explained in the next section.

[2]Although most other schools would consider something's having-disintegrated as nothing more than a mere absence, a permanent phenomenon that is neither caused nor capable of being a cause, Prāsaṅgikas argue that states such as "deadness" or "disintegratedness" is caused and can act as a cause, which is the basic meaning of being a functioning or effective thing. For instance, a flame's having-died is caused by the consumption of its fuel; moreover, the fuel's having-been-consumed is the cause of the light dying out. It may seem a very, very fine point, but for Prāsaṅgikas it allows them, without positing some other entity, to account for the way in which actions (karma), having-disintegrated, can produce effects in the future.

and accumulated, [261] the disintegratedness of the action is posited as the producer of effects without there being any need to posit, upon analyzing the imputed object, a thing that connects an effect with an action [such as]:[1]

- "acquisition" that is produced by actions
- a continuum of [mental] consciousness in which predispositions are infused
- "non-wastage of actions," a substantial entity that is like a seal witnessing a loan, etc.

The mere propounding that disintegratedness is a [functioning] thing is without analysis, like [saying] pots are things.

In the system of the Prāsaṅgika school, although it is propounded that there exist mere [functioning] things that are states of disintegratedness, it is like asserting that things that are pots exist because there is no analysis of the imputed object.[2]

---

[1]These are all ways to account for the continuation of karmic latencies until their fruition or elimination. Most of the sub-schools of the Vaibhāṣika are thought to agree that karmic latencies have a factor of adherence, "acquisition," that connects them to a specific sentient being. "Continuum of mind" is the basis for most other Buddhist schools; "non-wastage," which is a factor of non-deterioration that keeps latencies from disintegrating before they can ripen, is said to be the position of the other Vaibhāṣika sub-sects; and the mind-basis-of-all is the solution of the Cittamātra and Yogācāra-Svātantrika schools. Prāsaṅgikas will reject the need for any of these, which on the one hand it considers to be substantial entities, and on the other hand it considers to be the inventions of philosophers rather than something that accords with the conventions of the world. Disintegratedness is not substantial, and it *does* come from what the world says (since in the conventions of the world we *do* speak about death and other states of having-disintegrated as having been caused).

[2]This is a subtle point, but an important one for Prāsaṅgikas. All schools other than Prāsaṅgika are said to fall to an extreme of permanence because they feel that things have some kind of "pointable" existence. With regard to impermanent phenomena, for instance, they feel that there must be some illustration to which one can point or else the thing in question should be classified instead as a permanent phenomenon, if it exists at all. They cannot accept the fact that a functioning thing can be a mere nominal designation. Dzongkaba gives the example of how a man named Upagupta is not identical with the body and mind in dependence on which "Upagupta" is designated. This is Upagupta's mode of existence because he is empty of inherent existence. Nevertheless, Upagupta exists. Similarly, although there is nothing to which one can point that is the "disintegratedness" of an action (just as there was nothing to which one could point that was Upagupta), nevertheless there is a basis—the disintegrated action—in dependence on which "disintegratedness" can be designated (just as there is a basis—a body and mind—in dependence on which "Upagupta" can be designated). To insist that there must be something to which we can point is to engage in "ultimate analysis," the primary error of the non-Prāsaṅgika schools. The result, in any case, is that it is possible to assert that even when an actions's fruition

If harsh speech appears without having being destroyed to the innate [awareness] after a [long] time has passed, how could all that one has done previously not be remembered?

In accordance with Daktsang's assertions, if, for instance, harsh speech that occurred long ago, existing without destruction, [262] appeared to the innate awareness, how could all that one did before not be remembered? It would have to be remembered.

Non-Assertion of Autonomy and Self-Consciousness

Because they cannot [be established] without analysis, autonomous [reasons] and self-consciousness do not exist.

Because they cannot be posited without distinguishing the imputed object, autonomous reasons[1] and self-consciousness are not asserted to exist.

Distinctions About Pratyakṣa and True Cessations

When relating, *pratyakṣa* is for objects, not subjects.

When making designations relative to a pot and a sense direct perceiver apprehending a pot, *pratyakṣa* is applied chiefly to objects and secondarily to subjects. Therefore, the chief [use] of *pratyakṣa* is objects, not subjects.[2]

---

has been experienced, the action's disintegratedness, which functions as its "seed," does not cease. Once something has disintegrated, it will always be true that it has disintegrated.

[1]The disagreement between the Prāsaṅgika and Svātantrika schools over whether or not autonomous syllogisms exist is, at its heart, about what a consciousness is able to certify. For the Autonomist, the eye consciousness that certifies that an object *exists* also certifies the object's *mode of existence.* In other words, at the same time my eye consciousness sees an apple and enables me to certify that it exists, I am also able to certify the *way* it exists. Both schools agree that things appear as though they inherently exist. Therefore, my eye consciousness is certifying the *inherent* existence of the apple. Prāsaṅgikas completely disagree: an eye consciousness cannot certify anything more than the mere existence of what it sees. The syllogism that a Svātantrika uses is called "autonomous," but it might have been called "inherently existent" because they are synonyms. It is not really that the syllogism itself is autonomous, but that all of its elements—subject, reason, and example—appear to exist inherently, both to the stater of the syllogism and to the hearer of it. For an extensive analysis of this topic, see Hopkins, *Meditation,* 441–530.

[2]This term, which literally means "before the eyes," is used in two ways: to refer to direct perception and to refer to what is perceived, namely "manifest phenomena," or those phenomena

True cessations are the element of attributes[1] [i.e., the emptiness of inherent existence. Therefore, all] Superiors perceive selflessness [directly].

Since true cessations [263] are necessarily the element of attributes, the negation of subtle true establishment, it is asserted that the three [types of] Superiors directly perceive non-true existence.[2]

Distinctions About Nirvāṇas With and Without Remainder

Because it is explained that the extinction of the aggregates is unsuitable [in the sense of cutting the continuum of mind and body], and because it is explained that feelings and discriminations are destroyed, [nirvāṇas] without remainder and with remainder [involve] the extinction and non-extinction of mistaken [dualistic] appearances.

Statements of remainderless [nirvāṇa] and of extinction of the aggregates cannot [refer to] extinction at the present time. If they refer to cutting the continuum [of mind and body], since it is explained that feelings and discriminations are destroyed, there is no way to manifest [a remainderless nirvāṇa]. Therefore, statements that it is manifested are contradicted. Since it is explained in part by the fact that it [also] cannot apply to the future aggregates, extinction of the aggregates must refer to their extinction in the element of attributes. [264]

Therefore, nirvāṇas without and with remainder are regarded [respectively as] nirvāṇas on the occasions of the extinction and non-extinction of mistaken

---

that can appear to direct perception. Prāsaṅgikas, unlike others, reserve the term primarily for objects.

[1]The translation of *chos kyi dbyings/dharmadhātu* as "element of attributes" follows Hopkins. It is based on the etymology (by Maitreya in the *Discrimination of the Middle and the Extremes*) that the element of attributes is so called because meditation on it (emptiness) acts as a cause of the attributes (*chos, dharma*) of Superiors (*'phags pa, ārya*).

[2]True cessations are the absences of afflictions in the mind of persons who have irrevocably eliminated at least a portion of the afflictions. Their equation with emptiness makes again the point that to be a Superior, someone who has realized a true cessation, one must have realized emptiness, not anything more coarse such as is talked about in the lower tenet systems. Whether it is legitimate to make this equation is questionable; Jamyang Shayba quotes Candrakīrti and Dzongkaba, but the citations are at best ambiguous. Others, such as Paṇchen Sönam Drakba, author of textbooks for Drebung Loseling, disagree. However, by making this equation Jamyang Shayba is able to explain how persons who in one moment are realizing the emptiness of inherent existence can in the next moment, without switching objects of observation, be said to realize the true cessation of an affliction in their own continuums.

appearances to the mind, that is, of the existence and non-existence of the manifest appearance of true existence.[1]

Distinctions About the Two Obstructions and How They Are Abandoned

Predispositions [established by the conception of inherent existence] are obstructions to omniscience. Non-afflicted ignorance is also asserted.

[The following are scriptural sources for the assertion of non-afflicted ignorance.][2]

- Candrakīrti's *Commentary to the "Entrance to the Middle Way"* says, "Because ignorance that obstructs knowing [all] operates..."

---

[1]The lower schools and Prāsaṅgika mean different things by the terms "nirvāṇa with remainder" and "nirvāṇa without remainder." For the lower schools, these terms refer to a remainder of the mental and physical aggregates. First, an Arhat would actualize a nirvāṇa, within still having the mental and physical aggregates of mind and body, and later, at death, have a nirvāṇa without remainder of the aggregates. The Prāsaṅgika school uses the terms to refer to the presence or absence of dualistic appearance of inherent existence to ordinary consciousnesses, i.e., those not involved in directly realizing emptiness. An Arhat first manifests a nirvāṇa without remainder of mistaken dualistic appearance at the time of setting in one-pointed meditative equipoise on emptiness. However, due to the force of the obstructions to omniscience, after rising from that meditative stabilization the Arhat experiences false appearances; phenomena will continue to *appear* to exist inherently and, therefore, there is a "remainder" of dualistic appearance. Only the removal of the obstructions to omniscience, i.e., the attainment of Buddhahood, makes it possible to never again experience the "remainder" of false appearance. Only Buddhas have a nirvāṇa without remainder.

[2]The obstructions to omniscience are predispositions established by the afflictions of desire, etc., that cause the continued *appearance* of inherent existence even after one has eliminated ignorance and no longer *conceives* of things to exist that way. As predispositions, they would be classified as non-associated compositional factors (as opposed to matter or consciousness). However, Jamyang Shayba wants to call them "non-afflicted ignorance" (i.e., an ignorance that does not cause saṃsāra); and if they are ignorance, and ignorance is a consciousness, then they must be a consciousness, too. However, the sources that he cites (and that are reproduced by Losang Gönchok here) are hardly unambiguous. Janggya and Ngawang Belden point out that there are a host of scholars who disagree with Jamyang Shayba's view. Jamyang Shayba's best authority would appear to be Gyeltsap, who speaks of two kinds of obstructions to omniscience, the "seed" that are presumably non-associated compositional factors and the "manifest" that are consciousness—although Gyeltsap stops short of saying that the latter are a consciousness. In any case, this quotation appears only here in Losang Gönchok's commentary, not in Jamyang Shayba's!

- Dzongkaba's *Illumination of the Thought, Explanation of (Candrakīrti's) "Entrance to the Middle Way"* says, "Because the mere non-afflicted ignorance that has the character of obstructing knowing [all] thoroughly operates..." [265]
- Śāntideva's *Engaging in the Bodhisattva Deeds* (3.32) says, "It is the great sun that thoroughly removes the obscured vision of migrators' ignorance."
- Gyeltsap's *Explanation of (Śāntideva's) "Engaging in the Bodhisattva Deeds"* says: "...that removes thoroughly, that is, from the root, the non-afflicted ignorance of migrators, that is, the obscured vision that obstructs knowing [all]."

Moreover, [obstructions to omniscience that are consciousnesses exist] because regarding the obstructions to omniscience the two, seed and manifest [types], are explained.

- Dzongkaba's *Illumination of the Thought, Explanation of (Candrakīrti's) "Entrance to the Middle Way"* says: "Predispositions [established by] the afflictions are obstructions to omniscience. The effects of those, all the factors of mistaken dualistic perception, are included in [the obstructions to omniscience]."
- Gyeltsap's *Explanation of (Śāntideva's) "Engaging in the Bodhisattva Deeds"* [266] says: "The seed obstructions to omniscience are the final predispositions [established by] the afflictions, and the manifest [obstructions to omniscience] are the factors of appearance of things appearing to be truly existent, etc. However, it is not suitable to take whatever appears to be truly existent as necessarily being an obstruction to omniscience, etc."
- Dzongkaba's *Illumination of the Thought, Explanation of (Candrakīrti's) "Entrance to the Middle Way"* says: "Superiors who have not become awakened have not abandoned the ignorance that is the obstructions to omniscience, whereby in subsequent attainment they have conceptual consciousnesses that have the appearance [of true existence]..."

Such [explanations] exist in detail in Dzongkaba's *Great Exposition of the Stages of the Path*, but since it would be too much, I will not write it out. Those [explanations] in Kaydrup's *Opening the Eyes of the Fortunate* are just the same, and there is the clear example of Maudgalyāyana's not knowing—i.e., not being omniscient [although being a Superior]. [267]

This is what is to be included in the "etc." in Gyeltsap's *Explanation of (Śāntideva's) "Engaging in the Bodhisattva Deeds"* [cited earlier].

Until the afflictions are removed, abandonment of the obstructions to omniscience is not begun.

It is asserted that until the afflictions are removed, the abandonment of the obstructions to omniscience is not begun.[1] The sixth chapter of the *Excellent Golden Light Sūtra* called "Purification of Questions of Akṣayamati" explains in detail the twenty-two thorough obscurations, whereby in the Prāsaṅgika system also those must be regarded as objects of abandonment.

This sūtra teaches the Mādhyamika in general and the unique Prāsaṅgika school in particular in a literal way. It is as follows. The Teacher is asked, "If enlightenment and beings are not observed, how could a Bodhisattva [be observed]?" [268] Then the Teacher, in answer, explains that ultimately, enlightenment, beings, etc., are not observed and that all phenomena are nominalities and merely imputed. In that context, he extensively explains a presentation of the ten grounds and says that by reason of the indivisibility of the element of attributes that is to be realized, (1) it is not fitting that there be discordant vehicles, and (2) the teaching of three [final] vehicles is intended [to help those who would benefit from such a doctrine but is not Buddha's final thought].[2]

Therefore, that sūtra says, "Children of good family, [adhering] to signs regarding phenomena and persons...obstructs one regarding the Buddha ground." Regarding those, concerning the two [obstructions] of the first ground, the first [type of obstructions] are explained to be obstructions regarding the manifestation or production of a surpassing perfection of giving, [269] whereby they are attachments of thoroughly holding on to, or stains of adherence to, [persons and aggregates, such attachments or stains being] contradictory to the perfection of giving.[3]

---

[1]This is in contrast to the Yogācāra-Svātantrika school, where it is said that Bodhisattvas abandon both the afflictive obstructions and the obstructions to omniscience in stages as they proceed through the ten Bodhisattva grounds. Prāsaṅgikas think that this is absurd, since the afflictive obstructions are the cause of the stains that are the obstructions to omniscience. Candrakīrti asks, how you can remove the odor left by sesame oil or flowers until you have removed the oil itself?

[2]The element of attributes means emptiness, and the point is that there are not different objects of negation (different ignorant conceptions) that one addresses at different stages of the path, as others think, or different objects of negation for persons and other phenomena, but just one: inherent existence. Therefore, too, there is not more than one "final vehicle," since everyone must realize the emptiness of inherent existence in order to be liberated and in order to become a Buddha.

[3]On each of the ten Bodhisattva grounds that comprise the path of meditation, a specific virtue of giving, ethics, patience, etc., is perfected. (All of them are perfected continuously, but only one is completed at each stage.) One not only is removing the afflictive obstructions but also the "obstructions" to that particular perfection. On the first ground, whatever holds us back from perfect generosity is overcome. Even someone who has overcome all the afflictive obstructions (such as a former Hīnayāna Arhat who has come into the Bodhisattva path), much less others who have not, has bad habits from beginningless conditioning and is not capable yet of perfect

Regarding the second [type of obstructions], Dzongkaba's *Illumination of the Thought, Explanation of Candrakīrti's "Entrance"* says that the meaning of the statement, "At that time, all the [seeds for] paths going to bad migrations have ceased," in Candrakīrti's *Entrance to the Middle Way* is as follows. Seeds of paths to bad migrations have been abandoned, whereby [the second set of obstructions] are such seeds; not only that but also those potencies of actions that lead one into saṃsāra and are included within the levels of all three realms [are also included within this second type of obstruction]. Here [in the sūtra] it speaks of "obscurations of the fear of saṃsāra and bad migrations," and in Maitreya's *Ornament for Clear Realization* it says, "...thoroughly extinguished the [causal] branches [for being born in] the concentrations, etc."[1] [270]

The first [set of obstructions] of the second ground is easy to understand [from the statement] in that [sūtra], "The mistakenness of subtle infractions, that is, the stains of faulty ethics even in dreams." The second [type of obstructions] is taken as mistaken activities and behavior in dependence on body and speech, such as senselessly jumping like a monkey.[2]

Similarly, most of the others are seen to be provable as the positions of the Indian Prāsaṅgikas and the Foremost Father [Dzongkaba] and his spiritual sons. The statement by the Foremost Great Being [Dzongkaba] that on the first ground, what is abandoned is the stains of thoroughly holding on to [persons and aggregates] and the seeds of paths of bad migrations and that on the second ground what is abandoned is faulty ways opposes the statement that on the seventh ground and below, one abandons *merely* the afflictions [271] and that Arhats who have had prior realization [of nirvāṇa before entering the Mahāyāna] have nothing to be abandoned.[3]

---

generosity, etc.

[1]In other words, on those grounds (the first seven, anyway) one is also eliminating the afflictive obstructions, those that cause rebirth, whether that be bad migrations or even the birthplaces associated with the achievement of the mental concentrations (which are in the Form and Formless Realms).

[2]On the second ground one is eliminating obstructions to the perfection of ethics (the virtue of that ground) and one is also eliminating the predispositions that might cause one to behave badly in certain ways.

[3]It might be thought that those who become Arhats through following the Hīnayāna paths, once they enter the Bodhisattva path (as all are said to do), have nothing to do until after the seventh ground, when they eliminate the obstructions to omniscience. But as is now obvious, on each ground there are special obstructions to overcome so that one achieves the perfection of particular virtues. Although they have destroyed the afflictive obstructions and no longer conceive of inherent existence, they have not overcome the conditioning that prevents them from being perfectly generous, ethical, patient, and so on.

Gyeltsap's *Commentary on Maitreya's "Ornament for Clear Realization"* says that although the two, Hīnayāna Arhats and those on the Mahāyāna path of seeing, are the same in terms of directly realizing emptiness, they have a difference like Mount Meru and a mustard seed regarding their abilities to overcome the objects of abandonment.[1] Since the *Sūtra Unraveling the Thought* is similar to this, [such] must be asserted, and even the Cittamātra school does not identify this thorough obscuration [that is an obstruction for the first ground] as a conception of *self*. Both the Mādhyamika school and the Cittamātra school mainly identify this thorough obscuration from the point of view of partaking in the assumption of bad states that are in the opposite class of the respective ten perfections and call thorough obstructions "thorough obscurations"; [272] it does not appear to be definite that these are necessarily the mental factor, ignorance.

If the Prāsaṅgika school asserted these to be afflictive obstructions, it would be unsuitable to say that it did *not* assert them. If, [as some say,] a conception of objects as external objects, which is renowned as a conception of a self of phenomena in the Cittamātra system, is an afflictive obstruction, it would be contradictory [for them to be afflictive obstructions]. Therefore, if scholar's statements of such were taken to have [some other] intention, it would be better.[2]

Distinctions About How the Two Extremes are Cleared Away, Along with Subsidiary Topics

Through appearance the extreme of [inherent] existence is cleared away. Through emptiness the extreme of [utter] non-existence is cleared away.

The extreme of [true] existence is cleared away through ascertaining that appearances are dependent-arisings, and the extreme of non-existence is cleared away through emptiness, i.e., through refuting inherent existence.[3]

---

[1]Prāsaṅgikas say that anyone who is an Arhat has necessarily realized emptiness, not merely the less subtle selflessness that is described in the lower schools of tenets.

[2]This just seems to mean that some unspecified scholars have thought that the obstructions to perfect generosity, etc., were actually afflictive obstructions (the predispositions established by desire, hatred, and ignorance that cause rebirth, etc.) and that Losang Gönchok thinks that they have made a serious mistake.

[3]Other schools say that the extreme of non-existence or annihilation is cleared away by appearance (that is, the appearance of objects refutes that nothing exists) and the extreme of true existence is cleared away by emptiness, which is the absence of true existence. However, Prāsaṅgikas say that because the meaning of emptiness is the same as the meaning of dependent-arising, the reverse is also true. Because things are empty of own-existence, they must have a mode of existence of

For many unique [tenets] such as these, look in the *Great Exposition of the Middle Way.*

There are many [other] unique [Prāsaṅgika tenets], such as:

- The meditative equipoise of cessation realizes that [objects] are not established from their own side.[1] [273]
- In dependence on a mere contradictory consequence, an inferential consciousness realizing suchness is produced.[2]
- Even though even inferential cognition meets back to direct perception, it is sufficient that its experience [of its object] be incontrovertible; it is not necessary that direct perception be non-mistaken.[3]

These may be seen, i.e., ascertained, in (Jamyang Shayba's) *Decisive Analysis of the Middle Way* (called the *Great Exposition of the Middle Way*) and in the other books of this Foremost One[4] [Jamyang Shayba], etc.

---

depending on other things. Because they depend on other things, they must be empty of own-existence. Therefore, the appearance of dependently arising things refutes true existence, and realizing emptiness gives one conviction in the cause and effect of actions and eliminates doubts about conventional existence, thereby refuting the extreme of annihilation. In other words, understanding emptiness and dependent-arising is a middle way that eliminates the extremes, no matter where we begin.

[1]Jamyang Shayba does not explain this but only refers the reader to the works of Indian Mādhyamikas and those of Dzongkaba. In the meditative absorption of cessation, there is no manifest activity of the six types of consciousness. It is not evident how meditation on emptiness could be present at that time, but it is said to be a state attained only by Superiors, those who have realized emptiness.

[2]This refers to the reason why Prāsaṅgikas are so called; they believe that an understanding of emptiness can be induced in someone just by helping them to see that their own conception is untenable. They do not need to be presented with a positive proof but can infer that things must be dependent-arisings or that they must be only nominally existent once they understand that they are empty of independent existence.

[3]That direct perception is incorrect about the mode of being of the objects it apprehends, i.e., that it does not understand that the appearance of inherent existence is false, does not invalidate it with respect to just the object itself. Indeed, all perception of ordinary beings is mistaken because things appear to exist inherently, but they are nevertheless valid about the basic object itself. Therefore, inferences based upon sense direct perception are not necessarily invalidated, either.

[4]Losang Gönchok may not mean just Jamyang Shayba, but other "Foremost Ones" such as Dzongkaba, etc.

Valid Cognition in the Prāsaṅgika System

Valid cognition is explained as four: directly perceiving consciousnesses, inferential cognizing consciousnesses, [inferential valid cognition] comprehending [through an analogy], and scriptural. However, through the power of their objects of comprehension [these are condensed into] two: directly perceiving consciousnesses and inferential cognizing consciousnesses.

Valid cognition is explained as four: directly perceiving consciousnesses, inferential valid cognition [by the power of the fact], [inferential valid cognition] comprehending through an analogy, and scriptural valid cognition.[1] [274] However, in terms of their objects of comprehension they are condensed into two: directly perceiving consciousnesses and inferential cognizing consciousnesses.[2]

A direct valid cognition is a consciousness that, without [depending on] a sign, is incontrovertible regarding the manifest [object] that is the object of its mode of apprehension.

The definition of a direct valid cognition is asserted to be:

> a consciousness that, without depending on a sign, is incontrovertible regarding the manifest object of comprehension that is its object of the mode of apprehension.[3]

---

[1]In *Great Explanation of Tenets*, Jamyang Shayba defines valid cognition as: "an incontrovertible consciousness" *(mi bslu ba'i shes pa;* Gomang, 608.8), which means that it is correct; it is not deceived about its object. Other Buddhist schools understand *pramāṇa* to indicate *new* realization. According to this view, the first moment of an eye consciousness apprehending a pot, for instance, would be a valid (or "prime") cognition; later moments of that continuum would be *subsequent* cognizers. Prāsaṅgikas reject the requirement of novelty.

[2]In the list of four, the latter three types are all inferential and will be discussed by Losang Gönchok below. Inference by the power of the fact is the main type, being inference through the power of a reason. Inference comprehending through an analogy is to know something by way of an example, and scriptural inference is to accept what a scripture teaches, having ascertained that it is not contradicted by direct perception, inference, or other scriptures. For instance, the Buddha taught about the subtle workings of karma, which is not something that we who are without omniscience can establish or disprove by direct perception or inference. This is a "very hidden phenomenon." We can infer hidden phenomena in general but very hidden ones are different. Although in general the Buddha's statements are to be analyzed carefully, in some cases one simply trusts them.

[3]A manifest phenomenon is one that can be realized directly, without inference, such as the objects of the senses. A hidden phenomenon is the sort of thing that an ordinary being can only

The divisions are: sense direct perception, mental direct perception, and yogic direct perception.

When those are divided, there are three: sense direct perception, mental direct perception, and yogic direct perception. Regarding the middle one [mental direct perception], there are also conceptual directly perceiving consciousnesses.[1]

Whatever is a consciousness with dualistic appearance [275] is necessarily a direct valid perception regarding its appearance, but because of that is not necessarily a valid cognition.[2]

An inference is that which, in dependence on a sign, is incontrovertible regarding a hidden object.

The definition of an inferential valid cognition is:

> a consciousness that, in dependence on a sign or reason, is incontrovertible regarding the hidden object that is its object of the mode of apprehension.

Inferences [respectively] comprehending the [slightly] obscure, [hidden phenomena] through analogy, and the very obscure are asserted as inference, comprehension, and scriptural.

Regarding those, it is asserted that there are the three: (1) inferential cognitions that infer the merely hidden through the power of signs, (2) inferential cognitions comprehending through examples that understand the qualitative similarity of the example and the object, and (3) scriptural valid cognitions that, having taken a scripture free of [contradiction by] the three analyses [276] as a sign, realize very hidden phenomena.

---

newly realize through the power of inference. For instance, it takes inference to understand that sound is impermanent.

[1]Jamyang Shayba's position is that there are instances of conceptual mental direct perception, not that all instances of mental perception are necessarily conceptual. Dzongkaba says in his *Illumination of the Thought, Explanation of (Candrakīrti's) "Entrance to the Middle Way"* that there are instances of mental direct perception that are memory consciousnesses and, thus, necessarily conceptual. Jamyang Shayba also seems to assert that there are instances of conceptual mental direct perception that are feelings (*tshor ba, vedanā*). See Cozort, *Unique Tenets*, 251 *et seq*, for a full discussion of this topic.

[2]For instance, a wrong consciousness to which a single moon appears to be two moons is a direct valid cognition regarding the appearance of two moons; however, it is not a valid cognition because it is not non-deceptive.

[Whatever consciousness] induces ascertainment regarding the object of its mode of apprehension and is free from damage by other valid cognitions regarding that [object] is undeceived regarding that. Therefore, it is not contradictory to be a valid cognition even though mistaken.

Because whatever consciousness induces ascertainment regarding the object of its mode of apprehension and is free from damage by other valid cognitions of that [object] is incontrovertible regarding its object, it is not contradictory for it to be a valid cognition even if it is mistaken regarding its mode of apprehension.[1] [277]

The meaning of "non-deceptive" is explained in many contexts and is also explained as a conventionality. Because of that, like the term "substance," it does not have [only] one [meaning].

In general, since the meaning of "undeceived" must be explained in many contexts, it need not [as Daktsang says] refer only to being able to set itself up, because there are occasions when it is necessary to explain it even as a conventionality. Like the term "substance," it does not have to be explained as having only one meaning.

The Path

The means of achieving high status and definite goodness are two: faith and wisdom. Faith is a prerequisite for wisdom and makes one into a suitable vessel. Wisdom is the cause of liberation, the means of achieving the non-conceptual aim.

The principal means of achieving high status is faith in actions and their effects, the Four Noble Truths, and the Three Jewels. The principal means of achieving definite goodness is the wisdom realizing emptiness. [278] Concerning those two, faith of conviction in actions and their effects is a prerequisite for the wisdom realizing emptiness and makes one into a suitable vessel.[2] Wisdom is the

---

[1]As we have noted before, Prāsaṅgikas judge the validity of cognitions on the basis of whether they are accurate about the basic entity of their objects, not whether they are correct about the mode of existence of those objects.

[2]Faith of conviction refers to the preliminary conviction one might have, through contemplating the doctrines of Buddhism, that they are true and important. It is not a blind faith, for it is based upon reason, but on the other hand one may have a long way to go before one has the deep insight that brings complete certainty. It is obviously important to have faith as one begins to practice the spiritual path, or else one will lack the resolve and energy to attain deep insights.

cause, i.e., the means of being liberated from subtle and coarse saṃsāra. Non-conceptual exalted wisdom is the actual achiever of that aim.

All the modes of [Buddha's] doctrines are included in the stages of beings of low, middling, and superior [capacity] because they stem from two purposes.

[279] All the modes of doctrine of the Conqueror's sūtra and mantra are included in the stages of the paths of low, middling, and supreme beings, i.e., beings of small, middling, and great [capacity],[1] because the scriptures are only composed within being a means of achieving the two aims, temporary and final [of trainees].

From among the [paths of beings of] middling [capacity] are the two, Hearers and Solitary Realizers, and their paths. Mahāyāna [paths are in beings of] great [capacity]. [Therefore,] there are not four vehicles.

Moreover, since the two, Hearers and Solitary Realizers, are middling beings and their paths [are middling paths] and because Mahāyāna practitioners are beings of great [capacity] and their paths [are great paths, together they are] completely inclusive. Therefore, it is explained in Vajragarbha's *Commentary on the Condensation of the Hevajra Tantra*, etc., that there are not four vehicles.

Here, Hearers and Solitary Realizers have concordant realizations, eight grounds, and are divided by time and fruit.

Here in the Prāsaṅgika system, the realizations or paths, the means by which the two, Hearers and Solitary Realizers, progress, are similar.[2] Regarding the eight grounds, the approachers within the [280] the eight Approachers and [Abiders] in the fruit, are regarded as being within Superiors' paths. It is also explained that among learners there are no common beings.[3]

---

[1]An individual at the stage of a being of small capacity has understood the predicament of being caught in saṃsāra and turned to religious practice so that future rebirths will be good. A being of middle capacity has seen not just the suffering of bad migrations, but the whole sphere of saṃsāra as pervaded by suffering. Renunciation—the thought definitely to leave saṃsāra—is developed. Beings of great capacity are Bodhisattvas, beings under the influence of great compassion. Seeing the faults of saṃsāra and feeling a special closeness to all sentient beings, they seek the enlightenment of Buddhahood so that they might optimally lead all sentient beings to their own Buddhahood.

[2]That is, all the types of practitioners realize the same selflessnesses.

[3]This refers to the four degrees of enlightenment (Stream Enterer, Once Returner, Never Returner, and Arhat, which were first discussed in the Vaibhāṣika chapter), each of which is divided into an "Approacher" and an "Abider." To be any of these is to have realized emptiness, become a Superior, and no longer be a "common being." What this statement specifies is not only

Gyeltsap's *Commentary on (Maitreya's) "Sublime Continuum of the Mahāyāna"* says:

> The great compassion that thinks, "May all sentient beings of saṃsāra be free from suffering," occurs repeatedly even in Hearers and Solitary Realizer Superiors.

In accordance with that statement, [Prāsaṅgikas assert] that Hearers and Solitary Realizers have great compassion. However, it is not posited that Arhats become involved in the paths of beings of great [capacity] as long as they have not generated in their continuums the unusual attitude [of bearing the burden of other's welfare] from within the seven [cause and effect] precepts [to generate the altruistic aspiration to enlightenment] that is the special thought of powerful resolve.[1] When one cultivates within objects of observation and subjective aspects that are concordant with bearing the burden of others' welfare, [a path of a being of great capacity] is produced.

However, it is not firm until powerful resolve is surpassing. [281] Therefore, this differs from the order of one who, having entered the path of a great being from the beginning without previously having become an Arhat, generates gradually the great compassion taking up the burden of others' welfare and the unusual attitude.

[The Prāsaṅgika school] asserts that Hīnayāna Arhats are not non-learners.[2] They are distinguished as two, Hearers and Solitary Realizers, by way of:

- the extent of mind generation [that is, their motivation][3]

---

that emptiness is realized by all types of practitioners but that even an "Approacher" to Stream Enterer is a Superior; that is, there is first a moment of realization of emptiness that destroys afflictions (the "Approaching"), and in the next moment there is "Abiding" in the new state.

[1]The common stereotype of non-Mahāyāna practitioners is that they lack compassion, but here it is being made clear that they may have very great compassion. What they lack is *bodhicitta*, the aspiration to attain Buddhahood for the sake of others, and that may be because they do not think that it is reasonable to aspire to Buddhahood, which the Hīnayāna schools regard as an extremely rare state, not a universal possibility. Jamyang Shayba says in his *Great Exposition of Tenets* that "although they have great compassion, they do not have the great compassion bearing the burden of others' welfare" (Gomang, 616.16).

[2]In other words, even after they have attained the path of "no more learning" of their vehicle, they still have learning to do. They will definitely enter the Mahāyāna and generate the five paths serially, finally becoming Buddhas in order to bring about the welfare of limitless sentient beings.

[3]Identifying the differences between the motivations of Hearers and Solitary Realizers, Jamyang Shayba says in his *Great Exposition of Tenets* that due to their fear, Hearers wish for mere

- the length of time of accumulating the collections [of merit and wisdom][1]
- whether or not the fruit of Arhat depends on the words of others, etc.[2]

Similar [to presentations in other systems], Solitary Realizers [consist of] the Rhinoceros-like and the greater and lesser Congregating.

[Regarding the features of the Mahāyāna paths of practicing through belief,[3]] with a stable root, altruistic mind [282] **generation, the perfections are the vast branches.**

For the Mahāyāna, the root is the firm altruistic aspiration to enlightenment that has the broad branches that are the perfections of giving, ethics, patience, effort, concentration, and wisdom.

[The paths of] accumulation and preparation are differentiated by qualities, signs, meditation, and entity.

Moreover, the path of accumulation and the path of preparation of common beings are differentiated by:

- their qualities in accordance with the order of attaining the groups of the [thirty-seven] harmonies of enlightenment[4] [283]

---

liberation, while Solitary Realizers wish for perfect enlightenment, but selfishly (Gomang, 617.2–3). However, this is a bit of a distortion since he himself also says that both types are capable of great compassion. If they are "fearful" or "selfish," it is only because they believe in the first case that the purpose of the path is to eliminate suffering and in the second that it is not possible for them to save others as well as themselves.

[1]Solitary Realizers, at least the "Rhinoceros" type, accumulate merit over one hundred eons. This underscores the incredible importance of a teacher; to attain enlightenment without the aid of a teacher one must be a very intelligent and strong person, one who is born that way due to nearly countless virtuous lifetimes. Nevertheless, there are such persons. For the Hīnayāna schools, the Buddha is regarded as one since there was no Buddhism in his time; he had to find the truth by himself.

[2]Solitary Realizers are said not to depend on a teacher in their last life. The "Rhinoceros" type has no teacher at all, and the "Congregating" type has one only early on, achieving their final goal quite by themselves.

[3]Jamyang Shayba's outline in his *Great Exposition of Tenets* indicates that this section initiates his discussion of the Mahāyāna. The first topic is the "features of the grounds of practice through belief," which are a Bodhisattva's paths prior to becoming a Superior through the direct realization of emptiness (Gomang, 617.20).

[4]The thirty-seven harmonies with enlightenment are: the four mindful establishments, four

- signs of lineage and compassion, etc.[1]
- whether or not the [wisdom] arisen from meditation is most important[2]
- the entities of their definitions

There is no differentiation regarding [the exalted wisdom of] meditative equipoise on the ten grounds. [The grounds are differentiated by] the trainings and the accelerated increase of the twelve subsequent qualities of activities, etc.

Although there is no differentiation regarding the entity of the exalted wisdom of meditative equipoise [realizing emptiness] on the ten grounds,[3] [the grounds] are differentiated by way of, for instance, trainings, subsequent qualities, deeds, i.e., activities, powers, etc., that is to say, by the increase of the twelve [sets of good] qualities.[4]

---

thorough abandonments, four legs of manifestation, five faculties, five powers, seven branches of enlightenment, and the eight-branched superior path. (These were explained in the Vaibhāṣika chapter.) The path of accumulation is attained just by the generation of *bodhicitta*; the path of preparation, by a union of calm abiding and special insight with emptiness as its object, i.e., the inferential understanding of emptiness. In terms of the thirty-seven harmonies with enlightenment, not only does attaining the path of preparation involve a development of ability in meditation, but the fifth of the five powers and the fifth of the five faculties are specifical types of wisdom that are attained over the path of preparation.

[1]"Signs of lineage" means that the Bodhisattva is irreversible in the Mahāyāna lineage. It is attained on the four levels of the path of preparation.

[2]Jamyang Shayba comments that the path of accumulation is predominantly a state arisen from hearing and from thinking (rather than meditation). The path of preparation has states arisen from all three. However, since a meditator must attain calm abiding *prior* to attaining the path of preparation (since a union of calm abiding and special insight marks the beginning of the path of preparation), the path of accumulation also has states arisen from meditation (Gomang, 619.1–2).

[3]This means that the entity of each is a meditative stabilization directly realizing emptiness wherein there is neither the appearance nor the conception of inherent existence. However, the grounds are different in terms of a progression of increasing ability to serve as an actual antidote to progressively more subtle levels of the innate conception of inherent existence, then to serve as an actual antidote to the obstructions to omniscience.

[4]The good qualities are twelve types of extraordinary abilities: (1) seeing a number of Buddhas in one instant; (2) receiving the blessings of a number of Buddhas; (3) going to a number of Buddha lands; (4) illuminating those lands; (5) vibrating a number of worldly realms; (6) living for a number of eons; (7) seeing with true wisdom the past and future of a number of eons; (8) entering into and rising from a number of meditative stabilizations; (9) opening a number of different doors of doctrine; (10) ripening a number of sentient beings; (11) emanating a number

Each [ground] is also to be explained by way of eight: etymology, divisions, qualities, the supported, fruitions, the two signs [of irreversibility and dreams], abandonments, and antidotes.

Each ground is to be explained by way of the eight [topics]:

1 their etymologies[1]
2 their multiple modes of division[2]
3 the numerical increase of their twelve [sets of good] qualities
4 the mode of surpassing perfection—the supported[3]
5 their mode of apprehending fruitional births[4]
6 their two signs of irreversibility and dreams[5]

---

of versions of one's own body; and (12) surrounding each of the hundred bodies with a number of Bodhisattvas. On the Bodhisattva path of meditation, which follows the initial direct realization of emptiness that is the path of seeing, these are multiplied as one progresses from the first to the tenth ground into which the path is divided. First ground Bodhisattvas have these qualities hundredfold (i.e., can visit one hundred Buddha lands, emanate one hundred bodies, etc.). Second-ground Bodhisattvas have them thousandfold, third-ground Bodhisattvas have them hundred thousandfold, and so on.

[1]They have names, which are discussed by Nāgārjuna in his *Precious Garland.* For example, the first ground is called the Very Joyful because the Bodhisattva is rejoicing.

[2]Jamyang Shayba comments that divisions are by way of how Bodhisattvas train in the three trainings—morality, meditative stabilization, and wisdom—and in how the five uncontaminated aggregates are purified (Gomang, 620.2).

[3]On each ground, the meditator develops a different surpassing perfection. One attains the perfection of giving on the first ground, morality on the second ground, patience on the third, effort on the fourth, concentration on the fifth, wisdom on the sixth, skill in means on the seventh, prayer wishes on the eighth, power on the ninth, and exalted wisdom on the tenth.

[4]Nāgārjuna's *Precious Garland* (stanzas 441–60) presents a progression of fruitional rebirths of increasing power and influence. On the first ground, one is able to take birth as a monarch ruling Jambudvīpa (the southern continent of the four-continent world system). On the second, one takes birth as a monarch ruling the four continents. On the third, one takes birth as a monarch ruling the gods of the Land of the Thirty-Three. On the fourth, one takes birth as a monarch ruling the Land Without Combat. On the fifth, one takes birth as a monarch ruling the gods living in the Joyous Land. On the sixth, one takes birth as a monarch ruling the Land of Liking Emanation. On the seventh, one takes birth as a monarch ruling Controlling Others' Emanations. On the eighth, one takes birth as a great Brahma lord of a thousand worlds. On the ninth, one takes birth as a great Brahmā lord of a million worlds. On the tenth, one takes birth as the Devapūtra Maheśvara of the Highest Pure Land. Hopkins, *Buddhist Advice* 155–9.

[5]There are sixteen signs of irreversibility on the path of seeing. In addition, there are ten signs of omens in dreams, such as seeing the world system filled with treasures.

7 the difference between their objects of abandonment[1]
8 the difference between their antidotes[2] [284]

Since there is much [to be said] concerning these, they must be understood through [Jamyang Shayba's] commentary, etc.

Buddhahood

Regarding the effect, [the Buddha ground,] meditative equipoise and subsequent attainment do not alternate; they have become one entity. The movement of mind—conceptuality—has been thoroughly pacified. Thereby, abiding firmly [in meditative stabilization,] he does not rise [from meditative equipoise] but performs the activities of subsequent attainment.

Without the alternation of the two, the wisdom of meditative equipoise and the wisdom of subsequent attainment, both meditative equipoise and subsequent attainment have become one entity.[3] From that, the movement of his mind—all the collections of conceptuality—has been pacified without exception.[4] Thereby, since

[1]Each ground is associated with a particular quality, and as one perfects that quality, one is removing whatever obstructions remain to its optimal functioning. On the first ground, one removes the obstructions to generosity so that one's generosity becomes completely natural and free.

[2]The individual grounds' ability to act as antidotes bringing about purification increases ever higher because one advances to higher grounds through removing defects and increasing good qualities. (Gönchok Jikmay Wangbo's *Presentation of the Grounds and Paths,* 461.6–2.1).

[3]A Superior is someone who has directly realized emptiness, but until the attainment of Buddhahood, the direct realization of emptiness precludes the simultaneous perception of the objects whose emptiness is being understood. During the "exalted wisdom of meditative equipoise," emptiness directly appears to the mind without any elaboration of dualistic appearance (i.e., without the objects that *are* empty also appearing to mind). Subsequently, the Superior again perceives objects, which appear to inherently exist, although he or she does not assent to the appearance. The special quality of Buddhas is that both a phenomenon and its emptiness can appear simultaneously to their minds. Another way of putting this is that only for Buddha do the two truths, ultimate and conventional, appear simultaneously.

[4]Buddhas no longer have any conceptuality. Jamyang Shayba's commentary to this in his *Great Exposition of Tenets* (Gomang, 623.4–13) indicates that at Buddhahood one has overcome the "karmic winds" that are producers of conceptuality. In other words, in a condition of omniscience

his abiding in meditative stabilization is firm, he never rises from meditative equipoise, [285] but nevertheless performs the activities of the wisdom of subsequent attainment.[1]

All elaborations have vanished for the perspective of his perception of the element of attributes, but [for the perspective] of his non-analytical [perception], the diversity of phenomena are known, like an olive.

Moreover, for the perspective of his perception of emptiness—the element of attributes—all elaborations of conventionalities have vanished and do not exist. Still, for the perspective of his non-analytical perception of conventionalities, all the diversity of phenomena are known individually without confusion, like a wet olive fruit set in the palm of the hand.[2]

Because it is asserted that [Buddhas have] a single Body, or two, three, four, or five Bodies, that Subduers do not have a vast [Body] and that such [relies on] the perspective of others is mistaken.

The single Body is the Effect Truth Body.[3] The Truth Body for his own welfare and the Form Body for others' welfare are the Two [bodies]. [286] The Truth Body, Complete Enjoyment Body, and Emanation Body are the Three [Bodies].[4] Those three and the Nature Body are the Four [Bodies].[5] The five bodies that are the five exalted wisdoms [are the Five Bodies].[6] Because all the sūtras and

---

it is no longer necessary to have one's mind moved in one direction or another to have understanding.

[1]In other words, the Buddha can do whatever needs to be done, primarily teaching, without ever moving from his meditative equipoise on emptiness.

[2]A wet black olive in a palm is very distinctive, and so are all phenomena the Buddha observes, even though he observes all of them simultaneously.

[3]The omniscient consciousness of the Buddha is the Truth Body; this is what a Buddha really is. All of the other Bodies of Form are transmutations of the Truth Body, emanated for the sake of others.

[4]The Complete Enjoyment Body is a special form that teaches Bodhisattvas in pure lands; the Emanation Body is of several types, but all appear to ordinary beings in ordinary ways, such as the Buddha's appearance as an ordinary human in north India.

[5]The Nature Truth Body is the absence of all obstructions (i.e., both to liberation and to omniscience) in the continuum of a Buddha.

[6]A Buddha has five types of wisdom (really, just five ways of looking at a unitary phenomenon capable of infinite knowledge): mirror-like exalted wisdom; exalted wisdom of equality; exalted wisdom of individual realization; exalted wisdom of achieving activities; and exalted wisdom of

tantras assert that those exist, that the Kings of Subduers do not have a vast body and that such must rely on the perspective of others, their disciples, is very mistaken. [287]

Purity of adventitious defilements and natural purity are the Nature [Truth Body].

The true cessation that is a purification of the adventitious defilements—the two obstructions—and natural purity is the Nature Truth Body.[1]

The Wisdom Truth Body is the twenty-one divisions [of exalted wisdom], etc.

The twenty-one divisions of non-contaminated exalted wisdom are the Wisdom Truth Body.[2]

That which has the five [qualities] and does not withdraw its appearance is the Complete Enjoyment [Body].

The Complete Enjoyment Body has the five distinguishing features of:

- teacher
- preaching [of the Mahāyāna]
- spontaneous activity
- non-cessation, etc.[3]

---

the expanse of reality.

[1]A true cessation is an absence of a portion of the afflictions in the continuum of someone who has realized emptiness directly. A Buddha has all of the true cessations. It is a unique Prāsaṅgika tenet that true cessations are also emptinesses and ultimate truths. The Nature Truth Body is an emptiness in the sense that it is the Buddha's lack of obstructions and is said to have five characteristics: it is uncompounded, without differentiation, devoid of the two extremes, free from the three obstructions, and naturally clear light. It also has five qualities: incomprehensibility, innumerability, inconceivability, being unparalleled, and being the finality of purity (Gomang, 625.13 *et seq.).*

[2]The Wisdom Truth Body is also called the exalted knower of all aspects. The list of the twenty-one divisions of the Wisdom Truth Body is based on Maitreya's *Ornament for Clear Realization,* 8.2–6.

[3]The Complete Enjoyment Body is a body of special form that teaches Bodhisattvas. There are different enumerations of the five features of the Enjoyment Body. Losang Gönchok's list appears to be an abridgement of a longer formulation in Jamyang Shayba's *Great Exposition of Tenets:* "exalted body, the teacher; exalted speech, verbalization; exalted mind, uninterruptedly [fulfilling] the aims of transmigrators; spontaneity without striving; though displaying variously, undifferentiated like a precious jewel" (Gomang 627.14–7; Hopkins translation).

without withdrawing its appearance until the end of saṃsāra. [288]

Artisan, Birth, and Enlightenment are the three Emanation Bodies. All of space is filled with the voice that has the sixty harmonies.

Emanation Bodies are, for instance, the three: the Artisan Emanation Bodies, Birth Emanation Bodies, and Great Enlightenment Emanation Bodies [that display the twelve deeds of a Buddha].[1] All of space is filled with the voice that has the branches [i.e., qualities] of the sixty pleasant harmonies.[2]

The sport of the three secrecies pervades everywhere but is seen according to the lot [of sentient beings]. [A Buddha can] transform a moment into an eon, and vice versa. Also, [he can] set the stable and mobile in a hair-pore, just as [they were arrayed] in space, without [the hair-pore] becoming larger nor [the stable and mobile] becoming smaller.

The sport, i.e., creation, of the three inconceivable secrecies of body, speech, and mind pervades everywhere but is seen through being displayed by the power of the lot of what helps each trainee.[3] [Buddhas are able] to transform a moment into an eon and, conversely, to transform an eon into a moment, and to cause all the lands of the stable—environments—and all sentient beings who are the moving—beings—to fit into each hair-pore, like they are arrayed in space, [289] setting them [there] without the hair-pores becoming larger and without the lands of environments and beings becoming smaller.

Even though one remained, [blessed] by the Conquerors, expressing all of their marvelous qualities—the ten powers, the eighteen [qualities] unshared with others, etc.—one would not finish; it would be like [looking for] the end of space.

---

[1]Buddhas emanate in ordinary forms called Emanation Bodies, which are of three main types: Artisans (the appearance of a person such as a goldsmith or musician), Birth (the appearance as an object, animals, etc.), and Great Enlightenment (the appearance of one who displays the career of a Bodhisattva and then a Buddha).

[2]The sixty branches of speech are one of the three inconceivable mysteries of exalted body, speech, and mind.

[3]That is, ordinary people might not notice a Buddha's emanations. They are affected only if they have the sort of predispositions so that they might benefit from the emanation. The basic principle is that Buddhas can emanate limitlessly, but there is no point to the emanation unless it is helpful to others, particularly in leading them to enlightenment.

In brief, even if, one's lifespan having been blessed by the Conquerors, one remained expressing all of their marvelous qualities individually—the ten powers,[1] the eighteen unshared [qualities], etc.—one could not finish. It would be like looking for the limits of space.

Their spontaneous activities—whatever [is appropriate to] tame [trainees]—are displayed forever.

The activities of the Conquerors are displayed forever, continuously, in terms of all factors that are deeds—whatever would train any sentient being—effortlessly, spontaneously, for as long as saṃsāra lasts. [290]

[1]The ten powers are, from Maitreya's *Sublime Continuum* (3.5–6), "knowledges of sources and non-sources, of the fruitions of actions, of faculties, of dispositions, of interests, of paths proceeding everywhere, of the afflicted and undefiled concentrations, etc., of the mindfulness of [former] states, of the divine eye, and of the quiescence." *Great Exposition of Tenets* (Gomang, 629.12–4).

Secret Mantra

To indicate the distinctive features of the profound path of mantra, the uttermost peak of vehicles, [Jamyang Shayba sets forth the following verses]. Both sūtra and tantra are able to remove all the afflictive obstructions.

Both sūtra and tantra [paths] are able to remove all the afflictive obstructions. However, the simultaneous abandonment of the artificial and innate forms of the afflictive obstructions [291] is a distinctive feature of Highest [Yoga Tantra].[1]

Just as the supreme object is taught, whereas the supreme subject is hidden, so although the main defilements are taught, the supreme antidote is hidden. Therefore, the subtlest small obstructions to omniscience cannot [be removed by paths taught] in sūtras, [such being different] from mantra. Because of that, that the [objects of] abandonment and antidotes are similarly hidden is mistaken.

The supreme object, the profound emptiness, is taught in sūtra, but the supreme subject that realizes that, the path of innate great bliss, is hidden. Just so, the chief of the defilements, the nine cycles of the obstructions to omniscience, are taught, but the supreme antidote to those, the innate joy that unites bliss and

---

[1]Both the exoteric (sūtra) and esoteric (tantra, or mantra) paths can remove the obstructions to liberation, and the sūtra paths can also remove all but the very subtlest obstructions to omniscience. The esoteric path of Highest Yoga Tantra has special methods that allow the simultaneous abandonment of both the artificial and innate forms of the conception of inherent existence. Because one's own mind realizing emptiness is said to emanate as the form of a deity (a Complete Enjoyment Body Buddha, such as Kālacakra, Guhyasamāja, etc.), it is not necessary to alternate between mediation on emptiness and other phenomena as in the non-esoteric practice, as was discussed earlier. The vivid visualization of oneself as a deity also permits speedy collection of merit because of the capacities of Buddhas and because one can multiply tremendously the forms emanated. See, generally, Cozort, *Highest Yoga Tantra.*

emptiness indivisibly, is hidden.[1] Therefore, the subtlest of the small obstructions to omniscience cannot be abandoned by merely the paths that are taught as the means of abandonment in the class of sūtras, these being different from such mantra paths. For that reason, Daktsang is mistaken in explaining that the [object of] abandonment and the antidotes are similarly hidden.

Because [tantra] has more profound methods, the paths [of sūtra and mantra] differ greatly in terms of speed.

In general, [292] mantra has more profound methods for quickly obtaining a [Buddha's] Form Body,[2] and in particular, Highest [Yoga Tantra] has supremely profound methods for achieving an intimate grasp of the Three Bodies. Hence, there is a very great difference in speed between the paths of sūtra and mantra.[3]

The three, body, speech, and mind, have coarse, subtle, and very subtle [forms]. For the sake of purifying them, the vehicles and sūtra and tantra [advance one] higher and higher.

Moreover, since the three, body, speech, and mind, have three [forms]—coarse, subtle, and very subtle—the vehicles and sūtra and tantra [293] are more profound in terms of purifying them [as one goes] higher and higher.[4]

---

[1]The mantra path utilizes the bliss—the energy—that arises from sexual union to enhance the mind that realizes emptiness, providing a union of bliss and emptiness.

[2]A significant feature found in tantra but not in the Perfection Vehicle is deity yoga, whereby a meditator cultivates a similitude of a Buddha's Form Body, residence, resources, and activities. See, generally, *Tantra in Tibet,* translated by Hopkins.

[3]A practitioner of the Perfection Vehicle spends one period of countless eons on the path of accumulation to the path of seeing; then another period of countless eons on the path of meditation up to the lower half of the eighth Bodhisattva ground; then a final period of countless eons from the upper half of the eighth ground to the path of no more learning (Buddhahood). The three lower tantra sets provide methods that make progress from the path of accumulation to the path of seeing possible much faster than by Perfection Vehicle paths. Finally, Highest Yoga Tantra has additional methods not shared with either the Perfection Vehicle or the three lower tantra sets that allow for even speedier progress along the path for qualified trainees.

[4]With regard to the body, the coarse level is its elements (water, earth, etc.) and their evolutes; the subtle level is the channels, winds or energies, and drops, together called the subtle body; and the very subtle level is the fundamental "wind" in an "indestructible drop" in the heart. With regard to the mind, the coarse level is that of the sense consciousnesses; the subtle level is that of conceptuality; and the very subtle level is that of the actual "clear light" mind that dawns at the time of death or in tantric practice. Only the tantric practices involve working with the most subtle level.

Although the two others are explained in the lower [tantras and in sūtra], the third, while suitable to be the basis of [Buddha's] thought, is not [explicitly taught] in sūtra and the lower tantras.

Therefore, although the two, the coarse and the subtle, are explained in the lower [sets of tantras], Yoga Tantra and below, the third, the very subtle, although suitable to be a mere basis of [Buddha's] thought [when he taught something else], is not explicitly taught in the sūtras and lower tantras. It is clear in Highest [Yoga Tantra] in general and in the King of Tantras.

QUESTION: In what is [the very subtle] taught?

ANSWER: It is clearly and vastly taught in Highest Yoga Tantra in general, and in particular in the root and explanatory tantras of the glorious *Guhyasamāja Tantra*, the king among all tantras.

This is the tracks of passage to the peak for the ten million kings of fortunate adepts. It is established as the supreme secret path of the Conquerors of the three times.

It is well taught that this is the path for progressing, i.e., the tracks of passage, to the uttermost peak of ranks by the ten million kings of fortunate adepts. [294] And not only that, it is taught that it is the supreme secret path from which all the Conquerors of the three times proceeded and that it is established in the precious tantra sets in the statements of those valid beings who are scholars and adepts.

This has been the thirteenth chapter, the commentary on the occasion of distinguishing the differences between sūtra and tantra and establishing the great secret [mantra vehicle] as supreme.[1]

Sarva-maṅgalaṃ! (May All Beings be Happy!)

[1]The colophon has been omitted.

Emendations to the Tibetan Text

22.1 "By suffering," reading *sdug bsngal kyis* for *sdug bsngal kyi.*
39.2 "Vaidikas," reading *rig byed pa* for *rigs byed pa.*
42.2 "Pollution," reading *bslad pa* for *bslab pa.*
42.3 "Constituent," reading *khams* for *kham.*
42.4 "Constituent," reading *khams* for *kham.*
44.1 "Sign of liberation," reading *grol ba'i rtags* for *grol ba'i rtag.*
45.5 "Self which has the color of the sun," reading *nyi ma'i mdog can kyi bdag* for *nyi ma'i mdog can kyis bdag.*
81.2 "Boundaries," reading *mtshams* for *'tshams.*
126.5 "Which," reading *gyi* for *gyis.*
127.5 "System," reading *lugs* for *lung.*
128.5 "Followers of Reasoning," reading *rjes 'brang gis* for *rjes 'brang gi.*
131.5 "Must exist," reading *yod dgos pas* for *yod dgos pas so.*
134.3 "Wisdom," reading *ye shes* for *yi shes.*
143.5 "Dichotomy," reading *dngos* for *nges.*
209.2 "Non-observations,"reading *ma dmigs* for *dmigs* in accordance with Gomang 520.3.
211.2 "Is," reading *yin* for *min.*
224.2 "Stable," reading *brstan* for *bstan.*
238.2 "Conceptual," reading *rtag* for *rtags.*
244.3 "Comes," reading *song des* for *sogs nges* in accordance with Gomang.
250.2 "Initially," reading *dang por* for *dang po* following Gomang 586.7.
256.5 "Subsequent cognizers," reading *bcad shes* for *dpyad shes* in accordance with Gomang 599.9.
260.3 "Propounding," reading *smras dzam* for *smra dzam* in accordance with Gomang 600.22.
260.4 "Time passed," reading *dus song* for *dus sogs* in accordance with Gomang 600.22.
277.4 "Means of achieving"; Gomang reads *don grub phyir* instead of *don grub byed.*

278.4 "Not four"; Gomang reads *bzhi min zhes* instead of *bzhi min 'dir.*

282.1 "Signs, meditation, and entity"; Losang Gönchok's text reads *tshogs sbyor yon tan rtags sgom mang pos 'byed;* Gomang (14.22-15.1 and 617.21) reads *tshogs sbyor yon tan rtogs sgom ngo bos 'byed.* Jamyang Shayba's commentary in his *Great Exposition of Tenets* supports the reading of *rtags* (signs) and *ngo bos* (entity).

282.2 "Supported"; Jamyang Shayba's root text reads "supports" *(rten),* but Losang Gönchok follows Jamyang Shayba's own commentary (Gomang 621.1) in treating it as "the supported" (*brten pa).*

Tibetan Pronunciation and Transliteration

The following table indicates our transliteration and basic pronunciation systems for each Tibetan consonant; marks over certain sounds indicate that such a letter would be pronounced with a sharper, higher tone:

ཀ	ka	ḡa	ཁ	kha	ka	ག	ga	ga	ང	nga	nga/ n̄ga
ཅ	ca	j̄a	ཆ	cha	cha	ཇ	ja	ja	ཉ	nya	nya/ n̄ya
ཏ	ta	d̄a	ཐ	tha	ta	ད	da	da	ན	na	na/ n̄a
པ	pa	b̄a	ཕ	pha	pa	བ	ba	ba	མ	ma	ma/ m̄a
ཙ	tsa	d̄za	ཚ	tsha	tsa	ཛ	dza	dza	ཝ	wa	w̄a
ཞ	zha	sha	ཟ	za	sa	འ	ʻa	a	ཡ	ya	ya
ར	ra	ra	ལ	la	la	ཤ	sha	s̄ha	ས	sa	sa
ཧ	ha	ha	ཨ	a	a						

For the transliteration of Tibetan we follow the Wylie system[1] with the exception that we have not capitalized any letters.

For easy pronunciation, we have used Jeffrey Hopkins' system of "essay phonetics,"which approximates Lhasa pronunciation.[2] In the Hopkins system, the nasals (far right columns) are low in tone except when there is a superscribed or prefixed letter; a subscribed *la* is high in tone, except for *zla* which is pronounced "da"; *dbang* is pronounced "wang," *dbyangs*, "yang"; and the letters *ga* and *ba* are phoneticized as *k* and *p* when they are found in the suffix position. Since we want merely to give readers an approximate pronunciation, we have not used high tone markers, nor have we inserted hyphens between the syllables of Tibetan names.

A list of Tibetan names in both easy pronunciation and transliterated form is found below.

Amdo	a mdo
Batsap Nyimadrak	pa tshab nyi ma grags
Belden Chöjay	dpal ldan chos rje
Belden Drakba	dpal ldan grags pa
Beltsek	dpal brtseg
Daktsang Shayrab Rinchen	stag tshang shes rap rin chen
Dölboba Shayrap Gyeltsen	dol bo shes rab rgyal mtshan
Drashikyil	bkra shis 'khyil
Drebung	'bras spungs
Dromdönba	'brom ston pa
Dzongkaba Losang Drakba	tsong kha pa blo bzang grags pa
Gadamba (often seen as Kadampa)	bka' gdams pa
Gagyuba (often seen as Kagyudpa)	bka' rgyud pa
Ganden	dga' ldan
Ganden Jinchaling	dga' ldan byin chags gling
Ganggya Dingring	rgang gya'i lting ring
Ganggyamar	gangs rgya dmar
Gelukba	dge lugs pa
Gendün Gyatso	dge 'dun rgya mtsho
Gomang	sgo mang
Gönchok Jikmay Wangbo	dkon mchog 'jigs med dbang po
Gungtang Gönchok Denbay Drönmay	gung thang dkon mchog bstan pa'i sgron me
Gyeltsap Darma Rinchen	rgyal tshab dar ma rin chen
Gyumay	rgyud smad
Lhasa (pronounced Hlasa)	lha sa

[1]Wylie, 261–67.

[2]Hopkins, *Meditation*, 19–22.

Jambel Sampel	'jam dpal bsam 'phel
Jambel Trinlay Yönden Gyatso	'jam dpal 'phrin las yon tan rgya mtsho
Jamyang Shayba Ngawang Dzöndrü	'jam dbyangs bzhad pa ngag dbang btson 'grus
Jangdzay	byang rtse
Jangdzön	byang brston
Janggya Rolbay Dorjay	lcang kya rol pa'i rdo rje
Jaydzün Chögyi Gyeltsen	rje btsun chos kyi rgyal mtshan
Jonangba	jo nang pa
Jukdop	jug stobs
Kaydrup Gelek Belsang	mkhas grub dge legs dpal bzang
Losang Chögyi Nyima	blo bzang chos kyi nyi ma
Losang Dayang	blo bzang rta dbyangs
Losang Denbay Nyima	blo bzang bstan pa'i nyi ma
Losang Gönchok	blo bzang kun mchog
Loseling	blo gsal gling
Ngawang Belden	ngag dbang dpal ldan
Ngawang Drashi	ngag dbang bkra shis
Ngawang Losang Gyatso	ngag dbang blo bzang rgya mtsho
Ngok Lotsāwa Loden Sherab	rngog lo tsā ba blo ldan shes rap
Paṇchen Losang Chögyi Gyeltsen	paṇ chen blo bzang chos kyi rgyal mtshan
Paṇchen Śākya Chokden	paṇ chen shākya mchog ldan
Paṇchen Sönam Drakba	paṇ chen bsod nams grags pa
Purbujok	phur bu lcog
Rendawa	red mda' ba
Rongta Losang Damchö Gyatso	rong tha blo bzang dam chos rgya mtsho
Sagyaba	sa skya pa
Sera	se ra
Sönam Rinchen	bsod nams rin chen
Tangsakba	thang sag pa
Tügen Losang Chögyi Nyima	thu'u bkwan blo bzang chos kyi nyi ma
Tupden Gyatso	thub bstan rgya mtsho
Uba Losel	dbus pa blo gsal
Yangjen Gaway Lodrö	dbyangs can dga' ba'i blo gros
Yesheday	ye shes sde

Glossary of Technical Terms
(English-Sanskrit-Tibetan)

English	*Sanskrit*	*Tibetan*
abhidharma	abhidharma	chos mngon pa
able to set itself up	—	tshugs thub tu grub pa
absorption	samāpatti	snyoms 'jug
action	karma	las
affirming negation/negative	paryudāsapratiṣedha	ma yin dgag
afflicted mind	kliṣṭamanas	nyon yid
affliction	kleśa	nyon mongs
afflictive obstruction	kleśāvaraṅa	nyon sgrib
aggregate	skandha	phung po
aggregation	saṃghata	'dus pa
analysis	vicāra	dpyod pa
analytical cessation	pratisaṃkhyā-nirodha	so sor brtags 'gog
analytical meditation	—	dpyad sgom
Arhat	arhan/arhat	dgra bcom pa
artificial	parikalpita	kun btags
aspect	akārā	rnam pa
autonomous inference	svatantrānumāna	rang rgyud kyi rjes dpag
autonomous syllogism	svatantraprayoga	rang rgyud kyi sbyor ba
basis-of-all	ālaya	kun gzhi
basis of designation	—	gdags gzhi
belief	adhimokṣa	mos pa
bliss	sukha	bde ba
Blissful Pure Land	sukhāvatī	dbe ba can
Bodhisattva	bodhisattva	byang chub sems dpa'
body consciousness	kāyavijñāna	lus kyi rnam par shes pa
body sense	kāyendriya	lus kyi dbang po
Buddha	buddha	sangs rgyas

English	*Sanskrit*	*Tibetan*
calm abiding	śamatha	zhi gnas
cause	hetu	rgyu
character non-nature	lakṣaṇaniḥsvabhāvatā	mtshan nyid ngo bo nyid med pa nyid
Cittamātra	cittamātra	sems tsam
clairvoyance	abhijñā	mngon par shes pa
coarse selflessness	—	bdag med rags pa
common being	pṛthagjana	so skye bo
compassion	karuṇā	snying rje
Complete Enjoyment Body	saṃbhogakāya	longs spyod rdzogs pa'i sku
composite	saṃcita	bsags pa
compositional factor	saṃskāra	'du byed
concentration	dhyāna	bsam gtan
conception of self	ātmagrāha	bdag tu 'dzin pa
condition	pratyaya	rkyen
conditionality	idaṃpratyayatā	rkyen 'di pa tsam nyid
Conqueror	jina	rgyal ba
conscientiousness	apramāda	bag yod pa
consciousness	jñā/vijñāna	shes pa/rnam shes
consequence	prasaṅga	thal 'gyur
constituent	dhātu	khams
contact	sparśa	reg pa
contaminated	sāsrava	zag bcas
contaminated action	sāsravakarma	zag bcas kyi las
contamination	āsrava	zag pa
continuum	saṃtāna	rgyun/gyud
contradictory consequence	—	'gal brjod thal 'gyur
conventional analysis	—	tha snyad pa'i dpyod pa
conventional existence	saṃvṛtisat	kun rdzob tu yod pa
conventional truth/truth-for-a-concealer/obscurational truth	saṃvṛtisatya	kun rdzob bden pa
cooperative condition	sahakāripratyaya	lhan cig byed rkhyen
correct view	samyakdṛṣṭi	yang dag pa'i lta ba
counter-pervasion	vyatirekavyāpti	ldog khyab
creature/being/person	puruṣa	skyes bu
cyclic existence	saṃsāra	'khor ba
deed	karma	las
definitive	nītārtha	nges don
deity yoga	devayoga	lha'i rnal 'byor
dependent-arising	pratītyasamutpāda	rten 'byung
dependent phenomenon	paratantra	gzhan dbang
desire	rāga	'dod chags
Desire Realm	kāmadhātu	'dod khams

English	*Sanskrit*	*Tibetan*
determining factor	viniyata	yul nges
dharma	dharma	chos
direct cognition	—	mngon sum du rtogs pa
direct perception/perceiver	pratyakśa	mngon sum
discipline	vinaya	'dul ba
discrimination	saṃjñā	'du shes
disintegration	naṣṭa	'jig pa
disintegratedness	naṣṭa	zhig pa
dissimulation	śāṭhya	gyo
doubt	vicikitsā	the tshom
ear consciousness	śrotravijñāna	rna ba'i rnam par shes pa
ear sense	śrotrendriya	rna ba'i dbang po
effort	vīrya	brtson 'grus
elaborations	prapañca	spros pa
element of [superior] attributes	dharmadhātu	chos dbyings
Emanation Body	nirmāṇkāya	sprul sku
embarrassment	apatrāpya	khrel yod pa
emptiness	śūnyatā	stong pa nyid
Enjoyment Body	saṃbhogakāya	longs sku
enlightenment	bodhi	byang chub
equanimity	upekṣkā	btang snyoms
established atomically	—	rdul tu grub pa
excitement	auddhatya	rgod pa
existence able to set itself up	—	tshugs thub tu grub pa
existence by way of its own character	svalakṣaṇasiddhi	rang gi mtshan nyid kyis grub pa
existence from the object's side	—	rang ngos nas grub pa
existence through its own entityness/inherent existence	—	ngo bo nyid kyis grub pa
existence through its own power	—	rang dbang du grub pa
existent	sat	yod pa
existent base	—	gzhi grub
extreme	anta	mtha'
extreme of annihilation	ucchedānta	chad mtha'
extreme of permanence	śaśvatānta	rtag mtha'
eye consciousness	cakṣurvijñāna	mig gi rnam shes
feeling	vedanā	tshor ba
forbearance	kṣānti	bzod pa
form	rūpa	gzugs
Form Body	rūpakāya	gzugs sku
form constituent	rūpadhātu	gzugs kyi khams
form for the mental consciousness	dharmāyatanarūpa	chos kyi skye mched pa'i gzugs

English	*Sanskrit*	*Tibetan*
Form Realm	rūpadhātu	gzugs khams
form source	rūpāyatana	gzugs kyi skye mched
Formless Realm	ārūpyadhātu	gzugs med khams
fruit	phala	'bras bu
fruition consciousness	vipakavijñāna	rnam smin rnam shes
generally characterized phenomenon	sāmānyalakṣaṇa	spyi mtshan
generic object/generic image/meaning-generality	arthasāmānya	don spyi
giving	dāna	sbyin pa
great compassion	mahākaruṇā	snying rje chen po
Great One	mahat	chen po
gross object	sthūla	rags snang
ground	bhūmi	sa
Hearer	śrāvaka	nyan thos
hearing	śruta	thos pa
heat	uṣmagata	drod
higher knowledge	abhidharma	chos mngon pa
Highest Pure Land	akaniṣṭa	'og min
Highest Yoga Tantra	anuttarayogatantra	rnal 'byor bla med kyi rgyud
Hīnayāna	hīnayāna	theg dman
I	ahaṃ	nga
ignorance	avidyā	ma rig pa
impermanent	anitya	mi rtag pa
imputed	parikalpita	kun btags
imputed phenomenon	parikalpitadharma	kun btags pa'i chos
imputedly existent	prajñaptisat	btags yod
inference	anumāna	rjes dpag
inferential valid cognition	anumānapramāṇa	rjes dpag tshad ma
inherent existence	svabhāvasiddhi	rang bzhin gyis grub pa
innate	sahaja	lhan skyes
innate affliction	sahajakleśa	nyon mongs lhan skyes
intention	cetanā	sems pa
introspection	samprajanya	shes bzhin
investigation	vitarka	rtog pa, tshol ba
Joyous Land	tuṣita	dga' ldan
knowledge/higher knowledge	abhidharma	chos mngon pa
knowledge/wisdom	prajña	shes rab

English	*Sanskrit*	*Tibetan*
liberation	vimokṣa/mokṣa	thar pa
limitation	—	ming don gcig 'jig ma nges
lineage	gotra	rigs
love	maitrī	byams pa
Mādhyamika	mādhyamika	dbu ma pa
Mahāyāna	mahāyāna	theg chen
matter	kanthā	bem po
meditative absorption	samāpatti	snyoms 'jug
meditative stabilization	samāhita/samādhi	mnyam bzhag/ting nge 'dzin
mental and physical aggregates	skandha	phung po
mental consciousness	manovijñāna	yid kyi rnam shes
mental factor	caitta	sems byung
merit	puṇya	bsod nams
method	upāya	thabs
migrator	gati	'gro ba
mind	citta	sems
mind-basis-of-all	ālayavijñāna	kun gzhi rnam shes
mind of enlightenment	bodhicitta	byang chub kyi sems
mindfulness	smṛti	dran pa
natural existence/existence by way of [the object's] own character	svalakṣaṇasiddhi	rang gi mtshan nyid kyis grub pa
natural nirvana	—	rang bzhin myang 'das
Nature	prakṛti	rang bzhin
Nature Body	svabhāvikakāya	ngo bo nyid sku
negation/negative phenomenon	pratiṣedha	dgag pa
neutral	avyākṛta	lung du ma bstan pa
Never Returner	anāgāmin	phyir mi 'ong
nirvāṇa	nirvāṇa	mya ngan las 'das pa
Noble/Superior	ārya	'phags pa
nominal existence	—	ming tsam du yod pa
non-affirming negation/negative	prasajyapratiṣedha	med dgag
non-analytical cessation	apratisaṃkhyānirodha	so sor brtags min gyi 'gog pa
non-application	anabhisaṃskāra	'du mi byed pa
non-associated compositional factor	viprayuktasaṃskāra	ldan min 'du byed
non-attachment	alobha	ma chags pa
non-conceptual wisdom	nirvikalpajñāna	rnam par mi rtog pa'i ye shes
non-conscientiousness	pramāda	bag med pa
non-existent	asat	med pa
non-person compositional factor	—	gang zag ma yin pa'i ldan min 'du byed

English	*Sanskrit*	*Tibetan*
non-produced phenomenon/uncompounded phenomenon	asaṃskṛtadharma	'dus ma byas kyi chos
non-revelatory form	avijñāptirūpa	rnam par rig byed ma yin pa'i gzugs
non-thing	abhāva	dngos med
non-virtuous	akuśala	mi dge ba
non-wastage	avipranāśa	chud mi za ba
nose consciousness	ghrāṇavijñāna	sna'i rnam shes
nose sense	ghrāṇendriya	sna'i dbang po
not unable	anāgamya	mi lcogs med
object	viṣaya	yul
object of knowledge	jñeya	shes bya
object of negation	pratiṣedhya	dgag bya
object of observation	ālambana	dmigs yul/dmigs pa
objective existence	—	yul gyi steng nas grub pa
obscurational truth	saṃvṛtisatya	kun rdzob bden pa
observed object condition	ālambanapratyaya	dmigs rkyen
obstructions to liberation/afflictive obstructions	kleśāvaraṇa	nyon mong pa'i sgrib pa
obstructions to omniscience/obstructions to objects of knowledge	jñeyāvaraṇa	shes bya'i sgrib pa
obtainer	prāpti	thob pa
odor	gandha	dri
omnipresent factor	sarvatraga	kun 'gro
omniscience/exalted knower of all aspects	sarvākārajñāna	rnam pa thams cad mkhyen pa
Once Returner	āgāmin	phyir 'ong
only imputed	prajñaptimātra	btags tsam
other-approved inference	parasiddhānumāna	gzhan grags kyi rjes dpag
other-approved reason	parasiddhaliṅga	gzhan grags kyi rtags
other-approved syllogism	parasiddhaprayoga	gzhan grags kyi sbyor ba
other-powered	paratantra	gzhan dbang
own system	—	rang lugs
pain/suffering	duḥkha	sdug bsngal
path	mārga	lam
path of accumulation	saṃbhāramārga	tshogs lam
path of meditation	bhāvanāmārga	sgom lam
path of no more learning	aśaikṣamārga	mi slob lam
path of preparation	prayogamārga	sbyor lam
path of release	vimuktimārga	rnam grol lam
path of seeing	darśanamārga	mthong lam

English	*Sanskrit*	*Tibetan*
patience	kṣānti	bzod pa
peak	mūrdhan	rtse mo
perfection	pāramitā	phar phyin
Perfection Vehicle	pāramitāyāna	phar phyin kyi theg pa
permanent phenomenon	nitya	rtag pa
person	pudgala/puruṣa	gang zag
personal selflessness	pudgalanairātmya	gang zag gi bdag med
pervasions	vyāpti	khyab pa
phenomenon	dharma	chos
phenomenon-source	dharmāyatana	chos kyi skye mched
pleasure/bliss	sukhā	bde ba
position	pakṣa	phyogs
potency	vāsanā/bāla	bags chags/nus pa
Prāsaṅgika	prāsaṅgika	thal 'gyur pa
predicate of the probandum	sādhyadharma	bsgrub bya'i chos
predisposition	vāsanā	bags chags
preparation	sāmantaka	nyer bsdogs
probandum	sādhya	bsgrub bya
product	saṃkṛta	'dus byas
production non-nature	utpattiniḥsvabhāvatā	skye ba ngo bo nyid med pa nyid
proof	sādhana	sgrub byed
Proponent of Annihilation	ucchedavādin	chad par smra ba
Proponent of Permanence	śaśvatavādin	rtag par smra ba
quality	guṇa	yon tan
reality	dharmatā	chos nyid
reason	hetu	gtan tshigs
reasoning	yukti	rigs pa
referent object/determined object	—	zhen yul
requiring interpretation	neyārtha	drang don
resentment	upanāha	'khon 'dzin
root affliction	mūlakleśa	rtsa nyon
saṃsāra	saṃsāra	'khor ba
Sautrāntika	sautrāntika	mdo sde pa
Sautrāntika Following Scripture	āgamānusāra-Sautrāntika	lung gi rje su 'brang pa'i mdo sde pa
Sautrāntika Following Reasoning	nyāyānusāra-Sautrāntika	rigs gi rje su 'brang pa'i mdo sde pa
secondary affliction	upakleśa	nye nyon
seed	bīja	sa bon
self	ātman	bdag

English	*Sanskrit*	*Tibetan*
self-approved inference	svasiddhānumāna	rang grags rjes dpag
self-approved reason	svasiddhaliṅga	rang grags kyi rtags
self-consciousness/self-knower	svasaṃvedana	rang rig
self of persons	pudgalātman	gang zag gi bdag
self of phenomena	dharmātman	chos kyi bdag
self-sufficient	—	rang rkya ba
selflessness	nairātmya	bdag med
selflessness of persons	pudgalanairātmya	gang zag gi bdag med
selflessness of phenomena	dharmanairātmya	chos kyi bdag med
sense power	indriya	dbang po
sentient being	sattva	sems can
Solitary Realizer	pratyekabuddha	rang sangs rgyas
sound	śabda	sgra
source	āyatana	skye mched
space	ākāśa	nam mkha'
Spirit	puruṣa	gang zhag
special insight	vipaśyanā	lhag mthong
stabilization	samādhi	ting nge 'dzin
stabilizing meditation	—	'jog sgom
Stream Enterer	śrotāpanna	rgyun zhugs
subconscious awareness	buddhi	blo
subsequent cognition	—	bcad shes/dpyad shes
substantial cause	upādāna	nyer len
substantial entity	dravya	rdzas
substantial existence	dravyasat	rdzas su yod pa
substantially established	dravyasiddha	rdzas su grub pa
substantially existent	dravyasat	rdzas su yod pa
suchness	tathatā	de bzhin nyid/de kho na nyid
superimposition	āropa	sgro 'dogs
Superior	āryan	'phags pa
suppleness/pliancy	praśrabdhi	shin tu sbyangs pa
supramundane	lokottara	'jig rten las 'das pa
sūtra	sūtra	mdo
Svātantrika	svātantrika	rang rgyud pa
syllogism	prayoga	sbyor ba
synonym	ekārtha	don gcig
tangible object	spraṣṭavya	reg bya
tantra	tanra	rgyud
taste	rasa	ro
Tathāgata essence	tathāgatagarbha	de bzhin gshegs pa'i snying po
ten grounds	daśabhūmi	sa bcu
tenets/tenet system	siddhānta/siddhyanta	grub mtha'
thesis	pratijñā	dam bca'

English	*Sanskrit*	*Tibetan*
thing/actuality	bhāva	dngos po
thinking	cintā	bsam pa
thoroughly established	pariniṣpanna	yongs grub
Three Refuges	triśaraṇa	skyabs gsum
tongue consciousness	jihvāvijñāna	lce'i rnam par shes pa
tongue sense	jihvendriya	lce'i dbang po
true establishment	satyasiddhi/bhāva	bden par grub pa/dngos po
true existence	satyasat	bden par yod pa
truly established	satyasiddha	bden par grub pa
truly existent	satyasat	bden par yod pa
truth	satya	bden pa
Truth Body	dharmakāya	chos sku
ultimate	paramārtha	don dam pa
ultimate analysis	—	don dam pa'i dpyod pa
ultimate existence	paramārthasiddhi	don dam par grub pa
ultimate non-nature	paramārthaniḥsvabhāvatā	don dam pa ngo bo nyid med pa nyid
ultimate truth	paramārthasatya	don dam bden pa
uninterrupted path	ānantaryamārga	bar chad med lam
Vaibhāṣika	vaibhāṣika	bye brag smra ba
vajra	vajra	rdo rje
valid cognition/valid cognizer	pramāṇa	tshad ma
validly established	—	tshad mas grub pa
vehicle	yāna	theg pa
view	dṛṣṭi	lta ba
view of the transitory collection	satkāyadṛṣṭi	'jig tshogs la lta ba
virtuous/virtuous factor	kuśala	dge ba
visible form	rūpa	gzugs
wind/current of energy	prāṇa	rlung
wisdom	prajñā/jñāna	shes rab/ye shes
Wisdom Body	jñānakāya	ye shes chos sku
wrong view	mithyādṛṣṭi	log lta
Yogācāra	yogācāra	rnal 'byor spyod pa
yogic direct perception	yogi-pratyakṣa	rnal 'byor mngon sum

References

This is a list of texts to which we have referred in the introduction or which have been mentioned in Losang Gönchok's commentary. For an extensive bibliography of works related to tenets, particularly to Prāsaṅgika Mādhyamika, see Cozort, *Unique Tenets of the Middle Way Consequence School* (Snow Lion, 1998).

The Tibetan text herein translated is Losang Gönchok *(blo bzang dkon mchog), Word Commentary on the Root Text of (Jamyang Shayba's) "Tenets," The Clear Crystal Mirror (grub mtha' rtsa ba'i tshig tik shel dkar me long)*. Part of *Three Commentaries on the "Grub Mtha' Rtsa Ba Gdon Lṅa'i Sgra Dbyaṅs" of 'Jam-Dbyaṅs-Bzad-Pa'i-Rdo-Rje Nag-Dbaṅ-Brston-'Grus.* Delhi: Chophel Legden, 1978.

Sūtras and tantras are listed alphabetically by English translation (often with abbreviated titles), Indian and Tibetan treatises by author.

Sūtras and Tantras

Collection of Related Sayings (saṃyuktāgama). (See Bodhi.)

Descent to Laṅkā Sūtra (laṅkāvatārasūtra, lang kar gshegs pa'i mdo)

Diamond Cutter Sūtra (vajracchedikāsūtra, rdo rje gcod pa'i mdo).

Excellent Golden Light Sūtra (suvarṇaprabhāsottamasūtra, gser 'od dam pa)

Guhyasamāja Tantra (sarvatathāgatakāyavākchittarahasyaguhyasamājanāmamahākalpa-rāja, de bzhin gshegs pa thams cad kyi sku gsung thugs kyi gsang chen gsang ba 'dus pa zhes bya ba brtag pa'i rgyal po chen po).

Heart of Wisdom Sūtra (prajñāhṛdaya/bhagavatīprajñāpāramitāhṛdayasūtra, shes rab snying po/bCom ldan 'das ma shes rab kyi pha rol tu phyin pa'i snying po'i mdo).

Kālacakra Tantra (paramādibuddhoddhṛtaśrikālacakranāmatantrarāja, mchog gi dang po'i sangs rgyas las phyung ba rgyud kyi rgyal po dpal dus kyi 'khor lo).

Kāśyapa Chapter Sūtra (kāśyapaparivartasūtra, 'od srung gi le'u'i mdo).

King of Meditative Stabilizations Sūtra (samādhirājasūtra/sarvadharmasvabhāvasamatā-vipañcitasamādhirājasūtra, ting nge 'dzin rgyal po'i mdo, chos thams cad kyi rang bzhin mnyam pa nyid rnam par spros pa ting nge 'dzin rgyal po'i mdo).

Mahāyāna Abhidharma Sūtra (mahāyānābhidharmasūtra, theg pa chen po'i mngon pa'i chos kyi mdo [?]). Not extant except in fragments found in other works.

Meeting of Father and Son Sūtra (pitāputrasamāgamasūtra, yab dang sras mjal ba'i mdo).

Hundred Thousand Stanza Perfection of Wisdom Sūtra (śatasāhasrikāprajñāpāramitāsūtra, shes rab kyi pha rol tu phyin pa stong phrag brgya pa'i mdo).

Points of Controversy (kathāvatthu).

Sūtra on the Heavily Adorned (ghanavyūhasūtra, rgyan stug por bkod pa'i mdo).

Sūtra on the Ten Grounds (daśabhūmikasūtra, mdo sde sa bcu pa). (See Honda.)

Sūtra Unraveling the Thought (saṃdhinirmocanasūtra, dgongs pa nges par' grel pa'i mdo)

Tathāgatha Essence Sūtra (tathāgathagarbhasūtra, de bzhin gshegs pa'i snying po'i mdo).

Teaching of Akṣayamati Sūtra (akṣayamatinirdeśasūtra, blo gros mi zad pas bstan pa'i mdo)

Sanskrit and Tibetan Works

Āryadeva (*'phags pa lha*, second to third century, C.E.). *Four Hundred/Treatise of Four Hundred Stanzas (catuḥśatakaśāstrakārikā, bstan bcos bzhi brgya pa zhes bya ba'i tshig le'ur byas pa).*

Asaṅga (*thogs med*, c. 310–390). *Compendium of Ascertainments (nirnayasaṃgraha or viniścayasaṃgrahaṇī, gtan la dbab pa bsdu ba).*

________. *Compendium of Abhidharma (abhidharmasamuccaya, mngon pa kun btus).*

________. *Compendium of the Mahāyāna (mahāyānasaṃgraha, theg pa chen po bsdus pa).*

Asvabhāva (*ngo bo nyid med pa*, c. 450–530). *Connected Explanation of (Asaṅga's) "Compendium of the Mahāyāna" (mahāyānasaṃgrahopanibandhana, theg pa chen po'i bsdud pa'i bsad sbyar).*

Atīśa (982–1054). *Introduction to the Two Truths (satyadvayāvatāra, bden pa gnyis la 'jug pa).*

________. *Lamp for the Path to Enlightenment (bodhipathapradīpa, byang chub lam gyi sgron ma).*

Avalokitavrata (*spyan ras gzigs brtul zhugs*, seventh century). *Commentary on (Bhāvaviveka's) "Lamp for (Nāgārjuna's) 'Wisdom'" (prajñāpradīpaṭīkā, shes rab sgron ma'i rgya cher 'grel pa).*

Beltsek (*dpal brtseg*, eighth century). *Explanation of the Stages of Views (lta pa'i rim pa bshad pa).*

Bhāvaviveka (*legs ldan 'byed*, c.500–570). *Blaze of Reasoning, Commentary on the "Heart of the Middle Way" (madhyamakahṛdayavṛttitarkajvālā, dbu ma'i snying po'i 'grel pa rtog ge 'bar ba).*

________. *Heart of the Middle Way (madhyamakahṛdayakārikā, dbu ma'i snying po'i tshig le'ur byas pa).*

Buddhapālita (*sangs rgyas bskyangs*, c. 470–540). *Buddhapālita's Commentary on (Nāgārjuna's) "Treatise on the Middle Way" (buddhapālitamūlamadhyamakavṛtti, dbu ma rtsa ba'i 'grel pa buddha pā li ta).*

Candrakīrti (*zla ba grags pa*, seventh century). *Autocommentary on the "Entrance to (Nāgārjuna's) 'Treatise on the Middle Way'"* (*madhyamakāvatārabhāṣya, dbu ma la 'jug pa'i bshad pa/dbu ma la 'jug pa'i rang 'grel*).

________. *Clear Words, Commentary on (Nāgārjuna's) "Treatise on the Middle Way"* (*mūlmadhyamakavṛttiprasannapadā, dbu ma rtsa ba'i 'grel pa tshig gsal ba).*

________. *Commentary on (Āryadeva's) "Four Hundred Stanzas on the Yogic Deeds of Bodhisattvas"* (*bodhisattvayogacaryācatuḥśatakaṭīkā, byang chub sems dpa'i rnal 'byor spyod pa gzhi brgya pa'i rgya cher 'grel pa*).

________. *Commentary on (Nāgārjuna's) "Sixty Stanzas of Reasoning"* (*yuktiṣaṣṭikāvṛtti, rigs pa drug cu pa'i grel pa*).

________. *Entrance to (Nāgārjuna's) "Treatise on the Middle Way"* (*madhyamakāvatāra, dbu ma la 'jug pa*).

Daktsang Shayrab Rinchen (*stag tshang lo tsā ba shes rab rin chen*, born 1405). *Freedom from Extremes through Understanding All Tenets* (*grub mtha' kun shes nas mtha' bral grub pa*).

________. *Ocean of Good Explanations, Explanation of "Freedom from Extremes through Understanding All Tenets"* (*grub mtha' kun shes nas mtha' bral grub pa zhes bya ba'i bstan bcos rnam par bshad pa legs bshad kyi rgya mtsho*).

Dharmakīrti (*chos kyi grags pa*, seventh century). *Commentary on (Dignāga's) "Compendium on Valid Cognition"* (*pramāṇavārttikakārikā, tshad ma rnam 'grel gyi tshig le'ur byas pa*).

Dignāga (*phyogs glang*, c. 480–540). *Compendium on Valid Cognition* (*pramāṇa-samuccaya, tshad ma kun las btus pa*).

Dzongkaba Losang Drakba (*tsong kha pa blo bzang grags pa*, 1357–1419). *The Essence of Eloquence, Treatise Differentiating the Interpretable and the Definitive* (*drang ba dang nges pa'i don rnam par phye ba'i bstan bcos legs bshad snying po*).

________. *Golden Rosary of Eloquence/Extensive Explanation of (Maitreya's) "Treatise of Quintessential Instructions on the Perfection of Wisdom, Ornament for Clear Realization," As Well As Its Commentaries* (*legs bshad gser gyi phreng ba/Shes rab kyi pha rol tu phyin pa'i man ngag gi bstan bcos mngon par rtogs pa'i rgyan 'grel pa dang bcas pa'i rgya cher bshad pa*).

________. *Great Exposition of Special Insight* (*lhag mthong chen mo*; part of *Great Exposition of the Stages of the Path*).

________. *Great Exposition of the Stages of the Path/Stages of the Path to Enlightenment Thoroughly Teaching All the Stages of Practice of the Three Types of Beings* (*lam rim chen no/skyes bu gsum gyi rnyams su blang ba'i rim pa thams cad tshang bar ston pa'i byang chub lam gyi rim pa*).

________. *Illumination of the Thought, Extensive Explanation of (Candrakīrti's) "Entrance to (Nāgārjuna's) 'Treatise on the Middle Way'"* (*dbu ma la 'jug pa'i rgya cher bshad pa dgongs pa rab gsal*).

________. *Middling Exposition of the Stages of the Path/Small Exposition of the Stages of the Path To Enlightenment* (*lam rim 'bring/lam rim chung ngu*).

________. *Ocean of Reasoning, Explanation of (Nāgārjuna's) "Treatise on the Middle Way"/Great Commentary on (Nāgārjuna's) "Treatise on the Middle Way"* (*dbu ma rtsa ba'i tshig le'ur byas pa shes rab ces bya ba'i rnam bshad rigs pa'i rgya mtsho*).

Gönchok Jikmay Wangbo (*dkon mchog 'jigs med dbang po*, 1728–91). *Precious Garland of Tenets/Presentation of Tenets, A Precious Garland (grub pa'i mtha'i rnam par bzhag pa rin po che'i phreng ba*).

Great Exposition of Particulars (mahāvibhāṣā; sometimes attributed to Vasumitra; known by two names, *Ocean of Great Exposition* (*bye brag bzhad mtsho*) or *Treasury of Great Exposition* (*bye brag bzhad mdzod*).

Guṅaprabha (fourth century). *Vinayasūtra.*

Gyeltsap Dharma Rinchen (*rgyal tshab dar ma rin chen*, 1364–1432). *Explanation of (Dharmakīrti's) "Commentary on (Dignāga's) 'Compendium of Valid Cognition'"*

________. *Commentary on (Maitreya's) "Ornament for Clear Realization"* (*mngon par rtogs pa'i rgyan ma'i īka*).

________. *Explanation of (Śāntideva's) "Engaging in the Bodhisattva Deeds": Entrance of Conqueror Children* (*byang chub sems dpa'i spyod pa la 'jug pa'i rnam bshad rgyal sras 'jug ngogs*).

Jambel Trinlay Yönden Gyatso (*'jam dpal 'phrin las yon tan rgya mtsho*). *Festival for the Wise, Good Explanation Collecting All Points of the Collected Topics* (*bsdus grwa'i don kun bsdus pa legs bshad mkhas pa'i dga' ston*).

Jamyang Shayba Ngawang Dzöndrü (*'jam dbyangs bzhad pa ngag dbang brtson 'grus*, 1648–1721). *Great Exposition of the Middle Way/Analysis of (Candrakīrti's) "Entrance to (Nāgārjuna's) 'Treatise on the Middle Way,'" Treasury of Scripture and Reasoning, Thoroughly Illuminating the Profound Meaning [of Emptiness], Entrance for the Fortunate* (*dbu ma chen no/dbu ma 'jug pa'i mtha' dpyod lung rigs gter mdzod zab don kun gsal skal bzang 'jug ngogs*).

________. *Great Exposition of Tenets/Explanation of "Tenets," Sun of the Land of Samantabhadra Brilliantly Illuminating All Our Own and Others' Tenets and the Meaning of the Profound [Emptiness], Ocean of Scripture and Reasoning Fulfilling All Hopes of All Beings* (*grub mtha' chen mo/grub mtha'i rnam bshad rang gzhan grub mtha' kin dang zab don mchog tu gsal ba kun bzang zhing gi nyi ma lung rigs rgya mtsho skye dgu'i re ba kun skong*).

________. *Presentation of Tenets, Roar of the Five-Faced [Lion] Eradicating Error, Precious Lamp Illuminating the Good Path to Omniscience* (*grub mtha'i rnam par bzhag pa 'khrul spong gdong lnga'i sgra dbyangs kun mkhyen lam bzang gsal ba'i rin chen sgron me*).

Janggya Rolbay Dorjay (*lcang skya rol pa'i rdo rje* II, 1717–86). *Presentation of Tenets/Clear Exposition of the Presentations of Tenets, Beautiful Ornament for the Meru of the Subduer's Teaching* (*grub mtha'i rnam bzhag/grub pa'i mtha'i rnam par bzhag pa gsal bar bshad pa thub bstan lhun po'i mdzes rgyan*).

Jetāri (tenth century). *Discrimination of the Sugata* (*sugatamatavibhaṅghavṛtti, bder gzhegs gzhung gi rab byed*).

Jñānagarbha (eighth century). *Discrimination of the Two Truths* (*satyadvayavibhaṅga, bden gnyis rnam 'byed*).

Kamalaśīla (eighth century). *Illumination of the Middle Way* (*madhyamakāloka, dbu ma snang ba).*

Kaydrup Gelek Belsangbo (*mkhas sgrub dge legs dpal bzang po,* 1385–1438). *Thousand Dosages/Opening the Eyes of the Fortunate, Treatise Brilliantly Clarifying the Profound Emptiness* (*stong thun chen mo/zab no stong pa nyid rab tu gsal bar byed pa'i bstan bcos skal bzang mig 'byed).*

Longchen Rapjam *(klong chen rab 'byams/klong chen dri med 'od zer,* 1308–63). *Treasury of Tenets, Illuminating the Meaning of All Vehicles* (*theg pa mtha' dag gi don gsal bar byed pa grub pa'i mtha' rin po che'i mdzod*).

Losang Gönchok *(blo bzang dkon mchog). Word Commentary on the Root Text of (Jamyang Shayba's) "Tenets," Clear Crystal Mirror (grub mtha' rtsa ba'i tshig tik shel dkar me long*).

Maitreya *(byams pa). Discrimination of Phenomena and the Nature of Phenomena* (*dharmadharmatāvibhaṅga, chos dang chos nyid rnam par 'byed pa*).

———. *Discrimination of the Middle and the Extremes* (*madhyāntavibhaṅga dbus dang mtha' rnam par 'byed pa*).

———. *Ornament for the Mahāyāna Sūtras* (*mahāyānasūtralaṃkārakārikā, theg pa chen po'i mdo sde'i rgyan gyi tshig le'ur byas pa*).

———. *Ornament for Clear Realization (abhisamayālaṃkāra, mngon par rtogs pa'i rgyan*).

———. *Sublime Continuum of the Mahāyāna* (*mahāyānottaratantraśāstra theg pa chen po rgyud bla ma'i bstan bcos*).

Nāgārjuna *(klu sgrub,* first to second century, C.E.). *Essay on the Mind of Enlightenment (bodhicittavivarana byang chub sems kyi 'grel pa*).

———. *Precious Garland of Advice for the King* (*rājaparikathāratnāvalī, rgyal po la gtam bya ba rin po che'i phreng ba*).

———. *Refutation of Objections* (*vigrahavyāvartanīkārikā, rtsod pa bzlog pa'i tshig le'ur byas pa*).

———. *Treatise on the Middle Way/Fundamental Treatise on the Middle Way, Called "Wisdom"* (*madhyamakaśāstra/prajñānāmamūlamadhyamakākarikā, dbu ma'i bstan bcos/dbu ma rtsa ba'i tshig le'ur byas pa shes rab ces bya ba*).

Ngawang Belden *(ngag dbang dpal ldan,* b. 1797, a.k.a. Belden Chöjay). *Annotations for (Jamyang Shayba's) "Great Exposition of Tenets," Freeing the Knots of the Difficult Points, Precious Jewel of Clear Thought* (*grub mtha' chen mo'i mchan 'grel dka' gnad mdud grol blo gsal gces nor*).

Ngawang Losang Gyatso *(ngag dbang blo bzang rgya mtsho,* Fifth Dalai Lama, 1617–82). *Sacred Word of Mañjusrī, Instructions on the Stages of the Path to Enlightenment* (*byang chub lam gyi rim pa'i khrid yig 'jam pa'i dbyangs kyi zhal lung*).

Paṇchen Sönam Drakba *(pan chen bsod nams grags pa,* 1478–1554). *General Meaning of (Maitreya's) "Ornament for Clear Realization" (phar phyin spyi don/shes rab kyi pha rol tu phyin pa'i man ngag gi bstan bcos mngon par rtogs pa'i rgyan 'grel pa dang bcas pa'i rnam bshad snying po rgyan gyi don legs par bshad pa yum don gsal ba'i sgron me).*

Śāntarakṣita *(zhi ba 'tsho,* eighth century). *Compendium of Principles* (*tattvasamgraha-kārikā, de kho na nyid bsdus pa'i tshig le'ur byas pa*).

Śāntideva (*zhi ba lha,* ninth century). *Compendium of Instructions* (*śikṣāsamuccayakārikā bslab pa kun las btus pai' tshig le'ur byas pa*).

_______. *Engaging in the Bodhisattva Deeds* (*bodhisattvacaryāvatāra byang chub sems dpa'i spyod pa la 'jug pa*).

Tügen Losang Chögyi Nyima *(thu'u bkvan blo bzang chos kyi nyi ma,* 1737–1802). *Mirror of the Good Explanations Showing the Sources and Assertions of All Systems of Tenets (grub mtha' thams cad kyi khungs dang 'dod tshul ston pa legs bshad shel gyi me long*).

Vasubandhu *(dbyig gnyen,* c. 320–400). *Explanation of the "Treasury of Abhidharma" (abhidharmakośabhāṣyam, chos mngon pa'i mdzod kyi bshad pa).*

_______. *Thirty Stanzas (triṃśikākarikā, sum cu pa'i tshig le'ur byas pa, known as sum cu pa).*

_______. *Treasury of Abhidharma (abhidharmakośakārikā, chos mngon pa'i mdzod kyi tshig le'ur byas pa).*

Yesheday (*ye shes sde,* c. 800). *Differences Between Views* (*lta ba'i khyad par*).

Other Works

Bodhi, Bhikku. *Connected Discourses of the Buddha.* Boston: Wisdom, 2000.

Buescher, John. "The Buddhist Doctrine of Two Truths in the Vaibhāṣika and Theravāda Schools." Dissertation, University of Virginia, 1982.

Cozort, Daniel. *Highest Yoga Tantra.* Ithaca: Snow Lion, 1986.

_______. *Unique Tenets of the Middle Way Consequence School.* Ithaca: Snow Lion, 1998.

_______. "The Making of the Western Lama." In Heine and Prebish, *Buddhism in the Modern World.* Oxford, 2003.

Csikszentmihalyi, Mihalyi. *Flow: The Psychology of Optimal Experience.* New York: Harper & Row, 1990.

Dreyfus, Georges. *Recognizing Reality: Dharmakīrti's Philosophy and Its Tibetan Interpretations.* Albany: State University of New York, 1997.

_______. *The Sound of Two Hands Clapping.* Berkeley: University of California, 2003.

Gyatso, Ven. Jampa. "Climbing the Snow Mountain." *Mandala,* June 1998.

Hopkins, Jeffrey. *Buddhist Advice for Living and Liberation: Nāgārjuna's Precious Garland.* Ithaca: Snow Lion, 1998.

_______. *Maps of the Profound.* Ithaca: Snow Lion, 2003.

_______. *Emptiness Yoga.* Ithaca: Snow Lion, 1987.

_______. *Meditation on Emptiness.* London and Boston: Wisdom, 1983, 1996.

_______. "The Tibetan Genre of Doxography: Structuring a Worldview" in Cabezon and Jackson, *Tibetan Literature.* Ithaca: Snow Lion, 1996.

_______. *Emptiness in the Mind-Only School of Buddhism: Dynamic Responses.* Berkeley: University of California, 2001.

_______. *Reflections on Reality: The Three Natures and Non-Natures in the Mind-Only School: Dynamic Responses to Dzong-ka-ba's The Essence of Eloquence, Volume 2.* Berkeley: University of California, 2002.

———. *Tantra in Tibet.* Ithaca: Snow Lion, 1987.

Hopkins, Jeffrey, and Geshe Lhundup Sopa. *Cutting Through Appearances* (revised edition of *Practice and Theory of Tibetan Buddhism*). Ithaca: Snow Lion, 1989.

Honda, M. "An Annotated Translation of the 'Daśabhūmika.'" in D. Sinor, ed., *Studies in Southeast and Central Asia,* Satapiṭaka Series 74. New Delhi: 1968, pp. 115–276.

Klein, Anne C. *Knowing, Naming and Negation.* Ithaca: Snow Lion, 1991.

———, trans. and ed. *Path to the Middle: The Spoken Scholarship of Kensur Yeshey Tupden.* Albany: State University of New York, 1994.

Lati Rinbochay. *Mind in Tibetan Buddhism.* Elizabeth Napper, trans. and ed. Valois, NY: Snow Lion, 1980.

McClintock, Sara, and Georges Dreyfus. *The Svātantrika-Prāsaṅgika Distinction: What Difference Does a Difference Make?* Boston: Wisdom, 2002.

Nakamura, Hajime. *Indian Buddhism: A Survey with Bibliographical Notes.* Hirakata, Japan: Kurfs Publications, 1980. Rpt. Delhi: Motilal Banarsidass, 1987.

Napper, Elizabeth. *Dependent-Arising and Emptiness.* London and Boston: Wisdom, 1989.

Newland, Guy. *The Two Truths.* Ithaca: Snow Lion, 1992.

———. *Appearance and Reality.* Ithaca: Snow Lion, 1999.

Nietupski, Paul K. *Labrang.* Ithaca: Snow Lion, 1999.

Rabten, Geshe. *Life and Teachings of Geshe Rabten.* Translated and edited by B. Alan Wallace. London: George Allen & Unwin, 1980.

Schmitthausen, Lambert. *Ālayavijñāna: On the Origin and Early Development of a Central Concept of Yogācāra Philosophy.* Studia Philogica Buddhica Monograph Series IVa. Tokyo: International Institute for Buddhist Studies, 1987.

Sopa, Geshe Lhundup. *Lectures on Tibetan Religious Culture.* U. Wisconsin, unpublished mss., 1972.

Wylie, Turrell V. "A Standard System of Tibetan Transcription." *Harvard Journal of Asiatic Studies* 22: 261–7.

Further Reading

There is a wealth of scholarship on Buddhist philosophy, most of it very arcane. We presume that our readers will be inclined to work from the basis provided herein, a presentation of tenets from the point of view of the Tibetan Gelukba tradition. The list that follows is comprised of some books that might consulted to expand further on any of the topics presented in the present book.

Tenets in General

Sopa and Hopkins, *Cutting Through Appearances: The Practice and Theory of Tibetan Buddhism.* Ithaca: Snow Lion, 1990.

An annotated translation of *Precious Garland of Tenets,* a very short text written by Jamyang Shayba's next incarnation, Gönchok Jikmay Wangbo (1728–91). *Precious Garland of Tenets* follows the same organizational structure as Losang Gonchok's text, so the two books may easily be read together.

Hopkins, Jeffrey. *Maps of the Profound.* Ithaca and Boulder: Snow Lion, 2003.

A vast, annotated sourcebook on tenets that utilizes Jamyang Shayba's *Great Exposition of Tenets* along with Ngawang Belden's *Annotations* and many supplementary texts. This is the culmination of Prof. Hopkins' decades-long study of the *Great Exposition of Tenets.*

Vaibhāṣika

Buescher, John B. "The Buddhist Doctrine of Two Truths in the Vaibhāṣika and Theravāda Schools." Dissertation, University of Virginia, 1982. Available from University Microfilms.

Includes a portion of Ngawang Belden's *Explanation of the Conventional and the Ultimate in the Four Tenet Systems.*

Sautrāntika

Klein, Anne C. *Knowledge and Liberation: Tibetan Buddhist Epistemology in Support of Transformative Religious Experience.* Ithaca: Snow Lion, 1986. Also, Klein, *Knowing, Naming & Negation: A Sourcebook on Tibetan Sautrāntika.* Ithaca: Snow Lion, 1991.

Both books concern the central issues of the Sautrāntikas Following Reason. The second is a collection of key translations.

Perdue, Daniel E. *Debate in Tibetan Buddhism.* Ithaca: Snow Lion, 1992.

A rich introduction to the Collected Topics, the initial area of study undertaken at the beginning of Gelukba education. Distilled from the writings of Dignāga and Dharmakīrti, topics include cause and effect, parts and wholes, identity and difference, etc. Includes a complete explanation of monastic debating.

Lati Rinpoche and Elizabeth Napper, *Mind in Tibetan Buddhism.* Ithaca: Snow Lion, 1986.

An excellent beginner's book. The focus here is on the variety of minds and mental states, presented according to the Sautrāntikas Following Reason.

Dreyfus, Georges. *Recognizing Reality; Dharmakīrti's Philosophy and Its Tibetan Interpretations.* Albany: State University of New York Press, 1997.

Dharmakīrti is the main source for Sautrāntikas and Cittamātrins Following Reasoning. This brilliant work provides not only Gelukba, but also Sagyaba perspectives on Dharmakīrti.

Cittamātra

Hopkins, Jeffrey. *Emptiness in the Mind Only School.* Berkeley: Univ. of California, 2001. Also, Hopkins, *Reflections on Reality.* Berkeley: Univ. of California, 2002.

These two volumes present Dzongkaba's rich critique of Cittamātra in his *Essence of Eloquence*, perhaps his deepest work.

Wilson, Joe B. "The Meaning of Mind in the Mahāyāna Buddhist Philosophy of Mind-Only *(Cittamātra)...*" Dissertation, University of Virginia, 1984. Available from University Microfilms.

While focused upon the Cittamātra concepts of a mind-basis-of-all and afflicted mentality, this book discusses all of the main topics of the school.

Svātantrika-Mādhyamika

Lopez, Donald S. *A Study of Svātantrika.* Ithaca: Snow Lion, 1987.

Issues central to the Svātantrika school understanding of emptiness are presented clearly and compared to contrasting views held by the Prāsaṅgika school.

Prāsaṅgika -Mādhyamika

Hopkins, Jeffrey. *Meditation on Emptiness.* London and Boston: Wisdom, 1996 (second edition).

With sections on non-Buddhist schools and on the other Buddhist schools, this landmark book, although challenging for beginners, covers almost all of the topics of Buddhist tenets. It is particularly valuable for its extensive discussion of the sets of reasonings used by the Prāsaṅgika-Mādhyamika school for meditation on emptiness.

Cozort, Daniel. *Unique Tenets of the Middle Way Consequence School.* Ithaca: Snow Lion, 1998.
This book might best be seen as a complement to *Meditation on Emptiness,* discussing tenets that stem from the Prāsaṅgika school's presentation on emptiness. Much of the discussion concerns the Prāsaṅgika critique of the Cittamātra school.

Napper, Elizabeth. *Dependent-Arising and Emptiness.* London: Wisdom, 1989.
Even more than *Meditation on Emptiness* on the subject, based on the emptiness section of Dzongkaba's *Great Exposition of the Stages of the Path* and commentaries.

Newland, Guy Martin. *The Two Truths.* Ithaca: Snow Lion, 1992.
A thorough examination of the topic of the two truths seen through the eyes of Dzongkaba and later Gelukba scholars.

Hopkins, Jeffrey. *Emptiness Yoga.* Ithaca: Snow Lion, 1996 (second edition).
This book originated as a series of lectures given on the Prāsaṅgika chapter of Jang-gya's *Presentation of Tenets.* It is more conversational than some of the other books and will be for some the best place to start a more detailed study of Prāsaṅgika.

Tantra

Hopkins, Jeffrey. *The Tantric Distinction.* London and Boston: Wisdom, 1999 (revised edition).
A good beginner's book on the similarities and differences between sūtra and tantra, but which includes a discussion of all foundational topics.

Cozort, Daniel. *Highest Yoga Tantra* Ithaca: Snow Lion, 1986.
An introduction to tantra that is focuses on the general system of the Guhyasamāja tantra, with comparisons to Kālacakra.

Index